Introduction to
Classical &
New Testament
Greek

INTRODUCTION TO

Classical &
New Testament
Greek

A Unified Approach

MICHAEL BOLER

C E P

THE CATHOLIC EDUCATION PRESS
Washington, D.C.

Copyright © 2020

The Catholic Education Press

All rights reserved

The paper used in this publication meets the requirements of American
National Standards for Information Science—Permanence of Paper for
Printed Library Materials, ANSI Z39.48-1992.

∞

ISBN 978-1-949822-02-1 (paperback)

ISBN 978-1-949822-03-8 (ebook)

τῇ ἐμῇ τήθῃ

Contents

Introduction

For the Teacher

This book was born out of classroom experience. Having taught classical Greek at a Catholic liberal arts university, I found that I wanted two elements that currently available textbooks lacked. The first was more actual selections from Greek authors. While invented sentences work well for teaching the fundamentals of grammar, they fail to excite my students. Teaching at a university without a language requirement, I wanted to make the learning of classical Greek an exhilarating experience without sacrificing the necessary rigor. I began to bring in quotes and lines from ancient authors that I thought were illuminating. Gradually the idea of making a book entirely out of such quotations emerged. It has been my experience that the greatest factor in a student's decision to continue in their study of Greek is their interest in what they are reading. While not every sentence will light the fire of imagination for every student, it is my sincere hope that collectively these sentences will be interesting to the class in general and provide a bridge to discussions of the works from which they are taken.

Second, I found that many of my students wanted to read the New Testament. As a professor at a Catholic university, I have always sought to integrate the classical and early Christian traditions in all my language courses. I found that the classical textbooks made scant mention of the New Testament, while the New Testament textbooks did not include any classical Greek. In fact, most of my students were surprised to learn that the Greek of Plato and the Greek of the New Testament were the same language. Those that did know were under the impression that the Greek of the New Testament was simply a dumbed down version of classical Greek. To remedy this notion, I have an equal balance of classical and New Testament readings, with mentions of the differences when they arise.

Finally, I have sought in this book to remedy one of the greatest obstacles that the beginning student of Greek currently faces: a lack of knowledge of grammar. Most college age students today suffer from never having learned any principles of grammar in their previous schooling. This makes the acquisition of Greek grammar extremely difficult. I have therefore assumed in this book that the student has no knowledge of grammatical terms and concepts. To understand the structure of language itself is not a burden or a hurdle to be cleared in order to learn Greek. Rather, it is one of the greatest benefits a student can receive from learning another language. Time and again I have seen students grow in confidence when they learn with precision what was only vaguely sensed previously about language. Learning grammatical terminology aids the mind in understanding what languages are trying to communicate. This in turn not only grants the student greater insight into the English language but it frees the student from looking through only the prism of their own language. The result is the ability to triangulate, if you will, the reality that both languages seek to express in their own way. Those wishing to spend more time on grammar would do well to supplement this textbook with Donald Fairbairn's *Understanding Language: A Guide for Beginning Students of Greek & Latin* (Washington, DC: Catholic University of America Press, 2011).

Three Distinguishing Features of this Book

1. The Example Sentences

Starting with Chapter 2, each chapter contains 10 example sentences taken from classical and New Testament sources. These are real Greek sentences, not the paraphrased or invented sentences found in many textbooks. Each sentence contains an example of a grammatical concept introduced in that chapter. For the selections from the New Testament, no alterations of any kind have been made. For those from the classical authors, very minor changes are occasionally to be found. These changes consist primarily of adding the definite article and the word "to be" where it is merely implied in the original. In only a handful of cases has a word from the original sentence been changed. To the right of each sentence are notes. Vocabulary not included in the previous chapters will be given along with more advanced points of grammar that have not yet been introduced in the chapter.

2. Simplified Morphology and Syntax

I have sought to reduce the grammatical material the student must memorize to a minimum. This entails at times simplifying and passing over finer points of morphology or syntax. It is my hope that such economy will enable the student to progress in Greek with more confidence. After a foundation has been built, the student will then in a second-year course easily learn the exceptions and fill in the finer points.

3. Etymology and Discussion Topics

Each chapter concludes with "Etymology and Discussion Topics." Each entry examines the etymology of a vocabulary word or expands upon the context and meaning of one of the example sentences. It is hoped that these sections will both enrich the student's learning experience and lead to classroom discussion.

For the Student

What is Classical and New Testament Greek?

The language taught in this book is sometimes referred to as "classical Greek," "ancient Greek," or "Attic Greek." The term "Attic Greek" refers to the dialect used in ancient Athens (approximately 5th and 4th centuries B.C.E.), a city located in a region called Attica. There were other dialects used in ancient Greece. Herodotus wrote in the Ionian dialect, Sappho in the Aeolian dialect, and the Homeric epics were written in a literary dialect now commonly referred to as "Homeric Greek." The difference between the dialect used in classical Athens and the other dialects was not that great. This book has examples from Herodotus, Homer, and other non-Attic authors. The Attic equivalents to non-Attic forms will be given in the notes. When the Macedonians under Philip II and then Alexander conquered much of the East, Greek went from being spoken in small distinct geographical areas in Greece to becoming the official language of massive empires that ruled multitudes of peoples. Attic Greek, the dialect that predominated in cultural prestige at the time, became the basis for the "official" Greek of these empires, but its adoption by communities far away from Athens necessarily resulted in minor changes. The language that developed out of this became known as the common (koine) language. The New Testament is written in this Koine Greek. As you read the example sentences, you will occasionally come across differences between the later Koine and the earlier Attic dialect, which we shall call for convenience "classical." You will find, however, that they really are the same language and the differences are minor. The terms "classical Greek" and "Koine Greek" can give the erroneous impression that they are separate languages. Of course, Greek did not cease to be a language after the classical period. Its rich history continued through the Eastern Roman Empire (330 B.C.E.–1453 C.E.) and is still spoken this very day. While there are many similarities between modern and ancient Greek, there are many differences too, and students in Greece today must learn how to read classical Greek in school.

Why do so many English words come from Greek?

English words of Greek origin are found throughout the language, but they are particularly common in medical and academic vocabulary. Medical vocabulary is heavily based on Greek because of the influence of the early practitioners of medicine, the followers of Hippocrates. Academic and scientific vocabulary came either through French after the Norman conquest in the 11th century or directly during the 18th and 19th centuries, when new words (neologisms) were constantly invented to discuss rapidly expanding subjects of inquiry. To understand Greek (and her sister language Latin) is to understand the roots of intellectual inquiry in the English language.

Acknowledgments

This book has been years in the making, and I am heavily indebted to all those who have helped me along the way. First and foremost I would like to thank Trevor Lipscombe and the staff at Catholic Education Press, especially my editor Joel Kalvesmaki. His corralling of my sometimes meandering prose, tireless attention to detail, and knowledgeable suggestions have proven to be indispensable. I would also like to thank the readers of an early manuscript for their valuable suggestions. Two drafts of this book were used as the textbook for my Introduction to Ancient Greek course, and my students are responsible for many helpful additions and clarifications in the present edition. Sarah Ashour, Paul Roewe, Daniel Wagner, and David Strong were especially helpful in their reviews of the early chapters. Any errors or omissions are entirely my own.

I would also like to express my gratitude for the tireless support of my family, particularly my mother Nancy, father James, wife Megan, daughter Madeleine, and son Matthew.

Introduction to Classical & New Testament Greek

Chapter 1 ⌒

The Alphabet

The Greek alphabet consists of 24 letters, most of which were borrowed from the Phoenicians around the 8th century B.C.E. The exact shapes of the letters varied from region to region. The Athenian government officially adopted the Ionian alphabet in 403 B.C.E., which had already been in private use in the city. By 370 B.C.E. this alphabet was the standard throughout the Greek world. Greek texts were originally written using all capital letters. Scribes in the Eastern Roman Empire, commonly referred to as the Byzantine Empire, began around the ninth century to use a smaller minuscule script in place of the larger uncial script found in earlier manuscripts. The Greek alphabet employed today, with its uppercase and lowercase letters, is based on this minuscule script created by the Byzantines.

The pronunciation guide below is a close approximation to the pronunciation in classical Athens in the fifth and fourth centuries B.C.E. Modern scholarship can only approximate what Greek sounded like in that era. Pronunciation of Greek differed by both time and region. Some instructors insist on coming as close as possible to the ancient pronunciation, including using the pitch accents (see below). Others prefer to use the Modern Greek pronunciation. Many seminaries use a "Koine" pronunciation, based on the best available evidence from the time of the composition of the New Testament. This book offers a compromise, but only as a suggestion.

Name	Uppercase	Lowercase	*Letter* Pronunciation
alpha	A	α	short (α) = a as in f**a**ther
			long (ᾱ) = the same, but pronounced slightly longer
beta	B	β	b as in **b**oy
gamma	Γ	γ	g as in **g**irl; before κ, γ, ξ, χ: n as in si**n**g
delta	Δ	δ	d as in **d**og
epsilon	E	ε	e as in p**e**t
zeta	Z	ζ	sd as in wi**sd**om
eta	H	η	e as in th**ey**
theta	Θ	θ	th as in **th**ought (optional: th as in **Th**omas)
iota	I	ι	short (ι) = i as in p**i**n
			long (ῑ) = i as in p**i**ta
kappa	K	κ	k as in **k**angaroo
lambda	Λ	λ	l as in **l**amb
mu	M	μ	m as in **m**onth
nu	N	ν	n as in ti**n**
xi	Ξ	ξ	x as in bo**x**
omicron	O	o	short o, as in st**o**p
pi	Π	π	p as in to**p**
rho	P	ρ	r as in **r**un, but trilled
sigma	Σ	σ, ς	s as in **s**it; before β, γ, δ, μ: z as in **z**oo
tau	T	τ	t as in **t**in
upsilon	Υ	υ	short (υ) = u as in **ü**ber or the exclamation **ew**.
			long (ῡ) = the same, but pronounced slightly longer
phi	Φ	φ	p as in **ph**armacy (optional: p as in **p**ot, with a breath of air after the p)
chi	X	χ	c as in **c**art or Ba**ch**, with a puff of air after the c
psi	Ψ	ψ	ps as in ti**ps**y
omega	Ω	ω	o as in r**o**pe (optional: aw as in s**aw**)

- The optional, secondary pronunciations listed above (θ, φ, ω) are closer to the classical Athenian pronunciation than the main pronunciation, but they can be difficult for beginning students.
- Long and short vowels: The vowels ε and ο are always short; the vowels η and ω are always long. The vowels α, ι, and υ are sometimes long and sometimes short. Long α, ι, and υ are written ᾱ, ῑ, and ῡ, but not in this book. The long marks (called macrons) are listed in most dictionaries. You will not see them in printed Greek texts, but if you see ᾶ, ῖ, or ῦ (the vowels with an accent called the circumflex; see below), it must be long, as the circumflex accent cannot fall on a short vowel, except in a diphthong (see below).
- θ, φ, and χ were originally what are known as "aspirants." They were the letters τ, π, and κ followed by a puff of air, like the difference between the c sound in "back" and "Bach." They eventually turned into what are known as "fricatives," and were pronounced as "th" as in theater (θ), "ph" as in philosophy (φ), and "ch" as in the Hebrew name Chaim (χ). Aspirant theta and phi are difficult for English speakers to pronounce, so they are traditionally pronounced as fricatives.
- σ and ς are two versions of the same letter: sigma. There is no difference in pronunciation. ς is used when it is the last letter of a word; in all other positions σ is used.
- ω is difficult. Many linguists believe that it was originally a long drawn out "aw" sound. This is often difficult for English speakers to pronounce, however, and it is therefore customary to pronounce it as a long "o" sound.

Diphthongs

Diphthongs are two letters pronounced as one syllable. Just as we do not pronounce "house" as two syllables "ha-us," so also Greeks made certain vowel combinations one syllable.

Diphthongs	Pronunciation	Diphthongs	Pronunciation
αι	ai as in **high**	οι	oi as in **coin**
αυ	au as in **how**	ου	o as in **pool**
ει	ei as in **freight**	ηυ (rare)	same as ευ
ευ	a glide from ε to υ	υι (rare)	same as υ (ew as in **ew**, yuck) + y sound before vowels

ευ is a difficult diphthong for English speakers to pronounce. If you find that you cannot pronounce the quick glide from ε to υ, try pronouncing it as the "eu" in "euphemism," but without the initial "y" sound.

Occasionally you will encounter two vowels that form a diphthong, but which are to be pronounced separately. In such cases two little dots, called *diaeresis*, will be placed above the second vowel. E.g., πραϋς (*pra-us*) is two syllables, not one.

Subscripts

Vowel	Pronunciation
ᾳ	same as ᾱ
ῃ	same as η
ῳ	same as ω

Originally written αι, ηι, and ωι, these diphthongs were probably pronounced as glides from the first letter to a lightly pronounced ι, like ευ. By the second century B.C.E., the iota ceased to be pronounced but was still written after the first letter, i.e., adscript. In the Byzantine era, to save space, the iota began to be written below the first letter, i.e., subscript. While you do not need to pronounce the subscripts, *it is essential that you not ignore them*, as they provide crucial information when they occur. This is precisely why they continued to be written long after they ceased to be pronounced. If the first letter of an iota subscript is capitalized, the iota is written lower-case adscript, e.g., Αι, Ηι, Ωι.

Simplified Chart for Memorization: Alphabet

Letter	Pronunciation
α	a as in father
β	b as in **b**oy
γ	g as in **g**irl
δ	d as in **d**og
ε	e as in p**e**t
ζ	sd as in wi**sd**om
η	e as in th**ey**
θ	th as in **th**ought (optional: th as in **Th**omas)
ι	short (ι) = i as in p**i**n
	long (ī) = i as in p**i**ta
κ	k as in **k**angaroo
λ	l as in **l**amb
μ	m as in **m**onth
ν	n as in ti**n**
ξ	x as in bo**x**
o	short o, as in st**o**p
π	p as in to**p**
ρ	r as in **r**un, but trilled
σ, ς	s as in **s**it
τ	t as in **t**in
υ	u as in über or the exclamation **ew**.
φ	p as in **ph**armacy (optional: p as in **p**ot, with a breath of air after the p)
χ	c as in **c**art, with a puff of air after the c
ψ	ps as in ti**ps**y
ω	o as in r**o**pe (optional: aw as in s**aw**)

Simplified Chart for Memorization: Diphthongs and Subscripts

Diphthongs	Pronunciation
αι	ai as in h**igh**
αυ	au as in h**ow**
ει	ei as in fr**eigh**t
ευ	a glide from ε to υ (optional: eu as in **eu**phemism, but without the y sound before e)
οι	oi as in c**oin**
ου	o as in p**oo**l
ᾳ	same as ᾱ
ῃ	same as η
ῳ	same as ω

Breathings

When a word begins with a vowel, diphthong, or the consonant ρ and has what looks like a little c above it, you must add an "h" sound before the word. This is called a rough breathing mark. If you see a backwards "c" above a word that begins with a vowel or diphthong, you do not add an "h" sound before the letter. This is called a smooth breathing, although it probably would be more accurately described as a no-breathing mark. All words that begin with ρ take a rough breathing. All words that begin with a vowel or a diphthong take either a rough or a smooth breathing. If a word begins with a diphthong, the breathing mark is placed above the second vowel in the diphthong.

Smooth Breathing	Rough Breathing
ἀγών = agon	ἅγιος = hagios
οἶνος = oinos	οἱ = hoi

Accents

Greek accents were originally pitch accents, but they eventually became stress accents. Pitch accents are difficult for English speakers to recreate (unless they also happen to speak Chinese, Vietnamese, or one of the Scandinavian languages). It is therefore advisable to pronounce them as stress accents, which is in fact what is done in Modern Greek.

There are three classical Greek accent marks: the *acute* (´), the *circum-flex* (˜), and the *grave* (`).

- The *acute accent* (´) was originally a rise in pitch. ἀγών, ἅγιος.
- The *grave accent* (`) was either a fall in pitch or signified no pitch at all.
- The *circumflex accent* (˜) was originally a quick rise and fall in pitch. οἶνος, πνεῦμα. That up-down pronunciation was reflected in how it was originally written, as an acute followed by grave: ´`.

In practice, it is easiest to stress both the acute (´) and the circumflex (˜) accents and not to stress the grave (`), just like you ignore the smooth breathing mark in your pronunciation.

The rules of Greek accentuation are complex, with many exceptions. Native Greek speakers knew where the accent lay by practice, just as English speakers know that "assimilation" is accented assimilátion and not ássimilation or assimilatíon. The good news is that the accent will always be written for you (except for words that have no accent), so you simply stress whatever syllable has an acute or circumflex accent on it. There are patterns to Greek accents that can be beneficial to know. Therefore, a general guide to the rules of Greek accentuation is included in Appendix C.

Punctuation

The ancient Greeks themselves did not use punctuation (or spaces!), but the following punctuation marks are now standard. Most of the symbols are equivalent to English punctuation marks.

Greek Punctuation Mark	English Equivalent
.	. (the same)
,	, (the same)
;	?
· (middle dot)	; or :

Keep in mind that most of these marks have been inserted based on the judgment of a modern editor and not by the original author.

Capitalization

In contrast to English practice, the first word of a sentence is typically not capitalized. The practice today is to capitalize only proper nouns and the beginning of paragraphs. In addition, editions of the New Testament typically signal the start of a quotation not with a quotation mark, but by capitalizing the first word in the quotation. Therefore, the only places you will see capital Greek letters in this book will be in proper nouns and quotations of the New Testament. It is for this reason that it is recommended to memorize the lowercase letters first.

Exercise

Practice pronouncing the following Greek words:

ἄγγελος	ἰχθύς	Σωκράτης	θαυμάζω
βίος	λόγος	τρέπω	πρεσβύτερος
γράφω	μάθος	ὕβρις	ἁρπάζω
γένος	πάθος	φιλοσοφία	καιρός
δημοκρατία	ξένος	χάρις	ὅμοιος
ἐπιστήμη	ὀφθαλμός	ψυχή	νοῦς
ζωή	ποιητής	ὥρα	εὐδαιμονία
θεός	ῥῆμα	δαίμων	θεωρία

Chapter 2 ∿

Nouns • 1st Declension Nouns • 2nd Declension Nouns • The Definite Article • The Verb • εἰμί = To Be

Nouns

A noun is a part of speech (often called a "word class") that names persons, places, or things. Nouns are either common (city) or proper (Socrates). Nouns can also be concrete (book) or abstract (love).

Greek nouns have *gender*, *number*, and *case*.

Gender: Greek has three grammatical genders: *masculine, feminine*, and *neuter*. Every Greek noun will therefore be either masculine, feminine, or neuter. Gender is a grammatical concept. For example, the word for manliness "ἀνδρεία" is feminine, the word for rock "λίθος" is masculine, and the word for a young child "παιδίον" is neuter.

Number: Greek nouns are either singular (book) or plural (books). There is a rare third number, the dual, which is used for two items which form a natural pair, e.g., eyes. Since this number is so rare in Greek, it will not be included in this book, but you can see the forms for the dual in Appendix D.

Case: For the moment we will focus only on gender and number. We will discuss case in the next chapter.

Greek nouns fall into three *declensions*, which means that they more or less follow a certain spelling pattern when they *decline* (we will discuss this as well in the next chapter). You can therefore think of declensions as groups of nouns that have similar endings. In this chapter you will be introduced to two of the three Greek declensions.

1st Declension Nouns

Greek nouns of the 1st declension are almost exclusively feminine and end in either alpha (α) or eta (η). (Useful tip: when a 1st declension noun ends in α, it is always preceded by ε, ι, or ρ.)

Here are some common 1st declension nouns:

Feminine Nouns			
ψυχή	soul, spirit	χαρά	joy
ζωή	life	σοφία	wisdom
ἀρετή	excellence, virtue	ἀλήθεια	truth

2nd Declension Nouns

Greek nouns of the 2nd declension are almost exclusively masculine and neuter, with masculine nouns ending in ος and neuter nouns ending in ον. Here are some common 2nd declension nouns.

Masculine Nouns		*Neuter Nouns*	
λόγος	word, reason	βιβλίον	book
θεός	a god, God	ἔργον	work, deed
νόμος	law	δῶρον	gift

The Definite Article

The definite article in Greek is usually translated as "the," although there will be some exceptions, as we shall see. The difference between a *definite* and an *indefinite* article is that while the definite article points to some definite thing, the indefinite article does not. In English, the definite article is "the" and the indefinite article is "a/an."

The teacher is always learning.

We have in mind a *specific* and *definite* person we are talking about, hence the definite article, "the."

A teacher is always learning.

We don't have a definite or specific person in mind, hence the indefinite article, "a."

In Greek, the gender of the definite article is determined by the gender

of the noun the definite article is modifying, i.e., describing. You will sometimes hear that the noun governs the article, or that the article modifies or
is governed by the noun. That's just another way of saying that the definite
article follows whatever its corresponding noun does. Masculine nouns take
the masculine definite article ὁ, feminine nouns take the feminine definite
article ἡ, and neuter nouns take the neuter definite article τό.

Masculine Nouns		*Feminine Nouns*		*Neuter Nouns*	
ὁ λόγος	the word	ἡ ψυχή	the soul	τὸ βιβλίον	the book
ὁ θεός	the god / God	ἡ ζωή	the life	τὸ ἔργον	the deed
ὁ νόμος	the law	ἡ χαρά	the joy	τὸ δῶρον	the gift

While you will most often translate the definite article as "the," Greek often uses the definite article where English does not. For example, names in
Greek can take the definite article. While it may seem odd to say ὁ Πέτρος
"the Peter," it makes sense when you think about it. Proper names refer to
specific, or *definite* people. In your translations, however, it is not necessary
to translate the definite article in such situations, as constantly saying "the
Socrates" or "the Jesus" would be quite odd. ὁ Πέτρος can simply be translated "Peter."

Another place where Greek uses a definite article where English does not
is before abstract nouns such as "love" or "fear."

ἡ ἀγάπη = love
ὁ φόβος = fear

As you progress in your knowledge of Greek, context will tell you when to
translate the definite article. For the moment, translate the definite article as
"the." If it sounds ridiculous, leave it out.

The Verb

A verb is the part of speech that expresses an action or a state of being.
"Run," "walk," "stop," "go," "is," "becomes," "reads," "writes," and "learned" are
all English verbs.

Verbs in Greek have *person, number, tense, voice,* and *mood.* For the moment, we will focus only on *person* and *number.*

Person. Greek has three persons, 1st, 2nd, and 3rd. The 1st person refers
to the speaker, the 2nd person refers to the person spoken to, and the 3rd

person refers to a different subject. In English we primarily signify the person of a verb by a personal pronoun. "*I* read" (1st person), "*you* read" (2nd person), and "*he/she/it* reads" (3rd person). While Greek does have personal pronouns, since the spelling of the verb indicates the person, personal pronouns are therefore not necessary and are added primarily for emphasis.

Number. Just like nouns, verbs can be singular—"I *am*," "she *reads*"—or plural—"we *are*," "they *read*." Greek also has the dual number for verbs, but such rare forms will not be included in the book. You can find those forms in Appendix D.

εἰμί = To Be

The Greek word for "to be/exist" is εἰμί. Its forms are irregular, which means that they do not follow a predictable pattern and alas, they must simply be memorized.

	Singular		*Plural*	
1st person	εἰμί	I am	ἐσμέν	we are
2nd person	εἶ	you are	ἐστέ	you are
3rd person	ἐστί(ν)	he/she/it is	εἰσί(ν)	they are

For the 3rd person, although you see "he/she/it" and "they" in the translations, this can be a bit misleading, as these verbs will almost always have a noun for the subject of the sentence.

❡ νόμος, –ου, ὁ = law | δῶρον, –ου, τό = gift | θεός, –οῦ, ὁ = a god, God

ὁ νόμος δῶρόν ἐστιν.

The law is a gift.

ὁ θεός ἐστιν.

The god exists. / God exists.

As you can see in the first example with δῶρον, Greek often uses a noun without a definite article where English would use an indefinite article.

You may be puzzled by the (ν) at the end of the 3rd person endings. This is called a "movable ν." When ἐστί and εἰσί appear before a word that begins with a vowel (or at the end of a clause) the ν is added. When the next word begins with a consonant, it is left out. This is for phonetic reasons, much like the "movable n" of the indefinite article in English, e.g., *an* animal, but *a* person.

Greek has an odd exception to the rule that singular subjects take singular verbs and plural subjects take plural verbs. Greek *neuter plural* subjects always take singular verbs.

τὰ βιβλία δῶρά ἐστιν (not εἰσίν).

The books are gifts.

Vocabulary

In each chapter you will be given vocabulary based on the most common words from that chapter's sentences. It is accordingly necessary to memorize these words *before* beginning your example sentences. It will enable your translations to be quicker and therefore more enjoyable. Entries for nouns have four parts: the standard form (nominative, explained in the next chapter), the genitive ending (also explained in the next chapter), and the definite article, along with the most common definition. The genitive ending is given so that you will know what declension a noun belongs to. The article will tell you the gender of the noun. You will find this system employed not only in this book but in most dictionaries. Vocabulary entries marked with a ▸ are discussed in the Etymology and Discussion Topics section at the end of each chapter. The vocabulary section at the back of the book contains all of the vocabulary from the individual chapters.

ἀγάπη, –ης, ἡ = love

▸ ἀλήθεια, –ας, ἡ = truth

▸ ἀρετή, –ῆς, ἡ = excellence, virtue

▸ βιβλίον, –ου, τό = book, scroll

δῶρον, –ου, τό = gift

ἔργον, –ου, τό = work, deed

ζωή, –ῆς, ἡ = life

θεός, –οῦ, ὁ = a god, God

▸ λόγος, –ου, ὁ = word; reason

νόμος, –ου, ὁ = law; custom

σοφία, –ας, ἡ = wisdom

φόβος, –ου, ὁ = fear

χαρά, –ᾶς, ἡ = joy

ψυχή, –ῆς, ἡ = soul, spirit

καί (conj. and adv.) = (conj.) and; (adv.) also, even.

> ¶ Context will tell you whether καί is the conjunction or the adverb. For now, try "and." If that doesn't work for your translation, then try the adverb "also," or "even."

Sentences

1. ὁ θεὸς ἀγάπη ἐστίν. (1 John 4:8)

ὁ θεὸς ἀγάπη ἐστίν.

> ¶ Notice that Greek uses the definite article where English does not.

2. ὁ φόβος ἐστὶ προσδοκία κακοῦ. (Chrysippus, *Fragments*)

ὁ φόβος ἐστί προσδοκία κακοῦ.

> ¶ προσδοκία = expectation
>
> κακοῦ = of evil. This is in the genitive case, which we will discuss in the following chapter.

3. φόβος οὐκ ἔστιν ἐν τῇ ἀγάπῃ. (1 John 4:18)

> ¶ φόβος lacks the definite article here, but it is translated the same as ὁ φόβος in #2.
>
> οὐκ = not
>
> ἐν = in
>
> τῇ ἀγάπῃ = in love. This is the definite article and a noun in the dative case, which we will discuss in the following chapters.

4. ἐγώ εἰμι ἡ ὁδὸς καὶ ἡ ἀλήθεια καὶ ἡ ζωή. (John 14:6)

> ¶ ἐγώ = I. This is the 1st person personal pronoun, which you will learn in chapter 4.
>
> ὁδός = road, way. This is a rare feminine 2nd declension noun, hence the definite article ἡ and not ὁ.

5. ἐγὼ καὶ ὁ πατὴρ ἕν ἐσμεν. (John 10:30)

¶ ἐγώ = I

πατήρ = father. You will learn this 3rd declension masculine noun in chapter 8.

ἕν = one, a numerical adjective you will learn in chapter 22.

ἐσμεν: As you can see, the default translation "we are" doesn't quite work here since we have two subjects.

6. σὺ εἶ ὁ υἱὸς τοῦ θεοῦ. (John 1:49)

¶ σὺ = you. You will learn this 2nd person personal pronoun in chapter 4.

υἱός = son

τοῦ θεοῦ = of God. This is another genitive (τοῦ is the definite article, θεοῦ the noun) which you will learn in the following chapter.

7. ἡ εὐδαιμονία ἐστὶν εὔροια βίου. (Zeno of Citium, in Stobaeus, *Anthology*)

¶ εὐδαιμονία = happiness

εὔροια = good flow, prosperous course

βίου = of life (a genitive).

8. λύπης ἰατρός ἐστιν ὁ φίλος. (Menander, *Fragments*)

¶ λύπης = of grief (a genitive)

ὁ φίλος = friend

ἰατρός = physician

9. ὁ ὕπνος ἐστὶ σωμάτων σωτηρία. (Menander, *Fragments*)

¶ ὕπνος = sleep

σωτηρία = preservation; salvation

σωμάτων = of bodies (a genitive)

10. ἡ προπέτεια πολλοῖς ἐστιν αἰτία κακῶν. (Menander, *Fragments*)

¶ προπέτεια = rashness, haste

πολλοῖς = for many (a dative)

αἰτία = cause

κακῶν = of evils (a genitive)

Etymology and Discussion Topics

ἀλήθεια, –ας, ἡ = truth

Greek often attaches an alpha to the beginning of words to make a negative, much like the "un" in "unkind" and "unwise." Many English words derived from Greek, such as "amoral" and "agnostic," retain this negative alpha, called the "privative alpha." In the case of ἀλήθεια, the word is a combination of a privative alpha and a variation of the word λήθη, which means "forgetfulness."

ἀρετή, –ῆς, ἡ = excellence, virtue

This word is best translated as "excellence," although you will see it from time to time translated as "virtue." In Homer, ἀρετή is the word used to describe the skill of a warrior, but it can also be applied to the skill of a speaker, charioteer, etc. Later, it will come to refer to moral excellence, hence "virtue."

βιβλίον, –ου, τό = book, scroll

This Greek word is the reason why sometimes you will read works where "book" is used where you would expect "chapter," as in "Book Three of the *Iliad*." The reason is that ancient works like the *Iliad* were not usually written on a single scroll, but separated into different scrolls, hence βιβλίον A "Book One," βιβλίον B "Book Two," etc.

λόγος, –ου, ὁ = word, reason

This word was one of the most versatile nouns in the Greek language even before the New Testament. With the identification of Jesus as ὁ λόγος, this word takes on an even deeper meaning. Depending on the context, it can mean "word," "story," "reason," "account," and "explanation," among many other possibilities. After much study, you will eventually just think λόγος when you see the word, but for now you will need to think carefully about how to translate the word based on the context.

ὁ θεὸς ἀγάπη ἐστίν.

More will be said on Greek word order in the following chapters, but notice how Greek is not bound to word order like English. For your translations, however, it is usually best to use natural English word order. As in most places of doubt in this book, follow the advice of your instructor. Just because Greek does not have a rigid word order, it does not follow that word order is unimportant. On the contrary, one of the beautiful aspects of Greek is how a talented author can manipulate word order to create a desired effect. What might John be trying to accomplish by placing the two nouns next to each other in ὁ θεὸς ἀγάπη ἐστίν?

Chapter 3 ⁓

Subject and Predicate • Nouns: The Case System • Adjectives

Subject and Predicate

Before we discuss the case system, let's briefly explain the grammatical terms "subject" and "predicate." In simple terms, the subject is what or who the sentence is about, and the predicate is everything else. The subject can be quite long when it is modified by adjectives and other modifiers, and predicates can be quite complex. On a basic level, however, the subject is *what the sentence is about* and the predicate is *what you are saying about the subject.* Look at the following sentence:

Ancient Greek is a wonderfully complex language.

The subject is "Ancient Greek" and the predicate is "is a wonderfully complex language." "Ancient Greek" is what I am talking about, and "is a wonderfully complex language" is what I am saying about the subject, "Ancient Greek."

Nouns: The Case System

In English we can tell the function of a noun in a sentence by word order and through prepositions. Take the following two sentences:

The man eats the alligator.

The alligator eats the man.

Even though the words in these two sentences are exactly the same, they obviously communicate two very different scenarios. In English, we place the subject of the sentence before the verb and the object (more about objects later) after the verb.

In an *inflected* language such as Greek and Latin, the function of a noun is determined not by its placement in the sentence, but by the spelling of the noun. We can see traces of inflection in English.

Who sees you?

Whom do you see?

Likewise, in English, if we want to say something belongs to someone, we use the preposition "of" or an apostrophe and s, e.g., "The cloak of Plato" or "Plato's cloak." In an *inflected* language, ideas such as possession are communicated by the spelling of the noun, sometimes with the help of a preposition. Greek has five noun cases: nominative, genitive, dative, accusative, and vocative.

Nominative

This is the "subject" case. The nominative is the case under which all nouns and adjectives in your vocabulary (and all dictionaries) are listed.

In addition to being the subject of a sentence, a nominative can also be a *predicate nominative*. In the sentence "Socrates was a philosopher," both "Socrates" and "philosopher" would be in the nominative case, "Socrates" being the subject of the sentence and "philosopher" being a predicate nominative. Socrates is who the sentence is about, and "was a philosopher" is what is being said about Socrates. How do we tell what is the subject and what is the predicate nominative? Normally, the subject contains the definite article and the predicate nominative lacks one. In chapter 2, you had the following sentence:

ὁ θεὸς ἀγάπη ἐστίν. (1 John 4:8)

How do we know that this sentence should be translated "God is love" and not "Love is God"? The article in front of θεὸς and the absence of ἡ in front of ἀγάπη make it clear.

Genitive

The genitive case is used in Greek for several purposes, but can for the most part be translated with the preposition "of." Most genitives limit the

Start Chap 3 9/11/23,
memorize chart at PG 21.

scope of a noun. For example, "sword" is a noun that could refer to thousands of particular objects, but the "sword of Damocles" refers to one particular sword. "Love" could refer to many types of love, but "love of money" narrows the scope of the noun "love."

Dative

The dative case is the most varied in Greek and performs multiple roles which you will learn in subsequent chapters. The most common way to translate the dative is with "to" or "for."

Accusative

The accusative is most often the case of the *direct object*. In the sentence "Socrates taught *Plato*," Plato is the object directly affected by the verb "taught," and is hence the *direct object*.

Vocative

The vocative case is the case of address. In the sentence "Socrates, stop talking," Socrates is being addressed by the speaker and would be in the vocative case in Greek. In the sentence "Socrates would not stop talking," Socrates is the subject of the sentence and would be in the nominative case in Greek. Since the vocative is for the most part identical or very similar to the nominative, it is not suggested (although it is noble) to memorize the vocative for the different declensions. You already have enough to memorize, and the vocative is also usually identifiable by context or the use of the interjection ὦ "oh." In addition, the plural vocative is always identical to the plural nominative. Therefore, any vocatives will be given only for singular nouns, and in parentheses.

Greek Cases: A Simple Study Guide

Although the following chart is simplistic and there are exceptions, it is best to memorize this as you familiarize yourself with cases.

"subject" case	Nominative
"of" case	Genitive
"to/for" case	Dative
"object" case	Accusative
"address" case	Vocative

1st and 2nd Declensions: Model Nouns

For each declension, you will be asked to memorize a few model nouns. The reason for this is that if you memorize the declension of ψυχή, you will know how to decline any 1st declension noun you see that ends in the pattern –η, –ης, ἡ. Almost all Greek nouns fall into certain spelling patterns based upon adding endings to a stem (the part of the word that tends not to change). If, therefore, you memorize the endings of a few model nouns, you don't need to memorize all the declensions for every noun you encounter. We have here two model nouns for the 1st declension and two model nouns for the 2nd declension. The reason for two model nouns in the 1st declension is that, as you remember from last chapter, if the stem ends in ε, ι, or ρ, the singular endings will have an alpha (α) instead of the normal eta (η). For the second declension, we have one model noun for 2nd declension masculine nouns and one model noun for 2nd declension neuter nouns.

	1st Declension Feminine	1st Declension Feminine	2nd Declension Masculine	2nd Declension Neuter
	ψυχή = soul	χαρά = joy	λόγος = word	βιβλίον = book
Singular				
Nominative	ψυχ–ή	χαρ–ά	λόγ–ος	βιβλί–ον
Genitive	ψυχ–ῆς	χαρ–ᾶς	λόγ–ου	βιβλί–ου
Dative	ψυχ–ῇ	χαρ–ᾷ	λόγ–ῳ	βιβλί–ῳ
Accusative	ψυχ–ήν	χαρ–άν	λόγ–ον	βιβλί–ον
(Vocative)	(ψυχή)	(χαρά)	(λόγε)	(βιβλίον)
Plural				
Nominative	ψυχ–αί	χαρ–αί	λόγ–οι	βιβλί–α
Genitive	ψυχ–ῶν	χαρ–ῶν	λόγ–ων	βιβλί–ων
Dative	ψυχ–αῖς	χαρ–αῖς	λόγ–οις	βιβλί–οις
Accusative	ψυχ–άς	χαρ–άς	λόγ–ους	βιβλί–α

Notice how the nominative and accusative for the neuter noun βιβλίον are the same. This pattern holds for all neuter nouns.

Adjectives

Adjectives are words that *modify* nouns. The adjective "classical" modifies the noun "language" in the sentence "We should all study a *classical* language." In Greek, adjectives must *agree* with the nouns they modify in *gender*, *number*, and *case*.

Gender. As you learned in chapter 2, nouns have *gender* and are either masculine, feminine, or neuter. This means that masculine nouns must be modified by masculine adjectives, feminine nouns must be modified by feminine adjectives, and neuter nouns must be modified by neuter adjectives. Adjectives (usually) have endings for three genders to match the gender of the noun being modified.

Number. Agreement in *number* means that singular nouns are modified by singular adjectives and plural nouns are modified by plural adjectives.

Case. Finally, agreement in *case* means that nominative nouns must be modified by nominative adjectives, accusative nouns must be modified by accusative adjectives, etc.

Greek adjectives fall into 2 broad groups. The first group is called 1st and 2nd declension adjectives. The title can be a little misleading. This is really one group of adjectives, but it gets its name from the fact that its endings resemble the endings of the nouns of the 1st and 2nd declensions.

Our model adjective for 1st and 2nd declension adjectives is καλός, which means "beautiful, fine, noble."

	Masculine	Feminine	Neuter
Singular			
Nominative	καλ–ός	καλ–ή	καλ–όν
Genitive	καλ–οῦ	καλ–ῆς	καλ–οῦ
Dative	καλ–ῷ	καλ–ῇ	καλ–ῷ
Accusative	καλ–όν	καλ–ήν	καλ–όν
(Vocative)	(καλέ)	(καλή)	(καλόν)
Plural			
Nominative	καλ–οί	καλ–αί	καλ–ά
Genitive	καλ–ῶν	καλ–ῶν	καλ–ῶν
Dative	καλ–οῖς	καλ–αῖς	καλ–οῖς
Accusative	καλ–ούς	καλ–άς	καλ–ά

Good news. If you have already memorized the endings for ψυχή, λόγος, and βιβλίον, you have already memorized the endings for καλός. In your vocabulary and most dictionaries, 1st and 2nd declension adjectives will be listed as follows:

καλός, –ή, –όν (adj.) = beautiful, fine, noble

ἅγιος, –α, –ον (adj.) = holy

The –ος, –η, –ον endings tell you that this adjective declines exactly like your model adjective καλός. If the stem of the adjective ends in ε, ι, or ρ, the feminine singular endings will have α instead of η and will be listed like ἅγιος above.

The definite article "the" is likewise declined and must agree with the noun it is modifying in gender, number, and case.

	Masculine	Feminine	Neuter
Singular			
Nominative	ὁ	ἡ	τό
Genitive	του	τῆς	τοῦ
Dative	τῷ	τῇ	τῷ
Accusative	τόν	τήν	τό
Plural			
Nominative	οἱ	αἱ	τά
Genitive	τῶν	τῶν	τῶν
Dative	τοῖς	ταῖς	τοῖς
Accusative	τούς	τάς	τά

In Greek the preferred position to place the adjective is in the *attributive* position, which means right after the definite article. There are two forms of attributive word order, a shorter form and a longer form. The shorter form is more common, definite article + adjective + noun:

¶ ἀγαθός, –ή, –όν (adj.) = good | καλός, –ή, –όν (adj.) = beautiful

ὁ καλὸς λόγος

the beautiful word

αἱ καλαὶ ψυχαί

the beautiful souls

τὸ ἀγαθὸν βιβλίον

the good book

Occasionally you will see the longer form, definite article + noun + definite article + adjective:

ὁ λόγος ὁ καλός

the beautiful word

αἱ ψυχαὶ αἱ καλαί

the beautiful souls

τὸ βιβλίον τὸ ἀγαθόν

the good book

Both constructions are in the *attributive* position and are translated the same into English. While it might be tempting to ignore the term "attributive position," it is an extremely important concept. If an adjective is not in the attributive position, it is in the predicate position and therefore called a *predicate adjective*.

Look at the following example.

¶ χαλεπός, –ή, –όν (adj.) = difficult | τίμιος, –α, –ον (adj.) = valuable

τὸ χαλεπὸν βιβλίον ἐστὶ τίμιον.

The difficult book is valuable.

In this example the adjective χαλεπὸν "difficult" is in the attributive position and τίμιον "valuable" is in the predicate position. Even if we were to change the word order, the meaning of the sentence would stay the same, since the function of the adjectives is made clear by their attributive or predicate position.

τίμιον τὸ χαλεπὸν βιβλίον ἐστίν.

The difficult book is valuable.

Vocabulary

ἄρτος, –ου, ὁ = bread

βίος, –ου, ὁ = life

▶ ἡδονή, –ῆς, ἡ = pleasure

ὀργή, –ῆς, ἡ = anger

τιμή, –ῆς, ἡ = honor

χρόνος, –ου, ὁ = time

ἀγαθός, –ή, –όν (adj.) = good

ἀθάνατος, –ον (adj.) = immortal

❡ Some adjectives of the 1st and 2nd declension like ἀθάνατος, –ον lack feminine endings. They therefore use the masculine endings to modify both masculine and feminine nouns.

κακός, –ή, –όν (adj.) = bad, base, evil

▸ καλός, –ή, –όν (adj.) = beautiful, fine, noble

ξένος, –η, –ον (adj.) foreign, strange

οὐ (adv.) = not

❡ οὐ is used with verbs in the indicative mood. Before a word beginning with a vowel οὐ becomes οὐκ. Before a word beginning with a rough breathing, οὐ becomes οὐχ.

μή (adv.) = not

❡ μή is used with verbs not in the indicative mood. There are exceptions, but for now it is helpful to think οὐ/οὐκ/οὐχ = indicative, μή = imperative. However, οὐ, οὐκ, οὐχ, and μή are all translated the same in English.

Sentences

1. ἐγώ εἰμι ὁ ἄρτος τῆς ζωῆς. (John 6:35)

❡ ἐγώ = "I"

2. αἱ ἡδοναί εἰσι φθαρταί, αἱ τιμαί εἰσιν ἀθάνατοι. (Periander, in Diogenes Laertius, *Lives of Eminent Philosophers*)

❡ φθαρτός, –ή, –όν (adj.) = perishable

3. ἐγὼ οὐκ εἰμὶ ὁ Χριστός. (John 1:20)

❡ ἐγώ = "I"

Χριστός, –οῦ, ὁ = the Christ, the Messiah

4. ἀθάνατος ἡ ψυχή ἐστιν. (Clement of Rome, *First Homily*)

5. τὸ μέτρον ἐστὶν ἄριστον. (Cleobulus, in Diogenes Laertius, *Lives of Eminent Philosophers*)

❡ μέτρον, –ου, τό = the mean; moderation

ἄριστος, –η, –ον (adj.) = best

6. ὁ χρόνος ἰατρὸς τῶν πόνων ἐστίν. (Menander, *Fragments*)

❡ ἰατρός, –οῦ, ὁ = physician

πόνος, –ου, ὁ = toil, grief, suffering

▸ 7. τῷ σοφῷ ξένον οὐδέν ἐστιν. (Antisthenes, in Diogenes Laertius, *Lives of Eminent Philosophers*)

¶ ὁ σοφός = "the wise man"

οὐδέν = "nothing." Here it is nominative.

8. θεοῦ γάρ ἐσμεν συνεργοί. (1 Cor. 3:9)

¶ γάρ (conj.) = for (not a preposition)

συνεργός, –οῦ, ὁ = a co-worker, helper

▸ 9. ἀνελεύθεροι γάρ εἰσιν οἱ φιλάργυροι. (Menander, *Fragments*)

¶ γάρ (conj.) = for (not a preposition)

οἱ φιλάργυροι – "The greedy"

ἀνελεύθερος, –ον (adj.) = not free

10. μέγιστον ὀργῆς ἐστι φάρμακον ὁ λόγος. (Menander, *Fragments*)

¶ μέγιστος, –η, –ον (adj.) = greatest

▸ φάρμακον, –ου, τό = drug, remedy

Etymology and Discussion Topics

ἡδονή, –ῆς, ἡ = pleasure

From this word are derived the English words that denote pleasure, hedonism and the adjective hedonistic. Hedonism should not be confused with Epicureanism. In English, the adjective "epicurean" is most often used to denote what should properly be described as hedonistic. Keep an eye out for quotations by Epicurus in the following chapters and see if you can figure out the distinction between the philosophy of Epicurus and hedonism.

καλός, –ή, –όν (adj.) = beautiful, fine, noble

This adjective is sometimes difficult to translate. It means "beautiful," but it is often used to refer to nonphysical beauty, hence the translation "fine, noble." The idea of beauty, therefore, was both physical and ethical.

τῷ σοφῷ ξένον οὐδέν ἐστιν.

The adjective ξένος is the word from which our word "xenophobia" is derived. It means "foreign," but it can also mean "strange, unfamiliar." What do you think Antisthenes had in mind with the saying τῷ σοφῷ ξένον οὐδέν ἐστιν?

ἀνελεύθεροι γάρ εἰσιν οἱ φιλάργυροι.

You will encounter many such sayings of the famous Greek comic poet Menander in this book under the heading *Sententiae Menandri*. We are fortunate to possess such fantastic maxims and proverbs, but we are unfortunate not to have the contexts in which the vast majority of these lines were uttered. Take the sentence above, for example. The adjective ἀνελεύθεροι means "not free," but it can also mean servile or unpolished. Does this sentence mean that greedy people are "servile," or is one of Menander's characters saying that attachment to wealth and possessions inhibits our ability to be free?

φάρμακον, –ου τό = drug, remedy

This, like many Greek words, can have a positive and a negative meaning depending on the context. It is used for healing drugs, from which we get our word "pharmacy." It can also refer to a harmful drug, hence "poison." Finally, it can refer to a "charm" or a "potion." Euripides masterfully uses the ambiguity of φάρμακον in plays such as the *Medea* and *Hippolytus*.

Chapter 4 ⌒

Verbs • Present Active Indicative • Present Active Imperative •
Personal Pronouns: 1st and 2nd Person

Verbs

In classical Greek, verbs have *person, number, tense, voice,* and *mood.* In chapter 2 you learned about person (1st, 2nd, 3rd) and number (singular, plural). Below is a brief summary of *tense, voice,* and *mood.* We will go into greater detail as these tenses, voices, and moods are introduced in the coming chapters.

Tense

Strictly speaking, tense refers to the time of an action, yet Greek tenses also express aspect. Aspect will be covered in chapter 12. There are seven tenses in classical Greek: *present, future, imperfect, aorist, perfect, pluperfect,* and *future perfect.* We will discuss each tense in the coming chapters. This chapter will focus exclusively on the present tense.

Voice

Voice concerns where the action of a verb begins and where it ends. Like English, Greek has an *active* voice, where the action originates with the subject, "I am reading the book," and a *passive* voice, where the subject is the recipient of the action, "The books is read by me." In addition to the active and passive voices, Greek has a third voice, the *middle.* For the time being we will discuss only the active voice. We will discuss the middle and passive voices in chapter 14.

Mood

Mood concerns the manner in which the author views the action of the verb. Greek has four moods: *indicative, imperative, subjunctive,* and *optative*. Mood is one of the more difficult features of ancient Greek for English speakers. English relies on helper words and phrases like "may," "would," and "let us" to expresses concepts for which Greek uses different moods. In the first half of the book, we will focus only on the indicative and imperative moods.

Omega Verbs

Just as nouns fall into three groups with similar patterns, or declensions, Greek verbs fall into three groups with similar patterns, or conjugations: (1) omega verbs, (2) contract verbs (technically a subcategory of omega verbs), and (3) μι verbs.

This chapter will introduce *omega verbs,* so called because the form listed in the dictionary ends in the letter omega. Our model omega verb will be the Greek verb λύω, "to loosen." While it is far from the most exciting of verbs, λύω has been chosen as our model omega verb because of the regularity of its forms. The endings of omega verbs are made by attaching the endings to the stem of the verb, in this case λυ–. To find the present stem of a verb simply remove the omega. Although the endings below are actually a combination of something called a "thematic vowel" plus the endings, it is easier at this point to think of them (and memorize them) as single endings.

Present Active Indicative

Present (Tense) Active (Voice) Indicative (Mood) of λύω = to loosen			
	Singular		Plural
1st Person	λύ–ω "I loosen"	λύ–ομεν	"we loosen"
2nd Person	λύ–εις "you loosen"	λύ–ετε	"you loosen"
3rd Person	λύ–ει "he/she/it loosens"	λύ–ουσι(ν)	"they loosen"

The *indicative mood* states facts and is by far the most common mood in Greek. It *indicates* that things are a certain way. It is helpful to think of the indicative mood as the default mood.

Transitive and Intransitive Verbs

At this point it is helpful to distinguish between two types of verbs: *transitive* and *intransitive*. A transitive verb is a verb whose meaning "crosses" (from the Latin *transire*) from the subject to another noun called an object. In the English sentence "Socrates throws the book," the verb is transitive and takes the object "book." In the sentence "Socrates breathes," the verb is intransitive and does not take an object; its action affects only the subject "Socrates." Many verbs can be both transitive and intransitive. The verb "speaks" can be transitive ("In conversations Socrates always speaks the truth") or intransitive ("In conversations Socrates always speaks"). The distinction just described between transitive and intransitive is slightly artificial and simplistic. The concept will become more nuanced as you read more Greek, and will become very helpful when we come to the other voices (the middle and the passive) in chapter 14.

For the vast majority of transitive Greek verbs, any direct objects they take will be in the accusative case, the *accusative of direct object*. Certain Greek verbs take genitive and dative nouns, but your vocabulary in this book and in most dictionaries will give you this information. Therefore, if you don't see (+ genitive) or (+ dative) next to a transitive verb in the vocabulary, it takes an *accusative of direct object*. Finally, it is the custom to print all Greek verbs in dictionaries under the 1st person, singular, present, active, indicative form. The English definition will always be expressed in what is called an infinitive (more on infinitives in chapter 7): "to loosen," "to teach," "to live," etc.

❡ δεσμός, –οῦ, ὁ = chain | ἄνθρωπος, –ου, ὁ = human being, person, man

λύω τὸν δεσμόν.

I loosen the chain.

λύω τοὺς δεσμούς.

I loosen the chains.

ὁ ἄνθρωπος λύει τοὺς δεσμούς.

The person loosens the chains.

οἱ ἄνθρωποι τὸν δεσμὸν λύουσιν.

The people loosen the chain.

Remember that Greek does not have a rigid word order. The following two examples are translated exactly the same in English.

οἱ ἄνθρωποι τὸν δεσμὸν λύουσιν.

The people loosen the chain.

οἱ ἄνθρωποι λύουσι τὸν δεσμόν.

The people loosen the chain.

Present Active Imperative

As opposed to the indicative mood which states facts, the *imperative* mood commands.

Plato *listens* to Socrates. (Indicative)

Plato, *listen* to Socrates! (Imperative)

	Present Active Imperative of λύω			
	Singular		*Plural*	
2nd person	λῦ–ε	"loosen!"	λύ–ετε	"loosen!"
3rd person	λυ–έτω	"let him/her loosen!"	λυ–όντων	"let them loosen!"

Second person imperatives are commands and are common in English. We seldom use 3rd person imperatives and instead use the "let them…" construction, e.g., "Let them eat cake." Although this is the best way to translate Greek 3rd person imperatives in English, remember that they are 3rd person commands. You are not really commanding someone in the 2nd person to order someone in the 3rd person do something. Finally, you don't need to put an exclamation point after each translation of an imperative. They have been included in the above translations to clearly distinguish the imperative mood from the indicative mood.

Mood	Examples	
Indicative	ὁ ἄνθρωπος λύει τὸν δεσμόν.	The person loosens the chain.
Imperative	λῦε τὸν δεσμόν.	Loosen the chain. (Spoken to one person.)
Imperative	λύετε τὸν δεσμόν.	Loosen the chain. (Spoken to more than one person.)

(continues)

Mood	Examples	
Imperative	ὁ ἄνθρωπος λυέτω τὸν δεσμόν.	Let the person loosen the chain.
Indicative	οἱ ἄνθρωποι λύουσι τὸν δεσμόν.	The people loosen the chain.
Imperative	ἄνθρωποι, λύετε τὸν δεσμόν.	People, loosen the chain.
Imperative	οἱ ἄνθρωποι λυόντων τὸν δεσμόν.	Let the people loosen the chain.

You might ask, "Since the 2nd person plural is the same in the imperative as it is in the indicative, how will I know the difference? Why is the last example not 'People, you are loosening the chain'"? The answer is context. In real Greek context will make it clear which mood is intended.

Finally, there is no 1st person imperative. If someone wishes to command oneself, Greek has another expression that you will learn in chapter 32.

Present Imperative of εἰμί

Here is the present imperative of εἰμί, "to be."

	Singular	Plural
2nd Person	ἴσθι	ἔστε
3rd Person	ἔστω	ἔστων

¶ ταπεινός– ή, –όν (adj.) = humble | διδάσκαλος, –ου, ὁ = teacher | χαλεπός, –ή, –όν = difficult

ἴσθι ταπεινός.

Be humble.

οἱ διδάσκαλοι μὴ ἔστων χαλεποί.

Let the teachers not be difficult!

Personal Pronouns: 1st and 2nd Person

A pronoun is a word that "stands in" for a noun. The most common pronouns are called *personal* pronouns, e.g., "I," "you." We will encounter other types of pronouns in subsequent chapters. Because personal pronouns are so common, it is helpful now to learn the personal pronoun for the 1st and 2nd person. We will learn the 3rd person personal pronoun in chapter 6.

	1st Person Personal Pronoun		2nd Person Personal Pronoun	
Singular				
Nominative	ἐγώ	I	σύ	you
Genitive	ἐμοῦ (μου)	of me	σοῦ (σου)	of you
Dative	ἐμοί (μοι)	to/for me	σοί (σοι)	to/for you
Accusative	ἐμέ (με)	me	σέ (σε)	you
Plural				
Nominative	ἡμεῖς	we	ὑμεῖς	you
Genitive	ἡμῶν	of us	ὑμῶν	of you
Dative	ἡμῖν	to/for us	ὑμῖν	to/for you
Accusative	ἡμᾶς	us	ὑμᾶς	you

Remember that for the genitive and dative cases, the translations will vary as we learn more uses of these cases. You will notice alternate forms in the singular genitive, dative, and accusative cases enclosed in parentheses. There is no difference in translation.

Vocabulary

▸ ἄνθρωπος, –ου, ὁ = human being, person

ἐπιθυμία, –ας, ἡ = a desire, longing for (+ genitive)

▸ καρδία, –ας, ἡ = heart

καρπός, –οῦ, ὁ = fruit

κύριος, –ου, ὁ = lord

λίθος, –ου, ὁ = stone

υἱός, –οῦ, ὁ = son

ἀγαπητός, –ή, –όν (adj.) = beloved

ἀναμάρτητος, –ον (adj.) = unerring; blameless, without sin

δέ (conj.) = and, but

> ¶ The word δέ is a common Greek word used to connect clauses. With the exception of proverbs, Greek loves to have some word, such as δέ, to show the relationship of the current clause to the previous one. Context (or your notes if there is no context) will tell you whether you should translate δέ as "and" or "but," or if you should leave it untranslated.

εἰ = if

βάλλω = to throw

▸ γιγνώσκω (written γινώσκω in Koine) = to know

λέγω = to say, speak

φέρω = to bear, endure; bring forth

Sentences

1. κακὸν φέρουσι καρπὸν οἱ κακοὶ φίλοι. (Menander, *Fragments*)

> ❡ φίλος, –ου, ὁ = a friend

▸ 2. ἀργὸς μὴ ἴσθι. (Thales, in Stobaeus, *Anthology*)

> ❡ ἀργός, –ή, –όν (adj.) = not work-
> ing; lazy

3. ὁ δὲ θεὸς γινώσκει τὰς καρδίας ὑμῶν. (Luke 16:15)

> ❡ ὑμῶν = literally "of you." The
> genitive of the personal pronoun
> is used to indicate possession (see
> chapter 5). It is therefore possible
> to translate it as "your."
>
> δὲ: Here Jesus is contrasting how
> people present themselves to
> the world with how God sees
> them. Hence "but" is the correct
> translation here.

4. ὁ ἀναμάρτητος ὑμῶν πρῶτος ἐπ᾽ αὐτὴν βαλέτω λίθον. (John 8:7)

> ❡ ὁ ἀναμάρτητος ὑμῶν = "the
> blameless/sinless one of you." As
> we will see in chapter 6, Greek
> puts the definite article before an
> adjective to make it a noun.
>
> πρῶτος: technically an adjec-
> tive which can mean "before"
> or "first." Often Greek uses an
> adjective where we would use an
> adverb.
>
> ἐπ᾽ αὐτὴν = at her. "Her" is the
> woman caught in adultery in this
> famous passage from John. For
> the 3rd person personal pronoun,
> see chapter 6.
>
> βαλέτω: an aorist imperative, but
> for the time being, translate it as
> if it were the present imperative
> βαλλέτω.

5. λέγει αὐτῷ Σίμων Πέτρος, "Κύριε, ποῦ ὑπάγεις;" (John 13:36)

> ¶ αὐτῷ = "to him." The "him" in this passage is Jesus. Again, see chapter 6 for the 3rd person personal pronoun.
>
> Σίμων Πέτρος = Simon Peter
>
> Κύριε: It is the custom in most printed texts of scripture (though not in the manuscripts) to capitalize the beginning of a direct quotation. This book will keep this custom as well as add quotation marks.
>
> ποῦ (adv.) = where?
>
> ὑπάγω = to lead; to go away, withdraw.

► 6. μεγαλύνει ἡ ψυχή μου τὸν κύριον. (Luke 1:46)

> ¶ μεγαλύνω = to extol, magnify

7. σὺ εἶ ὁ υἱός μου ὁ ἀγαπητός. (Luke 3:22)

8. εἰ υἱὸς εἶ τοῦ θεοῦ, βάλε σεαυτὸν κάτω. (Matthew 4:6)

> ¶ βάλε: an aorist imperative, but for the time being, translate it as if it were the present imperative βάλλε.
>
> σεαυτὸν = yourself
>
> κάτω (adv.) = down

9. δίωκε δόξην καὶ ἀρετήν, φεῦγε δὲ ψόγον. (Menander, *Fragments*)

> ¶ διώκω = to pursue
>
> δόξα, –ης, ἡ = glory
>
> φεύγω = to flee
>
> ψόγος, –ου, ὁ = blame, censure

10. ἔστω δὲ ὁ λόγος ὑμῶν ναὶ ναί, οὒ οὔ. (Matthew 5:37)

> ¶ This is a difficult sentence. The idea is "let your X mean X, and your Y mean Y."
>
> ναί = yes.

Etymology and Discussion Topics

ἄνθρωπος, –ου, ὁ = human being, person

This common noun refers to both sexes, but because of the lack of a suitable English equivalent, it is most often translated as "man" in the general sense. All of our "anthro" words, e.g., anthropology, misanthrope, philanthropist, are derived from this noun.

καρδία, –ας, ἡ = heart

The majority of our medical terminology, like cardiology, comes from Greek as a result of the influence of the Hippocratic school on western medicine. The Hippocratic practitioners were quite different from those whom we would today call physicians. For example, an early Hippocratic oath contained a prohibition against putting a patient under the knife, and it also forbade the taking of money in exchange for services.

γιγνώσκω (written γινώσκω in Koine) = to know

This word and similar ones you will learn later with the γν– root signify "knowing." There are a great many English words derived from this root, e.g., Gnosticism, agnostic (notice the privative alpha), cognitive.

ἀργὸς μὴ ἴσθι.

The adjective ἀργός is a combination of an alpha privative and ἔργον, –ου, τό = work, and was originally spelled ἀεργός. The idea is that words modified by this adjective don't "do anything." This is the adjective in the famous passage from James 2:20 about "faith without works," which you will translate in chapter 8.

μεγαλύνει ἡ ψυχή μου τὸν κύριον. (Luke 1:46)

The Latin translation for μεγαλύνει is *magnificat*, hence the common title of Mary's hymn in Luke, "The Magnificat."

Chapter 5 ⚬⟋

Dative of Indirect Object • Dative of Respect • Genitive of Possession •
Objective Genitive • Prepositions

Dative of Indirect Object and Dative of Respect

When we first introduced the dative case, we described it as the "to/for" case. While we will learn other uses of the dative in this book, let's start with two of the most common.

Dative of Indirect Object

As we saw last chapter, the direct object is the noun *directly* affected by the verb and is put into the accusative case in Greek.

> ¶ λίθος, –ου, ὁ = stone

ὁ Πέτρος βάλλει τὸν λίθον.

Peter throws **the stone** (direct object).

Sometimes a person or an object is *indirectly* affected by the verb and is put into the dative case, hence the *dative of indirect object.*

> ¶ νέμω = "deal out, distribute, give"

ὁ Πέτρος νέμει τὰ βιβλία **τῷ Παύλῳ.**

Peter gives the scrolls **to Paul** (indirect object).

One very common use of the dative of indirect object occurs with reported speech. Words of speaking, like λέγω, use a dative of indirect object for the person to whom the speaker is talking. Greek views what is said as the direct object and the person to whom something is said as the indirect object.

ὁ Κρίτων λέγει τῷ Σωκράτει, "φεῦγε."

Crito says to Socrates, "Flee!"

Dative of Respect

Closely related to the dative of indirect object is the *dative of respect*, which indicates the person or thing for whom something is true or is done.

> ❡ ἀμαθία, –ας, ἡ = ignorance | θάνατος, –ου, ὁ = death |
> ἡσυχία, –ας, ἡ = peace | ταπεινός, –ή, –όν = humble |
> μένω = to remain

ἡ ἀμαθία θάνατός ἐστι τοῖς ἀνθρώποις.

Ignorance is death for humans.

ἡ ἡσυχία μένει τῷ ταπεινῷ ἀνθρώπῳ.

Peace remains for the humble person.

A helpful way to distinguish the dative of indirect object from the dative of respect is to be aware that datives of indirect object usually involve a transitive verb, while datives of respect usually involve an intransitive verb.

Genitive of Possession and Objective Genitive

The translation of the genitive case is usually easy, normally with "of." There are some important exceptions we will learn later. Even though at the moment you can probably get away with just translating the genitive as "of," it is helpful to know why you are translating it that way. Two common genitives, both of which can be translated with "of," are the *genitive of possession* and the *objective genitive*.

Genitive of Possession

The *genitive of possession* indicates the person or object to which a thing belongs. It need not always be a physical object.

> ¶ οἶκος, –ου, ὁ = house | κύριος, –ου, ὁ = lord |
> νόστος, –ου, ὁ = homecoming | Ἀχαιοί, –ῶν, οἱ = Achaeans

ὁ οἶκος τοῦ κυρίου

The house of the Lord

ὁ νόστος τῶν Ἀχαιῶν

The homecoming of the Achaeans

Objective Genitive

The *objective genitive* denotes the object of a verbal idea packed into a noun. Sometimes "for" is preferable to "of" in the translation of an objective genitive.

> ¶ φόβος, –ου, ὁ = fear | τιμή, –ῆς, ἡ = honor

ὁ φόβος τοῦ θανάτου

The fear of death

ἡ ἐπιθυμία τῆς τιμῆς

The desire of honor *or* The desire for honor

You can see how there is a big difference in meaning between the genitive of possession and the objective genitive. In the above two examples, the nouns in the genitive do not possess the nouns in the nominative.

Context will tell you if a genitive is a genitive of possession or an objective genitive. Consider the following example:

ἡ ἀγάπη τοῦ θεοῦ

The love of God

τοῦ θεοῦ would be a genitive of possession if it refers to the love God feels for human beings, but it would be an objective genitive if it refers to the love human beings feel for God. Don't worry. Even though you might doubt it at times, Greek authors will always strive for clarity and make their meaning clear through context.

Summary of Case Uses Learned Thus Far

As we progress in this book, we will periodically list all of the noun constructions that we have encountered. When you are translating the sentences, always be sure to identify these types of nouns. The extra effort demanded will not only improve your knowledge of Greek, but it will save you time in the long run when you translate more complex sentences.

Nominative	*Genitive*	*Dative*	*Accusative*
Subject	Genitive of Possession	Dative of Indirect Object	Direct Object
Predicate Nominative	Objective Genitive	Dative of Respect	

Subtleties of the Cases

Many of the grammatical terms you will encounter in this book are simplified. For example, there are some datives in this book that grammarians would not classify as a true dative of respect, but as another closely related dative such as the dative of interest. Likewise, many prefer the term subjective genitive to genitive of possession. However, in this book we will use terms such as dative of respect and genitive of possession as broad categories. The multitude of different uses of the cases can often be intimidating for beginning students of Greek. What grammarians have done is surveyed the vast amount of texts and accounted for a multitude of different uses for the different cases. They then try and categorize these uses. Often it is not clear which category a particular word might fall under, and sometimes the distinctions are artificial. This should in no way be taken as a condemnation of the excellent and indispensable work of grammarians. For the beginning student, however, it is beneficial to sacrifice strict accuracy of terms for ease of memorization. Therefore, this book uses very broad categories that can be more easily memorized. You can familiarize yourself with the intricacies of the different cases as you progress in your knowledge of Greek by consulting one of the many Greek grammars available.

Prepositions

A preposition is a word that expresses one word's relationship to another part of the sentence. Prepositions begin prepositional phrases, which consist of the preposition and an object of a preposition—a word or a phrase (more on phrases in chapter 10). The object of the preposition is everything governed by a preposition.

The book ***on the bottom shelf*** is hardly read.

In this sentence the preposition "on" and the object of the preposition "the bottom shelf" form the prepositional phrase "on the bottom shelf."

Socrates would talk ***with*** anyone.

In this sentence the preposition "with" and the object of the preposition "anyone" form the prepositional phrase "with anyone."

Just like English, Greek employs prepositions, even though Greek is not as dependent upon prepositions since it employs the different case endings. Many words are in the genitive, dative, or accusative because they are the *object of a preposition*. For example, the preposition ἐν "in" always takes a noun in the dative case. If, therefore, you see a noun in the dative after ἐν, you don't need to wonder what kind of dative it is (indirect object, respect, etc.). It is simply the object of a preposition that takes the dative case. All prepositions listed in this book and most dictionaries will list the case that the preposition takes (some prepositions take more than one case). It is very helpful to memorize this, but it is not absolutely necessary if you are already struggling with memorization. The preposition will almost always take the case of whatever noun you see directly after it.

ἐν τῷ οἴκῳ τοῦ θεοῦ
in the house of God

παρὰ τὸν νόμον
contrary to the law

Vocabulary

βασιλεία, –ας, ἡ = kingdom

▸ δόξα, –ης, ἡ = glory, power; opinion

▸ ἰατρός, –οῦ, ὁ = doctor

▸ κόσμος, –ου, ὁ = order; an ornament, decoration; the world

λύπη, –ης, ἡ = grief

μέτρον, –ου, τό = measure, moderation

παιδεία, –ας, ἡ = education

τέχνη, –ης, ἡ = art, skill

τύχη, –ης, ἡ = chance, fortune

μακάριος, –α, –ον (adj.) = blessed, happy

ἀνά = up (+ acc.)

διά = through (+ gen.); on account of (+ acc.)

εἰς = to, into (+ acc.)

ἐκ (ἐξ before vowel) = out of (+ gen.)

ἐν = in, among, with (+ dat.)

ἐντός = within (+ gen.)

ἐπί (ἐπ’ before vowel; ἐφ’ before rough breathing) = on, upon (+ gen.); on, by, for (+ dat.); to, against (+ acc.)

κατά (κατ’ before vowel; καθ’ before rough breathing) = down from, against (+ gen.); in accordance with (+ acc.)

μετά (μετ’ before vowel; μεθ’ before rough breathing) = among, with (+ gen.); after (+ acc.)

ὑπέρ = over, on behalf of (+ gen); over, beyond (+ acc.)

ὑπό (ὑπ’ before vowel; ὑφ’ before rough breathing) = under, by (+ gen.); under, by (+ dat.); under, toward (+ acc.)

Sentences

1. ἡ βασιλεία τοῦ θεοῦ ἐντὸς ὑμῶν ἐστιν. (Luke 17:21)

2. τῆς λύπης ἰατρός ἐστιν ἀνθρώποις ὁ λόγος. (Menander, *Fragments*)

> ¶ Although we don't have the original context for this sentence, a good translation for λόγος might be "talk" or even "reason."

3. ἡ παιδεία ἐν ταῖς εὐτυχίαις ἐστὶ κόσμος, ἐν δὲ ταῖς ἀτυχίαις καταφυγή. (Aristotle, in Diogenes Laertius, *Lives of Eminent Philosophers*)

> ¶ εὐτυχία, –ας, ἡ = good luck, success
>
> ἀτυχία, –ας, ἡ = bad luck, misfortune
>
> καταφυγή, –ῆς, ἡ = an escape

▶ 4. τυφλὴ καὶ δύστηνος ἀνθρώποις ἡ τύχη ἐστίν. (Menander, *Fragments*)

❡ τυφλός, –ή, –όν (adj.) = blind

δύστηνος, –ον (adj.) = wretched, disastrous

5. δὸς δόξαν τῷ θεῷ. (John 9:24)

❡ δὸς = give: 2nd person singular imperative of the verb δίδωμι, which you will learn in chapter 30.

6. ἄγει πρὸς τὸ φῶς τὴν ἀλήθειαν ὁ χρόνος. (Menander, *Fragments*)

❡ ἄγω = to drive, lead

πρός = toward (+ acc.)

φῶς = light: a 3rd declension neuter accusative.

7. κύριός ἐστιν τοῦ σαββάτου ὁ υἱὸς τοῦ ἀνθρώπου. (Luke 6:5)

❡ σάββατον, –ου, τό = the Sabbath

▶ 8. μακάριοι οἱ καθαροὶ τῇ καρδίᾳ. (Matthew 5:8)

❡ οἱ καθαροὶ = the pure. We will learn about such substantive adjectives in the following chapter. You will notice the lack of a verb in this sentence. Often you must supply it. In this sentence you must supply "are."

▶ 9. ἔργοις φιλόπονος ἴσθι, μὴ λόγοις μόνον. (Menander, *Fragments*)

❡ φιλόπονος, –ον (adj.) = fond of toil/work

μόνον (adv.) = only

10. δίκαιος ἴσθι καὶ τοῖς φίλοις καὶ τοῖς ξένοις. (Menander, *Fragments*)

❡ δίκαιος, –α, –ον (adj.) = just

καί…καί = both…and

τοῖς φίλοις = friends

τοῖς ξένοις = strangers

Etymology and Discussion Topics

δόξα, –ης, ἡ = glory, power; opinion

This is a versatile word with both positive and negative connotations. Its primary meaning concerns appearance or reputation. Its meaning of "glory" implies that it is a good reputation. In Plato and other philosophers, δόξα is contrasted unfavorably to knowledge and is best translated as "opinion." See chapter 6 for the peculiar –α, –ης ending.

ἰατρός, –οῦ, ὁ = physician

From this word come our medical words with the suffix –trician and –trics, e.g., pediatrician (παῖς), geriatrics (γέρων), and psychiatry (ψυχή).

κόσμος, –ου, ὁ = order; an ornament, decoration; the world

Pythagoras is said to have been the first person to refer to the universe as the cosmos on account of its beauty and symmetry. The connection between order and beauty is a staple of Greek thought.

τυφλὴ δὲ καὶ δύστηνος ἀνθρώποις ἡ τύχη ἐστίν.

An important concept in classical Greek thought is τύχη. Although it is sometimes translated as "fate," it is closely bound up with the ideas of chance and randomness. τύχη is not something upon which one can safely depend. When we say "justice is blind" or when we depict blind statues that hold the scales of justice, we mean something positive. In theory, justice should not look to the stature of the persons involved, but only to the facts of the case. When the ancients called τύχη blind, they meant something different. In the above sentence, what might the meaning of τυφλὴ be?

μακάριοι οἱ καθαροὶ τῇ καρδίᾳ.

The formula of "blessed/happy/prosperous" + a description of a type of person was common in ancient wisdom literature. When the New Testament was translated from Greek into Latin, μακάριοι was translated as *beati*, hence our designation of this passage as "the beatitudes."

ἔργοις φιλόπονος ἴσθι, μὴ λόγοις μόνον.

One of the most popular tropes in Greek thought is the contrast between word and deed or speech and action. Compare the above sentence to our expression "If you're going to talk the talk, you've got to walk the walk."

Chapter 6 ⟿

Substantive Adjectives • αὐτός • 1st Declension
Nouns Continued

Substantive Adjectives

In English we sometimes use an adjective with the definite article in place of a noun. "Free," "brave," and "meek" are adjectives, not nouns, but we can turn them into nouns by adding the definite article.

The land of *the free* and the home of *the brave*.

The meek shall inherit the earth.

These are called *substantive adjectives*. Greek uses substantive adjectives in place of nouns far more often than English does. They are, however, relatively easy to spot since they will almost always be immediately preceded by the definite article and will not be immediately followed by a matching noun. Greek uses masculine substantive adjectives to signify persons (ἄνθρωπος being the implied noun), and it uses neuter substantive adjectives to signify abstract concepts and things. Sometimes it might be necessary to add "man," "things," etc. to your translations. Context and common English usage will be the best guides.

¶ σοφός, –ή, –όν (adj.) = wise | καθαρός, –ά, –όν (adj.) = pure | πονηρός, –ή, –όν (adj.) = wicked, evil

οἱ καθαροὶ τῇ καρδίᾳ

the pure in heart

ὁ σοφός

the wise man/person

τὰ καλά

beautiful things

τὰ κακά

base/evil things

τὸ καλόν

the beautiful

τὸ πονηρόν

evil

αὐτός

The word αὐτός is a common and versatile word. It performs three functions.

(1) αὐτός: 3rd Person Personal Pronoun "he/she/it"

This is the most common use. As you can see in the figure below, it is declined almost exactly like your model adjective of the 1st and 2nd declension, καλός, the only exception being –ο instead of –ον for the neuter nominative and accusative singular.

	Masculine	*Feminine*	*Neuter*
Singular			
Nominative	αὐτ–ός	αὐτ–ή	αὐτ–ό
Genitive	αὐτ–οῦ	αὐτ–ῆς	αὐτ–οῦ
Dative	αὐτ–ῷ	αὐτ–ῇ	αὐτ–ῷ
Accusative	αὐτ–όν	αὐτ–ήν	αὐτ–ό

(continues)

	Masculine	Feminine	Neuter
Plural			
Nominative	αὐτ–**οί**	αὐτ–**αί**	αὐτ–**ά**
Genitive	αὐτ–**ῶν**	αὐτ–**ῶν**	αὐτ–**ῶν**
Dative	αὐτ–**οῖς**	αὐτ–**αῖς**	αὐτ–**οῖς**
Accusative	αὐτ–**ούς**	αὐτ–**άς**	αὐτ–**ά**

When αὐτός is the 3rd person personal pronoun, it agrees in gender and number with its antecedent, while its case is determined by the pronoun's function within the sentence, i.e., it's a nominative if it's the subject, accusative if it's the direct object, etc. The word *antecedent* (from the Latin *antecedere* "to go before") refers to what a pronoun stands in for or points back to. In other words, the antecedent is who the "he/she/him/her" is or what the "it" is.

> λέγει *αὐτῷ* Σίμων Πέτρος, "Κύριε, ποῦ ὑπάγεις;"
>
> Simon Peter says *to him*, "Lord, where are you going?"

In this sentence from chapter 4, αὐτῷ is masculine and singular because the antecedent (Jesus) is masculine and singular. You would know this from the context if you were reading the passage from John's gospel. In this sentence αὐτῷ is dative because it is a dative of indirect object.

> ὁ ἀναμάρτητος ὑμῶν πρῶτος ἐπ᾽ αὐτὴν βαλέτω λίθον. (John 8:7)
>
> Let the sinless one among you first throw a stone at **her**.

In this sentence from chapter 4, αὐτὴν is feminine and singular because γυνή (woman) from the passage is feminine and singular. Again, you would know this because of the context from the passage. αὐτὴν is accusative because it is the object of the preposition ἐπί, which means "against" when it takes the accusative case.

To recap: The gender and number of αὐτός as the 3rd person personal pronoun matches the gender and number of the antecedent, but its case is determined by its function in the sentence.

Classical/Koine Distinction

In Classical Greek, αὐτός is not used for the 3rd person personal pronoun in the nominative case. The reason for this is to avoid confusion with usage #2 below. In its place you will find other words such as the demonstrative pronoun οὗτος (chapter 18). In Koine, however, this rule becomes relaxed and you will see αὐτός used as a nominative 3rd person pronoun.

(2) Intensive Adjective

The second usage of αὐτός is as an intensive adjective. An intensive adjective stresses the noun it is modifying. In English we usually form the intensive by "very," e.g., "I saw the very books you mentioned," or by adding "–self," which can be quite confusing since we also use "–self" to form the reflexive pronoun.

Socrates *himself* taught me.

Read Plato's dialogues *themselves*, not translations of them.

ὁ Ὅμηρος αὐτός παιδεύει ἐμέ.

Homer *himself* teaches me.

ὁ Ὅμηρος φέρει τὰ βιβλία αὐτά.

Homer brings the books *themselves* (i.e., not summaries).

When αὐτός functions as an intensive adjective, it is *always in the predicate position*. As you remember from chapter 3, the predicate position means it does NOT immediately follow the definite article.

(3) "The same"

When αὐτός is in the attributive position, which means that it comes directly after the definite article, it means "the same."

ὁ αὐτός Ὅμηρος παιδεύει ἐμέ.

The *same* Homer (not another less famous Homer) teaches me.

ὁ Ὅμηρος φέρει τὰ αὐτὰ βιβλία.

Homer brings the *same* books (not other books).

When deciding on how to translate αὐτός, the following chart should help.

When αὐτός is…	…translate it this way	Example
"by itself," i.e., not next to a noun that it agrees with in gender, number, and case or following the definite article	3rd person personal pronoun	γιγνώσκω αὐτήν = I know her
modifying a noun but does NOT immediately follow the definite article (predicate position)	intensive adjective	αὐτὴ ἡ βασιλεία = the kingdom itself
immediately after the definite article (attributive position)	"the same"	ἡ αὐτὴ βασιλεία = the same kingdom

1st Declension Nouns Continued

In order to keep things simple, when you were introduced to 1st declension nouns in chapter 3, two import subcategories were not mentioned. Some 1st declension nouns have an alpha in the nominative, accusative, and vocative singular and an eta in the genitive and dative singular. These nouns will rarely cause you problems since you have already memorized their endings.

	θάλαττα = the sea	
	Singular	Plural
Nominative	θάλαττ–α	θάλαττ–αι
Genitive	θαλάττ–ης	θαλαττ–ῶν
Dative	θαλάττ–η	θαλάττ–αις
Accusative	θάλαττ–αν	θαλάττ–ας
(Vocative)	(θάλαττα)	

Another important category are masculine 1st declension nouns. These nouns are exactly like your model 1st declension nouns except in the nominative, genitive, and vocative singular cases.

| | μαθητής = student | | νεανίας = young man | |
	Singular	Plural	Singular	Plural
Nominative	μαθητ–ής	μαθητ–αί	νεανί–ας	νεανί–αι
Genitive	μαθητ–οῦ	μαθητ–ῶν	νεανί–ου	νεανι–ῶν
Dative	μαθητ–ῇ	μαθητ–αῖς	νεανί–ᾳ	νεανί–αις
Accusative	μαθητ–ήν	μαθητ–άς	νεανί–αν	νεανί–ας
(Vocative)	(μαθητά)		(νεανία)	

If, therefore, you see a noun with the endings –α, –ης, ἡ, it is declined like θάλαττα. If you see a noun with the ending –ης, –ου, ὁ or –ας, –ου, ὁ it is declined like μαθητής and νεανίας. The two possible nominative endings –ης or –ας are explained by the fact that when the stem of a 1st declension noun ends in ε, ι, or ρ, the nominative ends in α. Otherwise, it ends in η.

Vocabulary

ζῷον, –ου, τό = animal

θησαυρός, –οῦ, ὁ = store-room, treasure

The declension of the name *Jesus* is irregular.

Nominative	Ἰησοῦς
Genitive	Ἰησοῦ
Dative	Ἰησοῦ
Accusative	Ἰησοῦν
Vocative	Ἰησοῦ

The definite article will help you identify the case.

μαθητής, –οῦ, ὁ = student; disciple

οἶνος, –ου, ὁ = wine

▸ φίλος, –ου, ὁ = friend

▸ κοινός, –ή, –όν (adj.) = common; shared in common

πονηρός, –ά, –όν (adj.) = wicked, evil

φίλος, –η, –ον (adj.) = dear to, friendly to (+ dat.)

χαλεπός, –ή, –όν (adj.) = difficult, harsh

πρός = from (+gen.); at (+dat.); toward, against, to (+ acc.)

▶ γάρ (part.) = for

> ¶ This particle acts as a subordinating conjunction, giving the reason for the previous statement.

ἔχω = to have, hold

Sentences

1. αὐτὸς γὰρ ὁ πατὴρ φιλεῖ ὑμᾶς. (John 16:27)

> ¶ πατὴρ = father: a nominative masculine singular 3rd declension noun.
>
> φιλεῖ = loves: a 3rd person singular contract verb you will learn in chapter 24.

2. κοινὰ τὰ τῶν φίλων ἐστίν. (Traditional Proverb)

> ¶ Remember the odd quirk about Greek that neuter plural subjects always take singular verbs.

▶ 3. χαλεπὰ τὰ καλά ἐστιν. (Traditional Proverb)

4. μέτρον τοῦ βίου τὸ καλόν ἐστιν, οὐ τὸ τοῦ χρόνου μῆκος. (Plutarch, *Moralia*)

> ¶ μῆκος = length: a neuter nominative singular 3rd declension noun.

5. ὁ ἀγαθὸς ἄνθρωπος ἐκ τοῦ ἀγαθοῦ θησαυροῦ τῆς καρδίας προφέρει τὸ ἀγαθόν, καὶ ὁ πονηρὸς ἐκ τοῦ πονηροῦ προφέρει τὸ πονηρόν. (Luke 6:45)

> ¶ προφέρω = to bring forth

6. πάντα τῶν θεῶν ἐστι· φίλοι δὲ τοῖς σοφοῖς οἱ θεοί· κοινὰ δὲ τὰ τῶν φίλων·

πάντα ἄρα τῶν σοφῶν. (Diogenes the Cynic, in Diogenes Laertius, *Lives of Eminent*

Philosophers)

> ¶ πάντα = everything. This neuter nominative plural substantive will be learned in chapter 9.
>
> σοφός, –ή, –όν (adj.) = wise: here a substantive.
>
> τὰ = the things: it is common to have the article used substantively, especially with genitives
>
> ἄρα (part.) = then, therefore; see Etymology and Discussion Topics on γάρ.

7. φίλοις εὐτυχοῦσι καὶ ἀτυχοῦσιν ὁ αὐτὸς ἴσθι. (Periander, in Stobaeus, *Anthology*)

> ¶ εὐτυχοῦσι = to fortunate…; ἀτυχοῦσιν = to unfortunate…; both are dative masculine plural 3rd declension adjectives modifying φίλοις "friends."
>
> ἴσθι: 2nd person imperative of εἰμί.

8. περὶ τῶν αὐτῶν οὐδέποτε τὰ αὐτὰ λέγεις. (Socrates, in Xenophon, *Memorabilia*)

> ¶ περὶ + genitive = about
>
> οὐδέποτε (adv.) = never
>
> αὐτός in the attributive position is often used as a neuter substantive adjective, in which case you must supply the word "things."

9. ὁ Σωκράτης αὐτός ἐστιν καὶ ὁ ἄνθρωπος καὶ τὸ ζῷον. (Aristotle, *Metaphysics*)

> ¶ καὶ…καὶ… = both…and…
>
> Σωκράτης = Socrates, a 3rd declension noun you will learn in chapter 8. Here it is nominative masculine singular.

10. λέγει ἡ μήτηρ τοῦ Ἰησοῦ πρὸς αὐτόν, "Οἶνον οὐκ ἔχουσιν." (John 2:3)

> ¶ μήτηρ = mother: a nominative feminine singular 3rd declension noun; the 3rd declension is discussed in chapter 8.
>
> ἔχουσιν: the subject "they" are the hosts of the wedding at Cana.

Etymology and Discussion Topics

φίλος, –ου, ὁ = friend

This fascinating adjective was the source of much dispute in ancient Greece. Many scholars believe that this word was originally a possessive adjective, e.g., "my." In early Greek, φίλος is used primarily of kin and close relations. Only later does it begin to refer to a person based on their actions rather than blood or common social status. Hence, the famous play by Sophocles, *Antigone*, can be read as a fight about what this word means. Is a φίλος determined by one's actions (Creon) or by blood (Antigone)?

κοινός, –ή, –όν (adj.) = common; shared in common

This adjective is where we get our term "Koine Greek" from. After Alexander the Great conquered much of the East, Greek became an official language in much of the West and Near East. As Greek was originally comprised of many different dialects, the common dialect, largely based on the Attic dialect, was used to refer to this new "official" language.

γάρ (part.) = for

Particles are a class of words that change the meaning of clauses. For the more nuanced use of particles, see chapter 32. Particles like γάρ and ἄρα from sentence #6 often function as subordinating conjunctions. Greek uses conjunctions, words which "join" clauses together (from the Latin coniungere), more often than English. The subordinating conjunction γάρ is used primarily to state the reason or offer support for something stated in the previous clause. γάρ is also one of a group of words called "postpositives," which means that they refuse to be the first word in a clause. They usually come after the first word, but their position is not set. Finally, it is important to keep in mind that while the English word "for" can be a subordinating conjunction (for we are all sinners) or a preposition (for King and country), γάρ cannot be a preposition.

χαλεπὰ τὰ καλά ἐστιν.

The original form of this maxim is χαλεπὰ τὰ καλά. Like some of the early examples in this book, the implied verb has been added to aid in translation. Many Greek proverbs and maxims do not contain a verb. You must supply the appropriate form of "to be" in your translation. As you encounter more of these proverbs, it will become less awkward. We do something similar in English, e.g., "The Spartans were great warriors, not great cooks" instead of "The Spartans were great warriors; they were not great cooks."

Chapter 7 ⌒

Infinitives: Complementary Infinitive, Articular Infinitive •
Partitive Genitive • Elision

Infinitives: Complementary Infinitive, Articular Infinitive

As we saw in chapter 3, verbs have person (1st, 2nd, 3rd) and number (singular, plural). This is true for *finite* verbs, but there is a form of a verb called an *infinitive*. In English we form the infinitive by adding the word "to" to the present tense, e.g., "to teach," "to speak." Not being tied to a particular person and number, they are not defined and hence are called *infinitives*. Infinitives do have tense and voice, as do English infinitives, e.g., "to have taught" (past tense, active voice), "to be spoken" (present tense, passive voice). The English verb needs a helper word to express the infinitive; Greek needs only one word. For this chapter we will limit our discussion to the present active infinitive.

To form the present active infinitive of omega verbs, add –ειν to the present stem. Remember that we get the present stem by removing –ω from the 1st person singular of the present tense.

λύω = I loosen
λύειν = to loosen

λέγω = I speak
λέγειν = to speak

φέρω = I bear

φέρειν = to bear

παιδεύω = I teach

παιδεύειν = to teach

Remember that in your vocabulary and in all dictionaries Greek verbs are listed under their 1st person, singular, present, active, indicative form, even though the English definition is given in the infinitive.

εἶναι

The infinitive for εἰμί "to be" is irregular, εἶναι, and must be memorized.

Complementary Infinitive

One of the most common uses of the infinitive is the complementary infinitive, which *complements* the main verb in a clause or sentence. For example, in the sentence "I want to know," "want" is the main verb and "to know" is the complementary infinitive. There are many verbs in Greek which take complementary infinitives. Fortunately, most of their English equivalents also take complementary infinitives. Two such words are σπεύδω (to be eager) and ἐθέλω (to be willing).

¶ παιδεύω = to teach

σπεύδω παιδεύειν.

I am eager to teach.

ὁ Σίσυφος οὐ σπεύδει φέρειν τὸν λίθον.

Sisyphus is not eager to carry the stone.

οἱ διδάσκαλοι ἐθέλουσι παιδεύειν.

The teachers wish to teach.

θέλομεν ὑπάγειν.

We wish to depart.

Koine / Classical Difference

You will see the verb ἐθέλω in classical Greek spelled θέλω in Koine. There is no difference in meaning.

Articular Infinitive

Another common use of the infinitive is to act as a noun. We see this occasionally in English.

To die for one's beliefs is noble.

To live without wisdom is folly.

To refuse to study while expecting to excel is foolish.

However, English prefers to use the gerund (a noun formed from a verb, ending in –ing) in its place, and would rather say "Dying for one's beliefs is noble" and "Living without wisdom is folly." In your translations, it is best at the beginning not to try and change articular infinitives into gerunds. Sometimes, however, the English will sound too stilted and translating with an English gerund will be necessary.

Articular infinitives are easy to spot because they take the definite article. Articular infinitives are always considered neuter singular nouns and hence always take the definite article τό and are modified by neuter singular adjectives. Even though infinitives do not decline (a fact for which I am sure you are thankful), we can identify the case of an infinitive by the declension of its definite article.

> ¶ μανθάνω = to learn | ἐπιθυμία, –ας, ἡ = a desire for (+ genitive) |
> παιδεύω = to teach

τὸ παιδεύειν ἐστὶν καλόν.

To teach is noble.

ἡ τέχνη τοῦ παιδεύειν ἐστὶν ἐπιθυμία τοῦ μανθάνειν.

The art of teaching is a desire to learn.

Often the infinitive is used as a noun without the article. In such cases it is translated the same as you would translate an articular infinitive.

παιδεύειν ἐστὶν καλόν.

To teach is noble.

Partitive Genitive

The genitive is often used to signify the whole from which a *part* is taken. This is called a *partitive genitive*.

ὁ ἀναμάρτητος ὑμῶν
The sinless one of/among you

μόριον τῆς ψυχῆς
A piece of the soul

Elision

Greek words that end in short vowels usually drop that vowel when the next word begins with a vowel. An apostrophe is placed where the vowel would have been. Common elisions are δ' (δέ), ἀλλ' (ἀλλά), and γ' (γέ). See sentence #7 for an example.

Vocabulary

▸ βροτός, –οῦ, ὁ = a mortal man
  διδάσκαλος, –ου, ὁ = teacher, master
  πόνος, –ου, ὁ = hard work; toil

  ἄδικος, –ον (adj.) = unjust
  δίκαιος, –α, –ον (adj.) = just
  κενός, –ή, –όν (adj.) = empty
  χρηστός, –ή, –όν (adj.) = useful, serviceable

  αὐξάνω = to increase
  ἐθέλω (Koine θέλω) = to want, be willing
▸ δεῖ = it is necessary (+acc. and infinitive), there is a need of (+gen.)
▸ μανθάνω = to learn, understand
  μένω = to remain, stay
  νέμω = to deal out, distribute
▸ πράττω (Koine πράσσω) = to do
  γράφω = to write

Sentences

1. ἄδικόν ἐστιν τὸ λυπεῖν τοὺς φίλους. (Menander, *Fragments*)

> ¶ λυπέω = to cause pain, grieve

2. καλῶν οὐδὲν ἄνευ πόνου καὶ ἐπιμελείας οἱ θεοὶ νέμουσιν ἀνθρώποις.
   (Prodicus, *Fragments*)

> ¶ οὐδὲν = nothing. You will learn this word in chapter 22. It is neuter accusative singular and takes a partitive genitive in this sentence.
>
> ἄνευ (prep.) = without (+ gen.)
>
> ἐπιμέλεια, –ας, ἡ = care, diligence

3. ἐκεῖνον δεῖ αὐξάνειν, ἐμὲ δὲ ἐλαττοῦσθαι. (John 3:30)

> ¶ ἐκεῖνον = him. You will learn this demonstrative in chapter 18. It is masculine accusative singular. It is referring to Jesus. The speaker is John the Baptist.
>
> ἐλαττοῦσθαι = to decrease. This is a middle infinitive. You will learn the middle infinitive in chapter 14.

4. τὸ πολλὰ πράττειν ἐστὶ πανταχοῦ σαπρόν. (Menander, *Fragments*)

> ¶ πολλὰ = many things. You will learn this neuter accusative plural adjective in chapter 9.
>
> πανταχοῦ (adv.) = everywhere; absolutely
>
> σαπρός, –ά, –όν (adj.) = rotten; unsound

5. δίκαιος εἶναι μᾶλλον ἢ χρηστὸς θέλε. (Menander, *Fragments*)

> ¶ μᾶλλον ἢ = rather than
>
> When an adjective modifies the subject of a verb taking a complimentary infinitive, the adjective stays in the nominative case.

6. οὐ θέλω διὰ μέλανος καὶ καλάμου σοι γράφειν. (3 John 1:13)

> ¶ μέλανος = ink: gen. singular of μέλαν, a 3rd declension noun
>
> κάλαμος, –ου, ὁ = a reed; reed-pen

7. αἱ δ᾽ ἐλπίδες βόσκουσι τοὺς κενοὺς βροτῶν. (Menander, *Fragments*)

¶ ἐλπίδες = hopes: nominative plural of ἐλπίς, a 3rd declension noun you will learn in chapter 8.

βόσκω = to feed, nourish

8. ἄρτι μανθάνω. (Euripides, *Alcestis*)

¶ ἄρτι (adv.) = now

This line is uttered by Admetus in the play *Alcestis* when he realizes that he has made a great mistake.

9. ἐμοὶ γὰρ τὸ ζῆν Χριστὸς καὶ τὸ ἀποθανεῖν κέρδος. (Phil. 1:21)

¶ ζῆν = to live: an irregular infinitive you will learn in chapter 25.

Χριστός, -οῦ, ὁ = the Christ, the Messiah

ἀποθανεῖν = to die: an aorist infinitive you will learn in chapter 12.

κέρδος = gain, profit: a neuter nominative 3rd declension noun.

10. ὁ δὲ διὰ τὸ μένειν αὐτὸν εἰς τὸν αἰῶνα ἀπαράβατον ἔχει τὴν ἱερωσύνην. (Heb 7:24)

¶ ὁ δὲ: Often in a sustained narrative, Greek will use the definite article for the pronoun if the context makes it clear who the speaker is. In this case ὁ, "he," refers to Jesus.

εἰς τὸν αἰῶνα = forever

αἰῶνα: accusative of the 3rd declension noun αἰών, which you will learn in chapter 8.

ἀπαράβατος, ον (adj.) = unchangeable, permanent

ἱερωσύνη, −ης, ἡ = priesthood

Etymology and Discussion Topics

βροτός, –οῦ, ὁ = a mortal man

This is a poetic and archaic word for "man," used often in Homer but found rarely in prose. It is often used in opposition to θεός and ἀθάνατος. It is conjectured that the food of the gods, ambrosia (ἀμβροσία), was formed by combining the privative alpha (see chapter 2) and βροτός.

δεῖ and the subject infinitive

The impersonal verb δεῖ is not really an impersonal verb. When Greek uses this verb, it usually means that the infinitive is the subject of the verb. In other words, when δεῖ is used, the action described in the infinitive is "what is necessary." These are called "subject infinitives" because the infinitive acts as the subject of the verb. Since English uses the impersonal construction "it is…" so often, e.g., "it is necessary to…," "it is possible to…," it can be easier to think of verbs like δεῖ as impersonal verbs that take an infinitive.

μανθάνω = to learn; understand

This word is where we get our word "math," although in Greek it referred to all knowledge. This all-encompassing meaning of "math" can be seen in the word "polymath," which is a combination of the adjective πολύς ("much") and this root. A polymath is someone who is knowledgeable about many subjects.

Double taus and double sigmas

When Attic Greek has ττ, Koine (and other Greek dialects like Ionian) have σσ. There is no difference in meaning between πράττω and πράσσω or θαλάττα and θαλάσσα.

Chapter 8 ⟋

Nouns: 3rd Declension

Nouns: 3rd Declension

As we saw in chapter 2, Greek nouns fall into three groups, or *declensions*. While nouns of the 1st and 2nd declensions fall into predictable patterns, nouns of the 3rd declension display a greater variety. They are a bit trickier, but the good news is that this is the final declension for you to meet. After this chapter you will have learned the three noun declensions in Greek. Nouns of the 3rd declension can be masculine, feminine, or neuter, and follow the basic pattern below, albeit with some variations.

	Singular		Plural	
	m/f	*n*	*m/f*	*n*
Nominative	−ς / —	—	−ες	−α
Genitive	−ος	−ος	−ων	−ων
Dative	−ι	−ι	−σι(ν)	−σι(ν)
Accusative	−α/ν	—	−ας	−α

Note that the masculine and feminine 3rd declension nouns share the same endings. The gender of a 3rd declension noun cannot be determined by spelling, and will have to be memorized separately with each noun. If you don't remember the gender of a particular noun in a text, the definite article is usually there to aid you. In dictionaries the gender of all 3rd declension nouns will of course be signified by the inclusion of the definite article in the entry.

As you may remember from chapter 3, the variations in nouns are formed by adding endings to stems. To get the stem of the noun, we skip over the nominative, which is prone to contraction, and go to the genitive, which is much more stable. We must take the ending off of the genitive singular, in this case –ος. For the nominative case, the form ends with a sigma (ς) or it lacks an ending. To form the vocative singular (remember that in the plural the vocative is always the same as the nominative), Greek uses what is called the "pure" stem. The rules for forming the pure stem are not as easy as simply dropping the –ος from the genitive singular. Instead of memorizing the complicated rules, it is easier to simply memorize the vocative endings for each of your model nouns. You can then use that as a guideline for what 3rd declension vocatives look like. Remember to always look for a vocative when you see the interjection ὦ.

You may remember that you had two model nouns to memorize from the 1st declension and two from the 2nd declension. Because there is greater variation in the 3rd declension, you will have seven model nouns to memorize.

3rd Declension

	m	n	f	f	n	m	m
	divinity	body	grace	city	race	Socrates	king
Singular							
Nom.	δαίμων	σῶμα	χάρις	πόλις	γένος	Σωκράτης	βασιλ–εύς
Gen.	δαίμον–ος	σώματ–ος	χάριτ–ος	πόλ–εως	γέν–ους	Σωκράτ–ους	βασιλ–έως
Dat.	δαίμον–ι	σώματ–ι	χάριτ–ι	πόλ–ει	γέν–ει	Σωκράτ–ει	βασιλ–εῖ
Acc.	δαίμον–α	σῶμα	χάρι–ν	πόλι–ν	γένος	Σωκράτ–η	βασιλ–έα
(Voc.)	(δαῖμον)	(σῶμα)	(χάρι)	(πόλι)	(γένος)	(Σώκρατες)	(βασιλεῦ)
Plural							
Nom.	δαίμον–ες	σώματ–α	χάριτ–ες	πόλ–εις	γέν–η		βασιλ–εῖς
Gen.	δαιμόν–ων	σωμάτ–ων	χαρίτ–ων	πόλε–ων	γεν–ῶν		βασιλ–έων
Dat.	δαίμο–σι(ν)	σώμα–σι(ν)	χάρι–σι(ν)	πόλε–σι(ν)	γένε–σι(ν)		βασιλεῦ–σι(ν)
Acc.	δαίμον–ας	σώματ–α	χάριτ–ας	πόλ–εις	γέν–η		βασιλέ–ας

Think of these as the major patterns that all 3rd declension nouns follow. When in the dictionary you look up a noun like τεῖχος, –ους, τό = "wall," you know that it follows the pattern of your model noun γένος, –ους, τό. When you look up a noun like ἀγών, –ῶνος, ὁ = "contest," you know that it follows the pattern of your model noun δαίμων, –ονος, ὁ. This is why it is always crucial to memorize the genitive singular ending and gender of every noun in addition to the definition.

You will notice that one of your model nouns, Σωκράτης, exists only in the singular. Nouns declined like Σωκράτης are rare (τριήρης, –ους, ἡ = "trireme," being one). There are, however, quite a few names that follow this pattern. It is for this reason that you are asked to memorize the name Σωκράτης.

There are a few important nouns like πατήρ "father" and μήτηρ "mother" whose stem ends in –τερ. The ε drops or lengthens into η. Since you will look up these nouns in the dictionary and see the –τηρ, –τρος for the nominative and genitive singular endings, rather than memorizing these as model nouns, be mindful that (1) the ε can creep back into some of the forms (πατέρα not πάτρα) and (2) the ε is found in the vocative singular (μῆτερ). When you read Greek, you will find that these nouns will not cause you many problems.

	m	*f*
	father	*mother*
Singular		
Nom.	πατήρ	μήτηρ
Gen.	πατρ–**ός**	μητρ–**ός**
Dat.	πατρ–**ί**	μητρ–**ί**
Acc.	πατέρ–**α**	μητέρ–**α**
(Voc.)	(πάτερ)	(μῆτερ)
Plural		
Nom.	πατέρ–**ες**	μητέρ–**ες**
Gen.	πατέρ–**ων**	μητέρ–**ων**
Dat.	πατρά–**σι(ν)**	μητρά–**σι(ν)**
Acc.	πατέρ–**ας**	μητέρ–**ας**

Now that you have been introduced to Greek nouns, this is a good time to consult the beginning of Appendix A in the back of your book. In this appendix you will find the endings of all three declensions, the definite article, and all of your model nous. If you can memorize (and re-memorize) this chart, you are well on your way to reading Greek!

Vocabulary

▸ αἰών, –ῶνος, ὁ = age, generation

βασιλεύς, –έως, ὁ = king

γένος, –ους, τό = race; kind

▸ δαίμων, –ονος, ὁ = a divinity

▸ ἐλπίς, –ίδος, ἡ = hope, expectation

θάνατος, –ου, ὁ = death

μητήρ, –τρός, ἡ = mother

πατήρ, –τρός, ὁ = father

πίστις, –εως, ἡ = faith

▸ πόλις, –εως, ἡ = city

Σωκράτης, –ους, ὁ = Socrates

σῶμα, σώματος, τό = body

τέλος, –ους, τό = end, fulfillment

φρόνησις, –εως, ἡ = thought; practical wisdom, prudence

▸ χάρις, –ιτος, ἡ = favor; grace

▸ Χριστός, -οῦ, ὁ = the Christ, the Messiah

▸ ἴδιος, –α, –ον (adj.) = one's own, private

βλέπω = to see, look

παιδεύω = to teach

Sentences

1. στέρησις δέ ἐστιν αἰσθήσεως ὁ θάνατος. (Epicurus, *Letter to Menoeceus*)

> ❡ στέρησις, –εως, ἡ = deprivation
>
> αἴσθησις, –εως, ἡ = sense-perception

2. κατὰ τὴν ἰδίαν φρόνησιν οὐδεὶς εὐτυχεῖ. (Menander, *Fragments*)

> ❡ οὐδεὶς = no one: a nominative masculine noun you will learn in chapter 22.
>
> εὐτυχέω = to be fortunate

3. χάρις ὑμῖν καὶ εἰρήνη ἀπὸ θεοῦ πατρὸς ἡμῶν καὶ κυρίου Ἰησοῦ Χριστοῦ.
(1 Cor 1:3)

❡ As with many greetings, you must supply the imperative "be."

εἰρήνη, –ης, ἡ = peace

ἀπό (ἀπ᾽, ἀφ᾽) (prep.) = from (+ gen.)

4. ἡ χάρις τοῦ κυρίου Ἰησοῦ μεθ᾽ ὑμῶν. (1 Cor 16:23)

❡ St. Paul closes 1 Corinthians with this greeting, similar to the one with which he opened his letter in #3 above.

μεθ᾽ ὑμῶν = μετὰ ὑμῶν

5. ἀνάπαυσίς ἐστι τῶν κακῶν ἀπραξία. (Menander, *Fragments*)

❡ ἀνάπαυσις, –εως, ἡ = rest from a thing (+gen.)

ἀπραξία, –ας, ἡ = inaction

6. ἡ πίστις χωρὶς τῶν ἔργων ἀργή ἐστιν. (James 2:20)

❡ χωρίς (prep.) = without (+ gen.)

ἀργός, –ή, –όν (adj.) = not working; lazy

7. βουλὴ πονηρὰ χρηστὸν οὐκ ἔχει τέλος. (Menander, *Fragments*)

❡ βουλή, –ῆς, ἡ = plan

8. τὰ σώματα ὑμῶν μέλη Χριστοῦ ἐστιν. (1 Cor 6:15)

❡ μέλος, –ους τό = limb

9. ξίφος τιτρώσκει σῶμα, τὸν δὲ νοῦν λόγος. (Menander, *Fragments*)

❡ ξίφος, –ους τό = sword

τιτρώσκω = to wound, injure

νοῦν = mind: masculine accusative singular of νοῦς, a 3rd declension noun explained in chapter 14.

λόγος takes the implied verb τιτρώσκει.

10. βλέπομεν γὰρ ἄρτι δι᾽ ἐσόπτρου ἐν αἰνίγματι, τότε δὲ πρόσωπον πρὸς πρόσωπον. (1 Cor 13:12)

¶ ἄρτι (adv.) = now

ἔσοπτρον, –ου, τό = mirror

αἴνιγμα, –ατος, τό = a dark saying, riddle

τότε (adv.) = then

πρόσωπον, –ου, τό = face

Etymology and Discussion Topics

αἰών, –ῶνος, ὁ = age, generation

The common expression εἰς τοὺς αἰῶνας τῶν αἰώνων found in Scripture can roughly be translated as "unto the ages of ages." This phrase is common in liturgical prayer. The Vulgate translates this expression as "in saecula saeculorum." In English you will see many translations of this expression, from "for ever and ever" to "world without end."

δαίμων, –ονος, ὁ = a divinity

If you are wondering if we get our word "demon" from this noun, you are correct. It is used of evil spirits in the New Testament. In classical Greek, however, δαίμων was not always used in a negative sense. δαίμων referred to a divinity and could refer to a god, but was usually reserved for lower divinities, what we might call "spirits." When Socrates stood trial in 399 B.C.E., he told the jury that he had a δαίμων which looked after him and spoke to him whenever he was about to do something wrong.

ἐλπίς, –ίδος, ἡ = hope, expectation

This fascinating Greek word can mean both "hope" and "expectation." It is obviously used in a positive sense in Christianity, but in classical Greek it can be used in a negative sense as well. You have now learned the words for the three theological virtues: πίστις, ἐλπίς, and ἀγάπη.

πόλις, –εως, ἡ = city

This important Greek word is where we get our English word "political." It is a difficult word to translate because the Greeks distinguished between a physical city (ἄστυ, –εως, τό) and the people and government of that city (πόλις). This is why you will sometimes see "city-state" used to translate πόλις. In the classical period, what we today call "Greece" was not a unified country, but rather a collection of numerous autonomous πόλεις. As most Greeks did not live in the physical town (ἄστυ), the πόλις referred to both town and surrounding countryside. In fact, when the Greeks talked about cities, they did not say "I am going to Athens," or "Corinth is at war." Rather, they said "I am going to the Athenians," and "The Corinthians are at war." This is why you will find "Athens" in your vocabulary under Ἀθῆναι, –ῶν, αἱ.

χάρις, –ιτος, ἡ = favor; grace

The word χάρις and its uses are ancient and quite complex, but it concerns primarily an act of giving. It can be contrasted with the word μισθός, which means "wage" or "reward." χάρις is not given under compulsion nor is it someone's "right" or "due." It is freely given. χάρις can refer both to the act of giver and to the gratitude felt by the one receiving the favor. Our word gratitude comes from the Latin *gratia*, the very word the Romans used to translate χάρις. It is derived from the verb χαίρω "to rejoice," the same verb from which your model noun χαρά "joy" is derived.

Χριστός, –οῦ, ὁ = Christ

The adjective χριστός, –ή, –όν means "anointed." It is derived from the verb χρίω, which means to "anoint with sacred oil." One of the ways in which a king was inaugurated was with such an anointing. The Hebrew word "Messiah," the "anointed one" prophesied in the Old Testament, was translated as Χριστός in the Septuagint, a 3rd c. BCE translation of the Hebrew scriptures into Greek oftentimes abbreviated LXX. More often than not, the New Testament follows the wording of the Septuagint when it quotes the Old Testament. Whenever there was a reading of a Psalm that in English translations of the Bible sound generic, e.g., Psalm 132:10, "Do not reject your anointed one," early Christians saw in the Septuagint's wording an explicit prophecy about Jesus Christ.

ἴδιος, –α, –ον (adj.) = one's own, private

This adjective describes that which is private or peculiar to one's self. It was therefore used to describe what we would call a "layman." It is from this use of the word that we get our word "idiot." It is also where we get our linguistic word "idiom." Therefore, while you might be tempted to do so, don't read any pejorative sense into this Greek adjective when you are reading Greek lest you get some rather odd translations.

Chapter 9 ⟨⟩

Adjectives: 3rd Declension • Mixed Declension Adjectives •
Irregular Adjectives πᾶς, πολύς, and μέγας

Adjectives: 3rd Declension

Now that you have learned all three declensions of the Greek noun, it is
time to learn the remaining adjective declensions. Remember that the first
adjectives you learned were called adjectives of the 1st and 2nd declension.
3rd declension adjectives fall roughly into two categories. Just as you memorized καλός as your model adjective of the 1st and 2nd declension, if you
memorize two model adjectives for the 3rd declension, you can decline the
vast majority of 3rd declension adjectives.

Your two model adjectives of the 3rd declension will be εὐδαίμων "happy" and ἀληθής "true."

	εὐδαίμων, –ον (adj.) = happy			
	Singular		*Plural*	
	m/f	*n*	*m/f*	*n*
Nom.	εὐδαίμων	εὔδαιμον	εὐδαίμον–ες	εὐδαίμον–α
Gen.	εὐδαίμον–ος	εὐδαίμον–ος	εὐδαιμόν–ων	εὐδαιμόν–ων
Dat.	εὐδαίμον–ι	εὐδαίμον–ι	εὐδαίμο–σι(ν)	εὐδαίμο–σι(ν)
Acc.	εὐδαίμον–α	εὔδαιμον	εὐδαίμον–ας	εὐδαίμον–α
(Voc.)	(εὔδαιμον)	(εὔδαιμον)		

| ἀληθής, –ές (adj.) = true | | | |
| Singular | | Plural | |
m/f	n	m/f	n
Nom.	ἀληθ–ής	ἀληθ–ές	ἀληθ–εῖς	ἀληθ–ῆ
Gen.	ἀληθ–οῦς	ἀληθ–οῦς	ἀληθ–ῶν	ἀληθ–ῶν
Dat.	ἀληθ–εῖ	ἀληθ–εῖ	ἀληθέ–σι(ν)	ἀληθέ–σι(ν)
Acc.	ἀληθ–ῆ	ἀληθ–ές	ἀληθ–εῖς	ἀληθ–ῆ
(Voc.)	(ἀληθές)	(ἀληθές)		

As you can see, adjectives of the 3rd declension share endings for the masculine and feminine. These types of adjectives have endings that look similar to your model 3rd declension nouns.

It is important to remember that adjectives *modify* nouns, and that all adjectives *agree* with the nouns they modify in *gender*, *number*, and *case*. At this point, don't expect the spelling of the adjective and the noun to match. 3rd declension adjectives will often modify 1st and 2nd declension nouns and adjectives of the 1st and 2nd declension will often modify 3rd declension nouns, as the examples below illustrate.

ἡ καλὴ πόλις
the beautiful city

ὁ καλὸς βασιλεύς
the beautiful king

τὸ ἀληθὲς σῶμα
the true body

ὁ εὐδαίμων ἄνθρωπος
the happy person

Mixed Declension Adjectives

There is only one more group of adjectives to memorize. These are called *adjectives of mixed declension*, since they are made up of endings from adjectives of the 1st and 2nd declension (the feminine forms) and 3rd declension adjectives (masculine and neuter forms). Our model mixed declension adjective will be ἡδύς "sweet."

ἡδύς, –εῖα, –ύ (adj.) = sweet

	Singular			Plural		
	m	*f*	*n*	*m*	*f*	*n*
Nom.	ἡδ–ύς	ἡδεῖ–α	ἡδ–ύ	ἡδ–εῖς	ἡδεῖ–αι	ἡδ–έα
Gen.	ἡδ–έος	ἡδεῖ–ας	ἡδ–έος	ἡδ–έων	ἡδει–ῶν	ἡδ–έων
Dat.	ἡδ–εῖ	ἡδεί–ᾳ	ἡδ–εῖ	ἡδ–έσι(ν)	ἡδεί–αις	ἡδ–έσι(ν)
Acc.	ἡδ–ύν	ἡδεῖ–αν	ἡδ–ύ	ἡδ–εῖς	ἡδεί–ας	ἡδ–έα
(Voc.)	(ἡδύ)	(ἡδεῖα)	(ἡδύ)			

Irregular Adjectives πᾶς, πολύς, and μέγας

Three irregular adjectives are very common in Greek: πᾶς = all, πολύς = many, and μέγας = great. Their declensions are given below. Although you might think otherwise, this book is designed to keep what you must memorize to the absolute minimum. Since πᾶς, πολύς, and μέγας are only slightly irregular and for the most part follow the patterns of your four model adjectives (καλός, εὐδαίμων, ἀληθής, and ἡδύς), it is not necessary to memorize their declensions. If you are unsure of a particular form, you can refer back to these charts (all found in Appendix A). Since they are so common, after a while you will have them memorized simply by reading a lot of Greek.

πᾶς, πᾶσα, πᾶν (adj.) = all

	Singular			Plural		
	m	*f*	*n*	*m*	*f*	*n*
Nom.	πᾶ–ς	πᾶσ–α	πᾶν	πάντ–ες	πᾶσ–αι	πάντ–α
Gen.	παντ–ός	πάσ–ης	παντ–ός	πάντ–ων	πασ–ῶν	πάντ–ων
Dat.	παντ–ί	πάσ–ῃ	παντ–ί	πᾶ–σι(ν)	πάσ–αις	πᾶ–σι(ν)
Acc.	πάντ–α	πᾶσ–αν	πᾶν	πάντ–ας	πάσ–ας	πάντ–α

μέγας, μεγάλη, μέγα (adj.) = great, large

	Singular			Plural		
	m	*f*	*n*	*m*	*f*	*n*
Nom.	μέγας	μεγάλ–η	μέγα	μεγάλ–οι	μεγάλ–αι	μεγάλ–α
Gen.	μεγάλ–ου	μεγάλ–ης	μεγάλ–ου	μεγάλ–ων	μεγάλ–ων	μεγάλ–ων
Dat.	μεγάλ–ῳ	μεγάλ–ῃ	μεγάλ–ῳ	μεγάλ–οις	μεγάλ–αις	μεγάλ–οις
Acc.	μεγάν	μεγάλ–ην	μέγα	μεγάλ–ους	μεγάλ–ας	μεγάλ–α

	Singular			Plural		
	m	*f*	*n*	*m*	*f*	*n*
Nom.	πολ–ύς	πολλ–ή	πολ–ύ	πολλ–οί	πολλ–αί	πολλ–ά
Gen.	πολλ–οῦ	πολλ–ῆς	πολλ–οῦ	πολλ–ῶν	πολλ–ῶν	πολλ–ῶν
Dat.	πολλ–ῷ	πολλ–ῇ	πολλ–ῷ	πολλ–οῖς	πολλ–αῖς	πολλ–οῖς
Acc.	πολ–ύν	πολλ–ήν	πολ–ύ	πολλ–ούς	πολλ–άς	πολλ–ά

πολύς, πολλή, πολύ (adj.) = much, many

At this point it might be helpful to look at Appendix A in the back of your book (pp. 337–38), which contains all of your model adjectives. Now that you have finished nouns and adjectives, be sure to continually memorize your eleven model nouns and your four model adjectives. Don't worry if you forget the forms; it will happen. As you relearn them, you will forget fewer and fewer forms until you eventually know them all. Don't get discouraged when some forms slip from your mind.

Vocabulary

▸ ἀνήρ, ἀνδρός, ὁ = man; husband

▸ γυνή, γυναικός, ἡ = woman; wife

▸ θυμός, –οῦ, ὁ = soul, spirit; temper

  ἀληθής, –ές (adj.) = true

  ἄξιος, –α, –ον (adj.) = worthy; worthy of (+ gen.)

▸ εὐδαίμων, –ον (adj.) = fortunate, happy

  ἡδύς, ἡδεῖα, ἡδύ (adj.) = sweet

  μέγας, μεγάλη, μέγα (adj.) = great, large

▸ πᾶς, πᾶσα, πᾶν (adj.) = all

▸ πολύς, πολλή, πολύ (adj.) = much, many

▸ πιστεύω = to trust, have faith in (+ dat.)

Sentences

1. ἄξιος γὰρ ὁ ἐργάτης τοῦ μισθοῦ αὐτοῦ. (Luke 10:7)

> ¶ The verb "is" is implied.
>
> ἐργάτης, –ου, ὁ = worker
>
> μισθός, –οῦ, ὁ = wage, reward

2. Ἀχιλεῦ, δάμαζε θυμὸν μέγαν. (Homer, *Iliad*)

> ¶ Ἀχιλεύς, –έως, ὁ = Achilles
>
> δαμάζω = to tame, subdue
>
> You must supply the word "your" here in front of θυμὸν.

3. ἡ γὰρ σιωπὴ τοῖς σοφοῖσιν ἀπόκρισις. (Euripides, *Fragments*)

> ¶ σιωπή, –ῆς, ἡ = silence
>
> ἀπόκρισις, –εως, ἡ = answer, response
>
> σοφοῖσιν = σοφοῖς
>
> τοῖς σοφοῖσιν: a dative of respect, not indirect object.

4. μὴ δίωκε τἀφανῆ. (Menander, *Fragments*)

> ¶ διώκω = to hunt, pursue
>
> ἀφανής, –ές (adj.) = unclear
>
> τἀφανῆ = τὰ ἀφανῆ. This is called crasis, which will be explained in chapter 16.

5. πάντα στέγει, πάντα πιστεύει, πάντα ἐλπίζει, πάντα ὑπομένει. (1 Cor 13:7)

> ¶ This verse comes at the end of St. Paul's famous discussion of love. The implied subject of all the verbs is ἀγάπη.
>
> πιστεύω normally takes the dative, but it can take the accusative as it does here.
>
> στέγω = to sustain
>
> ἐλπίζω = to hope
>
> ὑπομένω = to be patient; endure

▶ 6. ῥίζα γὰρ πάντων τῶν κακῶν ἐστιν ἡ φιλαργυρία. (1 Tim 6:10)

❡ ῥίζα, –ας, ἡ = a root

φιλαργυρία, –ας, ἡ = love of money

7. καλὸν ἀληθὴς καὶ ἀτενὴς παρρησία. (Euripides, *Fragments*)

❡ The verb "is" is implied.

Notice that καλὸν is neuter singular and not feminine. Greek often uses a neuter adjective and you must supply "thing," i.e., "…is a beautiful thing." Sometimes such a translation can sound clunky, but it helps avoid confusion.

ἀτενής, –ές (adj.) = intent, earnest

παρρησία, –ας, ἡ = outspokenness, frankness

8. ἔστω δὲ ἡ προσποίησις τοῦ σωφρονεῖν ἀληθής. (Charondas, in Stobaeus, *Anthology*)

❡ προσποίησις, –εως, ἡ = a pretension or claim to a thing (+ gen.)

σωφρωνέω = to be temperate or moderate

9. ἡ παιδεία καθάπερ εὐδαίμων χώρα πάντα τὰ ἀγαθὰ φέρει. (Pythagoras, *Fragments*)

❡ καθάπερ (adv.) = just as

χώρα, –ας, ἡ = place; land

10. μετὰ τὴν δόσιν τάχιστα γηράσκει χάρις. (Menander, *Fragments*)

❡ δόσις, –εως, ἡ = giving

τάχιστα (adv.) = most quickly

γηράσκω = to grow old

Etymology and Discussion Topics

ἄνθρωπος, ἀνήρ, and γυνή

While ἄνθρωπος is used to refer to a generic human being, ἀνήρ and γυνή are used to refer to a man and a woman respectively. You will occasionally see ἀνήρ used for human being, but Greek prefers to use ἄνθρωπος. Because they refer to adults, ἀνήρ can also mean "husband" and γυνή can mean "wife."

θυμός, –ου, ὁ = soul, spirit; temper

θυμός is a notoriously tricky word to translate. Like ψυχή, it can refer to spirit or breath. θυμός differs from ψυχή in that it resembles how we use the word "heart." In addition to the good meaning of "courage/sprit," θυμός can also mean "temper" or even "wrath," and is frequently contrasted with ἐπιθυμία = desire (chap. 4). It is this last sense that Phoenix speaks of when he addresses Achilles in #2.

εὐδαίμων, –ον (adj.) = fortunate, happy

This adjective is a combination of the adverb εὐ "well" and your model noun δαίμων. It therefore literally means something like "to have a good divinity on your side." We have seen in the concept of τύχη how the ancient Greeks viewed human happiness and prosperity as something largely outside of one's control. This is not to say that one's actions were of no account, yet in the face of forces like τύχη, man's attempt to grasp happiness for himself was foolish. The philosophy of the Stoics can be viewed as a reaction to this notion. As you will see in some of the quotations from the Stoic philosophers, happiness for men does not depend on any δαίμων.

πᾶς, πᾶσα, πᾶν (adj.) = all

Numerous English words are formed from "pan." For example, pantheism (πᾶν + θεός) is the philosophy that sees God in all things. A pandemic (πᾶν + δῆμος "people") is something that effects all the people. Finally, a panoply (πᾶν + ὅπλον "shield") originally referred to a full set of armor, but in time came to mean an impressive array of any kind.

πολύς, πολλή, πολύ (adj.) = much, many

Don't confuse words like "political" and "policy," which come from πόλις, with words derived from πολύς. You can tell the difference by the spelling. Latin, and therefore most English derivatives, transliterate the

Greek upsilon with the letter y. From πολύς come words like polyphony (πολύς + φωνή "voice") and polymorphic (πολύς + μορφή "form").

πιστεύω = to trust, have faith in (+ dat.)

While this word is often translated as "to have faith," and it is related to the noun πίστις, it is more accurately translated as "trust." For early Christians, "faith" was not belief in a set of ideas, but trust in a person.

ῥίζα γὰρ πάντων τῶν κακῶν ἐστιν ἡ φιλαργυρία. (1 Tim 6:10)

φιλαργυρία is often mistranslated as "money." How does such a mistranslation alter the meaning of this verse?

Chapter 10 ⌐

*Adverbs • Sentences, Clauses, and Phrases • Relative Pronouns
and Relative Clauses • μέν ... δέ*

Adverbs

An *adverb* is a word that can modify a verb, an adjective, or another adverb.

Orpheus sang *well.* (modifies a verb)

Even *very* wild animals were captivated by his song. (modifies
    an adjective)

Orpheus sang *very* well. (modifies an adverb)

Adverbs cannot modify nouns, which is why you cannot say "The bravely Orpheus sang" in English.

To form an adverb from an adjective, English usually adds "-ly" to some form of the adjective.

beautiful → beautifully

happy → happily

true → truly

In Greek, an adverb is formed by replacing the genitive singular ending with ως.[1]

---

1. Technically an adverb is formed by taking the ν off the adjective's genitive plural ending and replacing the –ν with –ς, but this rule is easier to grasp if you think of ως as the adverbial ending.

καλός = beautiful → καλῶς = beautifully

εὐδαίμων = happy → εὐδαιμόνως = happily

ἀληθής = true → ἀληθῶς = truly

Greek can also use the neuter accusative ending (singular and plural) as an adverb.

μόνος, –η, –ον = alone → μόνον or μονῶς = only

δῆλος, –η, –ον = clear → δῆλον, δῆλα, or δήλως = clearly

In addition to adverbs formed from adjectives, Greek has many other adverbs that must be memorized. The good news is that they will be listed on their own in most dictionaries, and they don't change in spelling. Here are some common adverbs:

νῦν = now

πάλιν = again

ἀεί = always

Sentences, Clauses, and Phrases

Before we discuss the relative pronoun and relative clauses, it is important to explain some grammatical terms that this book will employ. While you might be tempted to pass over such information, an understanding of the difference between sentences, clauses, and phrases will not only make learning Greek easier, but it will also teach you about an important component of English grammar.

A *sentence* is a unit of speech that forms a complete thought, consisting of a *subject* and a *predicate*. In simplistic terms, the *subject* is what you are talking about, the *predicate* is what you are saying about the subject.

Diogenes disliked shoes.

"Diogenes" is the subject, "disliked shoes" is the predicate.

Sentences are made up of one or more *clauses*. A *clause* is a unit of speech that has a subject and a predicate, but is not necessarily a complete thought. There are two types of clauses. An *independent clause* expresses a complete thought and can therefore be a sentence. A *dependent clause* does not express a complete thought and cannot be a sentence. It *depends* upon an independent clause.

All independent clauses can be sentences. "Plato shunned politics" is an independent clause consisting of a subject "Plato" and a predicate "shunned politics." The clause "so that he could study philosophy" is not a complete thought and is therefore not an independent clause. It depends upon an independent clause like "Plato shunned politics" in order to make sense. The sentence "Plato shunned politics so that he could study philosophy" is a *sentence* made up of an independent clause, "Plato shunned politics," and a dependent clause, "so that he could study philosophy."

Clauses may contain *phrases*. A phrase is a small group of words that collectively convey a simple idea that no single word in the phrase could do on its own, such as "on account of money" and "in the highest" (prepositional phrases). A phrase does not have a subject or a predicate.

Relative Pronouns and Relative Clauses

As you learned in chapter 4, a pronoun stands in place of a noun. You have learned the personal pronouns. Instead of saying "Socrates was a philosopher. Socrates died in 399 B.C.E.," we can say "Socrates was a philosopher. *He* died in 399 B.C.E."

A *relative pronoun* is a pronoun that introduces a *relative clause*. It is called relative because it relates to a previously mentioned noun or pronoun. A relative clause is always a dependent clause; it will never form a complete sentence. In the sentence "Not all men *who have beards* are philosophers," "who have beards" is a relative clause introduced by the relative pronoun "who." If you are wondering if something is a relative clause, try putting brackets around it. The relative clause will not be a sentence. "Who have beards" is clearly not a sentence. However, when the relative clause is removed, what remains will always be a sentence. "Not all men are philosophers" is still a sentence consisting of a subject and a predicate.

The relative pronoun in Greek is as follows:

	Singular			Plural		
	m	*f*	*n*	*m*	*f*	*n*
Nom.	ὅς	ἥ	ὅ	οἵ	αἵ	ἅ
Gen.	οὗ	ἧς	οὗ	ὧν	ὧν	ὧν
Dat.	ᾧ	ᾗ	ᾧ	οἷς	αἷς	οἷς
Acc.	ὅν	ἥν	ὅ	οὕς	ἅς	ἅ

There are a couple of things that make memorizing and identifying relative pronouns easier.

First, the relative pronoun always has a rough breathing mark. Second, notice how similar the relative pronoun is to the definite article. With few exceptions (masculine and feminine nominatives), you simply remove the tau (τ) from the definite article and add a breathing mark.

An even easier way to memorize the relative pronoun is to remember that the relative pronoun consists of the endings of αὐτός with a breathing mark.

Let us look at two examples of a relative clause.

¶ φιλέω = to love | σοφία, –ας, ἡ = wisdom

ὁ διδάσκαλος ὅς παιδεύει τοὺς μαθητὰς φιλεῖ σοφίαν.

The teacher *who teaches the students* loves wisdom.

In this sentence, "who teaches the students" is a relative clause introduced by the relative pronoun ὅς. Remember our rule. If you take out the relative clause, what remains "The teacher loves wisdom" is still a sentence. On the contrary, a relative clause such as "who teaches the students" is not a sentence.

ὁ διδάσκαλος ὅν ὁ θεὸς παιδεύει φιλεῖ σοφίαν.

The teacher *whom God teaches* loves wisdom.

You will notice that in this sentence the case of the relative pronoun is in the accusative case. This brings us to our next important point: The *gender* and *number* of the relative pronoun is determined by the *antecedent*; the *case* is determined by the relative pronoun's function in the relative clause. As you remember from chapter 6, the *antecedent* is what the relative refers to, in other words, it is "who the who is" and "what the what is." In the first sentence (ὁ διδάσκαλος ὅς παιδεύει τοὺς μαθητὰς φιλεῖ σοφίαν), the antecedent of the relative ὅς was διδάσκαλος. It is masculine and singular because the antecedent διδάσκαλος is masculine and singular, but it is in the nominative case because it is the subject of the relative clause, not because διδάσκαλος is nominative. In the second sentence (ὁ διδάσκαλος ὅν ὁ θεὸς παιδεύει φιλεῖ σοφίαν), ὅν is again masculine and singular because the antecedent διδάσκαλος is masculine and singular. However, ὅν is accusative because it is the direct object in the relative clause.

μέν...δέ

One conspicuous feature of classical Greek is its fondness for expressing things by contrast of pairs. One of the ways it does this is by the μέν...δέ construction, where μέν marks the first clause and δέ marks the second clause.

> ¶ μωρία, –ας, ἡ = foolishness | ἰατρικός, –ή, –όν (adj.) = medical | τέχνη, –ης, ἡ = art | πλουτίζω = to enrich | ἀπορέω = to be poor | γραμματικός, –ή, –όν (adj.) = grammatical, academic

ὁ μὲν ἀγαθὸς ἄνθρωπος φέρει τὴν μωρίαν, ὁ δὲ κακὸς ἄνθρωπος ἔχει τὴν μωρίαν.

The good man bears foolishness, but the bad man has foolishness.

ἡ μὲν ἰατρικὴ τέχνη πλουτίζει, ἀπορεῖ δὲ ἡ γραμματικὴ τέχνη.

The medical art enriches, but the academic art is poor.

Sometimes the nouns are left out and the definite article alone is used.

οἱ μὲν γράφουσιν, οἱ δὲ λέγουσιν.

Some people write, some people speak.

When you see a μέν, look for a δέ in the next clause. Many instructors will ask that you translate μέν "on the one hand" and δέ as "on the other hand." This is another form of translation "training wheels" that can be cast off once you become comfortable with the construction. It is a bit clunky and not nearly as graceful as the μέν...δέ construction and therefore other instructors will allow you to leave μέν untranslated. The important thing is that you recognize this construction when you come upon it in your reading of Greek, and treat the two clauses as a pair to be contrasted or compared.

Vocabulary

ἀρχή, –ῆς, ἡ = beginning; first place, power

ἐκκλησία, –ας, ἡ = church

▶ ἔρως, –ωτος, ὁ = love

κέρδος, –ους, τό = gain, profit

αἰσχρός, –ή, –όν (adj.) = shameful

δυνατός, –ή, –όν (adj.) = strong; possible; able

ἕκαστος, –η, –ον (adj.) = each

νέος, –α, –ον (adj.) = new, young

ἀεί (adv.) = always

ἀπό (ἀπ’, ἀφ’) (prep.) = from (+ gen.)

νῦν (adv.) = now

οὕτως (οὕτω before consonants) (adv.) = thus, to such an extent

πάλιν (adv.) = back, again

ὡς (adv.) = as, like (see appendix E for more uses of ὡς)

Sentences

1. ὁ γὰρ πατὴρ φιλεῖ τὸν υἱὸν καὶ πάντα δείκνυσιν αὐτῷ ἃ αὐτὸς ποιεῖ. (John 5:20)

> ¶ φιλέω = to love
>
> δείκνυσιν = reveals: a third person singular μι verb (see chapter 30).
>
> ποιέω = to do

▸ 2. ὃν γὰρ θεοὶ φιλοῦσιν ἀποθνήσκει νέος. (Menander, *Fragments*)

> ¶ φιλέω = to love
>
> ἀποθνήσκω = to die

3. εἰ δυνατόν ἐστιν, παρελθάτω ἀπ’ ἐμοῦ τὸ ποτήριον τοῦτο· πλὴν οὐχ ὡς ἐγὼ θέλω ἀλλ’ ὡς σύ. (Matt 26:39)

> ¶ παρελθάτω = let pass: 3rd person singular aorist imperative. The subject is ποτήριον.
>
> τοῦτο = this: a demonstrative you will learn in chapter 18, which here modifies ποτήριον.
>
> πλήν (conj.) = except, but
>
> ἀλλ’ = ἀλλά (conj.) = but

4. τὸ γὰρ θανεῖν οὐκ αἰσχρόν, ἀλλ’ αἰσχρῶς θανεῖν. (Menander, *Fragments*)

> ¶ θανεῖν = to die: an aorist infinitive.
>
> ἀλλ’ = ἀλλά (conj.) = but
>
> You must supply the verb "is."

▶ 5. ὁ μὲν ἀγαθὸς ἀνὴρ οὐκ εὐθέως εὐδαίμων ἐξ ἀνάγκης ἐστίν, ὁ δὲ εὐδαίμων καὶ ἀγαθὸς ἀνήρ ἐστιν. (Archytas, in Stobaeus, *Anthology*)

> ❡ εὐθέως (adv.) = straightly; simply; at once
>
> ἐξ ἀνάγκης = by necessity; necessarily
>
> καὶ is here an adverb "also."

6. ἕκαστος ἴδιον ἔχει χάρισμα ἐκ θεοῦ, ὁ μὲν οὕτως, ὁ δὲ οὕτως. (1 Cor 7:7)

> ❡ χάρισμα, –ατος, τό = charism, gift
>
> οὕτως…οὕτως = in this way…in that way

7. ἔρως δίκαιος καρπὸν εὐθέως φέρει. (Menander, *Fragments*)

> ❡ εὐθέως (adv.) = straightly; simply; at once

8. πᾶν τὸ κέρδος ἄδικον ὃ φέρει βλάβην. (Menander, *Fragments*)

> ❡ You must supply the verb "is."
>
> βλάβη, –ης, ἡ = harm

9. ἐγὼ βρῶσιν ἔχω φαγεῖν ἣν ὑμεῖς οὐκ οἴδατε. (John 4:32)

> ❡ βρῶσις, –εως, ἡ = meat; food
>
> φαγεῖν = to eat: aorist infinitive of ἐσθίω "to eat." For the aorist, see chapter 12.
>
> οἴδατε = you [do not] know: 2nd person plural of οἶδα, a verb you will learn in chapter 27.

▶ 10. καὶ αὐτός ἐστιν ἡ κεφαλὴ τοῦ σώματος, τῆς ἐκκλησίας· ὅς ἐστιν ἀρχή, πρωτότοκος ἐκ τῶν νεκρῶν. (Col 1:18)

> ❡ αὐτός: the "he" is Jesus; see chapter 6 about the difference between classical and Koine Greek regarding the nominative of αὐτός.
>
> κεφαλή, –ῆς, ἡ = head
>
> πρωτότοκος, –ον (adj.) = firstborn
>
> νεκρός, –ά, ον (adj.) = dead

Etymology and Discussion Topics

ἔρως, φιλία, and ἀγάπη

These three words are all translated as "love." Upon closer examination, you will find that they in fact express different realities. When early Christians (and before that Greek Jews working on the Septuagint) thought about God's love for man, neither ἔρως nor φιλία worked. Because of its connection with Aphrodite and the fact that it was a deity, ἔρως had too much baggage. φιλία didn't work either: the adjective φίλος originally referred to what was one's own, especially kin and social status. It only gradually broadened over time. Because of this, the less common ἀγάπη was chosen to express divine love. This should not be taken to mean that ἀγάπη is in conflict or opposed to ἔρως. In fact, ἀγάπη has more in common with ἔρως than φιλία. For more on this complex and fascinating topic, read *The Four Loves* by C.S. Lewis and the introduction to *Deus Caritas Est* by Benedict XVI. See also chapter 26 Etymology and Discussion Topic.

ὃν γὰρ θεοὶ φιλοῦσιν ἀποθνῄσκει νέος.

Once again, not knowing the context allows for different interpretations of this line. This popular maxim is commonly held to mean that it is unfortunate that so many promising young people die early. It is also possible, however, that this is another example of the classical Greek dark sense of humor; it is better for one to die young and not experience the indignities of old age! For a great example of this sentiment, read the story of Cleobis and Biton in Herodotus (1.31).

ὁ μὲν ἀγαθὸς ἀνὴρ οὐκ εὐθέως εὐδαίμων ἐξ ἀνάγκης ἐστίν, ὁ δὲ εὐδαίμων καὶ ἀγαθὸς ἀνήρ ἐστιν.

What is Archytas saying in this line? We can see in the μέν clause the common ancient belief that happiness depends to a great extent on forces outside of man's control, yet what is he saying about happiness with the δέ clause?

καὶ αὐτός ἐστιν ἡ κεφαλὴ τοῦ σώματος, τῆς ἐκκλησίας· ὅς ἐστιν ἀρχή, πρωτότοκος ἐκ τῶν νεκρῶν. (Col 1:18)

While it is considered terrible English to begin a sentence with a relative pronoun, Greek has no issue whatsoever doing so, nor is it considered bad style.

Chapter 11 ⌒

Future Tense • Principal Parts of the Verb •
Direct and Indirect Statements

Future Tense

In chapter 4, you learned the about verb tenses. You also learned the forms of the present tense. Here are the forms of the future tense, active voice, indicative mood. There is no future imperative in Greek.

	Singular		*Plural*	
1st	λύ–σω	"I will loosen"	λύ–σομεν	"we will loosen"
2nd	λύ–σεις	"you will loosen"	λύ–σετε	"you will loosen"
3rd	λύ–σει	"he/she/it will loosen"	λύ–σουσι(ν)	"they will loosen"

If you have memorized the present active indicative forms of λύω, forming the future active tense is easy. You simply add a sigma before the present endings.

οἱ διδάσκαλοι παιδεύουσι τοὺς μαθητάς.

The teachers teach the students. (present tense)

οἱ διδάσκαλοι παιδεύσουσι τοὺς μαθητάς.

The teachers will teach the students. (future tense)

The same principle is applied to form the future infinitive. Simply add σ before the infinitive ending.

Present Infinitive: λύ–ειν

Future Infinitive: λύ–σειν

We will discuss how to translate the future infinitive in the section on indirect statement below.

In a simple world, all futures for omega verbs would be as easy as adding a sigma before the present active indicative endings. However, some consonants preceding a sigma were difficult to pronounce, and the form was simplified. We observe a similar spelling change in the English word "sympathy," a combination of the preposition *syn* (σύν) and *pathy* from the Greek noun for passion (πάθος), where we instinctively change the n to an m. In other instances, certain consonants preceding a sigma produced a sound for which they already had a single letter. For example, whenever a kappa (κ) was followed by a sigma (σ), they wrote ξ instead of κς. "I will drag" is therefore written as ἕλξω, not ἕλκσω, as you might expect.

Below is a chart of the major spelling peculiarities that are important for the future tense. If you are able to memorize these changes, fantastic. If not, don't be discouraged. As you read more Greek, you will eventually come to expect such changes.

A stem ending in…	…plus…	…results in:
π, β, φ (labials[1])	σ	ψ
τ, δ, θ (dentals[2])	σ	σ
κ, γ, χ (palatals[3])	σ	ξ

1 π, β, and φ are called labials because you use your lips to pronounce them.

2 τ, δ, and θ are called dentals because you press your tongue to the back of your teeth to pronounce them.

3 κ, γ, and χ are called palatals because you use the palate of your mouth to pronounce them.

¶ σπεύδω = to hasten | οὔποτε = never | ἀεὶ = always

οἱ διδάσκαλοι ἀεὶ λέξουσιν (hypothetically λέγσουσιν).

The teachers will always talk.

οἱ μαθηταὶ οὔποτε σπεύσουσι (hypothetically σπεύδσουσιν) γράφειν.

The students will never hasten to write.

πολλάκις οἱ διδάσκαλοι κακῶς γράψουσιν (hypothetically γράφσουσιν).

Often the teachers will write poorly.

Principal Parts of the Verb

When someone learns English, there is no way to know that the past tense of "drink" is "drank," but the past tense of "think" is "thought." Dictionaries for people learning English will therefore list the tenses of English verbs to aid the one learning English. In Greek, those who write dictionaries provide the information to form any tense of the Greek verb. They do this by giving you the *principal parts* for each verb. There are 6 principal parts for the Greek verb. They are all 1st person singular forms in the indicative mood. You already know the first principal part. It is the present active indicative form. This is the form that all verbs will be alphabetized under in a dictionary.

The 6 principal parts are listed below. Remember that all principal parts are 1st person singular indicative.

1. Present Active
2. Future Active
3. Aorist Active
4. Perfect Active
5. Perfect Middle/Passive
6. Aorist Passive

Now that you know the future tense, you have now met the first two principal parts. In the vocabulary at the back of this book, you will find all the principal parts for each verb. In the vocabulary in each individual chapter, verbs will be listed with the principal parts whose tenses have been introduced by that point. If you see a — in place or a principal part, this signifies that the verb lacks this principal part or that it is extremely rare. If you see [   ] in place of a principal part, this signifies that this principal part does exist, but that you have not yet learned the form. It is important for you to memorize the principal parts of a verb in addition to the definition. From time immemorial teachers have been telling their students the importance of memorizing the principal parts, and students have been ignoring them. If you won't memorize all six, at least memorize the first three. Not only are these tenses more common, but the forms will give you an idea of any important spelling changes that might occur.

Direct and Indirect Statements

Look at the following two statements:

Socrates says, "The unexamined life is not worth living."

Socrates says that the unexamined life is not worth living.

Both of the above sentences contain a statement of Socrates. The first example contains a *direct* statement. The words of Socrates are given in quotation marks. In the second sentence, the words of Socrates are given *indirectly*, hence they are an *indirect statement*.

Greek has three ways of expressing indirect statement. (1) ὅτι / ὡς, (2) *accusative and infinitive*, and (3) *accusative and participle*. As you will see in the sections below, Greek uses indirect statement after many verbs other than those signifying speech. The term "indirect statement" can thus be a little misleading.

(1) *ὅτι / ὡς*. This form of indirect statement is the easiest for speakers of English to grasp. After verbs of speaking, ὅτι (less frequently ὡς) is used to introduce the indirect statement and can be translated as "that."

ὁ διδάσκαλος λέγει ὅτι ἡ ἀρετή ἐστι χαλεπή.

The teacher says that excellence is difficult.

(2) *Accusative and Infinitive*. Used primarily with verbs of thinking and believing, Greek changes what would have been the verb of the direct statement into the corresponding infinitive, and it changes what would have been the nominative of the direct statement to the accusative case. We occasionally do this in English. Consider the following examples:

Polyphemus ate his guests. I think that *he is a poor host*.

Polyphemus ate his guests. I consider *him to be a poor host*.

The direct statement is "he is a poor host." In the first sentence, the standard English use of a verb introducing indirect statement, followed by "that," is used. In the second sentence, we can see the vestiges of an English case system. We change the subject "he" to our equivalent of the accusative case "him," and we change the finite verb "is" to the corresponding infinitive "to be." As you can see, we seldom employ this construction in English, and it is limited to a few verbs. Greek uses this method with far more frequency.

> ¶ φησι = says: 3rd person singular verb of φήμι, a verb you will be introduced to in chapter 17

ὁ διδάσκαλός φησι τὴν ἀρετὴν εἶναι χαλεπήν.

The teacher says that excellence is difficult.

The direct statement is ἡ ἀρετή ἐστι χαλεπή, "excellence is difficult." The nominative ἡ ἀρετή is changed into the accusative τὴν ἀρετὴν and the finite verb ἐστι is changed into the infinitive εἶναι. Because an adjective always agrees with the noun it is modifying in gender, number, and case, χαλεπή is changed to the accusative χαλεπήν.

> ¶ πόνος, –ου, ὁ = toil

ὁ φιλόσοφός φησι τὸν πόνον παιδεύειν τοὺς μαθητάς.

The philosopher says that toil teaches the students.

In this sentence, the direct statement would have been ὁ πόνος παιδεύει τοὺς μαθητάς. The nominative ὁ πόνος is changed into the accusative τὸν πόνον, and the finite verb παιδεύει is changed into the infinitive παιδεύειν. In this sentence we have two accusatives. How do we know that the sentence should not read "The philosopher says that the students teach toil." Well, first of all, the context. While students might teach patience, "the students teach toil" does not make as much sense as "toil teaches the students." Second, a writer will often use word order to tell you what the original nominative was by placing it before the direct object.

You will likely be tempted to translate indirect statements using the accusative and infinitive construction literally. While you should ultimately defer to the advice of your instructor, this is often not the best way to proceed. While a literal translation might sometimes be possible, far more often it will not work. Instead, you should insert "that" into your translation and translate the sentence as you would an indirect statement in the ὅτι / ὡς construction.

One exception to the rule that the subject must be put into the accusative occurs when the subject of the indirect statement is the subject of the verb that introduces the indirect statement.

ὁ διδάσκαλός φησι παιδεύειν τοὺς μαθητάς.

The teacher says that he teaches the students.

Since the subject (διδάσκαλός) of the verb (φησι) introducing the indirect statement is the subject of the verb (παιδεύειν) in indirect statement, a repetition of the subject in the accusative case is not needed. If there are any modifiers of the subject, they remain in the nominative case.

ὁ διδάσκαλός φησιν αὐτὸς παιδεύειν τοὺς μαθητάς.

The teacher says that he himself (i.e., not a teaching assistant) teaches the students.

You will notice that the verb used in the example for the ὅτι / ὡς construction was λέγει, while the verb used for the accusative and infinitive example was φησιν. As mentioned above, verbs that signify mere speech, like λέγω, tend to take the ὅτι / ὡς construction, while verbs of asserting or claiming prefer the accusative and infinitive construction. Even though both λέγει and φησιν can be translated as "says," λέγω generally refers to mere speech while φημί is used for what one believes to be true, more like "assert."

All of the examples above expressed present time in indirect statement. In the next chapter, we will learn how to express past and future time in indirect statement.

(3) *Accusative and Participle.* The last type of indirect statement is the rarest of the three and is preferred by verbs of *perception*. We will discuss this third type in chapter 21 after we introduce the participle. You will eventually find that it follows the same rules as the accusative and infinitive construction, but uses a participle instead of an infinitive.

Vocabulary

ἀδελφός, –οῦ, ὁ = brother

▸ ᾅδης, –ου, ὁ = death, the underworld; (later) hell; capitalized by modern editors (Ἅιδης) when referring to the god Hades.

▸ γῆ, γῆς, ἡ (older form γαῖα, –ας, ἡ) = earth

▸ πέτρα, –ας, ἡ = a rock

πύλη, –ης, ἡ = a gate

ἀληθινός, –ή, –όν (adj.) trustful, true
ἄλλος, –η, –ο (adj.) = another; other

ἀλλά (conj.) = but

ὅτι = "that," when introducing indirect statement; because

περί (prep.) = concerning, about (+ gen.); around (+ dat.); around (+ acc.)

χωρίς (prep. and adv.) = (prep.) without (+ gen.); (adv.) separately

ἄγω, ἄξω = to lead

νομίζω, νομιῶ = to think, consider

πέμπω, πέμψω = to send

Sentences

1. ὁ παιδείας ἀμύητος πῶς ἄλλους ἀνθρώπους παιδεύσει; (Aesop, *Fables*)

> ¶ ἀμύητος, –ον (adj.) = uninitiated; uninitiated in (+ gen)
>
> πῶς (adv.) = how?

2. κἀγὼ δέ σοι λέγω ὅτι σὺ εἶ Πέτρος, καὶ ἐπὶ ταύτῃ τῇ πέτρᾳ οἰκοδομήσω μου τὴν ἐκκλησίαν, καὶ πύλαι ᾅδου οὐ κατισχύσουσιν αὐτῆς. (Matthew 16:18)

> ¶ κἀγὼ = καὶ ἐγώ.
>
> Πέτρος, –ου, ὁ = Peter
>
> ταύτῃ = this: a demonstrative you will learn in chapter 18.
>
> οἰκοδομέω = to build
>
> κατισχύω = to overpower (+ gen.)

3. οἴδαμεν δὲ ὅτι τοῖς ἀγαπῶσιν τὸν θεὸν πάντα συνεργεῖ εἰς ἀγαθόν. (Rom 8:28)

> ¶ οἴδαμεν = we know: a verb you will learn in chapter 27
>
> τοῖς ἀγαπῶσιν = for those loving: the participle in a dative of respect, which you will learn in chapters 19–21.
>
> συνεργέω = to work together

4. νόμιζε τοὺς ἀληθινοὺς φίλους εἶναι ἀδελφούς. (Menander, *Fragments*)

> ¶ νομίζω can often mean "consider."

5. ἄξεις ἀλύπως τὸν βίον χωρὶς γάμου. (Menander, *Fragments*)

> ¶ ἀλύπως (adv.) = painless
>
> γάμος, –ου, ὁ = marriage

6. ἕκαστος γὰρ τὸ ἴδιον φορτίον βαστάσει. (Gal 6:5)

> ¶ βαστάζω, βαστάσω = to bear, carry
>
> φορτίον, –ου, ὁ = load, burden

7. θεὸν σέβου καὶ πάντα πράξεις εὐθέως. (Menander, *Fragments*)

> ¶ σέβου = revere, worship. This is the 2nd person imperative of a deponent verb. Deponent verbs will be introduced in chapter 15.
>
> εὐθέως (adv.) = straightly, directly. Here it probably has the sense of "correctly."

8. ἀλλά σ’ ἐς Ηλύσιον πεδίον καὶ πείρατα γαίης ἀθάνατοι πέμψουσιν.
   (Homer, *Odyssey*)

> ¶ σ’ = σε
>
> ἐς = εἰς
>
> πεῖραρ, –ατος τό = epic for πέρας, –ατος, τό = end, limit
>
> Ηλύσιος, –α, –ον (adj.) = Elysian. The Elysian field was reportedly where certain heroes spent their afterlife. The speaker is Proteus and the σε is Menelaus.
>
> πεδίον, –ου, τό = field, plain
>
> γαίης = epic for γῆς

9. ἀλλὰ μάτην ὁ πρόθυμος ἀεὶ πόνον ἕξει. (Euripides, *Children of Heracles*)

> ¶ μάτην (adv.) = in vain
>
> πρόθυμος, ον (adj.) = eager
>
> ἕξει: future of ἔχω.

10. πολλαὶ μέν ἐσμεν, λέξομεν δὲ συντόμως. (Aeschylus, *Eumenides*)

> ¶ συντόμως (adv.) = concisely, briefly
>
> πολλαὶ: feminine because these words are spoken by the Furies, in this play no fans of long wordy speeches.

Etymology and Discussion Topics

ᾄδης (Ἅιδης), –ου ὁ

Remember that when a letter with a subscript is capitalized, the subscript can then be written below the A (see above) or after it, adscript (Ἅι). In classical Greek, this word could refer both to the god Hades and to the realm over which Hades ruled, the underworld. A very common construction was the preposition ἐν + the genitive, ἐν Ἅιδου. As you know, the preposition ἐν takes the dative case, not the genitive case. The missing word that is to be supplied is the dative οἴκῳ (house). Thus ἐν Ἅιδου means "In the house of Hades" or simply, "In Hades."

γῆ, γῆς, ἡ (older form γαῖα, –ας, ἡ) = earth

Many gods and goddesses are simply transliterations of Greek words. Gaia (γαῖα) means "earth," Thanatos (θάνατος) means "death," and Nike (νίκη) means "victory."

πέτρα, –ας, ἡ = a rock

As you can see in the second sentence, Peter (Πέτρος) is called the rock (πέτρα) of the Church.

Chapter 12 ✐

Expressing Past Time in Greek • Imperfect Tense • Aorist Tense •
Aorist Active Imperative • Imperfect of εἰμί

Expressing Past Time in Greek

Imperfect and Aorist

Greek has two main tenses used to express the past, the *imperfect* and
the *aorist*.[1] The *imperfect* tense describes an action that is viewed as ongoing
in the past, or taking part over a period of time. In contrast, the *aorist* tense
does not. The aorist can be said to view the action as a single event. Two examples from English will make this distinction clear.

> The student *was laughing* at the appearance of the professor in his
> regalia. (imperfect)
>
> The student *laughed* at the joke of the professor. (aorist)

In the first sentence, the author is viewing the laughter of the student as
continuing over a period of time, as the general ridiculousness of academic
regalia warrants. In the second sentence, the laugh of the student is imagined
as a single, brief event.

The imperfect tense expresses *ongoing*, *habitual*, or *continual* aspect,
while the aorist tense expresses *simple* aspect. However, you will often find
the aorist used where you could argue that the action is ongoing and not
simple. For this reason, it is helpful to think of the aorist as the "default"

---

1. The pluperfect, which also expresses past time, will be discussed in chapter 29.

past tense, while the imperfect is used when the author wants to stress the *ongoing*, *habitual*, or *continual* aspect of an action in the past.

Does this mean, for example, that you always have to translate the imperfect of "to say" as "used to say," or "was saying"? That depends. It can be very helpful to do so in order to form in your mind a clear distinction between the imperfect and the aorist tenses. After some time, when you feel comfortable with the distinction, you can cast off the training wheels, so to speak, and translate the two tenses the same when proper English warrants. However, noticing an author's choice of past tense can be crucial to the proper understanding of a sentence. While often translated as "Jesus said," you should pay attention to whether the imperfect or the aorist tense is used. You will notice that the imperfect tense comes before sayings that were probably repeated over and over. After all, the disciples often were not the quickest learners!

More about Aspect

At the risk of confusing you more, let's talk more about this term "aspect" used above. Greek tenses express both time and aspect. While time naturally refers to when an action occurs, aspect refers to the type of action involved. Greek has three aspects, *imperfect* (ongoing/habitual), *aorist* (simple), and *perfect* (completed). We will discuss the perfective aspect (the rarest aspect) in chapter 27. For now, let us focus on the difference between imperfect and aoristic aspect. As we said, while the aorist is technically the "simple" aspect, it is easiest to think of it as the default aspect. If the author wants to stress continual aspect in the past, the imperfect is used.

For the present and future tenses, you will find that aspect will never be too difficult of an issue. Context will determine how to translate the sentences. For the most part, you will tend to translate them in the simple way (aorist), only using the "is —ing" or "will be —ing" (imperfect) translation when the context demands it.

> ¶ μάθημα, –ατος, τό = lesson

ὁ διδάσκαλος παδεύει μάθημα χαλεπόν.

The teacher teaches a difficult lesson. / The teacher is teaching a difficult lesson.

ὁ διδάσκαλος παδεύσει μάθημα χαλεπόν.

The teacher will teach a difficult lesson. / The teacher will be teaching a difficult lesson.

For the past, however, there are separate forms for the aoristic and imperfect aspects: the *aorist* and *imperfect* respectively.

In the following table the left side demonstrates your model verb λύω, and the right side the endings you will need to memorize.

Imperfect Active Indicative				
λύω		Endings		
Singular	*Plural*	*Singular*	*Plural*	
1st	ἔλυ–**ον**	ἐλύ–**ομεν**	ον	ομεν
2nd	ἔλυ–**ες**	ἐλύ–**ετε**	ες	ετε
3rd	ἔλυ–**ε(ν)**	ἔλυ–**ον**	ε(ν)	ον

Imperfect Tense

The imperfect tense is formed from the present stem. How do we find the present stem? First, remove any prepositions that are prefixed. We take the personal ending ω off of the 1st principal part of the verb. Hence the present stem of λύω is λυ, and the present stem of παιδεύω is παιδευ.

To form the imperfect tense, add the imperfect endings *and* add an augment. An augment is the addition of the letter epsilon (ε) to the beginning of the word. The addition of ε to the beginning of a verb is called a *syllabic* augment, because with the addition of ε, an extra syllable is added to the word.

ὁ διδάσκαλος ἐπαίδευε τοὺς μαθητάς.

The teacher was teaching the students. / The teacher used to teach the students.

There is one more type of augment, the *temporal* augment. A *temporal* augment occurs when you add the augment to a verb that starts with a vowel or diphthong.[2] The vowel or diphthong is lengthened and it takes longer to say, hence its name, the *temporal* augment. Augmented verbs can often cause frustration with beginning students because it is hard to know where to look in a dictionary, which alphabetizes by the first principle part, not by augmented forms. Syllabic augments are easier to spot since they all begin with an epsilon. If you see a word that starts with an epsilon and you can't find it in a dictionary, remove the epsilon and try finding the verb that way. Temporal augments are more difficult, since it is not as easy as removing one

2. A few verbs that begin with a vowel take a syllabic augment.

letter. Below is a list of common temporal augments. If you see a word that you think might have a temporal augment, try looking for the present stem with the following chart. After a while, you will begin to recognize these common temporal augments.

If a stem begins with…	…after temporal augmentation it becomes
α, ε	η
ο	ω
αι, ει	η
αυ, ευ	ηυ
οι	ῳ

In compound verbs, which are verbs that consist of a preposition and a verb, like ἐπιγράφω "to write upon," from ἐπί (upon) + γράφω (write), the augment is placed after the preposition, not before it. The augment overrides any vowel the prefix ends in, e.g., ἐπέγραφον = I was writing.

¶ ἀκούω = to hear | σκῶμμα, σκώματος, τό = a joke | νομοθέτης, –ου, ὁ = lawmaker

οἱ μαθηταὶ οὐκ ἤθελον ἀκούειν τὸ σκῶμμα τοῦ διδασκάλου.

The students were not wanting to hear the joke of the teacher.

οἱ νομοθέται τοὺς λίθους ἐπέγραφον.

The lawmakers used to write on stones.

Aorist Tense

	Aorist Active Indicative			
	λύω		Endings	
	Singular	Plural	Singular	Plural
1st	ἔλυ–σα	ἐλύ–σαμεν	σα	σαμεν
2nd	ἔλυ–σας	ἐλύ–σατε	σας	σατε
3rd	ἔλυ–σε(ν)	ἔλυ–σαν	σε(ν)	σαν

The aorist tense, as opposed to the imperfect tense, expresses action in the past that is not viewed as ongoing. The aorist is formed from the aorist stem, which can be found via the third principal part.[3]

The majority of aorist stems end in sigma and have endings like λύω above. These verbs are called 1st aorists. A few verbs lack the sigma but otherwise are identical, e.g., ἔμεινα, ἔμεινας, ἔμεινεν, etc. There is another large group of aorists called 2nd aorists. With very few exceptions, verbs have *either* a 1st or a 2nd aorist, not both. There is no difference in meaning. The endings of 2nd aorists are found below. Instead of our model verb λύω, which has a 1st aorist, the 2nd aorist of the verb λείπω "to leave" is given below.

	2nd Aorist Active Indicative			
	λείπω		Endings	
	Singular	Plural	Singular	Plural
1st	ἔλιπ–**ον**	ἐλίπ–**ομεν**	ον	ομεν
2nd	ἔλιπ–**ες**	ἐλίπ–**ετε**	ες	ετε
3rd	ἔλιπ–**ε(ν)**	ἐλίπ–**ον**	ε(ν)	ον

If these endings look familiar, that is because you just learned them. The 2nd aorist endings are identical to the imperfect endings. How then do you tell the difference between the imperfect and a 2nd aorist? Remember that the aorist tense is formed from the aorist stem, which is found in the 3rd principal part, while the imperfect tense is formed from the present stem, which is found in the 1st principal part. Look at the first three principal parts of the verb λείπω "to leave." λείπω, λείψω, ἔλιπον.

This is why memorizing the principal parts of verbs is so crucial. When you see a third principal part that ends in –σα, you know it has a 1st aorist. When you see a third principal part that ends in –ον, you know it has a 2nd aorist. ἐλείπομεν "we used to leave/were leaving," is imperfect; ἐλίπομεν "we left" is aorist.

ὁ Σωκράτης ἔλιπεν.

Socrates left.

ἐλύσαμεν τοὺς δεσμοὺς τοῦ Σωκράτους.

We loosened the chains of Socrates.

---

3. Technically, the sigma in the aorist tense is part of the aorist stem and not an ending, but for memorization purposes it is easier to memorize the sigma as part of the ending.

Aorist Active Imperative

In chapter 4 you learned the *imperative* mood. While the indicative states facts, the imperative commands. You also learned the endings for the present active imperative. The aorist also takes the imperative. Below are the endings for the aorist active imperative.

<table>
<tr><td colspan="4" align="center">*Aorist Active Imperative of λύω*</td></tr>
<tr><td></td><td>*Singular*</td><td>*Plural*</td><td></td></tr>
<tr><td>2nd</td><td>λῦ–σον "loosen!"</td><td>λύ–σατε "loosen!"</td><td></td></tr>
<tr><td>3rd</td><td>λυ–σάτω "let him/her loosen!"</td><td>λυ–σάντων "let them loosen!"</td><td></td></tr>
</table>

You can see how similar the endings are to the present imperatives below.

<table>
<tr><td colspan="4" align="center">*Present Active Imperative of λύω*</td></tr>
<tr><td></td><td>*Singular*</td><td>*Plural*</td><td></td></tr>
<tr><td>2nd</td><td>λῦ–ε "loosen!"</td><td>λύ–ετε "loosen!"</td><td></td></tr>
<tr><td>3rd</td><td>λυ–έτω "let him/her loosen!"</td><td>λυ–όντων "let them loosen!"</td><td></td></tr>
</table>

In addition to the sigma of the aorist stem, with the exception of the 2nd person singular, you simply have an alpha in place of the epsilon and omicron of the present endings. It is also important to note that *augments are found only in the indicative mood*. The aorist imperative drops the augment.

Verbs with 2nd aorists form their aorist active imperative by taking the endings of the present active imperative. Remember that the stem is what distinguishes 2nd aorist imperatives from their respective present imperative.

<table>
<tr><td colspan="5" align="center">*λείπω, λείψω, ἔλιπον = to leave*</td></tr>
<tr><td></td><td colspan="2">*Present Active Imperative*</td><td colspan="2">*Aorist Active Imperative*</td></tr>
<tr><td></td><td>*Singular*</td><td>*Plural*</td><td>*Singular*</td><td>*Plural*</td></tr>
<tr><td>2nd</td><td>λείπ–ε</td><td>λείπ–ετε</td><td>λίπ–ε</td><td>λίπ–ετε</td></tr>
<tr><td>3rd</td><td>λειπ–έτω</td><td>λειπ–όντων</td><td>λιπ–έτω</td><td>λιπ–όντων</td></tr>
</table>

Translation of the Present and Aorist Imperative

At this point you might be wondering why the translations are the same for both imperatives above, and how on earth can someone command someone to do something in the past. The answer is that when it comes to the imperative (and other moods you will learn later), *the tense signifies aspect, not time*. It is counterintuitive to say that a tense has nothing to do with time, but in the imperative mood, that is the case.[4] Remember when we talked about imperfect versus aoristic aspect. The present imperative represents imperfect aspect while the aorist imperative represents aoristic aspect. Since we lack the ability to express aspect in English, "Be honest" could mean "Always be honest in the course of your life" or it could refer to a specific instance where the speaker wants the truth, "Did you really memorize the 3rd declension? Be honest." In English, when we want to express a habitual command, we have to add words like "keep," "stay," and "always." In Greek, aspect performs this task. Look at the following two sentences.

¶ πάσχω = to experience | γράμμα, –ατος, τό = letter

γράφε ἅ πασχεῖς.

Write what you experience.

γράψον τὸ γράμμα ἄλφα.

Write the letter alpha.

While you would translate γράφε and γράψον the same "write," the present imperative (γράφε) expresses a habitual command, while the aorist imperative (γράψον) expresses a one-time command.

Let's look at real examples from the New Testament. In the popular proverb given in Luke 4:23, Ἰατρέ, θεράπευσον σεαυτόν, "Physician. Heal thyself," the aorist imperative (θεράπευσον) is used. (We will learn reflexive pronouns like σεαυτόν in chapter 29.) In contrast, in Matthew 7:1 when Jesus says μὴ κρίνετε "Don't judge," the present imperative (imperfect aspect) is used since it is a habitual or continual command.

Finally, the aorist active infinitive ending is given below. Verbs with 2nd aorists like λείπω attach the present infinitive ending to the aorist stem.

1st Aorist Infinitive		2nd Aorist Infinitive	
σαι	λῦ–**σαι**	ειν	λίπ–**ειν**

Because only the indicative mood has the augment, the aorist active infinitive is added to the aorist stem but does not have an augment. When you see an aorist infinitive not in indirect statement, the same rules of aspect apply. If the author wants to stress imperfect aspect, the present infinitive is used;

---

4. Aspect in Greek moods is more nuanced than indicated here, but for the student learning about aspect, it is easiest at this point to think of the indicative mood as the only mood that stresses time, while the other moods express aspect.

if not, the aorist infinitive is used. You will learn how to translate the aorist infinitive in indirect statement in chapter 13.

Imperfect of εἰμί

The irregular verb εἰμί does not have an aorist tense, only the imperfect. Note the alternate forms for the 1st person singular and the 2nd person plural. There is no difference in meaning.

| | *Imperfect Active Indicative of εἰμί "to be"* | |
	Singular	*Plural*
1st	ἦ or ἦν	ἦμεν
2nd	ἦσθα	ἦτε or ἦστε
3rd	ἦν	ἦσαν

Vocabulary

γλῶττα (Koine γλῶσσα) –ης, ἡ = tongue; language

γόνυ, –ατος, τό = knee

▸ οὐρανός, –οῦ, ὁ = sky; heaven

▸ πνεῦμα, –ατος, τό = air, breath; spirit

βραδύς, –εῖα, –ύ (adj.) = dull; slow

νήπιος, –α, –ον (adj.) = childish; as substantive noun = a child.

ταχύς, –εῖα, –ύ (adj.) = swift, quick

εὖ (adv.) = well

ἀκούω, [   ], ἤκουσα = to hear (+ gen. of persons, + acc. of sounds).

▸ ἀποκαλύπτω, ἀποκαλύψω, ἀπεκάλυψα = to uncover, reveal

ἀποκρύπτω, ἀποκρύψω, ἀπέκρυψα = to hide, conceal

λαμβάνω, [   ], ἔλαβον = to take, seize; receive; understand

μερίζω, [   ], ἐμέρισα = to allot, assign

Sentences

▶ 1. ἐν ἀρχῇ ἦν ὁ λόγος, καὶ ὁ λόγος ἦν πρὸς τὸν θεόν, καὶ θεὸς ἦν ὁ λόγος.

   (John 1:1)

> ¶ While πρός can be translated "with" + the accusative, see the Etymology and Discussion Topics at the end of this chapter for a more literal translation.

2. χαλεπὸν τὸ εὖ γνῶναι. (Pittacus, in Stobaeus, *Anthology*)

> ¶ γνῶναι: aorist active infinitive of γιγνώσκω "to know."

3. Λακεδαιμόνιοι τριακοσίους εἰς Θερμοπύλας ἔπεμψαν. (Stobaeus, *Anthology*)

> ¶ Λακεδαιμόνιος, –α, –ον (adj.) = Spartan: here used as a substantive adjective "The Spartans."
>
> τριακόσιοι, –αι, –α (adj.) = 300. This adjective lacks singular endings. You must supply "soldiers" after τριακοσίους.
>
> ▶ θερμοπύλαι, –ῶν, αἱ = Thermopylae
>
> ἔπεμψαν: aorist of πέμπω

4. ἡ γλῶσσα πολλοὺς εἰς ὄλεθρον ἤγαγεν. (Menander, *Fragments*)

> ¶ πολλούς: supply ἀνθρώπους.
>
> ὄλεθρος, –ου, ὁ = destruction, ruin
>
> ἤγαγεν: aorist of ἄγω.

5. οὐχὶ ἐμώρανεν ὁ θεὸς τὴν σοφίαν τοῦ κόσμου; (1 Cor 1:20)

> ¶ οὐχὶ = not. οὐχὶ is used in questions that expect the response "yes," so here "Did God not…?"
>
> The aorist of μωραίνω "to make silly or foolish" is ἐμώρανα, a verb that lacks the sigma, as discussed above.

6. ἑκάστῳ ὡς ὁ θεὸς ἐμέρισεν μέτρον πίστεως. (Rom 12:3)

> ❡ ὡς: here "as." Paul is exhorting his audience not to put themselves above others.

7. ἐξομολογοῦμαί σοι, πάτερ, κύριε τοῦ οὐρανοῦ καὶ τῆς γῆς, ὅτι ἀπέκρυψας ταῦτα ἀπὸ σοφῶν καὶ συνετῶν, καὶ ἀπεκάλυψας αὐτὰ νηπίοις. (Luke 10:21)

> ❡ ἐξομολογοῦμαί = I give you (σοι) thanks. This is a deponent verb. See chapter 15.
>
> ὅτι: here "because"
>
> ταῦτα = these things: neuter accusative plural
>
> συνετός, –ή, –όν (adj.) = intelligent

8. ἡ πολλῶν ἀνδρῶν γόνατ᾽ ἔλυσε. (Homer, *Odyssey*)

> ❡ ἡ: the definite article is used in this line to refer to Helen of Troy
>
> γόνατ᾽ = γόνατα

9. ἡμεῖς δὲ οὐ τὸ πνεῦμα τοῦ κόσμου ἐλάβομεν ἀλλὰ τὸ πνεῦμα τὸ ἐκ τοῦ θεοῦ. (1 Cor 2:12)

10. ἔστω δὲ πᾶς ἄνθρωπος ταχὺς εἰς τὸ ἀκοῦσαι, βραδὺς εἰς τὸ λαλῆσαι, βραδὺς εἰς ὀργήν. (James 1:19)

> ❡ λαλῆσαι: the aorist active infinitive of λαλέω, "to speak."

Etymology and Discussion Topics

οὐρανός, –οῦ, ὁ = sky; heaven

This word literally means "sky." You will often hear that the planet Uranus was named after the Greek god of the sky. However, as you can see, it is merely a transliteration of the Greek word for sky. The god's name is "sky." In Christianity, this is the word that will be used for "heaven." It is used in both the singular οὐρανός "heaven" and plural οὐρανοί "heavens" without a difference in meaning.

πνεῦμα, –ατος, τό = air, breath; spirit

From this Greek word come English words like "pneumonia" and "pneumatic." The Romans will later translate this word as "spiritus" in Latin, hence "Spiritus Sanctus."

ἀποκαλύπτω, ἀποκαλύψω, ἐκάλυψα = to uncover, reveal

When we hear the word "apocalypse," we often think of a catastrophe (another word derived from Greek) or disaster. This is due to many of the scenes described in the final book of the New Testament, ἀποκάλυψις, the 3rd declension noun form of the verb ἀποκαλύπτω. This verb is formed from the preposition ἀπό = from and καλύπτω = to cover, veil, thus "taking away or removing that which covers or veils." The book is about the revelation of the future, hence its more common translation "Revelation."

πρὸς τὸν θεόν

From the opening line of John's Gospel, "πρὸς τὸν θεόν" is a difficult prepositional phrase to translate into English. While it can mean "with," when πρός takes the accusative case it primarily signifies motion or direction toward something. It can, however, also express reciprocal action. "With" therefore is an acceptable translation, but it loses something of the trinitarian nature of the Greek.

θερμοπύλαι, –ῶν, αἱ = Thermopylae

The famous battle ground Thermopylae was a natural defensive position, so used as late as the Second World War. It is believed to have been named on account of the neighboring hot springs, hence θερμός, –ή, –όν "hot" + gates πύλαι = Θερμοπύλαι.

Chapter 13 ❧

Indirect Statement in the Past and Future • Time Constructions

Indirect Statement in the Past and Future

In chapter 11 you learned how Greek expresses indirect statements in the present tense. In this chapter you will learn how Greek expresses indirect statements in the past and future. Although we will look at the different constructions separately, the principle remains the same: the tense of the verb in what would have been the direct statement *remains unchanged* by the verb that introduces the indirect statement.

ὅτι / ὡς Construction. In constructions of this type, the tense of the verb in the indirect statement remains unchanged by the tense of the verb that introduces the indirect statement.

❡ ὑψηλός, –ή, –όν (adj.) = sublime

ὁ διδάσκαλος ἀεὶ λέγει ὅτι ὁ Πλάτων ἐστὶν ὑψηλός.
The teacher always says that Plato is sublime.

ὁ διδάσκαλος ἀεὶ λέξει ὅτι ὁ Πλάτων ἐστὶν ὑψηλός.
The teacher will always say that Plato is sublime.

ὁ διδάσκαλος ἀεὶ ἔλεγεν ὅτι ὁ Πλάτων ἐστὶν μικρός.
The teacher was always saying that Plato was short.

Although the verb that introduces the indirect statement (λέγω) changes from the present (λέγει) to the future (λέξει) to the imperfect (ἔλεγεν), the tense of the verb in the indirect statement stays the same (ἐστὶν). You will notice, however, that while the Greek verb in indirect statement remains unchanged, the *English translation changes* when the verb that introduces the indirect statement is in a past tense, as in the final example. English does not, however, change the tense when the indirect statement is still true, as in the following example.

ὁ διδάσκαλος ἀεὶ ἔλεγεν ὅτι ὁ Πλάτων ἐστὶν ὑψηλός.

The teacher was always saying that Plato is sublime.

Plato is still sublime, but he is no longer short, having died long ago.

Accusative and Infinitive Construction. As you remember from chapter 11, the subject of the indirect statement is changed into the accusative case, and the verb is changed into the corresponding tense of the infinitive.

❡ δοξάζω, δοξάσω, ἐδόξασα = to think, believe

ὁ διδάσκαλος δοξάζει τὸν Πλάτονα εἶναι ὑψηλόν.

The teacher believes that Plato is sublime.

ὁ διδάσκαλος δοξάσει τὸν Πλάτονα εἶναι ὑψηλόν.

The teacher will believe that Plato is sublime.

ὁ διδάσκαλος ἐδόξασε τὸν Πλάτονα εἶναι μικρόν.

The teacher believed that Plato was short.

ὁ διδάσκαλος ἐδόξασε τὸν Πλάτονα εἶναι ὑψηλόν.

The teacher believed that Plato is sublime.

Let's look at some examples where the tense in the indirect statement is other than present.

❡ ὑβρίζω, —, ὕβρισα = to insult | βλάπτω, βλάψω, ἔβλαψα = to harm | δικαστής, –οῦ, ὁ = juror

ὁ διδάσκαλος λέγει ὅτι ὁ Σωκράτης ὕβρισε (aorist) τοὺς δικαστάς.

The teacher says that Socrates insulted the jurors.

ὁ διδάσκαλος λέξει ὅτι ὁ Σωκράτης ὕβρισε (aorist) τοὺς δικαστάς.

The teacher will say that Socrates insulted the jurors.

ὁ διδάσκαλος ἔλεγεν ὅτι ὁ Σωκράτης ὕβρισε (aorist) τοὺς δικαστάς.

The teacher was saying that Socrates had insulted the jurors.

ὁ Σωκράτης ἔλεγεν ὅτι ὁ Ἀλκιβιάδης βλάψει (future) τὴν πόλιν.

Socrates was saying that Alcibiades would harm the city.

ὁ διδάσκαλος δοξάζει τὸν Σωκράτην ὑβρίσαι (aorist infinitive) τοὺς δικαστάς.

The teacher believes that Socrates insulted the jurors.

ὁ διδάσκαλος δοξάσει τὸν Σωκράτην ὑβρίσαι (aorist infinitive) τοὺς δικαστάς.

The teacher will believe that Socrates insulted the jurors.

ὁ διδάσκαλος ἐδόξασε τὸν Σωκράτην ὑβρίσαι (aorist infinitive) τοὺς δικαστάς.

The teacher believed that Socrates had insulted the jurors.

ὁ Σωκράτης ἐδόξασε τὸν Ἀλκιβιάδην βλάψειν (future infinitive) τὴν πόλιν.

Socrates believed that Alcibiades would harm the city.

Notice that while English retains the tense of the indirect statement when that statement is introduced by a verb in the present tense or future tense, the tense of the indirect statement changes when introduced by a verb in a past tense (unless the indirect statement continues to be true). It is crucial to remember that this confusion is a result of English, not Greek. The Greek method is simple and consistent. Whatever the tense of the indirect statement, that tense is retained either in the indicative in the ὅτι / ὡς construction or in the infinitive in the accusative and infinitive construction. Although we will learn the third construction (accusative and participle) in chapter 21, you will be happy to know that the exact same rules listed above apply.

Finally, there is one other way of thinking about tenses in indirect statement. You can remember that the tense in the indirect statement remains unchanged, or you can memorize this chart.

When in an indirect statement you see...	...it describes an action that happens...
present infinitive	*at the same time* as the verb that introduced the indirect statement
aorist infinitive	*before* the verb that introduced the indirect statement.
future infinitive	*after* the verb that introduced the indirect statement.

If you go back over all of the examples above, you will see that this principle applies as well. Both ways of explaining tense in indirect statement are correct, so choose which one works better for you.

Time Constructions

Greek has three ways of expressing time.

Genitive of Time within Which: Greek uses the *genitive* to express the time within which an action occurs.

Accusative of Duration of Time: Greek uses the *accusative* to express the duration of time for which an action occurs.

Dative of Time When: Greek uses the *dative* to express when an action occurs.

The following English examples illustrate the difference between these three methods of expressing time.

The baby cried out during the night.

Here the speaker is stating that at some particular time during the night, the baby cried out. The baby didn't cry out the whole night, or many times during the night. Instead of *during the night*, Greek would put the word night (νύξ) in the genitive case (νύκτος).

The baby cried through the night.

Here the speaker is stating that the baby cried the entire night, not just at some particular point during the night. Greek would put the word night (νύξ) in the accusative case (νύκτα).

The baby cried at night.

Here the speaker is not specifying whether it was at one point during the night or the entire night that the baby cried. They are either too sleep deprived to remember or simply do not care to specify. Here Greek would put the word night (νύξ) in the dative case (νύκτι).

No preposition is needed in any of these constructions, although the later the Greek is, the more often you will see the use of a preposition.

¶ καθεύδω, καθευδήσω, ἐκαθεύδησα = to sleep | μάθημα, μαθήματος, τό = a lesson

οἱ μαθηταὶ ἐκαθεύδησαν τοῦ μαθήματος τοῦ διδασκάλου.

The students slept during the lesson of the teacher.

This sentence states that at some point in the lesson, the students fell asleep.

οἱ μαθηταὶ ἐκαθεύδησαν τὸ μάθημα τοῦ διδασκάλου.

The students slept through the lesson of the teacher.

This sentence states that the students slept through the entire lesson.

οἱ μαθηταὶ ἐκαθεύδησαν τῷ μαθήματι τοῦ διδασκάλου.

The students slept at the lesson of the teacher.

This sentence merely states that they slept at the lesson, neither specifying at which point nor for how long they slept.

Summary of Case Uses Learned Thus Far

Nominative	*Genitive*	*Dative*	*Accusative*
Subject	Genitive of Possession	Dative of Indirect Object	Direct Object
Predicate Nominative	Objective Genitive	Dative of Respect	Accusative of Duration of Time
	Partitive Genitive	Dative of Time When	
	Genitive of Time within Which		

Vocabulary

βουλή, –ῆς, ἡ = counsel, direction

ἔτος, ἔτους, τό = year

ἡμέρα, –ας, ἡ = day

νύξ, νυκτός, ἡ = night

ὄνομα, ὀνόματος, τό = name

ῥῆμα, ῥήματος, τό = saying, word

φιλοσοφία, –ας, ἡ = philosophy

φιλόσοφος, –ου, ὁ = a philosopher

φῶς, φωτός, τό = light

ἅγιος, –α, –ον (adj.) = holy

▸ γλυκύς, –εῖα, –ύ (adj.) = sweet

ἔπειτα (adv.) = then

διδάσκω, διδάξω, ἐδίδαξα = to teach, explain

ὀνομάζω, ὀνομάσω, ὠνόμασα = to name, call

εἶπον: the 2nd aorist of λέγω, "to say." The first three principal parts are λέγω, λέξω, εἶπον.

Sentences

1. τῇ νυκτὶ βουλὴ τοῖς σοφοῖσι γίγνεται. (Menander, *Fragments*)

> ¶ σοφοῖσι = σοφοῖς
>
> γίγνεται = comes: 3rd person singular of γίγνομαι, a deponent verb you will learn in chapter 15.

2. ἔπειτα μετὰ τρία ἔτη ἀνῆλθον εἰς Ἱεροσόλυμα ἱστορῆσαι Κηφᾶν, καὶ ἐπέμεινα πρὸς αὐτὸν ἡμέρας δεκαπέντε. (Gal 1:18)

> ¶ τρία = three: here neuter accusative plural, modifying ἔτη.
>
> ἀνῆλθον = I went up to: 1st person singular aorist of ἀνέρχομαι, a deponent verb. The speaker is Paul.
>
> Ἱεροσόλυμα, –ων, τά = Jerusalem
>
> ἱστορῆσαι: aorist infinitive of ἱστορέω = to inquire; to visit.
>
> Κηφᾶς, –ᾶ, ὁ = Cephas, Peter's Aramaic name
>
> ἐπιμένω, [   ], ἐπέμεινα = to stay, remain in a place
>
> δεκαπέντε = fifteen: indeclinable adjective

3. φιλοσοφίαν πρῶτος ὠνόμασε Πυθαγόρας καὶ ἑαυτὸν φιλόσοφον, μηδένα γὰρ
ἔλεγεν εἶναι σοφὸν ἀλλὰ θεόν. (Diogenes Laertius, *Lives of Eminent Philosophers*)

> ¶ πρῶτος, –η, –ον (adj.) = first
>
> ὠνόμασε: aorist of ὀνομάζω
>
> ▶ Πυθαγόρας, –ου, ὁ = Pythagoras:
> an ancient mathematician and
> philosopher
>
> ἑαυτὸν = himself: a masculine,
> singular, accusative reflexive
> pronoun; reflexive pronouns are
> discussed in chapter 29.
>
> μηδένα = no one: here masculine,
> singular accusative

▶ 4. τῆς παιδείας ἔφη τὰς μὲν ῥίζας εἶναι πικράς, τὸν δὲ καρπὸν γλυκύν. (Aristotle, in
Diogenes Laertius, *Lives of Eminent Philosophers*)

> ¶ ἔφη = said: 3rd person, singular,
> aorist of φημί. The subject is the
> understood "Aristotle."
>
> ῥίζα, –ης, ἡ = a root
>
> πικρός, –ά, –όν (adj.) = sharp,
> bitter

5. οὐ πιστεύεις ὅτι ἐγὼ ἐν τῷ πατρὶ καὶ ὁ πατὴρ ἐν ἐμοί ἐστιν; τὰ ῥήματα ἃ
ἐγὼ λαλῶ ὑμῖν ἀπ’ ἐμαυτοῦ οὐ λαλῶ· ὁ δὲ πατὴρ ἐν ἐμοὶ μένων ποιεῖ τὰ ἔργα
αὐτοῦ. (John 14:10)

> ¶ λαλῶ = I say: the speaker is Jesus.
>
> ἐμαυτοῦ = myself: genitive, singu-
> lar, masculine reflexive pronoun
>
> ἐν ἐμοὶ μένων ποιεῖ = remaining in
> me, does…
>
> μένων: circumstantial participle
> you will learn in chapter 20.

6. ἐν ἐκείνῃ τῇ ἡμέρᾳ γνώσεσθε ὑμεῖς ὅτι ἐγὼ ἐν τῷ πατρί μου καὶ ὑμεῖς ἐν ἐμοὶ
κἀγὼ ἐν ὑμῖν. (John 14:20)

> ¶ ἐκεῖνος, –η, –ο = that: a demon-
> strative you will learn in chapter
> 18.
>
> γνώσεσθε = you will know: 2nd
> person plural future of γιγνώσκω.
> See chapter 15 for future depo-
> nents.
>
> κἀγὼ = καὶ ἐγὼ: see chapter 16
> on crasis.

▶ 7. καὶ ἰδοὺ ἐγὼ μεθ' ὑμῶν εἰμι πάσας τὰς ἡμέρας ἕως τῆς συντελείας τοῦ αἰῶνος.
(Matt. 28:20)

> ¶ ἰδοὺ = behold
>
> μεθ' ὑμῶν = μετὰ ὑμῶν.
>
> ἕως (prep.) = until (+ gen.)
>
> συντέλεια, –ας, ἡ = completion, end

8. ἦν δὲ ἄνθρωπος ἐκ τῶν Φαρισαίων, Νικόδημος ὄνομα αὐτῷ, ἄρχων τῶν
Ἰουδαίων· οὗτος ἦλθεν πρὸς αὐτὸν νυκτὸς καὶ εἶπεν αὐτῷ, "Ραββί, οἴδαμεν
ὅτι ἀπὸ θεοῦ ἐλήλυθας διδάσκαλος." (John 3:1–2)

> ¶ Φαρισαῖος, –ου, ὁ = a Pharisee
>
> Νικόδημος, –ου, ὁ = Nicodemus
>
> ὄνομα αὐτῷ = whose name was: literally, "there was a name to him." You will learn this use of the dative in chapter 26.
>
> ἄρχων, –οντος, ὁ = a ruler
>
> Ἰουδαῖος, –ου, ὁ = a Jew
>
> οὗτος = he: i.e., Nicodemus, literally "this one," a demonstrative you will learn in chapter 18.
>
> ἦλθεν = came: 3rd person singular aorist of ἔρχομαι, a deponent verb
>
> ῥαββίς, –ίδος, ὁ = a rabbi, teacher: here a vocative.
>
> οἴδαμεν = we know: a 1st person plural irregular verb you will learn in chapter 27
>
> ἐλήλυθας = you have come: 2nd person singular perfect (see chapter 27) of ἔρχομαι.

9. τὸ γὰρ ἅγιον πνεῦμα διδάξει ὑμᾶς ἐν αὐτῇ τῇ ὥρᾳ ἃ δεῖ εἰπεῖν. (Luke 12:12)

> ¶ ὥρα, –ας, ἡ = any period of time; hour, season

10. ὁ Ἀναξαγόρας ἔλεγεν ὅτι ἡ σελήνη ἀπὸ τοῦ ἡλίου ἔχει τὸ φῶς. (Socrates, in Plato, *Cratylus*)

> ¶ Ἀναξαγόρας –ου, ὁ = Anaxagoras: an early Greek philosopher
> σελήνη, –ης, ἡ = the moon
> ἥλιος, –ου, ὁ = the sun

Etymology and Discussion Topics

γλυκύς, –εῖα, –ύ (adj.) = sweet

From this adjective come our many English words related to sugar, e.g., glucose, glycogen, and hypoglycemic. Homer and other Greek poets were fond of using this word to describe various things, from sleep (γλυκὺς ὕπνος) to desire (γλυκὺς ἵμερος).

Πυθαγόρας

Pythagoras of Samos was one of the most famous thinkers of the ancient world. In addition to his interest in mathematics, he was credited with the invention of the term "philosophy," as your sentence explains.

τῆς παιδείας ἔφη τὰς μὲν ῥίζας εἶναι πικράς, τὸν δὲ καρπὸν γλυκύν.

Be sure to remember this great metaphor when you experience frustration with learning morphology or syntax!

καὶ ἰδοὺ ἐγὼ μεθ᾽ ὑμῶν εἰμι πάσας τὰς ἡμέρας ἕως τῆς συντελείας τοῦ αἰῶνος. (Matt. 28:20)

This is the very last line of Matthew's Gospel. Is there any significance in this line to the choice of an accusative of duration as opposed to the other time constructions?

Chapter 14 ~⌐

The Middle and Passive Voice • Genitive of Agent (with ὑπό) •
Present and Imperfect Middle/Passive

The Middle and Passive Voice

In chapter 4 you learned about voice, and in particular the *active* voice. This chapter will introduce you to the *middle* and *passive* voices. Since the middle can take some getting used to, let's start with an explanation of the passive voice.

The Passive Voice

In contrast to the active voice, where the subject performs the action, in the passive voice the subject receives the action. English doesn't have unique forms for verbs in the passive voice, instead, the passive construction combines a form of the verb, "to be," with the past participle. Examples of this passive construction include, "the ball *is thrown*," and "the presents *are received*." Only transitive verbs, i.e., those that can take a direct object, allow passive constructions. You cannot use the passive voice with intransitive verbs like "to be" or "to become." Compare these sentences.

A. The teacher *throws* the cellphone out of the window.

B. The cellphone *is thrown* out of the window.

In sentence A, the subject is "teacher," the (active) verb is "throws," the direct object is "cellphone," and "out of the window" is a prepositional phrase. In sentence B, the subject is cellphone," the (passive) verb is "is thrown," and "out of the window" is a preposition phrase.

Let's look at the next two sentences.

C. The student *follows* the cellphone out of the window.

D. The cellphone *is followed* out of the window by the student.

In sentence C, the subject is "student," the (active) verb is "follows," "the cellphone" is the direct object, and "out of the window" is a prepositional phrase. In sentence D, the subject is "cellphone," the (passive) verb is "is followed," and the original subject of sentence A, the student (who very much loves his cellphone), is in the prepositional phrase "by the student."

Below are some Greek examples.

❡ μωρός, –ά, –όν (adj.) = foolish | καταφρονέω = to despise

E. οἱ μωροὶ καταφρονοῦσι τὴν σοφίαν.

The foolish (people) despise wisdom.

F. ἡ σοφία καταφρονεῖται ὑπὸ τῶν μωρῶν.

Wisdom is despised by the foolish (people).

In sentence E, the subject is "μωροὶ," the (active) verb is "καταφρονοῦσι," and the direct object is "σοφίαν." In sentence F, the subject is "σοφία," the (passive) verb is "καταφρονεῖται," and "ὑπὸ τῶν μωρῶν" is a prepositional phrase.

Genitive of Agent (with ὑπό)

In a passive construction Greek uses the preposition ὑπό + the genitive to signify the agent of the action in the verb, i.e., what would have been the subject if the verb were active. In sentence F, ὑπὸ τῶν μωρῶν is a genitive of agent.

Summary of Case Uses Learned Thus Far

Nominative	*Genitive*	*Dative*	*Accusative*
Subject	Genitive of Possession	Dative of Indirect Object	Direct Object
Predicate Nominative	Objective Genitive		Accusative of Duration of Time
	Partitive Genitive	Dative of Respect	
	Genitive of Time within Which	Dative of Time When	
	Genitive of Agent (with ὑπό)		

Middle Voice

Now that we have discussed the passive voice, we come to the middle voice, a voice that English does not have. This can be quite a difficult concept for students to become comfortable with, as there really is no English equivalent. While the subject of a verb in the active voice is the agent of the action, and the subject of a verb in the passive voice is the recipient of the action, the middle voice is used when the subject is seen as *both the agent and the recipient* of the action. In English we usually express this relationship by the use of the reflexive pronoun. Consider these English sentences below.

Socrates taught Plato. (active)

Plato was taught by Socrates. (passive)

Socrates taught himself. (middle)

Look at the following sentences. The imperfect will be used since you have not learned the aorist middle and passive tenses.

¶ λούω, λούσω, ἔλουσα = to wash | ἵππος, –ου, ὁ = horse

ὁ Ἀλκιβιάδης ἔλουεν τὸν ἵππον.

Alcibiades washed the horse. (active)

ὁ ἵππος ἐλούετο ὑπὸ τοῦ Ἀλκιβιάδου.

The horse was washed by Alcibiades. (passive)

ὁ Διογένης οὔποτ᾽ ἐλούετο.

Diogenes never washed himself. (middle)

So how does the middle really work?

That being said, you will rarely translate the middle voice with "himself/herself/itself" in real Greek. In the majority of cases, when you encounter a Greek verb in the middle voice it will either be (1) a deponent verb, (2) a special middle meaning, or (3) an intransitive verb. We will learn about deponent verbs in the next chapter. Let's talk about options 2 and 3.

(2) *Special meaning*. When you look up a verb in a dictionary (or in the vocabulary section at the back of this book), it will obviously list the definition. Many verbs will then have a different entry for the middle voice after the heading "med.," which is short for the Latin word *medium*, or it will simply say "middle," as the vocabulary in this book does. This is your dictionary's way of telling you that there is a special middle meaning of the verb.

For example, under πείθω, you will find the definition "to persuade." You will then see (middle) "to obey (+ dat.)." Most of the time, the "special" middle translation of a word makes sense if you think about what the middle voice signifies. Take a look at the following three examples in Greek.

G. ἡ σοφία πείθει τὸν σοφόν. (active)

Wisdom persuades the wise man.

H. ὁ σοφὸς πείθεται ὑπὸ τῆς σοφίας. (passive)

The wise man is persuaded by wisdom.

I. ὁ σοφὸς πείθεται τῇ σοφίᾳ. (middle)

The wise man obeys wisdom.

Now you can see that the middle meaning "obey" derives from the middle sense of "persuading oneself." For the majority of cases, it is far easier and safer to just look up the middle meaning rather than to try to extrapolate the definition from the nature of the middle voice. When you are memorizing vocabulary, it is therefore helpful to memorize the middle meaning of a verb if it has a special middle meaning.

(3) *Verb used intransitively*. As you remember from chapter 4, a *transitive* verb is a verb that takes a direct object; an *intransitive* verb is a verb that does not take a direct object. Although we introduced the concept of transitive and intransitive verbs in chapter 4, it is helpful to review the concept at this point.

The verb "need" is transitive and needs a direct object to complete its meaning. If someone were to say "I need," you would probably look at him with a puzzled look and wonder what he needs. The verb "to be," for example, cannot take a direct object and is therefore intransitive. Other English intransitive verbs include "to happen" and "to sleep." Transitive verbs can be expressed passively as well as actively. Intransitive verbs, on the contrary, cannot be put into the passive voice. What is the passive of the word "to be"? You cannot say "is beed" any more than you can say "is happened." You can, however, say "is needed," as in "An understanding of the difference between transitive and intransitive verbs *is needed* if one is to understand Greek verbs."

There are many verbs, however, which can be used both transitively and intransitively. Examples include "to run" and "to speak." Take a look at the following examples.

J. Actions *speak* louder than words. (intransitive)

K. Socrates *speaks* the truth. (transitive)

L. Any idiot can *run*. (intransitive)

M. It takes a special kind of idiot to *run* a marathon. (transitive)

In J and L, there was not a direct object, while K and M contained direct objects (truth/marathon).

What does this have to do with the Greek middle? Greek normally uses the active voice if the verb is transitive and needs a direct object, but it will often prefer the middle if an intransitive sense is used, although the active voice is also capable of being used intransitively.

ὁ φόβος παύει τὴν καρδίαν τοῦ ἀνθρώπου.

Fear stops the heart of man.

ὁ φόβος παύεται ἐν τῇ εὐχῇ.

Fear stops in prayer.

That being said, the middle voice can also be used transitively. You will often encounter a middle verb where it is translated just like the active voice, but you can see how the action pertains to the subject. Sometimes, however, it can be difficult to see why an author chooses the middle instead of the active voice. With time and patience, the initial exasperation with the middle voice can turn into an appreciation for the wonderful subtleties this mood communicates.

Present and Imperfect Middle/Passive

Now that we have seen how the middle and passive voices work, let us look at the forms. For all but two tenses (future and aorist) the forms for the middle and the passive voices are identical. Context will tell you whether a verb is middle or passive. Hint: If there is a genitive of agent, it is passive. This is why the *forms* will be called middle/passive. In an actual Greek sentence, the form will be *either* middle *or* passive, but not both.

Present Middle/Passive

	Present Middle/Passive Indicative			
	λύω		Endings	
	Singular	Plural	Singular	Plural
1st	λύ–ομαι	λυ–όμεθα	μαι	μεθα
2nd	λύ–η/ει	λύ–εσθε	σαι	σθε
3rd	λύ–εται	λύ–ονται	ται	νται

The present middle passive endings of your model verb are formed by adding a thematic vowel (an omicron or an epsilon) to the endings given above, often called "primary" endings. While it is important to memorize these endings (they will come into play again in later chapters), it is also helpful to memorize the combination of the thematic vowel + endings in a model verb, since this is how you will see them in Greek sentences. The second person singular endings of middle/passive omega verbs go through some changes and result in the quite different looking endings seen above. Both the η and the ει forms are commonly found, and must therefore be memorized.

Imperfect Middle/Passive

	Imperfect Middle/Passive Indicative			
	λύω		Endings	
	Singular	Plural	Singular	Plural
1st	ἐλυ–όμην	ἐλυ–όμεθα	μην	μεθα
2nd	ἐλύ–ου	ἐλύ–εσθε	σο	σθε
3rd	ἐλύ–ετο	ἐλύ–οντο	το	ντο

The imperfect middle passive endings of your model verb are formed by adding a thematic vowel to the endings given above, often called "secondary" endings. Again, while it is important to memorize these endings, it is also helpful to memorize the combination of the thematic vowel + endings in a model verb, since this is how you will see them in Greek sentences. Finally, just like the second person singular of the present middle/passive, the second person singular ending of the imperfect middle/passive undergoes some changes.

Present Middle/Passive Imperative and Infinitive

Just like the indicative, the forms for the present middle and passive imperatives are the same. Context will tell you whether it is a middle or a passive imperative, but passive imperatives are less common than middle imperatives. In fact, a great many middle imperatives are imperatives of deponent verbs, which you will learn about in the next chapter.

	Singular		Plural	
2nd	λύ–ου	be loosened!	λύ–εσθε	be loosened!
3rd	λυ–έσθω	let him/her be loosened!	λυ–έσθων	let them be loosened!

Please note that the passive translations are given above. The middle of λύου would be "loosen/ untie yourself," etc.

The present middle and passive infinitive is –εσθαι.

λύ–εσθαι

"to be loosened" (passive) / "to loosen/untie oneself" (middle)

Vocabulary

ἀσθένεια, –ας, ἡ = weakness

δύναμις, –εως, ἡ = power, might

νοῦς, νοῦ, νῷ, νοῦν, ὁ = mind. These contracted forms are best thought of as irregular and must be memorized.

παιδίον, –ου, τό = young child

πλῆθος, –ους, τό = number; the multitude

πόλεμος, –ου, ὁ = war

▶ ἄρχω, ἄρξω, ἦρξα = to rule (+ gen.); to begin; (middle) to begin

πείθω, πείσω, ἔπεισα = to persuade; (middle) to obey (+ dat)

σώζω, σώσω, ἔσωσα = to save

▶ τρέπω, τρέψω, ἔτρεψα = to turn; (middle) turn or betake oneself

φυλάττω (Koine φυλάσσω), φυλάξω, ἐφύλαξα = to guard; (middle) be on guard against

Sentences

1. καὶ μὴ συσχηματίζεσθε τῷ αἰῶνι τούτῳ, ἀλλὰ μεταμορφοῦσθε τῇ
ἀνακαινώσει τοῦ νοός. (Rom 12:2)

> ¶ συσχηματίζω = to correct,
> remodel; (middle) to conform
> (oneself) to (+ dat.)
>
> τούτῳ = this: a dative singular
> demonstrative (see chapter 18),
> here modifying αἰῶνι.
>
> μεταμορφοῦσθε: 2nd person
> plural middle/passive imperative
> of μεταμορφόω = to transform
>
> ἀνακαίνωσις, –εως, ἡ = renewal
>
> νοός: a later Koine form of νοῦ
> (genitive singular).

2. ὁ ἄνθρωπος ἀτυχῶν σῴζεται ὑπὸ τῆς ἐλπίδος. (Menander, *Fragments*)

> ¶ ἀτυχῶν = unlucky: a participle
> (see chapter 19) modifying
> ἄνθρωπος

▸ 3. ἀρκεῖ σοι ἡ χάρις μου· ἡ γὰρ δύναμις ἐν ἀσθενείᾳ τελεῖται. (2 Cor 12:9)

> ¶ ἀρκεῖ = suffices, is enough
> (+ dat.): 3rd person singular
> present indicative of ἀρκέω, a
> contract verb (chapter 24).
>
> σοι: the "you" here is St. Paul.
>
> μου: the speaker here is God.
>
> τελεῖται: 3rd person singular
> present indicative passive of
> τελέω, here "to perfect," another
> contract verb.

4. τὸ δὲ παιδίον ηὔξανεν καὶ ἐκραταιοῦτο πληρούμενον σοφίᾳ, καὶ χάρις θεοῦ
ἦν ἐπ᾽ αὐτό. (Luke 2:40)

> ¶ ηὔξανεν: aorist active of αὐξάνω
>
> ἐκραταιοῦτο = grew strong: 3rd
> person singular indicative middle
> of κραταιόω, a contract verb.
>
> πληρούμενον = filled with
> (+ dat.): a participle (chapter 19)
> modifying παιδίον.

5. πείθεται γὰρ τὸ πλῆθος τοῖς δημαγωγοῖς. (Aristotle, *Politics*)

> ¶ ▸ δημαγωγός, –οῦ,
> ὁ = demagogue

6. καὶ εἰς ἐπιθυμίας αἰσχρὰς καὶ ψυχοβλαβεῖς μὴ τρέπεσθε, ἀλλ᾽ ὁλοψύχως τὰς ἐντολὰς τοῦ Θεοῦ φυλάξατε. (John Chrysostom, *Sermons*)

> ❡ ψυχοβλαβής, –ές (adj.) = soul-destroying
>
> ὁλοψύχως (adv.) = with one's whole soul
>
> ἐντολή, –ῆς, ἡ = command, commandment

7. ὁ γέρων πάμπρωτος ὑφαίνειν ἤρχετο μῆτιν Νέστωρ. (Homer, *Iliad*)

> ❡ This line describes the second of the three speakers to speak in the famous embassy to Achilles in Book 9 of the *Iliad*.
>
> γέρων, –οντος, ὁ = old man
>
> πάμπρωτος, η, ον (adj.) = first of all
>
> ὑφαίνω = to weave
>
> ἤρχετο: imperfect middle of ἄρχω
>
> μῆτις, –τιδος, ἡ = wisdom; plan
>
> Νέστωρ, –ορος, ὁ = Nestor

8. ἄρχεται δὲ ὁ πόλεμος ἐνθένδε ἤδη Ἀθηναίων καὶ Πελοποννησίων καὶ τῶν ἑκατέροις συμμάχων. (Thucydides, *History of the Peloponnesian War*)

> ❡ This is the opening line of Book 2 of Thucydides' famous account of the Peloponnesian War.
>
> ἐνθένδε ἤδη = now really
>
> Ἀθηναῖοι, –ων, οἱ = Athenians
>
> Πελοποννήσιοι, –ων, οἱ = Peloponnesians
>
> ἑκάτερος, –α, –ον (adj.) = each other
>
> σύμμαχος, -η, -ον (adj.) = ally

9. ὑφ᾽ ἡδονῆς ὁ φρόνιμος οὐχ ἁλίσκεται. (Menander, *Fragments*)

> ❡ φρόνιμος, –ον (adj.) = prudent
>
> ἁλίσκεται = is caught, succumbs to: a 3rd person singular present indicative of a deponent verb (see chapter 15).

10. ὁ Σωκράτης οὔτε πείθεται οὔτε πείθει ἡμᾶς. (Plato, *Crito*)

¶ In the *Crito*, Socrates here imagines the laws of Athens speaking about Socrates if he were to flee Athens to escape justice. Socrates decides to stay and accept his execution.

οὔτε...οὔτε = neither...nor

ἡμᾶς: the laws of Athens

Etymology and Discussion Topics

ἄρχω, ἄρξω, ἦρξα = to rule; (middle) to begin

From this verb (and the nouns ἀρχή and ἄρχων) come English words with the prefix "arch" such as "archbishop" and "archenemy." While "to rule" and "to begin" might seem to be very different meanings, it makes sense upon closer examination. From the meaning of "first" comes both the idea of beginning as well as the idea of authority or preeminence.

τρέπω, τρέψω, ἔτρεψα = to turn; (middle) turn or betake oneself

Believe it or not, the trophies that one might receive for say, an athletic event, get their name from this Greek verb. In ancient Greece, after a victorious battle troops would build a monument, often from the discarded weapons of the enemy, to the gods to commemorate their victory. Such monuments were usually erected at the site where the enemy "turned," hence the name "trophy."

ἀρκεῖ σοι ἡ χάρις μου· ἡ γὰρ δύναμις ἐν ἀσθενείᾳ τελεῖται. (2 Cor 12:9)

The verb τελέω is a contract verb that will be introduced in chapter 24, but this is a good place to discuss this verb and its related noun, τέλος. The verb τελέω means "to complete or finish," but it contains the idea of "completion" or "fulfillment." The noun τέλος can thus be an "end," but it can also be something's natural end. It is from this meaning that we get our word "teleology," a very important term not only for philosophers such as Aristotle, but for Christianity as well.

δημαγωγός, –οῦ, ὁ = demagogue

This word is a combination of δῆμος "the people" + the verb ἄγω "to lead." A demagogue is therefore one who "leads the people." Just as is the case today, this word had a negative connotation in ancient Greece.

Chapter 15 ～

Deponent Verbs • Future Middle • Aorist Middle •
Future of εἰμί

Deponent Verbs

A *deponent* verb is a verb which has only middle and passive forms, but is active in meaning. It is helpful to think of them as normal verbs that, for whatever reason, do not have any active forms, but should nevertheless be translated actively. How do you tell if a verb is deponent? Simple. Look up the verb in your vocabulary or a dictionary. If the principal parts are passive and not active (the first principal part ends in μαι not ω), it is a deponent verb. Here are some very common deponent verbs.

ἔρχομαι = to come/go

βούλομαι = to want

γίγνομαι = to become

Many deponent verbs will be incapable of being translated passively. You can't say "is come" or "is become." For those deponent verbs that could theoretically be translated passively, "is wanted," you will nevertheless still translate them actively.

There are some Greek verbs called *semi-deponents*. These are verbs that are deponent in some tenses and not others. Once again, look at the verb's first four principal parts; if any one of them has a middle or passive ending, that tense is deponent.

βλέπω, βλέψομαι, ἔβλεψα = to look

As you can see, βλέπω has active forms in the present and aorist tenses. In the future tense, however, it lacks active forms. You would translate βλέψομαι "I will look," as though it were active. βλέπω is therefore a semi-deponent.

Future Middle

As mentioned previously, the only tenses in which there exist separate forms for the middle and passive voices are the future and aorist. The future middle is formed by adding the primary middle endings (with a thematic vowel) to the 2nd principal part.

Future Middle Indicative

	λύω		Endings	
	Singular	*Plural*	*Singular*	*Plural*
1st	λύ–σομαι	λυ–σόμεθα	μαι	μεθα
2nd	λύ–σῃ/ει	λύ–σεσθε	σαι[a]	σθε
3rd	λύ–σεται	λύ–σονται	ται	νται

a. As in the case of the present and imperfect, the 2nd person singular undergoes contraction.

As you can see, the future middle is simply the present middle/passive with a sigma before the endings.

Future Middle Infinitive

The future middle infinitive is formed by attaching –εσθαι to the future stem (2nd principal part). The future middle infinitive of λύω is λύ–σεσθαι.

Aorist Middle

The aorist middle is formed by adding the secondary middle/passive endings (with a thematic vowel) to the aorist stem. Again, while the sigma is technically part of the aorist stem, it is easier to memorize it as part of the endings.

	2nd Aorist Middle/Passive Indicative			
	λύω		*Endings*	
	Singular	*Plural*	*Singular*	*Plural*
1st	ἐλυ–σάμην	ἐλυ–σάμεθα	μην	μεθα
2nd	ἐλύ–σω	ἐλύ–σασθε	σο[a]	σθε
3rd	ἐλύ–σατο	ἐλύ–σαντο	το	ντο

a. As in the case of the present and imperfect, the 2nd person singular undergoes contraction.

Aorist Middle Infinitive

The aorist middle infinitive is formed by attaching –ασθαι to the aorist active stem (3rd principal part). The aorist middle infinitive of λύω is λύ–σασθαι. Remember that infinitives will never have an augment.

Aorist Middle Imperative

The aorist middle imperative is formed by adding these endings to the aorist active stem (3rd principal part). Remember that the indicative is the only mood which takes an augment.

	Singular	*Plural*
2nd	λῦ–σαι	λύ–σασθε
3rd	λυ–σάσθω	λυ–σάσθων

Future of εἰμί

εἰμί is a semi-deponent verb. You have now learned all three tenses (present, future, and imperfect) of εἰμί.

	Singular		*Plural*	
1st	ἔσομαι	I will be	ἐσόμεθα	we will be
2nd	ἔσῃ (ἔσει)	you will be	ἔσεσθε	you will be
3rd	ἔσται	he/she/it will be	ἔσονται	they will be

Vocabulary

δικαιοσύνη, –ης, ἡ = righteousness, justice

θέλημα, –ματος, τό = will

σός, –ή, –όν (adj.) = your

οὖν (adv.) = certainly; then, therefore

βούλομαι, βουλήσομαι, —, = to want

▸ γίγνομαι (Koine γίνομαι), γενήσομαι, ἐγενόμην = to come into being, become

δύναμαι, δυνήσομαι, —, = to be able

ἐργάζομαι —, εἰργασάμην = to work, make

▸ ἔρχομαι, ἐλεύσομαι, ἦλθον = to go; come

▸ θαυμάζω, θαυμάσω, ἐθαύμασα = to wonder, marvel

Sentences

1. ὡς μὲν βούλομαι, οὐ δύναμαι· ὡς δὲ δύναμαι, οὐ βούλομαι. (Theocritus, in Stobaeus, *Anthology*)

> ❡ When asked why he did not write prose, this was the response of Theocritus.

2. ἔρχεσθε καὶ ὄψεσθε. (John 1:39)

> ❡ This is Jesus' response when asked by two future disciples where he was staying.
>
> ὁράω, ὄψομαι, εἶδον = to see. ὁράω is a contract verb with a future deponent (ὄψομαι) whose present forms you will learn in chapter 25.

3. φιλόπονος ἴσθι καὶ βίον κτήσῃ καλόν. (Menander, *Fragments*)

> ❡ φιλόπονος, –ον (adj.) = industrious
>
> ἴσθι: imperative of εἰμί.
>
> κτάομαι, κτήσομαι, ἐκτησάμην = to acquire

4. διὰ τὸ θαυμάζειν οἱ ἄνθρωποι καὶ νῦν καὶ τὸ πρῶτον ἤρξαντο φιλοσοφεῖν.

(Aristotle, *Metaphysics*)

¶ τὸ πρῶτον = previously

ἤρξαντο: aorist of ἄρχω.

φιλοσοφέω = to philosophize

▶ 5. καὶ ὁ λόγος σὰρξ ἐγένετο καὶ ἐσκήνωσεν ἐν ἡμῖν. (John 1:14)

¶ σάρξ, σαρκός, ὁ = flesh

σκηνόω, σκηνώσω, ἐσκήνωσα =
to dwell

6. ὀργὴ γὰρ ἀνδρὸς δικαιοσύνην θεοῦ οὐκ ἐργάζεται. (James 1:20)

7. βουλόμεθα πλουτεῖν πάντες, ἀλλ᾽ οὐ δυνάμεθα. (Menander, *Fragments*)

¶ πλουτέω, πλουτήσω, ἐπλούτησα =
to be wealthy

8. πάτερ, εἰ βούλει παρένεγκε τοῦτο τὸ ποτήριον ἀπ᾽ ἐμοῦ· πλὴν μὴ τὸ θέλημά
μου ἀλλὰ τὸ σὸν γινέσθω. (Luke 22:42)

¶ παραφέρω, παροίσω, παρήνεγκα =
bring forward; turn aside

τοῦτο = this: a demonstrative you
will learn in chapter 18

ποτήριον, −ου, τό = cup

πλὴν = (prep.) except (+ gen.);
(conj.) save that, but

9. ἐνδύσασθε οὖν ὡς ἐκλεκτοὶ τοῦ θεοῦ, ἅγιοι καὶ ἠγαπημένοι, σπλάγχνα
οἰκτιρμοῦ, χρηστότητα, ταπεινοφροσύνην, πραΰτητα, μακροθυμίαν. (Col 3:12)

¶ ἐνδύω, ἐνδύσω, ἐνέδυσα = to clothe;
(middle) to put on, dress (oneself)

ἐκλεκτός, −ή, −όν (adj.) = picked
out; chosen

ἠγαπημένοι = beloved

σπλάγχνον, −ου, τό = (often in
plural) innards, the seat of feelings

οἰκτιρμός, −οῦ, ὁ = pity, compas-
sions

χρηστότης, −τητος, ἡ = goodness

ταπεινοφροσύνη, −ης, ἡ = humility

πραΰτης, −τητος, ἡ = mildness,
gentleness

μακροθυμία, −ας, ἡ = patience

10. ἐν ἀρχῇ ἦν ὁ λόγος, καὶ ὁ λόγος ἦν πρὸς τὸν θεόν, καὶ θεὸς ἦν ὁ λόγος. οὗτος ἦν ἐν ἀρχῇ πρὸς τὸν θεόν. πάντα δι᾿ αὐτοῦ ἐγένετο, καὶ χωρὶς αὐτοῦ ἐγένετο οὐδὲ ἕν. (John 1:1–3)

¶ You translated the first line in chapter 12.

οὗτος = this one: a demonstrative you will learn in chapter 18, here referring to the λόγος.

οὐδὲ ἕν = not one thing: here the subject of ἐγένετο

Etymology and Discussion Topics

γίγνομαι (Koine γίνομαι), γενήσομαι, ἐγενόμην = to come into being, become

This very important deponent verb can be difficult to translate into English. The basic meaning of γίγνομαι is "to come into being." You will often, however, find that a better English translation will be "to be," rather than "to become." While you may often be forced for the sake of clarity to translate γίγνομαι as "to be," try and keep in mind the basic meaning of "becoming." Finally, as you saw in #5, γίγνομαι, like εἰμί, can take a predicate nominative.

ἔρχομαι, ἐλεύσομαι, ἦλθον = to go; come

This extremely common Greek verb has principal parts that do not look like each other. It is a combination of what were originally separate words, hence the different stems you see in the present, future, and aorist. While ἔρχομαι is deponent in the present and future, it is not a deponent in the aorist.

θαυμάζω, θαυμάσω, ἐθαύμασα = to wonder, marvel

In addition to being used to describe the wonder of the first philosophers, θαυμάζω is used by Matthew, Mark, and Luke to describe people's reactions to the words and deeds of Jesus in the synoptic gospels.

καὶ ὁ λόγος σὰρξ ἐγένετο καὶ ἐσκήνωσεν ἐν ἡμῖν. (John 1:14)

While σκηνόω does mean "to dwell," it is related to the Greek word for "tent," σκηνή. Furthermore, John uses this word, σκηνή, for the Jewish temple. You can therefore see how much of John's allusion is missed by simply translating ἐσκήνωσεν as "dwelt."

Chapter 16 ⁓

Aorist Passive • Future Passive • Crasis

Aorist Passive

The aorist passive is formed from the aorist passive stem, which is obtained by removing the personal ending from the 6th principal part. The 6th and final principal part (you will learn the 4th and 5th principal parts in chapters 27 and 28) of our model verb λύω is ἐλύθην. Remember that in your vocabulary, the principal parts of verbs that you have not yet learned will be signified by [   ].

Aorist Passive Indicative

	λύω		Endings	
	Singular	*Plural*	*Singular*	*Plural*
1st	ἐλύ–θην	ἐλύ–θημεν	ν	μεν
2nd	ἐλύ–θης	ἐλύ–θητε	ς	τε
3rd	ἐλύ–θη	ἐλύ–θησαν	–	σαν

Although the θη is technically part of the aorist passive stem and not an ending, it is easiest for memorization purposes to include it in the ending, as the distinctive θη is helpful when identifying the aorist passive.

Aorist Passive Imperative

Aorist Passive Imperative

	Singular	*Plural*
2nd	λύ–θητι	λύ–θητε
3rd	λυ–θήτω	λυ–θέντων

Finally, as you learned in chapter 12, it is important to remember that in the imperative mood, tense signifies *aspect not time*.

Aorist Passive Infinitive

The aorist passive infinitive ending is –ναι, which is attached to the aorist passive stem. Remember that only the indicative mood takes the augment.

The aorist passive infinitive of λύω = λυ–**θῆναι**.

> ¶ κατακρίνω = to condemn | δεσμός, –οῦ, ὁ = chain

ὁ δεσμὸς ἐλύθη ὑπὸ τοῦ Σωκράτους.

The chain was loosened by Socrates.

οἱ φιλόσοφοι κατεκρίθησαν ὑπὸ τῶν πολλῶν.

The philosophers were condemned by the many.

λυθέντων οἱ μαθηταὶ ἀπὸ τῶν κακῶν διδασκάλων.

Let the students be freed from the bad teachers!

Future Passive

The future passive is formed by adding the future middle endings to the aorist passive stem (6th principal part) without the augment.

	Future Passive Indicative	
	Singular	*Plural*
1st	λυ–**θήσομαι**	λυ–**θησόμεθα**
2nd	λυ–**θήσῃ/σει**	λυ–**θήσεσθε**
3rd	λυ–**θήσεται**	λυ–**θήσονται**

Again, although the θη is technically part of the aorist passive stem and is not an ending, it is easiest for memorization purposes to include it in the ending.

Future Passive Infinitive

The future passive infinitive ending is –σεσθαι, which is attached to the aorist passive stem.

The future passive infinitive of λύω is λυ–**θήσεσθαι**.

¶ πῶς = how | δεσμός, –οῦ, ὁ = chain

πῶς λυθήσονται οἱ δεσμοὶ τοῦ θανάτου;

How will the chains of death be loosened?

ἡ ἀλήθεια ἀποκαλυφθήσεται.

The truth will be revealed.

Crasis

In chapter 7 you learned about elision, where the last vowel of a word is removed if the next word begins with a vowel. In its place the symbol ' is used, e.g., ἐπ' ἀρετῇ, κατ' ἀρετήν. Sometimes two words are combined, and the resulting word loses one or two of the original letters. This is called crasis (κρᾶσις "mingling") and is signified by the coronis symbol, which looks identical to a smooth breathing symbol. Don't worry, there are relatively few words that permit crasis, and they are confined largely to words that are frequently found together, much like our English "I'm" and "you're." An easy way to spot examples of crasis is to look for a smooth breathing over a syllable that begins with a consonant. This will be a coronis since the smooth breathing mark can be found over only those words that begin with a vowel or a diphthong (or the consonant ρ). Some common examples of crasis are κἀγώ "and I" (καὶ + ἐγώ) and ταὐτά "the same things" (τὰ + αὐτά). Be sure not to confuse ταὐτά with ταῦτα, the neuter plural nominative and accusative of οὗτος you will learn in chapter 18.

Vocabulary

ἀνδρεία, –ας, ἡ = manliness, bravery

ἐλεήμων, –ον (adj.) = merciful

ἐμός, ή, όν (adj.) = my

καθαρός, ή, όν (adj.) = pure, clean

μόνος, η, ον (adj.) = alone, only

πραΰς, εῖα, –ύ (adj.) = gentle, meek

ἕνεκεν (sometimes written ἕνεκα) (prep.) = on account of (+ gen.)

διακονέω, διακονήσω, διηκόνησα, —, —, ἐδιακονήθην = to minister, serve

▸ καλέω, —, ἐκάλεσα, —, —, ἐκλήθην = to call, name

▸ ὁράω (imperf. ἑώρων), ὄψομαι, εἶδον, [   ], [   ], ὤφθην = to see, behold

παρακαλέω, [   ], παρεκάλεσα, παρεκλήθην = to summon; encourage, comfort

ποιέω, ποιήσω, ἐποίησα, [   ], [   ], ἐποιήθην = to make; to do.

Sentences

1. ἐγὼ μόνος ἐσώθην ὑπὸ τῆς ἐμῆς εὐσεβείας. (Chariton, *Chaereas and Callirhoë*)

> ¶ ἐσώθην: aorist passive of σῴζω
>
> εὐσέβεια, –ας, ἡ = reverence, piety

2. τόλμα ἀλόγιστος ἀνδρεία φιλέταιρος ἐνομίσθη. (Thucydides, *History of the Peloponnesian War*)

> ¶ This famous line comes from Thucydides' description of civil strife in Book 3 of his *History of the Peloponnesian War*, in which he laments the fact that words had to change their meaning.
>
> τόλμα, –ας, ἡ = boldness, courage
>
> ἀλόγιστος, –ον (adj.) = thoughtless, foolish
>
> φιλέταιρος, –ον (adj.) = loyal, partisan
>
> ἐνομίσθη: aorist passive of νομίζω

▶ 3. καὶ γὰρ ὁ υἱὸς τοῦ ἀνθρώπου οὐκ ἦλθεν διακονηθῆναι ἀλλὰ διακονῆσαι.
(Mark 10:45)

¶ καὶ γὰρ = for indeed

ἦλθεν: aorist of ἔρχομαι

▶ 4. ὃ θέλεις φέρε κἀγὼ αὐτὸ ἀγαθὸν ποιήσω. (Epictetus, *Discourses*)

¶ ὃ θέλεις φέρε = bring what you wish: the sense of these words is similar to our "come what may."

5. χρυσὸς ἀνοίγει πάντα κἀΐδου πύλας. (Menander, *Fragments*)

¶ χρυσός, –οῦ, ὁ = gold

ἀνοίγω = to open

κἀΐδου: crasis for καὶ ἀΐδου. καὶ is adverbial "even." ἀΐδου is an alternative spelling of ᾅδου (chap. 11 vocabulary).

6. λογίζομαι γὰρ ὅτι οὐκ ἄξια τὰ παθήματα τοῦ νῦν καιροῦ πρὸς τὴν μέλλουσαν δόξαν ἀποκαλυφθῆναι εἰς ἡμᾶς. (Romans 8:18)

¶ λογίζομαι = to think

πάθημα, –ματος, τό = suffering

τοῦ νῦν καιροῦ = the present time

πρὸς = in comparison to

μέλλουσαν = coming, future: modifies δόξαν here (+ inf.), "the glory about to be…"

ἀποκαλυφθῆναι: aorist passive infinitive of ἀποκαλύπτω (chap. 12 vocabulary)

7. ὁ δὲ ἀγαπῶν με ἀγαπηθήσεται ὑπὸ τοῦ πατρός μου, κἀγὼ ἀγαπήσω αὐτὸν καὶ ἐμφανίσω αὐτῷ ἐμαυτόν. (John 14:21)

¶ ὁ δὲ ἀγαπῶν με = the one loving me: the participle will be introduced in chapter 19.

ἀγαπηθήσεται: future passive of ἀγαπάω = to love.

ἀγαπήσω: future of ἀγαπάω.

κἀγὼ = καὶ ἐγὼ

ἐμαυτόν = myself: an accusative reflexive pronoun you will learn in chapter 29.

ἐμφανίσω: future of ἐμφανίζω = to reveal

8. καὶ ἐπλήσθη πνεύματος ἁγίου ἡ Ἐλισάβετ. (Luke 1:41)

> ¶ ἐπλήσθη: aorist passive of
> πίμπλημι = to fill, here + gen. for
> the filling substance.
>
> Ἐλισάβετ = Elizabeth

9. πᾶς ὁ ὑψῶν ἑαυτὸν ταπεινωθήσεται καὶ ὁ ταπεινῶν ἑαυτὸν ὑψωθήσεται.
   (Matthew 23:12)

> ¶ πᾶς ὁ ὑψῶν ἑαυτὸν = everyone
> exalting himself: another parti-
> ciple (chapter 19) and reflexive
> pronoun (chapter 29).
>
> ταπεινόω = to lower, humble
>
> ὁ ταπεινῶν ἑαυτὸν = the one
> humbling himself
>
> ὑψόω = to raise, exalt

▸ 10. The Beatitudes

μακάριοι οἱ πτωχοὶ τῷ πνεύματι, ὅτι αὐτῶν ἐστιν ἡ βασιλεία τῶν οὐρανῶν.

μακάριοι οἱ πενθοῦντες, ὅτι αὐτοὶ παρακληθήσονται.

μακάριοι οἱ πραεῖς, ὅτι αὐτοὶ κληρονομήσουσι τὴν γῆν.

μακάριοι οἱ πεινῶντες καὶ διψῶντες τὴν δικαιοσύνην, ὅτι αὐτοὶ
    χορτασθήσονται.

μακάριοι οἱ ἐλεήμονες, ὅτι αὐτοὶ ἐλεηθήσονται.

μακάριοι οἱ καθαροὶ τῇ καρδίᾳ, ὅτι αὐτοὶ τὸν θεὸν ὄψονται.

μακάριοι οἱ εἰρηνοποιοί, ὅτι αὐτοὶ υἱοὶ θεοῦ κληθήσονται.

μακάριοι οἱ δεδιωγμένοι ἕνεκεν δικαιοσύνης, ὅτι αὐτῶν ἐστιν ἡ βασιλεία
    τῶν οὐρανῶν.
                                        (Matthew 5:3–10)

> ¶ πτωχός, –ή, –όν (adj.) = beggarly;
> poor
>
> πενθοῦντες = those who grieve:
> a masculine nominative plural
> participle (chapter 19) used as a
> substantive adjective.
>
> κληρονομέω, κληρονομήσω = to
> inherit
>
> πεινῶντες καὶ διψῶντες τὴν
> δικαιοσύνην = those hungering
> and thirsting for righteousness:
> two masculine nominative plural
> participles (chapter 19) used as a
> substantive adjectives.
>
> χορτάζω, χορτάσω, ἐχόρτασα, —,
> [   ], ἐχορτάσθην = to feed, fill

ἐλεέω, ἐλεήσω, ἠλέησα, [   ], —,
ἠλεήθην = to have pity/mercy on

ὁράω, ὄψομαι, εἶδον, —, —, ὤφθην
= to see

εἰρηνοποιός, –οῦ, ὁ = peacemaker

οἱ δεδιωγμένοι = those persecuted:
a masculine nominative plural
perfect participle of διώκω
(= pursue), used as a substantive
adjective.

Etymology and Discussion Topics

καλέω

The verb καλέω is a contract verb whose present and imperfect tenses we will learn in chapter 24. For now, it should be noted that when it means "to call/name," καλέω takes a predicate nominative.

ὁράω (imperf. ἑώρων), ὄψομαι, εἶδον, [   ], [   ], ὤφθην = to see, behold

And you thought φέρω was a complicated verb! ὁράω is made up of stems from three different verbs. The aorist εἶδον originally began with an old letter, the digamma, ϝ, which is believed to have made the "w" sound. When it dropped out, the syllabic augment ε merged with the ι to make the diphthong ει. The verb οἶδα "to know," which you will learn in chapter 27, is from the same stem as εἶδον. Sophocles brilliantly plays on this relationship between sight and knowledge with Tiresias and Oedipus in his play *Oedipus Tyrannus*. Furthermore, the name Οἰδίπους sounds very similar to οἶδά που. "Perhaps I know."

καὶ γὰρ ὁ υἱὸς τοῦ ἀνθρώπου οὐκ ἦλθεν διακονηθῆναι ἀλλὰ διακονῆσαι.
(Mark 10:45)

As you can see in this example, the infinitive can be used to express purpose.

ὃ θέλεις φέρε κἀγὼ αὐτὸ ἀγαθὸν ποιήσω. (Epictetus)

As a stoic philosopher, Epictetus is stating that outside circumstances do not dictate whether or not an event is good for him, only his reaction to that event can be good or bad.

The Beatitudes

While we often take the beatitudes for granted, upon closer examination one can see how they in fact extol people who are the antitheses of those once considered μακάριοι in the pre-Christian world. The adjective πτωχός is used to describe a beggar, grief was to be avoided, and fame was sought in war, not peace.

Chapter 17 ~~~

Irregular Aorists • Irregular Verbs

Irregular Aorists

A few verbs in Greek have irregular second aorists. Although the number of such verbs is small, they are very important verbs. If you have already memorized the forms of εἰμί and your model verb λύω, it would be helpful to memorize the irregular aorists in this chapter. If, however, you are still struggling with memorization, focus your efforts on memorizing εἰμί and λύω and refer to this chapter when you encounter the following verbs.

Two important Greek verbs, βαίνω = to step, go, and γιγνώσκω = to know, form their aorist active (3rd principal part) in the following way.

βαίνω = To Step, Go

The 3rd principal part of βαίνω "to step, go" is ἔβην.

<table>
<thead>
<tr><th colspan="5" align="center">*Aorist Active Indicative*</th></tr>
<tr><th></th><th colspan="2" align="center">*Singular*</th><th colspan="2" align="center">*Plural*</th></tr>
</thead>
<tbody>
<tr><td>*1st*</td><td>ἔβη–**ν**</td><td>I stepped</td><td>ἔβη–**μεν**</td><td>we stepped</td></tr>
<tr><td>*2nd*</td><td>ἔβη–**ς**</td><td>you stepped</td><td>ἔβη–**τε**</td><td>you stepped</td></tr>
<tr><td>*3rd*</td><td>ἔβη</td><td>he/she/it stepped</td><td>ἔβη–**σαν**</td><td>they stepped</td></tr>
</tbody>
</table>

Aorist Infinitive Active

The aorist infinitive active of βαίνω is βῆ–ναι.

Aorist Active Imperative

	Aorist Active Imperative	
	Singular	Plural
2nd	βῆ–θι	βῆ–τε
3rd	βή–τω	βά–ντων

You will notice that the endings (not the stem) look like the endings of the aorist passive you learned last chapter.

γιγνώσκω = To Know

The 3rd principal part of γιγνώσκω "to know" is ἔγνων.

	Aorist Active Indicative			
	Singular		Plural	
1st	ἔγνω–ν	I knew	ἔγνω–μεν	we knew
2nd	ἔγνω–ς	you knew	ἔγνω–τε	you knew
3rd	ἔγνω	he/she/it knew	ἔγνω–σαν	they knew

Aorist Active Infinitive

The aorist active infinitive is γνῶ–ναι

Aorist Active Imperative

	Aorist Active Imperative	
	Singular	Plural
2nd	γνῶ–θι	γνῶ–τε
3rd	γνώ–τω	γνό–ντων

Irregular Verbs

Three other irregular verbs are presented below.

φημί

The irregular verb φημί "to say, declare" is technically a μι verb (chapter 30), but for the moment it is best memorized as an irregular verb. φημί takes the accusative and infinitive in indirect statement.

	φημί, φήσω, ἔφησα = to say, assert			
	Present Active Indicative		*Imperfect Active Indicative*	
	Singular	*Plural*	*Singular*	*Plural*
1st	φημί	φαμέν	ἔφην	ἔφαμεν
2nd	φῄς	φατέ	ἔφησθα/ ἔφης	ἔφατε
3rd	φησί(ν)	φασί(ν)	ἔφη	ἔφασαν

The aorist, ἔφησα, is a regular 1st aorist like ἔλυσα. Although one would think that the aorist would be used to introduce both direct and indirect statements, Greeks preferred to use the imperfect tense rather than the aorist. In such cases, therefore, it would usually be a mistake to translate the imperfect as an ongoing or habitual action. ἔφη most often simply means "he/she said."

Aorist Active Infinitive

The aorist active infinitive is φά–**ναι**.

Aorist Active Imperative

	Aorist Active Imperative	
	Singular	*Plural*
2nd	φα–**θί**	φά–**τε**
3rd	φά–**τω**	φά–**ντων**

εἶμι = To Go

This irregular verb looks very similar to the verb εἰμί "to be." You will notice that the 2nd person singular is identical to the 2nd person singular of εἰμί. For the 1st person singular, only the accent will enable you to distinguish it from εἰμί. This verb has only one principal part, but the present often has a future sense of "will go." You will find it used in place of the future of ἔρχομαι. Unfortunately for those learning Greek, two sets of endings are found for many of the imperfect forms.

	εἶμι = to go			
	Present Active Indicative		*Imperfect Active Indicative*	
	Singular	*Plural*	*Singular*	*Plural*
1st	εἶμι	ἴμεν	ᾖα or ᾔειν	ᾖμεν
2nd	εἶ	ἴτε	ᾔεισθα or ᾔεις	ᾖτε
3rd	εἶσι(ν)	ἴασι(ν)	ᾔειν or ᾔει	ᾖσαν or ᾔεσαν

Present Active Infinitive

The present active infinitive is ἰέ–ναι.

Present Active Imperative

	Present Active Imperative	
	Singular	*Plural*
2nd	ἴ–θι	ἴ–τε
3rd	ἴ–τω	ἰό–ντων

To recap, while it is important to be familiar with the verbs introduced in this chapter, it is far more important to memorize all the forms of εἰμί and your model verb λύω. Next in importance are the aorists of βαίνω and γιγνώσκω, followed by φημί and εἶμι.

Vocabulary

αἴνιγμα, –ατος, τό = riddle

▸ Ζεύς, Διός, Διί, Δία, ὁ = Zeus

δειλός, –ή, –όν (adj.) = cowardly; lowborn

κλεινός, –ή, –όν (adj.) = famous, renowned

βαίνω, βήσομαι, ἔβην, [   ], [   ], ἐβάθην = to step; go

γιγνώσκω, γνώσομαι, ἔγνων, [   ], [   ], ἐγνώσθην = to know

εἶμι = to go, come

ἐλέγχω, ἐλέγξω, ἤλεγξα, —, [   ], ἠλέγχθην = to cross-examine, question

ὑπάγω, ὑπάξω, ὑπήγαγον, —, —, ὑπήχθην = to lead under; go away

φημί, φήσω, ἔφησα—, —, — = to say, assert

οὔ φημί = to deny

Sentences

1. ἔγνων ὡς θεὸς ἦσθα. (*Homeric Hymn to Aphrodite*)

▶ 2. ἡ μὲν ἔβη πρὸς δῶμα Διὸς θυγάτηρ Ἀφροδίτη. (Homer, *Iliad*)

⁋ This line follows the meeting of Aphrodite and Hera, in which they devise a plan to deceive Zeus.

δῶμα, –ατος, τό = home. It is here Aphrodite's home. Διὸς goes with θυγάτηρ.

θυγάτηρ, –τρός, ἡ = daughter

3. Οἰδίπους εἰμί, ὃς τὰ κλείν' αἰνίγματ' ἔγνων καὶ μέγιστος ἦν ἀνήρ.
(Euripides, *Phoenician Women*)

⁋ The speaker is Oedipus.

κλείν' αἰνίγματ' = κλείνα αἰνίγματα

Οἰδίπους, –ποδος, ὁ = Oedipus

μέγιστος, –η, –ον (adj.) = greatest

4. ἐν τῷ κόσμῳ ἦν, καὶ ὁ κόσμος δι' αὐτοῦ ἐγένετο, καὶ ὁ κόσμος αὐτὸν οὐκ ἔγνω. (John 1:10)

⁋ ἦν: the subject is the λόγος mentioned in John's prologue.

5. φονέα σέ φημι τἀνδρὸς ὃν ζητεῖς κυρεῖν. (Sophocles, *Oedipus Tyrannus*)

⁋ These words are spoken by the seer Tiresias to Oedipus, who has summoned the seer to help him find the killer of King Laius.

φονεύς, –έως, ὁ = murderer

τἀνδρὸς = τοῦ ἀνδρός, i.e., Laius

ζητέω = to seek

κυρέω = to find

6. εἰ μέν σοι δοκῶ ἐγὼ καλῶς λέγειν, φάθι, εἰ δὲ μή, ἔλεγχε καὶ μὴ ἐπίτρεπε.
(Socrates, in Plato, *Gorgias*)

⁋ δοκέω = to seem

ἔλεγχε: supply "με" as the direct object.

ἐπιτρέπω = to overturn; give up, yield

▶ 7. αὐτόματοι δ' ἀγαθοὶ δειλῶν ἐπὶ δαῖτας ἴασιν. (Traditional Proverb)

> ¶ αὐτόματος, –η, –ον (adj.) = acting on one's own will, of one's own accord
>
> The subject is the substantive adjective ἀγαθοὶ, "The good of their own accord go…"
>
> δαίτη = meal, feast

8. ἔφη αὐτῷ ὁ Ἰησοῦς, "Εἰ θέλεις τέλειος εἶναι, ὕπαγε πώλησόν σου τὰ ὑπάρχοντα καὶ δὸς τοῖς πτωχοῖς, καὶ ἕξεις θησαυρὸν ἐν οὐρανοῖς."
(Matthew 19:21)

> ¶ αὐτῷ: the "him" in this passage is the young rich man who asked what he still needed to be perfect.
>
> τέλειος, –α, –ον (adj.) = perfect
>
> πωλέω, πωλήσω, ἐπώλησα = to sell
>
> τὰ ὑπάρχοντα = "possessions," a neuter accusative plural substantive participle (chapter 19)
>
> δός - "give," 2nd person singular aorist imperative of δίδωμι, a μι verb you will learn in chapter 30.
>
> πτωχός, –ή, –όν (adj.) = beggarly, poor
>
> ἕξεις: future of ἔχω

9. τοὺς βουλομένους ἀθανάτους εἶναι ἔφη δεῖν εὐσεβῶς καὶ δικαίως ζῆν.

(Antisthenes, in Diogenes Laertius, *Lives of Eminent Philosophers*)

> ¶ βουλομένους = "those wishing," accusative plural participle (see chapter 19 for form; chapter 15 for vocabulary).
>
> ἔφη δεῖν = "he said that it was necessary that…"; δεῖν is the infinitive of the impersonal verb δεῖ (this chapter's vocabulary), which in turn takes an accusative and infinitive construction.
>
> εὐσεβῶς (adv.) = piously
>
> ζῆν: present infinitive of ζάω "to live."

▶ 10. ἄνδρα μοι ἔννεπε, Μοῦσα, πολύτροπον, ὃς μάλα πολλὰ

πλάγχθη, ἐπεὶ Τροίης ἱερὸν πτολίεθρον ἔπερσε·

πολλῶν δ᾽ ἀνθρώπων ἴδεν ἄστεα καὶ νόον ἔγνω. (Homer, *Odyssey*)

❡ These are the opening lines of the *Odyssey*.

ἐνέπω = to tell

μοῦσα, –ης, ἡ = muse

πολύτροπος, –ον (adj.) = turning many ways; much traveled; shifty, versatile

μάλα πολλὰ: a tricky phrase to translate; "in many ways," or "far and often."

πλάγχθη: 3rd person aorist (note the poetic lack of an augment) passive of πλάζω = to turn aside.

ἐπεί (conj.) = when; after

Τροίη, –ης, ἡ = Troy

ἱερός, –ή, –όν (adj.) = holy

πτολίεθρον, –ου, τό = citadel

πέρθω, πέρσω, ἔπερσα = to sack, plunder

ἴδεν = εἶδε, aorist of ὁράω

ἄστυ, –εως, τό = city

νόον = νοῦν, acc. of νοῦς.

Etymology and Discussion Topics

Ζεύς

You might have been wondering how you get from the nominative Ζεύς to the genitive Διός. These were originally two different words that at some point were combined. Most likely, the nominative Ζεύς was superimposed upon the other form.

ἡ μὲν ἔβη πρὸς δῶμα Διὸς θυγάτηρ Ἀφροδίτη

Notice how far away the definite article ἡ is from its noun Ἀφροδίτη. In epic poetry you will often find names and epithets at the end of the line. The reason for this is metrical. Common phrases such as swift-footed Achilles (πόδας ὠκὺς Ἀχιλλεύς), rosy-fingered Dawn (ῥοδοδάκτυλος Ἠώς), and Aphrodite Daughter of Zeus (Διὸς θυγάτηρ Ἀφροδίτη) fit nicely at the end of a dactylic hexameter line of poetry. Greek can also postpone a noun well after its definite article and still make sense. If you are hearing the lines spoken or sung, you would hear the feminine nominative definite article and then the verb, followed by the rest of the sentence. You would know that the subject of the sentence was a feminine singular noun, and you would be waiting for that noun to be spoken. In some cases, as in the above example, context would tell you what the subject was as soon as you heard the definite article. In other cases, you would be in suspense until the subject was spoken.

αὐτόματοι δ᾽ ἀγαθοὶ δειλῶν ἐπὶ δαῖτας ἴασιν

This proverb was quoted by the poet Bacchylides and the philosopher Plato. What do you suppose the meaning is?

ἄνδρα μοι ἔννεπε

While English is to a large extent bound by word order, Greek is freer to arrange words. In epic poetry, the initial word of the poem is often significant. While our English translations usually start with the verb, e.g., "Tell Muse" and "Sing goddess," the first word of the *Odyssey* is ἄνδρα, as it is a poem about Odysseus. Similarly, the first word of the *Iliad* is μῆνιν, the "wrath" of Achilles.

Chapter 18 ∾

Demonstratives

Demonstratives

A demonstrative (from the Latin *demonstrare* "to point out") points out a noun or idea. Our two most common demonstratives in English are "this" and "that." We usually use "this" to point to something close to the speaker and "that" to point to something farther away from the speaker.

Imagine someone walks into a coffee shop. The customer looks at the counter and sees a cup of coffee. The customer could say, "How much is the cup of coffee in front of me?" However, a far simpler way would be to point at the coffee and say "How much is *this*?" Suppose that the barista responds "It is two dollars." The customer then sees someone at a table drinking a different looking coffee. "And how much is *that* coffee?" To which the barista replies, "Eight dollars." The customer, quite perplexed, asks, "Why is *this* one only two dollars, while *that* one is eight dollars." The barista replies, "*This* one is coffee, but *that* one has coffee and ice." Now imagine that if in the proceeding dialogue we were not allowed to use the demonstratives *this* and *that*. You can imagine how unwieldy that would be. Demonstratives therefore both simplify language and make it more effective.

In addition to pointing out nouns, demonstratives can point out whole sentences or ideas. Notice the line above, "You can imagine how unwieldy *that* would be." Instead of saying, "You can imagine how unwieldy it would be if in the proceeding dialogue we were not allowed to use the demonstratives this and that," we can simply say, "You can imagine how unwieldy *that* would be."

Demonstratives can be either *adjectives*, in which case they modify nouns in gender, number, and case, or they can be *pronouns*, in which case they agree with their antecedent in gender and number, but their case is determined by its function in the sentence.

In Greek, there are three demonstratives that you must learn. Let us look at the two words that most easily correspond to the English "this" and "that."

	οὗτος, αὕτη, τοῦτο = *this*			ἐκεῖνος, ἐκείνη, ἐκεῖνο = *that*		
	m	*f*	*n*	*m*	*f*	*n*
Singular						
Nom.	οὗτ–ος	αὕτ–η	τοῦτ–ο	ἐκεῖν–ος	ἐκείν–η	ἐκεῖν–ο
Gen.	τούτ–ου	ταύτ–ης	τούτ–ου	ἐκείν–ου	ἐκείν–ης	ἐκείν–ου
Dat.	τούτ–ῳ	ταύτ–ῃ	τούτ–ῳ	ἐκείν–ῳ	ἐκείν–ῃ	ἐκείν–ῳ
Acc.	τούτ–ον	ταύτ–ην	τοῦτ–ο	ἐκεῖν–ον	ἐκείν–ην	ἐκεῖν–ο
Plural						
Nom.	οὗτ–οι	αὗτ–αι	ταῦτ–α	ἐκεῖν–οι	ἐκεῖν–αι	ἐκεῖν–α
Gen.	τούτ–ων	τούτ–ων	τούτ–ων	ἐκείν–ων	ἐκείν–ων	ἐκείν–ων
Dat.	τούτ–οις	ταύτ–αις	τούτ–οις	ἐκείν–οις	ἐκείν–αις	ἐκείν–οις
Acc.	τούτ–ους	ταύτ–ας	ταῦτ–α	ἐκείν–ους	ἐκείν–ας	ἐκεῖν–α

The good news is that if you have already memorized the declension of αὐτός, –ή, –ό, you already know the endings of οὗτος and ἐκεῖνος. The endings are identical.

When demonstratives function as adjectives and hence modify nouns, they take the predicate position, not the attributive position. As you remember from chapter 3, the attributive position is right after the definite article, the predicate position is not right after the definite article. Unlike English, which does not say "this the book," Greek most often includes the definite article as well. As in the case of the definite article with names, when translating you will leave out the definite article.

τοῦτο τὸ βιβλίον ἐστὶν κακόν, ἐκεῖνο δὲ τὸ βιβλίον ἐστὶν ἀγαθόν.

This book is bad, but that book is good.

In addition to modifying nouns, a demonstrative can function as a pronoun.

¶ γηράσκω = to grow old | οὔποτε (adv.) = never

ἡ ἀρετή ἐστιν ἀεὶ καλή. τὸ σῶμα γηράσκει, ἐκείνη δὲ οὔποτε γηράσκει.

Excellence is always beautiful. The body grows old, but *that* never grows old.

When functioning as a pronoun, the demonstrative must agree with its *antecedent* (what the *this* or *that* refers to) in gender and number, but, as in the case of other pronouns, its case is determined by the role it plays in the sentence. When a demonstrative refers not to a single word, but to an idea, Greek uses the neuter singular.

¶ βαρύς, –εῖα, –ύ (adj.) = heavy; tiresome

οἱ διδάσκαλοι φιλοῦσιν λέγειν. βαρύ ἐστι τοῦτο τοῖς μαθηταῖς.

The teachers love to talk. *This* is tiresome to the students.

Remember that because of the inflected nature of Greek, the language is not bound to English word order.

Finally, when speaking of two things, ἐκεῖνος and οὗτος are used where English often says "the former" and "the latter." οὗτος is used to refer to "the latter" and ἐκεῖνος is used to refer to "the former." The reason for this is that Greek views what was just said as the closer "this," and what was said previously as being the farther away "that." You can choose to translate such sentences with "the former" and the "latter," but you can also translate them literally with "this" and "that."

Διογένης καὶ Πλάτων ἦσαν φιλόσοφοι. οὗτος μὲν ἐλούετο, ἐκεῖνος δὲ οὐκ ἐλούετο.

Diogenes and Plato were Philosophers. The latter (or "this one") bathed, but the former (or "that one") did not bathe.

In this sentence οὗτος refers to Plato, and ἐκεῖνος refers to Diogenes.

ὅδε

ὅδε is another common Greek demonstrative. It can usually be translated as "this." The forms of this demonstrative are quite simple. As you can see, it is merely the definite article with –δε attached to the end.

		ὅδε = *this*	
	m	*f*	*n*
Singular			
Nom.	ὅδε	ἥδε	τόδε
Gen.	τοῦδε	τῆσδε	τοῦδε
Dat.	τῷδε	τῇδε	τῷδε
Acc.	τόνδε	τήνδε	τόδε
Plural			
Nom.	οἵδε	αἵδε	τάδε
Gen.	τῶνδε	τῶνδε	τῶνδε
Dat.	τοῖσδε	ταῖσδε	τοῖσδε
Acc.	τούσδε	τάσδε	τάδε

Like, οὗτος, it points out something close to the speaker. It can be helpful to think of it as a closer version of οὗτος, even though you will often translate it the same. Another common use of this demonstrative is to use the neuter to designate what will immediately follow. Any of the three translations for the sentence below are possible.

¶ θαῦμα, –ατος, τό = wonder | ταπεινοφροσύνη, –ης, ἡ = humility

σῷζε ἐν τῷ βίῳ σοῦ τάδε· τὸ θαῦμα καί ἡ ταπεινοφροσύνη.

Preserve these in your life: wonder and humility. / Preserve in your life the following: wonder and humility. / Preserve these things in your life: wonder and humility.

Vocabulary

ἁμαρτωλός, –οῦ, ὁ = sinner

▸ καιρός, –οῦ, ὁ = due measure; season, opportunity

σοφός, –ή, –όν (adj.) = wise

▸ σοφός, –οῦ, ὁ = wise man, sage

στρατηγός, –οῦ, ὁ = general

ἐκεῖνος, ἐκείνη, ἐκεῖνο = that; the former

ὅδε, ἥδε, τόδε = this; the following

οὗτος, αὕτη, τοῦτο = this; the latter

αὖ (adv.) = again; moreover

ἤ (conj.) = or; than

προσεύχομαι, προσεύξομαι, προσηυξάμην, —, —, — = to pray

Sentences

1. ἡ βασιλεία ἡ ἐμὴ οὐκ ἔστιν ἐκ τοῦ κόσμου τούτου. (John 18:36)

2. τοῦτο μόνον θέλω μαθεῖν ἀφ᾽ ὑμῶν, ἐξ ἔργων νόμου τὸ πνεῦμα ἐλάβετε ἢ ἐξ ἀκοῆς πίστεως; (Gal 3:2)

> ¶ Remember that θέλω is the Koine spelling of ἐθέλω.
>
> ἀκοή, –ῆς, ἡ = hearing

3. οὗτος ἁμαρτωλοὺς προσδέχεται καὶ συνεσθίει αὐτοῖς. (Luke 15:2)

> ¶ οὗτος: Jesus.
>
> προσδέχομαι = to receive, admit
>
> συνεσθίω = to eat with (+ dat.)

4. ἀδιαλείπτως προσεύχεσθε, ἐν παντὶ εὐχαριστεῖτε· τοῦτο γὰρ θέλημα θεοῦ ἐν Χριστῷ Ἰησοῦ εἰς ὑμᾶς. (1 Thess 5:17–18)

> ¶ ἀδιαλείπτως (adv.) = continuously
>
> εὐχαριστεῖτε: 2nd person plural present imperative of εὐχαριστέω = to give thanks: a contract verb (see chapter 24).

5. σοφοὶ δὲ ἐνομίζοντο οἵδε· Θαλῆς, Σόλων, Περίανδρος, Κλεόβουλος, Χείλων, Βίας, Πιττακός. (Diogenes Laertius, *Lives of Eminent Philosophers*)

> ¶ This is a list of the "Seven Sages" of ancient Greece. All the names are in the nominative.

6. ἦν Λακεδαιμόνιος Χείλων σοφός, ὃς τάδ' ἔλεξε· μηδὲν ἄγαν· καιρῷ πάντα
πρόσεστι καλά. (Diogenes Laertius, *Lives of Eminent Philosophers*)

¶ ▸ Λακεδαιμόνιος, –η, –ον (adj.) = Spartan

Χείλων: One of the seven sages listed in the previous sentence.

ἔλεξε: while εἶπον is the most common aorist of λέγω, you will occasionally see the 1st aorist ἔλεξα.

μηδὲν ἄγαν: usually translated "Nothing in excess," this maxim is literally "[Do] nothing excessively."

ἄγαν (adv.) = very much; too much, excessively

πρόσειμι = to be added to, belong to (+ dat.)

7. τὸ πνεῦμα τὸ ἅγιον ὃ πέμψει ὁ πατὴρ ἐν τῷ ὀνόματί μου, ἐκεῖνος ὑμᾶς διδάξει
πάντα καὶ ὑπομνήσει ὑμᾶς πάντα ἃ εἶπον ὑμῖν ἐγώ. (John 14:26)

¶ ὑπομιμνήσκω, ὑπομνήσω, ὑπέμνησα = to remind; bring to one's mind

8. καὶ ἔλεγεν, "Αββα ὁ πατήρ, πάντα δυνατά σοι· παρένεγκε τὸ ποτήριον τοῦτο
ἀπ' ἐμοῦ· ἀλλ' οὐ τί ἐγὼ θέλω ἀλλὰ τί σύ." (Mark 14:36)

¶ ἔλεγεν: the grammatical subject is Jesus.

Αββα = Abba: Aramaic for "father."

ὁ πατήρ: Mark's explanation to the reader of what Αββα means.

παρένεγκε: aorist imperative of παραφέρω. See chapter 12 for augmentation in compound verbs.

ποτήριον, –ου, τό = cup

τί = what: an interrogative pronoun you will learn in chapter 25

9. οὔτε γὰρ ὁ ἐλλείπων τῇ ὀργῇ οὔτε ὁ ὑπερβάλλων ἐπαινετός ἐστιν, ἀλλ' ὁ
μέσως ἔχων πρὸς ταῦτα, οὗτος πρᾷς. (Aristotle, *Magna Moralia*)

¶ οὔτε…οὔτε = neither…nor

ὁ ἐλλείπων = the one lacking: you
will learn the participle in chapter
19.

ὀργῇ: a dative of respect here

ὁ ὑπερβάλλων = the one exceed-
ing: another participle you will
learn in chapter 19.

ἐπαινετός, –ή, –όν (adj.) = praise-
worthy

ἀλλ' = ἀλλά

ὁ μέσως ἔχων = the one being
moderate: another participle you
will learn in chapter 19.

πρὸς: here "with respect to" or
"regarding"

10. Socrates: ὅς ἀγαθὸς ῥαψῳδός ἐστιν, οὗτος καὶ ἀγαθὸς στρατηγός ἐστιν;
Ion: μάλιστα, ὦ Σώκρατες.
Socrates: οὐκοῦν καὶ ὅς ἀγαθὸς στρατηγός ἐστιν, ἀγαθὸς καὶ ῥαψῳδός
ἐστιν;
Ion: οὐκ αὖ μοι δοκεῖ τοῦτο.
Socrates: ἀλλ' ἐκεῖνο δοκεῖ σοι, ὅς ἀγαθὸς ῥαψῳδός, καὶ στρατηγὸς ἀγαθὸς
εἶναι;
Ion: πάνυ γε.

(Plato, *Ion*)

¶ The speakers are Socrates and the
rhapsode Ion. A rhapsode was a
professional reciter of epic poetry,
particularly Homer. The dialogue
Ion concerns whether poetry is
an art.

ὅς: here "he who" or "whoever."

καὶ: here adverbial "also."

μάλιστα (adv.) = most of all;
absolutely

οὐκοῦν = surely then

δοκέω = to seem; to seem right

πάνυ γε = by all means, no doubt

Etymology and Discussion Topics

καιρός, –οῦ, ὁ

The Greek words χρόνος and καιρός express different facets of time. While χρόνος usually refers to linear time, καιρός expresses the notion of the proper time or moment for something. If we were to say "There is not enough time to read all the great books," we would be speaking of χρόνος, while if we were to say "It is always a good time to read a great book," we would be speaking of καιρός.

σοφός, –ή, –όν

The substantive of this adjective (σοφός, –οῦ, ὁ) is so common that it is often used as a noun and is listed as such in dictionaries.

Λακεδαιμόνιος, –η, –ον

It might come as a surprise to learn that the Spartans rarely referred to themselves as Σπαρτιᾶται "Spartans." The word Σπάρτη referred to the physical city, but the Spartans preferred to refer to themselves as Lacedaemonians (Λακεδαιμόνιοι). The ancient writer Pausanias says that the Spartans would often distinguish themselves in battle by wearing red cloaks (there were no uniforms for most hoplite armies) and using shields with the letter lambda (Λ) painted on the front.

Chapter 19 ~

Introduction to Participles

A participle is a verbal adjective, and it accordingly shares properties of both the verb and the adjective. Roughly speaking, English has two primary participles, the active participle, which ends in "-ing," and the passive participle, which ends in "−ed".

The *shouting* professor. (active participle)

The *amused* student. (passive participle)

Both "shouting" and "amused" function as adjectives in the previous two examples, modifying the nouns "professor" and "student." However, participles can also act like verbs and take objects and other modifiers.

A professor *shouting* about the greatness of Homer must be expected.

The student *amused* by such a professor must also be expected.

In English, we are not overly fond of participles. In contrast, Greek loves to use participles. An understanding of how participles work is therefore crucial to appreciating the beauty of the Greek language. Over the next three chapters you will learn the different ways Greek uses the participle. First, you must learn the forms of the participle.

Greek participles, like adjectives, modify nouns in gender, number, and case. Like verbs, participles have *tense* (present, future, aorist, and perfect) and *voice* (active, middle, and passive). While the future and perfect participles do occur (you will learn the perfect participle in chapter 27), by far the majority of participles are either present or aorist. We will learn about how the participle expresses time and aspect in the next chapter.

Participle of εἰμί

First, it is important to memorize the forms of the present participle of the word "to be."

	εἰμί = to be		
	m	*f*	*n*
Singular			
Nom.	ὤν	οὖσα	ὄν
Gen.	ὄντος	οὖσης	ὄντος
Dat.	ὄντι	οὖσῃ	ὄντι
Acc.	ὄντα	οὖσαν	ὄν
Plural			
Nom.	ὄντες	οὖσαι	ὄντα
Gen.	ὄντων	οὖσῶν	ὄντων
Dat.	οὖσι(ν)	οὖσαις	οὖσι(ν)
Acc.	ὄντας	οὖσας	ὄντα

Participles of λύω

Here are the forms of the present, future, and aorist participles for our model verb λύω.

	Present Active			*Present Middle/Passive*		
	m	*f*	*n*	*m*	*f*	*n*
Singular						
Nom.	λύ–ων	λύ–ουσα	λῦ–ον	λυ–όμενος	λυ–ομένη	λυ–όμενον
Gen.	λύ–οντος	λυ–ούσης	λύ–οντος	λυ–ομένου	λυ–ομένης	λυ–ομένου
Dat.	λύ–οντι	λυ–ούσῃ	λύ–οντι	λυ–ομένῳ	λυ–ομένῃ	λυ–ομένῳ
Acc.	λύ–οντα	λύ–ουσαν	λῦ–ον	λυ–όμενον	λυ–ομένην	λυ–όμενον
Plural						
Nom.	λύ–οντες	λύ–ουσαι	λύ–οντα	λυ–όμενοι	λυ–όμεναι	λυ–όμενα
Gen.	λυ–όντων	λυ–ουσῶν	λυ–όντων	λυ–ομένων	λυ–ομένων	λυ–ομένων
Dat.	λύ–ουσι(ν)	λυ–ούσαις	λύ–ουσι(ν)	λυ–ομένοις	λυ–ομέναις	λυ–ομένοις
Acc.	λύ–οντας	λυ–ούσας	λύ–οντα	λυ–ομένους	λυ–ομένας	λυ–όμενα

	Future Active			Future Middle		
	m	*f*	*n*	*m*	*f*	*n*
Singular						
Nom.	λύ–σων	λύ–σουσα	λῦ–σον	λυ–σόμενος	λυ–σομένη	λυ–σόμενον
Gen.	λύ–σοντος	λυ–σούσης	λύ–σοντος	λυ–σομένου	λυ–σομένης	λυ–σομένου
Dat.	λύ–σοντι	λυ–σούσῃ	λύ–σοντι	λυ–σομένῳ	λυ–σομένῃ	λυ–σομένῳ
Acc.	λύ–σοντα	λύ–σουσαν	λῦ–σον	λυ–σόμενον	λυ–σομένην	λυ–σόμενον
Plural						
Nom.	λύ–σοντες	λύ–σουσαι	λύ–σοντα	λυ–σόμενοι	λυ–σόμεναι	λυ–σόμενα
Gen.	λυ–σόντων	λυ–σουσῶν	λυ–σόντων	λυ–σομένων	λυ–σομένων	λυ–σομένων
Dat.	λύ–σουσι(ν)	λυ–σούσαις	λύ–σουσι(ν)	λυ–σομένοις	λυ–σομέναις	λυ–σομένοις
Acc.	λύ–σοντας	λυ–σούσας	λύ–σοντα	λυ–σομένους	λυ–σομένας	λυ–σόμενα

	Aorist Active			Aorist Middle		
	m	*f*	*n*	*m*	*f*	*n*
Singular						
Nom.	λύ–σας	λύ–σασα	λῦ–σαν	λυ–σάμενος	λυ–σαμένη	λυ–σάμενον
Gen.	λύ–σαντος	λυ–σάσης	λύ–σαντος	λυ–σαμένου	λυ–σαμένης	λυ–σομένου
Dat.	λύ–σαντι	λυ–σάσῃ	λύ–σαντι	λυ–σαμένῳ	λυ–σαμένῃ	λυ–σομένῳ
Acc.	λύ–σαντα	λύ–σασαν	λῦ–σαν	λυ–σάμενον	λυ–σαμένην	λυ–σάμενον
Plural						
Nom.	λύ–σαντες	λύ–σασαι	λύ–σαντα	λυ–σάμενοι	λυ–σάμεναι	λυ–σάμενα
Gen.	λυ–σάντων	λυ–σασῶν	λυ–σάντων	λυ–σαμένων	λυ–σαμένων	λυ–σομένων
Dat.	λύ–σασι(ν)	λυ–σάσαις	λύ–σασι(ν)	λυ–σαμένοις	λυ–σαμέναις	λυ–σομένοις
Acc.	λύ–σαντας	λυ–σάσας	λύ–σαντα	λυ–σαμένους	λυ–σαμένας	λυ–σάμενα

	Future Passive			Aorist Passive		
	m	*f*	*n*	*m*	*f*	*n*
Singular						
Nom.	λυ–θησόμενος	λυ–θησομένη	λυ–θησόμενον	λυ–θείς	λυ–θεῖσα	λυ–θέν
Gen.	λυ–θησομένου	λυ–θησομένης	λυ–θησομένου	λυ–θέντος	λυ–θείσης	λυ–θέντος
Dat.	λυ–θησομένῳ	λυ–θησομένῃ	λυ–θησομένῳ	λυ–θέντι	λυ–θείσῃ	λυ–θέντι
Acc.	λυ–θησόμενον	λυ–θησομένην	λυ–θησόμενον	λυ–θέντα	λυ–θεῖσαν	λυ–θέν
Plural						
Nom.	λυ–θησόμενοι	λυ–θησόμεναι	λυ–θησόμενα	λυ–θέντες	λυ–θεῖσαι	λυ–θέντα
Gen.	λυ–θησομένων	λυ–θησομένων	λυ–θησομένων	λυ–θέντων	λυ–θεισῶν	λυ–θέντων
Dat.	λυ–θησομένοις	λυ–θησομέναις	λυ–θησομένοις	λυ–θεῖσι(ν)	λυ–θείσαις	λυ–θεῖσι(ν)
Acc.	λυ–θησομένους	λυ–θησομένας	λυ–θησόμενα	λυ–θέντας	λυ–θείσας	λυ–θέντα

At this point you might be feeling a bit overwhelmed with all the new participles you must memorize. Fear not. If you have memorized your model adjectives thus far, you will have an easier time memorizing the participles. The masculine and neuter active participles resemble 3rd declension adjectives, while the feminine active forms resemble adjectives of the 1st and 2nd declension. The forms ending in –μενος are by far the easiest, as they are identical to the endings of 1st and 2nd declension adjectives after the μεν. The chart below should put you more at ease.

Participle	Endings look like
Present Active	*Exactly* like the participle of εἰμί.
Present Middle/Passive	–ομεν– plus the –ος, –η, –ον endings of καλός
Future Active	–σ– + present active participle endings
Future Middle	–σ– + present middle/passive participle endings
Future Passive	–θη– + future middle participle endings
Aorist Active	Except for the nominative, the masculine and neuter resemble the present active participle endings, but with –σα– in place of –ο– before the endings, e.g., –σαντος / –οντος. The feminine endings resemble first declension endings.
Aorist Middle	Like the future middle endings, but with –σα– instead of –σο–, e.g., –σαμενος / –σομενος.

(continues)

Participle	Endings look like
Aorist Passive	Except for the nominative, the masculine and neuter resemble the present active participle endings, but with –θε– in place of –ο– before the endings, e.g., –θεντος / –οντος. The feminine endings resemble first declension endings.

Therefore, if you memorize the present participles of εἰμί (which look a lot like the 3rd declension endings) and you have already memorized καλός, you already know almost all these forms.

The Greek participle is capable of several functions. It can be *attributive*, *circumstantial*, or *supplementary*. Recognizing which one of these functions a participle is performing is crucial to understanding the meaning of a sentence. In this chapter we will focus on the first usage, the attributive participle.

Attributive Participle

In chapter 3 you were introduced to the attributive and predicate positions of adjectives. The attributive position means that the adjective is placed immediately after the definite article. This usually means between the article and the noun (ὁ καλὸς λόγος = the beautiful word), but you will occasionally see it after a second definite article (ὁ λόγος ὁ καλός = the beautiful word) with no difference in translation. Since participles are verbal adjectives, they can function as ordinary attributive adjectives, agreeing with their noun in gender, number, and case. If the participle is modifying a noun and it is in the attributive position, just treat it like a simple adjective. Since a participle is a verbal adjective, it can also act take an object. A participle will never, however, be the main verb in a sentence.

> ⸆ ἀείδω = to sing | βαρύς, –εῖα, –ύ (adj.) = heavy; tiresome | εὔδοξος, –ον (adj.) = esteemed | πλεονεξία, –ας, ἡ = greediness | δυσδαίμων, –ον (adj.) = unhappy

ὁ ἀείδων ἄνθρωπός ἐστι βαρύς.

The singing man is tiresome.

ὁ ἀείδων τὴν ἀλήθειαν ἄνθρωπός ἐστιν εὔδοξος.

The man singing the truth is esteemed.

οἱ ἄνθρωποι οἱ πεισθέντες ὑπὸ πλεονεξίας γίγνονται δυσδαίμονες.

Men persuaded by greed become unhappy.

When Greek uses attributive participles in this way, it is often necessary to add a "that" or "who" in your translation. οἱ ἄνθρωποι οἱ πεισθέντες ὑπὸ πλεονεξίας could be translated "men who are persuaded by greed" as well as "men persuaded by greed." This is particularly useful when the participle is being used as a substantive adjective, e.g., οἱ παιδεύοντες could be translated as "those who teach" as well as "those teaching." Although it will be necessary at times to translate attributive participles in this way, it should always be kept in mind that they are not relative clauses.

Vocabulary

▸ ἁμαρτία, –ας, ἡ = mistake; sin

βλάβη, –ης, ἡ = harm

κοιλία, –ας, ἡ = womb

ποιητής, –οῦ, ὁ = poet

αἰώνιος, –ον (adj.) = eternal

δοῦλος, –η, –ον (adj.) = servile; as substantive "slave"

▸ ἀμὴν (adv.) = verily, in truth; so be it

οὐκέτι (adv.) = no longer

ὥσπερ (adv.) = as if, just as

δέομαι, δεήσομαι, —, —, [   ], ἐδεήθην = to need, lack; have need of (+gen.)

φεύγω, φεύξομαι, ἔφυγον, [   ], —, — = to flee

Sentences

1. πάντα δυνατὰ τῷ πιστεύοντι. (Mark 9:23)

⁋ The verb ἐστίν is understood in this sentence.

2. φεῦγ' ἡδονὴν φέρουσαν ὑστέρην βλάβην. (Alexis, *Fragments*)

⁋ φεῦγ' = φεῦγε

ὕστερος, –α, –ον (adj.) = later

3. οὐ δεῖ ὥσπερ καθεύδοντας ποιεῖν καὶ λέγειν. (Heraclitus, *Fragments*)

> ¶ οὐ δεῖ: translate as if it were writ-
> ten δεῖ οὐ; supply "we" or "people"
> as the object of δεῖ. Remember
> that δεῖ takes the accusative and
> infinitive construction.
>
> καθεύδω = to sleep

▶ 4. ὁ μὴ δαρεὶς ἄνθρωπος οὐ παιδεύεται. (Menander, *Fragments*)

> ¶ δαρεὶς: aorist passive participle
> of δέρω = to skin, thrash, so ὁ μὴ
> δαρεὶς ἄνθρωπος = the person not
> thrashed

5. τὰ γὰρ βλεπόμενα πρόσκαιρα, τὰ δὲ μὴ βλεπόμενα αἰώνια. (2 Cor 4:18)

> ¶ πρόσκαιρος, –ον (adj.) = occasion-
> al; temporary

6. ἀμὴν ἀμὴν λέγω ὑμῖν, ὁ πιστεύων ἔχει ζωὴν αἰώνιον. (John 6:47)

7. Ἀμὴν ἀμὴν λέγω ὑμῖν ὅτι πᾶς ὁ ποιῶν τὴν ἁμαρτίαν δοῦλός ἐστιν τῆς
ἁμαρτίας. (John 8:34)

▶ 8. καὶ ἀνεφώνησεν κραυγῇ μεγάλῃ καὶ εἶπεν, "Εὐλογημένη σὺ ἐν γυναιξίν, καὶ
εὐλογημένος ὁ καρπὸς τῆς κοιλίας σου." (Luke 1:42)

> ¶ ἀνεφώνησεν: aorist of ἀναφωνέω =
> to shout, proclaim: the grammat-
> ical subject is Elizabeth, and her
> words are addressed to Mary.
>
> κραυγή, –ῆς, ἡ = a shout
>
> μεγάλῃ: see μέγας (chap. 9 vocab-
> ulary)
>
> εἶπεν: aorist of λέγω (chap. 4
> vocabulary)
>
> Εὐλογημένη: present passive parti-
> ciple of εὐλογέω = to praise; bless
>
> Again, the verbs "are" and "is" are
> to be supplied in the quotation.

▸ 9. ἀνὴρ δίκαιός ἐστιν οὐχ ὁ μὴ ἀδικῶν. (Philemon, *Fragments*)

¶ Remember that the predicate nominative need not follow the verb. The definite article, not word order, is the key to distinguishing a subject from a predicate nominative.

ἀδικέω = to be unjust

10. δέομαι ποιητοῦ δεξιοῦ. οἱ μὲν γὰρ οὐκέτ᾽ εἰσίν, οἱ δ᾽ ὄντες κακοί.

(Aristophanes, *Frogs*)

¶ These words are spoken by the god Dionysus in Aristophanes' play *Frogs*, in which the god travels to the underworld to see who the better poet is, Aeschylus or Euripides, both of whom had died.

δεξιός, –ά, –όν (adj.) = right; skillful

οὐκέτ᾽ = οὐκέτι

οἱ μὲν: the skillful poets

Again, you must supply the implied verb "are" after οἱ δ᾽ ὄντες. As you have seen, Greek often leaves out the word "to be" and leaves it implied, especially in short clauses. From this point on, your notes will no longer alert you to when this occurs in your sentences.

Etymology and Discussion Topics

ἁμαρτία, –ας, ἡ = mistake; sin

While this word means "sin" in the New Testament, it would be a mistake to always translate ἁμαρτία as "sin" in classical authors. The original meaning of ἁμαρτία and the verb ἁμαρτάνω is closer to "mistake" than "sin." In Homer ἁμαρτάνω is used when javelins miss their target. In its original classical sense ἁμαρτία often implies various levels of culpability. While "sin" implies the culpability of the doer of the action, classical ἁμαρτία speaks more often to the role of τύχη in the universe and man's limited capacity to think and act correctly.

ἀμὴν (adv.) = verily, in truth; so be it

This adverb is a transliteration of an Aramaic word. In the New Testament it is used to affirm, intensify, and strengthen what precedes or follows.

ὁ μὴ δαρεὶς ἄνθρωπος οὐ παιδεύεται.

Perhaps at this point in your study of Greek you might agree with this sentence of Menander. Joking aside, what do you think this sentence implies about the nature of education? How might education be likened to being "flayed" or "thrashed." Is education the accumulation of knowledge or the subtraction of false assumptions?

Εὐλογημένη σὺ ἐν γυναιξίν, καὶ εὐλογημένος ὁ καρπὸς τῆς κοιλίας σου.
(Luke 1:42)

These famous words spoken by Elizabeth form the second line of the "Hail Mary," the first line coming from the address of the angel to Mary earlier in Luke's Gospel (1:28).

ἀνὴρ δίκαιός ἐστιν οὐχ ὁ μὴ ἀδικῶν.

What do you think this sentence says about justice? Is merely avoiding injustice sufficient?

Chapter 20 ⌒

Now that you have learned the attributive use of the participle in chapter 19, let's look at another use of the participle.

Circumstantial Participle

By far the two most common uses of the participle are the *attributive* and the *circumstantial*. Most of the time, therefore, when you see a participle, you will have to decide between these two uses. The good news is that distinguishing between the two is relatively straightforward. While the attributive participle is always in the *attributive* position, the circumstantial participle is always in the *predicate* position. Remember that the predicate position means that the participle is *not* in the attributive position, i.e., not directly after the definite article.

The circumstantial participle describes the circumstances under which the main action of the sentence takes place. They occur in phrases that describe the nouns they modify and are called *participial phrases*. In these constructions, *the subject of the participle will be identical to the subject of the main verb in the independent clause*. The circumstantial participle, while it can take objects since it is a verbal adjective, can never be the main verb of a sentence.

❡ θέλγω = to charm | πολίτης, –ου, ὁ = citizen

λέγων τὴν ἀλήθειαν, ὁ διδάσκαλος ἐπαίδευε τοὺς μαθητάς.

Speaking the truth, the teacher was educating the students.

θελχθέντες ὑπὸ τοῦ δημαγωγοῦ, οἱ πολῖται ἥμαρτον.

Having been charmed by the demagogue, the citizens erred.

As you can see from the above sentences, the tense of circumstantial participles express both time *and* aspect. In chapter 13 you learned that the tense of a verb in indirect statement is relative to the tense of the main verb in the sentence. Likewise, the tense of the circumstantial participle is interpreted relative to the tense of the main verb.

present participle	action *at the same time* as the main verb.
aorist participle	action *before* the main verb.
future participle	action *after* the main verb.

Just as the present infinitive expresses imperfect aspect (there is no imperfect infinitive) and the aorist infinitive expresses aoristic aspect, so too the present participle expresses imperfect aspect (there is no imperfect participle) and the aorist participle expresses aoristic aspect.

In the first example (λέγων τὴν ἀλήθειαν, ὁ διδάσκαλος ἐπαίδευε τοὺς μαθητάς), the present active participle λέγων expresses time contemporaneous with the main verb and imperfect aspect, i.e., the teacher was speaking the truth while he was teaching, and the author views the action of speaking the truth as ongoing (imperfect aspect).

In the second example (θελχθέντες ὑπὸ τοῦ δημαγωγοῦ, οἱ πολῖται ἥμαρτον), the aorist passive participle θελχθέντες expresses time prior to the main verb and aoristic aspect. The citizens are first charmed and then make the mistake. The use of the aoristic aspect shows that the citizens being charmed was most likely a single event.

As verbal adjectives, circumstantial participles agree with the nouns they modify in gender, number, and case, even though they are frequently far removed from the nouns they modify, as in our two examples above.

Circumstantial participles can expresses a variety of relationships to the action of the main verb, but the most common are temporal (when), causal (since), concessive (although), and conditional (if). We will examine the conditional (if) in chapter 35.

If we look at the sentence above (λέγων τὴν ἀλήθειαν, ὁ διδάσκαλος ἐπαίδευε τοὺς μαθητάς), we see that the circumstantial participle is most likely temporal, and could be translated "When he was speaking the truth, the teacher was educating the students." In the second sentence, the meaning is probably causal. θελχθέντες ὑπὸ τοῦ δημαγωγοῦ, οἱ πολῖται ἥμαρτον could be translated as "Since they had been charmed by the demagogue, the citizens erred." If we were to negate either sentences, the circumstantial participles would be concessive (contrasting the action described in the participle with the action in the main verb).

> λέγων τὴν ἀλήθειαν, ὁ διδάσκαλος οὐκ ἐπαίδευε τοὺς μαθητάς.
>
> Although he was speaking the truth, the teacher was not educating the students.

> θελχθέντες ὑπὸ τοῦ δημαγωγοῦ, οἱ πολῖται οὐχ ἥμαρτον.
>
> Although they had been charmed by the demagogue, the citizens did not err.

It is important that you be aware of the temporal, causal, concessive, and conditional aspects of circumstantial participles. In every case, context will be your aid in determining which type of circumstantial participle it is. Many instructors and books will insist that you identify which type of circumstantial participle you see and then translate it accordingly. I would, however, discourage you from doing this. It is far easier to translate the participles literally. I believe this is beneficial for the following reasons.

(1) It is far less complicated for the beginning student.

(2) The English word roughly corresponds to the Greek one. While the Greeks were aware that a circumstantial participle could have these different meanings, they used the same word in each case.

(3) Very often there is no way to tell whether the author has in mind a temporal or a causal participle. Take, for example the first sentence (λέγων τὴν ἀλήθειαν, ὁ διδάσκαλος ἐπαίδευε τοὺς μαθητάς). This could be translated "When he was speaking the truth, the teacher was educating the students" or "Since he was speaking the truth, the teacher was educating the students." Context tells us that the participle λέγων is not concessive. "Although he was speaking the truth, the teacher was educating the students" would not make any sense. Very often, however, a Greek author will use a circumstantial participle that could be either temporal or causal. It is far easier to translate the participles literally, all the while keeping in mind the different types of circumstantial participles. Remember, you are learning Greek in order to read

Greek, not translate Greek into beautiful English. The use of translation is a tool that you must use until your Greek reaches an advanced level, at which time you can cast off translations like training wheels on a bicycle.

Vocabulary

▸ ἄγγελος, –ου, ὁ = messenger; angel

▸ γράμμα, –ατος, τό = letter; in plural "writings"

ἔλεος, –ου, ὁ = pity, mercy

πλοῦτος, –ου, ὁ = wealth

▸ ἕτερος, –α, –ον (adj.) = other

καινός, –ή, –όν (adj.) = new

νεκρός, –ά, –όν (adj.) = dead

βλάπτω, βλάψω, ἔβλαψα, [   ], [   ], —, ἐβλάβην = to harm

ἡγέομαι, ἡγήσομαι, ἡγησάμην, —, [   ], — = to think, believe (+ inf. in indirect statement)

πίνω, πίομαι, ἔπιον, [   ], [   ], ἐπόθην = to drink

πίπτω, πεσοῦμαι, ἔπεσον, [   ], —, — = to fall; fail

ταράσσω, ταράξω, ἐτάραξα, [   ], [   ], ἐταράχθη = to shake; disturb

Sentences

1. ὁ γραμμάτων ἄπειρος οὐ βλέπει βλέπων. (Menander, *Fragments*)

¶ ἄπειρος, –ον (adj.) = without experience of (+gen.)

2. ἀδικεῖ Σωκράτης, οὓς μὲν ἡ πόλις νομίζει θεοὺς οὐ νομίζων, ἕτερα δὲ καινὰ δαιμόνια εἰσηγούμενος. (Xenophon, *Memorabilia*)

¶ This is one of the charges that Socrates will be convicted of and sentenced to death for.

ἀδικέω = to be unjust

δαιμόνιον, –ου, τό = divinity; lesser god.

εἰσηγέομαι = to introduce, propose

3. ὡς τὸν αὐτὸν οἶνον πίνοντες οἱ μὲν παροινοῦσιν οἱ δὲ πραΰνονται, οὕτω καὶ
πλοῦτον. (Ariston, in Stobaeus, *Anthology*)

> ❡ ὡς…οὕτω καὶ = just as…so also
>
> οἱ μὲν… οἱ δὲ: can be translated as "some…others…"
>
> παροινέω = to behave ill at wine
>
> πραΰνω = to calm; middle: to become calm
>
> πλοῦτον = "concerning wealth," an accusative of respect you will learn in chapter 38.

4. βλάπτει τὸν ἄνδρα θυμὸς εἰς ὀργὴν πεσών. (Menander, *Fragments*)

> ❡ πεσών: aorist active participle of πίπτω

5. ἡγεῖται δὲ πάντα ταῦτα τὰ κτήματα οὐδενὸς ἄξια καὶ ἡμᾶς οὐδὲν εἶναι—
λέγω ὑμῖν—εἰρωνευόμενος δὲ καὶ παίζων πάντα τὸν βίον πρὸς τοὺς
ἀνθρώπους διατελεῖ. (Plato, *Symposium*)

> ❡ ἡγεῖται: the grammatical subject is Socrates. The speaker of these words is Alcibiades in Plato's *Symposium*.
>
> κτῆμα, –ατος, τό = possession
>
> οὐδενὸς = of nothing: gen. singular of οὐδὲν (see chapter 22)
>
> λέγω ὑμῖν: this aside is not grammatically part of the sentence, like our expression "let me tell you," which we might stick in the middle of a sentence.
>
> εἰρωνεύομαι = to feign ignorance
>
> παίζω = to play, jest
>
> διατελεῖ: he spends, he lives

6. ὁ δὲ θεὸς πλούσιος ὢν ἐν ἐλέει, διὰ τὴν πολλὴν ἀγάπην αὐτοῦ ἣν ἠγάπησεν ἡμᾶς, καὶ ὄντας ἡμᾶς νεκροὺς τοῖς παραπτώμασιν συνεζωοποίησεν τῷ Χριστῷ. (Eph 2:4–5)

¶ πλούσιος, –α, –ον (adj.) = rich

ἠγάπησεν = loved: 3rd person singular aorist active of ἀγαπάω

καὶ: here adverbial "even"

παράπτωμα, –ατος, τό = transgression: παραπτώμασιν is here a dative of respect with νεκρούς.

συζωοποιέω = to bring to life with (+ dat.): the subject is θεός.

▶ 7. καὶ ἐταράχθη Ζαχαρίας ἰδών, καὶ φόβος ἐπέπεσεν ἐπ' αὐτόν. εἶπεν δὲ πρὸς αὐτὸν ὁ ἄγγελος, "Μὴ φοβοῦ, Ζαχαρία, διότι εἰσηκούσθη ἡ δέησίς σου, καὶ ἡ γυνή σου Ἐλισάβετ γεννήσει υἱόν σοι, καὶ καλέσεις τὸ ὄνομα αὐτοῦ Ἰωάννην." (Luke 1:12–13)

¶ Luke 1:11, the passage just prior to this sentence, describes how an angel of God appeared to Zachariah.

Ζαχαρίας, –ου, ὁ = Zachariah, the father of John the Baptist

ἰδών - aorist active participle of ὁράω. The implied direct object of ἰδών is the angel.

ἐπιπίπτω = to fall upon

φοβέομαι = to be afraid

διότι (conj.) = since

δέησις, –εως, ἡ = need, prayer, supplication

εἰσηκούσθη: aorist passive of εἰσακούω = to harken, answer

γεννήσει: future active of γεννάω = to bear, give birth to

καλέσεις: future active of καλέω = to call, name (chap. 16 vocabulary)

Ἰωάννης, –ου, ὁ = John

8. ἄνθρωπον ὄντα δεῖ φρονεῖν τἀνθρώπινα. (Menander, *Fragments*)

> ¶ φρονέω = to think
>
> τἀνθρώπινα = τά ἀνθρώπινα
>
> ἀνθρώπινος, –η, –ον (adj.) = human

9. ὃς ἐν μορφῇ θεοῦ ὑπάρχων οὐχ ἁρπαγμὸν ἡγήσατο τὸ εἶναι ἴσα θεῷ, ἀλλὰ ἑαυτὸν ἐκένωσεν μορφὴν δούλου λαβών. (Phil 2:6–7)

> ¶ ὅς: the antecedent is Jesus.
>
> μορφή, –ῆς, ἡ = form
>
> ὑπάρχων: participle of ὑπάρχω, here "being."
>
> ἁρπαγμός, –οῦ, ὁ = something to be grasped or seized.
>
> ἡγήσατο: aorist middle of ἡγέομαι (see this chapter's vocabulary)
>
> τὸ εἶναι ἴσα θεῷ = equality with God: the customary way to translate such an articular
>
> ἴσα = like: an adverb that takes a dative.
>
> ἐκένωσεν: aorist of κενόω = to empty
>
> ἑαυτὸν = himself: a reflexive pronoun you will learn in chapter 29.
>
> λαβών: aorist participle of λαμβάνω

10. ἀκούσας δέ τις τῶν συνανακειμένων ταῦτα εἶπεν αὐτῷ, Μακάριος ὅστις φάγεται ἄρτον ἐν τῇ βασιλείᾳ τοῦ θεοῦ. (Luke 14:15)

> ¶ τις τῶν συνανακειμένων = one of the guests
>
> τις: an indefinite pronoun you will learn in chapter 25
>
> εἶπεν: the subject is τις
>
> αὐτῷ: Jesus
>
> ὅστις = whoever: an indefinite relative pronoun you will learn in chapter 35
>
> φάγεται = eats: aorist middle of ἐσθίω = to eat

Etymology and Discussion Topics

ἄγγελος, –ου, ὁ = messenger; angel

This word literally means "messenger" and can denote a human or a divine messenger. We get our word "angel" from this word on account of the many instances where it is used for a divine messenger. In your translations, ἄγγελος τοῦ θεοῦ can be translated "angel of God" or simply "messenger of God."

γράμμα, –ατος, τό = letter; in plural "writings"

From this word comes your favorite English word, "grammar." The original meaning of γράμμα is something drawn, whether a picture, a diagram, or another drawn thing. In the plural, it almost always refers to a piece of writing.

ἕτερος, –α, –ον (adj.) = other

The adjective ἕτερος means "other" or "different." From this word comes our prefix "hetero," (heterogeneous) as opposed to the prefix "homo" (homogenous), which comes from the adjective ὅμος "same." In theology heterodoxy (ἕτερος + δόξα) "other opinion" is contrasted with orthodoxy (ὀρθός + δόξα) "correct opinion."

καὶ ἐταράχθη Ζαχαρίας

You will most often see ἐταράχθη translated as "disturbed" or "troubled" in the passages such as this one and in the annunciation (Luke 1:29). While this is certainly permissible, the translation can mask the initially terrifying experience that is narrated. This verb is used in Homer when Poseidon violently "shakes" the sea. It is also used to describe armies being thrown into disorder. While "troubled" is an acceptable translation, some of the power of the Greek verb can be lost in such a translation.

Chapter 21 ⌒

Supplementary Participle • Participle in Indirect Statement •
Future Participle to Express Purpose • Genitive Absolute

Supplementary Participle

Certain verbs in Greek take a participle to complete their meaning. In chapter 7 you learned about the complementary infinitive. Certain verbs, like βούλομαι "to want" and ἐθέλω "to wish," take an infinitive to complete their meaning, e.g., βούλομαι μανθάνειν "I want to learn." Similarly, some verbs take a participle to complete their meaning. These participles are called *supplementary*. How do you know if a verb takes a supplementary participle? Good news: your vocabulary and dictionary will say (+ participle) and give the meaning under that word. Two such words are the middle voices of παύω and ἄρχω (παύομαι "to stop" and ἄρχομαι "to begin.")

> ὁ φιλόσοφος οὐ παύεται λέγων.
>
> The philosopher doesn't stop speaking.
>
> ὁ φιλόσοφος ἄρχεται λέγων.
>
> The philosopher begins speaking.

Sometimes the translation will be easy, as in the above example with "stop speaking." In other instances, English would prefer an infinitive, as in the second example where we would prefer to say "begins to speak" rather than "begins speaking." As a general rule, it is easiest to try and translate participles literally unless it would sound very awkward. Once you become more familiar with how participles work, you can allow yourself more flexibility in your translations.

The supplementary participle can modify the subject, as in the above examples, or the object.

ὁ χρόνος ἔπαυσε τὸν φιλόσοφον λέγοντα.

Time stopped the philosopher (from) talking.

There are two very important Greek verbs that take a supplementary participle, τυγχάνω and λανθάνω.

τυγχάνω

τυγχάνω means roughly "to happen." In English, we use an infinitive to complete the meaning of this verb.

He happens to be a philosopher.

She happens to have a talent for writing Greek verse.

Greek students happen to be smarter than Latin students.

In Greek, τυγχάνω takes the participle. It is almost always impossible to translate the participle literally. Instead, translate the participle as if it were an infinitive.

❡ ὤν: present participle of εἰμί | ἐλθών: aorist participle of ἔρχομαι

ὁ Σωκράτης τυγχάνει ὢν μικρός.

Socrates happens to be small.

ὁ Πλάτων ἔτυχεν ἐλθὼν εἰς Σικελίαν.

Plato happened to go to Sicily.

λανθάνω

λανθάνω is a notoriously tricky verb. It means "to escape the notice of someone." It is used to express an action that is done without the knowledge of someone. The action is expressed by the supplementary participle, and the person who does not notice is put into the accusative case. It is impossible to translate this verb literally in English.

λανθάνω λέγων τὸν φιλόσοφον.

I am speaking without the knowledge of the philosopher. / The philosopher doesn't notice that I am speaking.

This could be translated in a number of ways, but the important part is that the subject "I" is the one doing the action "speaking" and it escapes the notice of the accusative "the philosopher."

Participle in Indirect Statement

Another type of supplementary participle is a participle in indirect statement. In chapter 11 you learned that Greek has three ways of expressing indirect statement. With verbs of speaking ὅτι or ὡς + indicative is used. With verbs of assertion or belief the accusative + infinitive is used. With verbs of perception, the construction is like the accusative + infinitive, but the verb is put into the participle, not the infinitive.

¶ αἰσθάνομαι = to perceive | μάθημα, μαθήματος, τό = a lesson

αἰσθάνομαι τὸν φιλόσοφον ὄντα σοφόν.

I perceive that the philosopher is wise.

ὁ μαθητὴς ἤκουσε τὸ μάθημα παιδευόμενον ὑπὸ τοῦ κακοῦ φιλοσόφου.

The student heard that the lesson was being taught by the bad philosopher. (i.e., the student heard this piece of information from someone else.)

If the participle is in attributive position, it is not in indirect statement.

ὁ μαθητὴς ἤκουσε τὸ παιδευόμενον μάθημα ὑπὸ τοῦ κακοῦ φιλοσόφου.

The student heard the lesson being taught by the bad philosopher. (i.e., the student actually heard the lesson being taught by the bad philosopher).

As in the case of the circumstantial participle, the tense of the participle in indirect statement indicates both time and aspect. Remember that the participle in indirect statement is relative to the time of the main verb. This is why the present participle παιδευόμενον is translated as "was being taught" in the previous example.

Future Participle to Express Purpose

As mentioned previously in chapter 19, by far the most common tenses of the participle are the present and the aorist. The future participle is largely confined to two uses. The first is to express subsequent time in indirect statement.

ὁ μαθητὴς ἤκουσε τὸν κακὸν φιλόσοφον παιδεύσοντα τὸ μάθημα.

The student heard that the bad philosopher would be teaching the lesson.

Another place you will encounter the future participle is to express purpose, often introduced by verbs of motion.

πέμπω τὸν ἄγγελον παιδεύσοντα τὴν ἀλήθειαν.

I am sending a messenger to teach the truth.

Genitive Absolute

The genitive absolute is technically a circumstantial participle where the subject is different from the subject of the main verb, but it is easier to think of it as its own construction. For those of you who have studied Latin, the genitive absolute is the equivalent of the ablative absolute in Latin.

As you saw in the last chapter, the subject of a circumstantial participial phrase is the subject of the main verb in the sentence.

λέγων τὴν ἀλήθειαν, ὁ διδάσκαλος ἐπαίδευε τοὺς μαθητάς.

Speaking the truth, the teacher was educating the students.

The subject of λέγων is the subject of ἐπαίδευε, i.e., the teacher. What if we want to use a sentence that expresses the circumstances under which the action takes place, but we want the subject of the participle to be different from the subject of the main verb? We use the genitive absolute construction. It is called the genitive absolute (from the Latin *absolutus* "detached") because the noun and participle in the genitive are separate from the subject of the sentence. Both the subject of the genitive absolute and its participle are placed in the genitive case, but you will translate them exactly as you would other circumstantial participial phrases.

¶ ὑπομένω = to persevere

μαθήματος ὄντος χαλεποῦ, ὁ μαθητὴς ὑπέμενεν.

The lesson being difficult, the student persevered.

Again, although it is important to recognize that this participle is probably concessive "although," the meaning is still clear if you translate the participle literally. One of the most common uses of the genitive absolute is to report sayings. Very often Greek likes to say, for example, "Someone having once asked Socrates X, he responded Y." The first part is often expressed with a genitive absolute.

¶ δυσχεραίνω = to become annoyed

εἰπόντος ποιητοῦ ὅτι ἡ ζωή ἐστι καλή, Διογένης ἐδυσχέρανα.

A poet having said that life is beautiful, Diogenes became annoyed.

Summary of Case Uses Learned Thus Far

Nominative	Genitive	Dative	Accusative
Subject	Genitive of Possession	Dative of Indirect Object	Direct Object
Predicate Nominative	Objective Genitive		
	Partitive Genitive	Dative of Respect	Accusative of Duration of Time
	Genitive of Time within Which	Dative of Time When	
	Genitive of Agent (with ὑπό)		
	Genitive Absolute		

Vocabulary

δόλος, –ου, ὁ = craft; treachery

▸ Ἑλλάς, –άδος, ἡ = Greece

πρόσωπον, –ου, τό = face

▸ σοφιστής, –οῦ, ὁ = sophist

τόπος, –ου, ὁ = place

εἶτα (adv.) = then, next

ἐπεί (sometimes spelled ἐπειδὴ) (adv.) = when, since, after

ἁμαρτάνω, ἁμαρτήσομαι, ἥμαρτον, [   ], [   ], ἡμαρτήθην = to err; sin

ἀναγκάζω, ἀναγκάσω, ἠνάγκασα, [   ], [   ], ἠναγκάσθην = to force, compel; often has a complementary infinitive

λανθάνω, λήσω, ἔλαθον, [   ], [   ], ἐλήσθην = to escape someone's notice; to forget (+ gen.)

παύω, παύσω, ἔπαυσα, [   ], [   ], ἐπαύθην = to stop; (middle) to stop/cease (+ part.)

πορεύω, πορεύσω, ἐπόρευσα, [   ], [   ], ἐπορεύθην = to carry; (middle/passive) to go, walk

τρέφω, θρέψω, ἔθρεψα, [   ], [   ], ἐτράφην = to nourish; rear

τυγχάνω, τεύξομαι, ἔτυχον, [   ] = to occur, to happen to (+ dat.); to happen to (+ part.) chance upon, obtain (+ gen.)

Sentences

1. εἰ δὲ τυγχάνεις κακὸς ὤν, ἡ κακία σε βλάπτει καὶ οὐχ ἡ φυγή. (Musonius, in Stobaeus, *Anthology*)

❡ This sentence is taken from a passage about exile. Notice Musonius's stoicism on the indifference of externals.

κακία, –ας, ἡ = badness

φυγή, –ῆς, ἡ = exile

2. ὁ σοφιστὴς τυγχάνει ὢν ἔμπορος ἢ κάπηλος τῶν ἀγωγίμων ὑφ' ὧν ψυχὴ
τρέφεται; (Plato, *Protagoras*)

❡ ἔμπορος, –ου, ὁ = merchant

κάπηλος, –ου, ὁ = a huckster, dealer

ἀγώγιμον, –ου, τό = portable wares, provisions

ὑφ' ὧν = ὑπὸ ὧν

3. οὐδεὶς ποιῶν πονηρὰ λανθάνει θεόν. (Menander, *Fragments*)

❡ οὐδεὶς = no one: masculine nominative singular. See chapter 22.

4. εἶδεν ὁ Ἰησοῦς τὸν Ναθαναὴλ ἐρχόμενον πρὸς αὐτὸν καὶ λέγει περὶ αὐτοῦ,
"Ἴδε ἀληθῶς Ἰσραηλίτης ἐν ᾧ δόλος οὐκ ἔστιν." (John 1:47)

❡ εἶδεν: aorist of ὁράω

Ναθαναὴλ (indeclinable), ὁ = Nathaniel

Ἴδε: aorist imperative of ὁράω

Ἰσραηλίτης, –ου, ὁ = Israelite

5. αὐτοὶ δ' ἁμαρτάνοντες οὐ γιγνώσκομεν. (Euripides, *Fragments*)

❡ Remember that in indirect statement, if the subject of the indirect statement is the same as the verb that introduces the indirect statement, the nominative is used instead of the accusative for any of the subject's modifiers. See Chapter 11.

6. λέγουσι ὅτι τῆς μητρὸς ἀναγκαζούσης αὐτὸν γῆμαι ἔλεγεν, "οὐδέπω καιρός."
εἶτα, ἐπειδὴ παρήβησεν, ἔλεγεν, "οὐκέτι καιρός." (Thales, in Diogenes Laertius,
Lives of Eminent Philosophers)

❡ Diogenes Laertius recounts this story about the philosopher Thales. λέγουσι "they say" is used when a story is told without a source being named.

ἔλεγεν: the subject is Thales

γῆμαι = to marry: aorist infinitive of a contract verb (chapter 24), complementary to ἀναγκάζω

οὐδέπω (adv.) = not yet

παρήβησεν: 3rd person aorist singular of παρηβάω = to be elderly; past one's prime

7. γενομένης δὲ ἡμέρας ἐξελθὼν ἐπορεύθη εἰς ἔρημον τόπον. (Luke 4:42)

> ¶ The subject of the sentence is Jesus.
>
> ἐξελθών: aorist participle of ἐξέρχομαι = to depart
>
> ἐπορεύθη: aorist passive of πορεύω
>
> ▶ ἔρημος, –ον (adj.) = deserted, solitary

8. ἐμφόβων δὲ γενομένων αὐτῶν καὶ κλινουσῶν τὰ πρόσωπα εἰς τὴν γῆν εἶπαν πρὸς αὐτάς, "Τί ζητεῖτε τὸν ζῶντα μετὰ τῶν νεκρῶν;" (Luke 24:5)

> ¶ This sentence is taken from the end of Luke's gospel. The subject of the genitive absolute is the women who came to the tomb of Jesus. The subject of εἶπαν is the angels (two men with radiant clothing) at the tomb.
>
> ἔμφοβος, –ον (adj.) = fearful
>
> κλίνω = to bend
>
> εἶπαν: Koine for εἶπον, 3rd person plural aorist active of λέγω.
>
> αὐτάς: the women who had come to the tomb
>
> Τί = why
>
> ζητεῖτε: 2nd person plural present of the contract verb ζητέω = to seek
>
> ζῶντα: accusative masculine singular present participle (here a substantive adjective) of the contract verb ζάω = to live

9. καὶ ὑστερήσαντος οἴνου λέγει ἡ μήτηρ τοῦ Ἰησοῦ πρὸς αὐτόν, "Οἶνον οὐκ ἔχουσιν." (John 2:3)

> ¶ This sentence is taken from the Wedding at Cana. The οἶνος is the wine that was being served at the wedding.
>
> ὑστερήσαντος: aorist active participle of the contract verb ὑστερέω = to lag behind; to be wanting

10. ὁ βάρβαρος τῷ μεγάλῳ στόλῳ ἐπὶ τὴν Ἑλλάδα δουλωσόμενος ἦλθεν.

(*Thucydides, History of the Peloponnesian War*)

¶ ▶ βάρβαρος, –ου, ὁ = barbarian; foreigner: Thucydides is here referring to the second Persian War of 480 B.C.E.

τῷ μεγάλῳ στόλῳ = with a great expedition: a dative of means, a construction you will learn in chapter 24.

στόλος, –ου, ὁ = expedition

δουλωσόμενος: future middle participle of the contract verb δουλόω = to enslave; (middle) to enslave to oneself.

ἦλθεν: aorist of ἔρχομαι

Etymology and Discussion Topics

Ἑλλάς, –άδος, ἡ = Greece

It might come as a surprise to learn that the Greeks did not refer to themselves as "Greek." The Romans called the Greeks Graeci. They referred to themselves as Ἕλληνες and Greece as Ἑλλάς, named for the mythical hero Hellen, the son of Deucalion. Although the term originally referred to a specific region in ancient Thessaly, in time it came to be used for all Greek-speaking peoples.

σοφιστής, –οῦ, ὁ = sophist

The word *sophist*, formed from the same root at σοφός and σοφία, did not originally have a negative connotation. The seven sages of the ancient world, along with other respected wise men, were called sophists. The word later became specifically attached to those late 5th century B.C.E. men who taught rhetoric and other subjects for a fee. Plato and others viewed such men with suspicion and are largely responsible for the term being one of reproach.

ἔρημος, –ον (adj.) = deserted, solitary

This adjective means "deserted" or "solitary." English usually translates this word, and the noun ἐρημία, as "desert." One need not, however, imagine the Greek word as a dry and arid place. Our word *desert* comes from the Latin *desertus*, which means "abandoned." The important aspect of ἔρημος is its solitude, not an abundance of sand or other things we often associate with a desert.

βάρβαρος, –ου, ὁ = barbarian; foreigner

A "barbarian" was someone who did not speak Greek. It was often used to describe the Persians specifically, and thus it became a pejorative word after the two Persian wars. It was not, however, always used derisively; sometimes it was used without prejudice to simply refer to a foreigner.

Chapter 22 ⌒

Numbers • Result Clauses

Numbers

Numbers in Greek are usually treated as adjectives, as they are in English. The good news for beginning students is that most numbers are indeclinable. The numbers 1–4 are declinable and agree with their noun in gender, number, and case. For obvious reasons there is no plural for the adjective "one" and no singular for "two," "three," and "four."

	One			Two	Three		Four	
	m	*f*	*n*	*m/f/n*	*m/f*	*n*	*m/f*	*n*
Nom.	εἷς	μία	ἕν	δύο	τρεῖς	τρία	τέτταρες	τέτταρα
Gen.	ἑνός	μιᾶς	ἑνός	δυοῖν	τριῶν	τριῶν	τεττάρων	τεττάρων
Dat.	ἑνί	μιᾷ	ἑνί	δυοῖν	τρισί(ν)	τρισί(ν)	τέτταρσι(ν)	τέτταρσι(ν)
Acc.	ἕνα	μίαν	ἕν	δύο	τρεῖς	τρία	τέτταρας	τέτταρα

At this point, memorizing "one" and "three" should be easier, as the masculine and neuter endings resemble 3rd declension endings and the feminine μία has the endings of χαρά. The odd looking endings of δύο are not just another set of endings that Greek designed to perplex beginning students. They are in fact a modified version of the other number you were told about in chapter 2, the dual. For the dual endings, see appendix D. Cardinal numbers, like those listed above, count. Ordinal numbers (first, second, third) order. Ordinal numbers follow the endings of adjectives of the 1st and 2nd declension, e.g., πρῶτος, –η, –ον "first," δεύτερος, –α, –ον "second." For a list of the most common numbers, see appendix A. The only ones that you need to know are 1–3. The rest of the numbers can be looked up as you come across them in your readings.

No One, Nothing

οὐδείς, οὐδεμία, οὐδέν (adj.) = no one, nothing

This very common substantive adjective is a combination of οὐδ(ε) + the endings for "one," thus literally "no one." The masculine is used for people (the feminine forms are rare) and the neuter for things, "no one" and "nothing" respectively. The plural is extremely rare. The neuter οὐδέν is often used adverbially "not at all." As you learned in chapter 3, Greek uses the negative οὐ with the indicative mood (and a few other constructions) and μή with the other moods. Whenever μή would be appropriate, simply replace οὐ with μή, e.g., μηδείς, μηδέν for οὐδείς, οὐδέν.

	οὐδείς, οὐδεμία, οὐδέν (adj.) = no one, nothing		
	m	*f*	*n*
Nom.	οὐδ–είς	οὐδε–μία	οὐδ–έν
Gen.	οὐδ–ενός	οὐδε–μιᾶς	οὐδ–ενός
Dat.	οὐδ–ενί	οὐδε–μιᾷ	οὐδ–ενί
Acc.	οὐδ–ένα	οὐδε–μίαν	οὐδ–έν

Result Clauses

A result clause states that something happened as a result of the action in the main verb.

The professor talked for so long that the audience fell asleep.

In this sentence the result clause is "that the audience fell asleep." The fact that the audience fell asleep is the *result* of the long talk of the professor. In English, we introduce result clauses by "that," "so that," or sometimes "with the result that." In Greek, result clauses are introduced by ὥστε. However, Greek has two result clauses, actual and natural.

Actual Result Clause

The actual result clause most closely resembles an English result clause and consists of ὥστε + a verb in the indicative.

¶ φεύγω, φεύξομαι, ἔφυγον, [   ], —, — = to flee

ὁ Σωκράτης οὕτως ἀληθῶς εἶπεν ὥστε βαρὺς ἦν τοῖς πολλοῖς.

Socrates spoke so truthfully that he was tiresome to many.

ὁ Σωκράτης ἦν οὕτω δίκαιος ὥστε οὐκ ἔφυγε τὸν θάνατον.

Socrates was so just that he did not flee death.

All result clauses are dependent clauses and can never be sentences on their own. If you encounter a result clause (if you see ὥστε a result clause will most likely follow), the main verb of the sentence cannot be a part of the result clause.

Natural Result Clause

In contrast to an actual result clause, which states that such and such result *actually* followed from the main verb, Greek has another type of result clause which states that such and such would *naturally* follow from the main verb.

A natural result clause consists of ὥστε + an infinitive.

¶ ἐκπλήττω, ἐκπλήξω, ἐξέπληξα = to amaze

τὸ παιδίον ἔχει τὴν σοφίαν ὥστε ἐκπλῆξαι τοὺς φιλοσόφους.

The child has wisdom so as to amaze the philosophers.

In natural result clauses, the tense of the infinite expresses *aspect*, not time, which is why the aorist infinitive is used above. If the subject of the natural result clause is the same as the subject of the main verb, as in this sentence, the subject of the infinitive does not need to be repeated in the natural result clause. If the subject of the natural result clause is different from the subject of the verb that introduced the natural result clause, it is put into the accusative.

¶ θαυμάζω = to marvel, be amazed

τὸ παιδίον ἔχει τὴν σοφίαν ὥστε τοὺς φιλοσόφους θαυμάσαι.

The child has wisdom so as to make the philosophers marvel.

As you can see, it is often difficult to translate natural result clauses the same way every time. The important distinction is that while an actual result clause says that a particular result actually happened, a natural result clause does not stress that it did happen, only that it would naturally follow from that action. For this reason you will most often see actual result clauses introduced by a verb in the past tense. That being said, you will often find, especially in the New Testament, ὥστε + infinitive used where the event being described actually happened. Context will tell you whether the action expressed by the infinitive actually happened or was only probable. Finally, you will often see ὥστε begin a sentence. In such cases ὥστε can usually be translated as "therefore" or "and so," and it will signify that what follows is a result of what was stated in the previous sentence.

Since actual result clauses take the indicative, the negative, if it is used, is οὐ. Since natural result clauses take the infinitive, the negative, if used, is μή.

Vocabulary

βάπτισμα, –ατος, τό = baptism

▶ ἐπιστήμη, –ης, ἡ = knowledge

σάρξ, σαρκός, ἡ = flesh

δύο, δυοῖν (adj.) = two

εἷς, μία, ἕν (adj.) = one

▶ ἔσχατος, –η, –ον (adj.) = furthest, last

οὐδείς, οὐδεμία, οὐδέν (adj.) = no one, nothing

πρῶτος, –η, –ον (adj.) = first

τοσοῦτος, τοσαύτη, τοσοῦτο (adj.) = so much, thus much

τρεῖς, τρία (adj.) = three

καθώς (adv.) = just as

ὥστε (conj.) = so that, so as; therefore

ἐπίσταμαι, ἐπιστήσομαι, —, —, —, ἠπιστήθην = to understand, know; know how to (+inf.)

▶ χορτάζω, χορτάσω, ἐχόρτασα, —, [   ], ἐχορτάσθην = to feed, feed until full

χωρίζω, χωρίσω, ἐχώρισα, —, [   ], ἐχωρίσθην = to divide, separate

Sentences

1. οὐδεὶς τὸ μέλλον ἀσφαλῶς ἐπίσταται. (Menander, *Fragments*)

> ¶ ἀσφαλῶς (adv.) = with certainty
>
> τὸ μέλλον = the future: literally "the about to be," a substantive attributive participle from μέλλω = to be about to

2. ὁ Σωκράτης ἔλεγε καὶ ἓν μόνον ἀγαθὸν εἶναι, τὴν ἐπιστήμην, καὶ ἓν μόνον κακόν, τὴν ἀμαθίαν. (Diogenes Laertius, *Lives of Eminent Philosophers*)

> ¶ καὶ … καί = both … and
>
> ἀμαθία, –ας, ἡ = ignorance

3. ἐρωτηθεὶς τί ἐστι φίλος ὁ Ἀριστοτέλης ἔφη, "μία ψυχὴ δύο σώμασιν ἐνοικοῦσα." (Diogenes Laertius, *Lives of Eminent Philosophers*)

> ¶ ἐρωτηθεὶς: aorist passive participle of the contract verb ἐρωτάω = to ask
>
> τί = what
>
> φίλος: the noun, not the adjective, hence τί ἐστι φίλος = what is a friend?
>
> Ἀριστοτέλης, –ους, ὁ = Aristotle
>
> δύο: the undeclined δύο is used here for the dative δυοῖν.
>
> ἐνοικέω = to inhabit, dwell in (+ dat.)

4. οὕτως γὰρ ἠγάπησεν ὁ θεὸς τὸν κόσμον, ὥστε τὸν υἱὸν τὸν μονογενῆ ἔδωκεν. (John 3:16)

> ¶ ἀγαπάω, ἀγαπήσω, ἠγάπησα = to love
>
> μονογενής, –ές (adj.) = only-begotten
>
> ἔδωκεν = gave: 3rd person singular aorist of δίδωμι, a μι verb you will learn in chapter 30.

5. καὶ ἰδοὺ εἰσὶν ἔσχατοι οἳ ἔσονται πρῶτοι, καὶ εἰσὶν πρῶτοι οἳ ἔσονται ἔσχατοι. (Luke 13:30)

> ¶ ἰδοὺ: aorist of ὁράω

6. τέλος δὲ οἱ Στοϊκοί φασιν εἶναι τὸ εὐδαιμονεῖν, οὗ ἕνεκα πάντα πράττεται,
   αὐτὸ δὲ πράττεται οὐδενὸς ἕνεκα. (Stobaeus, *Anthology*)

> ¶ ▸ Στωϊκός, –ή, –όν (adj.) = Stoic;
> οἱ Στοϊκοί = "The Stoics"
>
> φασιν: 3rd plural of φημί
>
> εὐδαιμονέω = to be happy

7. εἷς ἄρτος, ἓν σῶμα οἱ πολλοί ἐσμεν, οἱ γὰρ πάντες ἐκ τοῦ ἑνὸς ἄρτου
   μετέχομεν. (1 Cor 10:17)

> ¶ μετέχω = to partake of, share in
> (+ gen.)

8. καὶ λέγουσιν αὐτῷ οἱ μαθηταί, "Πόθεν ἡμῖν ἐν ἐρημίᾳ ἄρτοι τοσοῦτοι ὥστε
   χορτάσαι ὄχλον τοσοῦτον;" (Matthew 15:33)

> ¶ αὐτῷ: Jesus
>
> πόθεν (adv.) = from where?
>
> ἐρημία, –ας, ἡ = desert, wilderness
>
> ὄχλος, –ου, ὁ = crowd

9. καταλείψει ἄνθρωπος τὸν πατέρα καὶ τὴν μητέρα καὶ κολληθήσεται τῇ
   γυναικὶ αὐτοῦ, καὶ ἔσονται οἱ δύο εἰς σάρκα μίαν. ὥστε οὐκέτι εἰσὶν δύο ἀλλὰ
   σὰρξ μία. ὃ οὖν ὁ θεὸς συνέζευξεν ἄνθρωπος μὴ χωριζέτω. (Matthew 19:5–6)

> ¶ καταλείπω, καταλείψω = to leave
> behind
>
> κολληθήσεται: future passive of
> κολλάω = to fasten together, unite
> with (+dat.)
>
> συνέζευξεν: aorist of συζεύγνυμι
> = to join together: a μι verb (see
> chapter 30).

10. καὶ ἰδοὺ σεισμὸς μέγας ἐγένετο ἐν τῇ θαλάσσῃ, ὥστε τὸ πλοῖον καλύπτεσθαι
    ὑπὸ τῶν κυμάτων· αὐτὸς δὲ ἐκάθευδεν. (Matthew 8:24)

> ¶ ἰδού = behold
>
> σεισμός, –οῦ, ὁ = a shaking, quake
>
> ἐγένετο: 2nd aorist of γίγνομαι
>
> θαλάσσῃ = θαλάττῃ
>
> πλοῖον, –ου, τό = boat
>
> καλύπτω = to cover
>
> κῦμα, –ατος, τό = a wave
>
> αὐτὸς: i.e., Jesus
>
> ἐκάθευδεν: imperfect of καθεύδω
> = to sleep

Etymology and Discussion Topics

ἐπιστήμη, –ης, ἡ = knowledge

Plato contrasts ἐπιστήμη "knowledge" with δόξα, in the sense of "opinion." The important philosophical branch of epistemology concerns human knowledge. The word ἐπιστήμη is a combination of the preposition ἐπί "upon," and the μι verb ἵστημι "to stand." ἐπιστήμη thus denotes something that one can firmly stand or rest upon, the foundation upon which something can be safely built.

ἔσχατος, –η, –ον (adj.) = furthest, last

From this word comes the theological word "eschatology," which studies the end times.

χορτάζω, χορτάσω, ἐχόρτασα, —, —, ἐχορτάσθην = to feed, feed until full

In many parts of the developed world, we take it for granted that "to eat" means "to eat until full." For most of human history, and in many parts of the world today, that is simply not the case. The verb χορτάζω was used in reference to livestock in the sense of "to fatten," where a farmer would feed an animal in order that they be large enough to provide suitable meat when slaughtered. When χορτάζω is used for humans, it has the sense of being full, or satisfied. While ἐσθίω means merely to eat, χορτάζω implies satisfaction and lack of want. An appreciation of the difference between ἐσθίω and χορτάζω gives insight into New Testament passages such as #8 and the sermon on the mount (Matthew 5:6).

Στωϊκός, –ή, –όν (adj.) = Stoic

Stoicism was a philosophical school founded by Zeno of Citium in the early part of the 3rd century B.C.E. The name "Stoicism" comes from the word στοά, –ᾶς, ἡ = a colonnade, i.e., a roofed building with pillars. Zeno taught in a particular building in the Athenian agora called the ποικιλὴ στοά "the painted colonnade." Zeno and his followers were therefore known as Stoics. Our English adjective "stoic" derives its meaning from the ethical doctrine of the Stoics, which regarded outside events as "indifferent" to human happiness.

Chapter 23 ⌁

Degrees of Adjectives: Positive, Comparative, Superlative • Comparative and Superlative Adverbs • Genitive of Comparison • Dative of Degree of Difference

Degrees of Adjectives: Positive, Comparative, Superlative

Adjectives have three degrees. Although you might not have heard any of these terms, you are probably already familiar with the underlying concepts.

The *positive* degree is the normal translation of your adjective, e.g., "short," "long," "easy," "difficult," "wise," "foolish." All the adjectives you have learned thus far have been in the positive degree.

The *comparative* degree states that the modified noun has more of the quality specified by the adjective compared to something else, e.g., "short-er," "longer," "easier," "more difficult," "wiser," "more foolish." In English, we typically form the comparative by adding "–er" to one syllable adjectives and "more + adjective" for polysyllabic adjectives, but there are exceptions, especially with two-syllable adjectives.

The *superlative* degree states that the modified noun has the most of the quality of the adjective, e.g., "shortest," "longest," "easiest," "most difficult," "wisest," "most foolish." Likewise, we typically form the superlative by adding "–est" to one syllable adjectives and "most + adjective" for polysyllabic adjectives.

You have already been learning the Greek positive degree of adjectives. The comparative degree is formed with the endings –τερος, –α, –ον and the superlative adjective with the endings –τατος, –η, –ον. See chapter 3 for a refresher on why the feminine singular of –τερα has the alpha and the feminine singular of –τατη has the eta.

Formation of the Comparative Adjective

The comparative of most adjectives consists of the stem + ο/ω + –τερος, –α, –ον. There is a reason why some adjectives have omicron and some omega before the endings, but it is not necessary to memorize it.[1] Likewise, some 3rd declension adjectives do not include a thematic vowel before the endings. However, this will not cause you any problems because the stem and the distinctive –τερος, –α, –ον endings enable you to identify the forms. Below is the comparative for the adjective σοφός, –ή, –όν "wise."

	σοφώτερος, –τερα, –τερον = wiser		
	m	*f*	*n*
Singular			
Nom.	σοφώ–τερος	σοφω–τέρα	σοφώ–τερον
Gen.	σοφω–τέρου	σοφω–τέρας	σοφω–τέρου
Dat.	σοφω–τέρῳ	σοφω–τέρᾳ	σοφω–τέρῳ
Acc.	σοφώ–τερον	σοφω–τέραν	σοφώ–τερον
(Vocative)	(σοφώτερε)	(σοφωτέρα)	(σοφώτερον)
Plural			
Nom.	σοφώ–τεροι	σοφώ–τεραι	σοφώ–τερα
Gen.	σοφω–τέρων	σοφω–τέρων	σοφω–τέρων
Dat.	σοφω–τέροις	σοφω–τέραις	σοφω–τέροις
Acc.	σοφω–τέρους	σοφω–τέρας	σοφώ–τερα

Irregular Comparatives

In English, many of our most common adjectives form their comparatives not only with different endings, but with different stems. The comparative of "good" is not "gooder," but "better." The comparative of "bad" is not "badder," but "worse." Likewise, in Greek many common adjectives have irregular comparatives. Some adjectives, including your model adjective καλός, –ή, –όν, don't use the –τερος endings. Rather, they form their comparative in the following manner.

---

1. If the last syllable of the stem is long (see appendix C on long and short syllables), the thematic vowel is an omicron. If it is short, the thematic vowel is an omega.

	καλλίων, –ιον = *more beautiful*	
	m/f	*n*
Singular		
Nom.	καλλ–ίων	κάλλ–ιον
Gen.	καλλ–ίονος	καλλ–ίονος
Dat.	καλλ–ίονι	καλλ–ίονι
Acc.	καλλ–ίονα (καλλ–ίω)	κάλλ–ιον
(Vocative)	(κάλλιον)	(κάλλιον)
Plural		
Nom.	καλλ–ίονες	καλλ–ίονα (καλλ–ίω)
Gen.	καλλ–ιόνων	καλλ–ιόνων
Dat.	καλλ–ίοσι(ν)	καλλ–ίοσι(ν)
Acc.	καλλ–ίονας	καλλ–ίονα (καλλ–ίω)

You will notice that the masculine and feminine accusative singular has an alternate form. This is actually a contraction (the ν drops out and the o + α = ω) and is quite common. The good news is that if you have memorized your model 3rd declension adjective εὐδαίμων, forming this comparative is easy. Simply add an iota before the endings of εὐδαίμων.

Don't worry, your vocabulary will tell you the positive degree of these irregulars. The good news is that their endings are either like καλλίων, –ιον, or sometimes the iota drops out and the endings are like εὐδαίμων.

Finally, there is one more way to form the comparative. Just like our English "more + adjective," Greek can add μᾶλλον "more" + the positive degree of the adjective. All attributive participles and some adjectives can be joined with μᾶλλον to form the comparative.

Formation of the Superlative Adjective

To form the superlative, instead of the endings –τερος, –τερα, –τερον, add the endings –τατος, –τατη, –τατον.

σοφώτατος, –τατη, –τατον = wisest

	m	f	n
Singular			
Nom.	σοφώ–τατος	σοφω–τάτη	σοφώ–τατον
Gen.	σοφω–τάτου	σοφω–τάτης	σοφω–τάτου
Dat.	σοφω–τάτῳ	σοφω–τάτῃ	σοφω–τάτῳ
Acc.	σοφώ–τατον	σοφω–τάτην	σοφώ–τατον
(Vocative)	(σοφώτατε)	(σοφωτάτη)	(σοφώτατον)
Plural			
Nom.	σοφώ–τατοι	σοφώ–ταται	σοφώ–τατα
Gen.	σοφω–τάτων	σοφω–τάτων	σοφω–τάτων
Dat.	σοφω–τάτοις	σοφω–τάταις	σοφω–τάτοις
Acc.	σοφω–τάτους	σοφω–τάτας	σοφώ–τατα

Irregular Superlatives

Those adjectives who form their superlatives with –ίων, –ιον instead of –τερος, –τερα, –τερον form their superlatives not with –τατος, –τατη, –τατον but with –ιστος, –ιστη, –ιστον.

κάλλιστος, –ιστη, –ιστον = most beautiful

	m	f	n
Singular			
Nom.	κάλλ–ιστος	καλλ–ίστη	κάλλ–ιστον
Gen.	καλλ–ίστου	καλλ–ίστης	καλλ–ίστου
Dat.	καλλ–ίστῳ	καλλ–ίστῃ	καλλ–ίστῳ
Acc.	κάλλ–ιστον	καλλ–ίστην	κάλλ–ιστον
(Vocative)	(κάλλιστε)	(καλλίστη)	(κάλλιστον)
Plural			
Nom.	κάλλ–ιστοι	κάλλ–ισται	κάλλ–ιστα
Gen.	καλλ–ίστων	καλλ–ίστων	καλλ–ίστων
Dat.	καλλ–ίστοις	καλλ–ίσταις	καλλ–ίστοις
Acc.	καλλ–ίστους	καλλ–ίστας	κάλλ–ιστα

The endings consist of –ιστ + the endings of your model adjective καλός.

Finally, there is one more way to form the superlative. Just like our English "most + adjective," Greek can add μάλιστα "most" + the positive degree of the adjective. All attributive participles and some adjectives form their superlatives with μάλιστα.

Comparative and Superlative Adverbs

Just as adjectives have positive, comparative, and superlative degrees, so too do adverbs, e.g., "quickly, "more quickly," "most quickly." The comparative adverb is the neuter accusative singular of the corresponding comparative adjective and the superlative adverb is the neuter accusative plural of the corresponding superlative adjective. Once again, you can also use μᾶλλον + adverb to form the comparative adverb and μάλιστα + adverb to form the superlative adverb.

Below are two simplified charts of what has been discussed so far.

	Formation of Adjectives	
	Comparative	*Superlative*
Most adjectives	−τερος, −τερα, −τερον	−τατος, −τατη, −τατον
	(σοφώτερος, −τερα, −τερον)	(σοφώτατος, −τατη, −τατον)
Some adjectives	−ιων, −ιον	−ιστος, −ιστη, −ιστον
	(καλλίων, −ιον)	(κάλλιστος, −ιστη, −ιστον)
Alternate way	μάλλον + adjective	μάλιστα + adjective
	(μάλλον σοφός)	(μάλιστα σοφός)

	Formation of Adverbs		
	Positive	*Comparative*	*Superlative*
Most adverbs	−ως	−τερον	−τατα
	(σοφῶς)	(σοφώτερον)	(σοφώτατα)
Some adverbs	−ως	−ιον	−ιστα
	(καλῶς)	(κάλλιον)	(κάλλιστα)
Alternate way	καλῶς	μᾶλλον + adverb	μάλιστα + adverb
		(μᾶλλον καλῶς)	(μάλιστα καλῶς)

Genitive of Comparison

There are two ways to express comparison in Greek. The easy way is to use the word ἤ "than." When doing so, the second item in the comparison is put into the same case as the thing it is being compared to.

ὁ Ὀδυσσεύς ἐστι σοφώτερος ἢ Πολύφημος.

Odysseus is wiser than Polyphemus.

The other way is to use a genitive *without* ἤ. This is called a genitive of comparison.

ὁ Ὀδυσσεύς ἐστι σοφώτερος Πολυφήμου.

Odysseus is wiser than Polyphemus.

As you can see, your English translation will be the same regardless of whether you see ἤ or a genitive of comparison.

Dative of Degree of Difference

In comparisons with comparatives and superlatives, the dative is used to express the degree to which the comparison is true.

ὁ Σωκράτης ἐστὶ πολλῷ σοφώτατος τῶν Ἑλλήνων.

Socrates is by far (lit. by much) the wisest of the Greeks.

Summary of Case Uses Learned Thus Far

Nominative	Genitive	Dative	Accusative
Subject	Genitive of Possession	Dative of Indirect Object	Direct Object
Predicate Nominative	Objective Genitive	Dative of Respect	Accusative of Duration of Time
	Partitive Genitive	Dative of Time When	
	Genitive of Time within Which	Dative of Degree of Difference	
	Genitive of Agent (with ὑπό)		
	Genitive Absolute		
	Genitive of Comparison		

Vocabulary

διακονία, –ας, ἡ = service

κτῆμα, –ατος, τό = a possession

▶ πάθος, –ους, τό = experience, suffering

συγγνώμη, –ης, ἡ = pardon, forgiveness

τροφή, –ῆς, ἡ = nourishment, food

▶ βελτίων, –ίον (comp. adj. of ἀγαθός) = better

▶ κρείττων, –ον (Koine κρείσσων, –ον) (comp. adj. of ἀγαθός) = stronger

μείζων, –ον (comp. adj. of μέγας) = greater

μάλα (adv.) = very

μάλιστα (supl. adv. of μάλα) = most

μᾶλλον (comp. adv. of μάλα) = more

κράζω, κράξω, ἔκραξα, [   ], —, — = to croak, scream

Sentences

▶ 1. ἀνδρῶν ἁπάντων Σωκράτης σοφώτατος. (Oracle at Delphi, in Diogenes Laertius, *Lives of Eminent Philosophers*)

¶ ἁπάντων = πάντων: ἅπας, ἅπασα, ἅπαν is a strengthened form of πᾶς, but often you must translate it the same.

2. συγγνώμη τιμωρίας κρείσσων. (Pittacus, in Diogenes Laertius, *Lives of Eminent Philosophers*

¶ τιμωρία, –ας, ἡ = vengeance

3. νυνὶ δὲ μένει πίστις, ἐλπίς, ἀγάπη, τὰ τρία ταῦτα· μείζων δὲ τούτων ἡ ἀγάπη. (1 Cor 13:13)

¶ νυνί = now: a strengthened form of νῦν. Paul is referring to the here and now as opposed to the afterlife.

τούτων: best taken as a partitive genitive

4. οὐκ ἔστι σοφίας κτῆμα τιμιώτερον. (Menander, *Fragments*)

> ¶ τίμιος, –α, –ον (adj.) = valuable

5. ἡ γὰρ ψυχὴ πλεῖόν ἐστιν τῆς τροφῆς καὶ τὸ σῶμα τοῦ ἐνδύματος. (Luke 12:23)

> ¶ ψυχὴ: in this context, "life"
>
> πλείων, –ον (comp. of πολύς) = more: one would expect the feminine πλείων here, but the neuter is often used for "more."
>
> ἔνδυμα, –ατος, τό = clothing

6. φιλοσόφου τοῦτο τὸ πάθος, τὸ θαυμάζειν· οὐ γὰρ ἄλλη ἀρχὴ φιλοσοφίας ἢ αὕτη. (Socrates, in Plato, *Theatetus*)

> ¶ This line is spoken by Socrates to Theatetus, who has just admitted to Socrates that his head is spinning from wonder at the complex philosophical concepts they have been discussing.

7. ὑμεῖς δὲ οὐχ οὕτως, ἀλλ᾽ ὁ μείζων ἐν ὑμῖν γινέσθω ὡς ὁ νεώτερος, καὶ ὁ ἡγούμενος ὡς ὁ διακονῶν. (Luke 22:26)

> ¶ γινέσθω: classical γιγνέσθω, from γίγνομαι
>
> νεώτερος: comparative of νέος, –α, –ον
>
> ἡγούμενος, –ου, ὁ = leader
>
> διακονῶν: attributive substantive participle of διακονέω = to serve

8. ὁ δὲ πολλῷ μᾶλλον ἔκραζεν, "Υἱὲ Δαυίδ, ἐλέησόν με." (Mark 10:48)

> ¶ ὁ = Bartimaeus, a blind man
>
> πολλῷ μᾶλλον: he had been told to be quiet after shouting after Jesus the first time.
>
> Δαυίδ = David: an indeclinable noun; the context makes it clear it is genitive.
>
> ἐλεέω, ἐλεήσω, ἠλέησα = to have mercy on, show pity toward: remember that the imperative mood has no augment.

9. βέλτιόν ἐστι τὸ σῶμά γ᾽ ἢ ψυχὴν νοσεῖν. (Menander, *Fragments*)

> ¶ Supply νοσεῖν with σῶμα.
>
> γ᾽ = γε = indeed
>
> νοσέω = to be sick

10. εἰ γὰρ ἡ διακονία τῆς κατακρίσεως δόξα, πολλῷ μᾶλλον περισσεύει ἡ διακονία τῆς δικαιοσύνης δόξῃ. (2 Cor 3:9)

> ¶ κατάκρισις, –εως, ἡ = condemnation
>
> δόξα: although a noun, best translated as an adjective.
>
> περισσεύω = to abound
>
> δόξῃ = in glory

Etymology and Discussion Topics

πάθος, –ους, τό = experience, suffering

This word is often difficult to translate. Its basic meaning is "to suffer." While it very often has the negative connotation of suffering, it also can have the positive sense of "experience." In his play *Agamemnon*, the playwright Aeschylus has his chorus state that through suffering comes understanding. This sentiment is wonderfully expressed in just two words, πάθει μάθος. For the use of the dative to mean "through" see chapter 24 on the dative of means. In addition to experience and sufferings, early Christians used πάθος of temptations.

βελτίων and κρείσσων

The adjective ἀγαθός, –ή, –όν has three comparatives. If "good" in the sense of worth is meant, the comparative is βελτίων "better." If "good" in the sense of ability is meant, the comparative is ἀμείνων "better." If "good" in the sense of strength is meant, the comparative is κρείττων (Koine κρείσσων) "stronger/better."

ἀνδρῶν ἁπάντων Σωκράτης σοφώτατος.

This is the famous response that Socrates claims was the cause of resentment towards him, although Socrates quotes this oracle rather differently at his trial. Socrates states that he was very much perplexed by this oracle as he did not believe he possessed wisdom. He therefore sought someone who was wise, thinking that he could then dismiss this oracle and cease to be perplexed. After inquiring of different people who professed to have wisdom, such as politicians and poets, and finding them lacking, Socrates concludes that he is wise because he at least is aware of his own ignorance.

Chapter 24 ⌐

Introduction to Contract Verbs • Epsilon Contract Verbs •
Liquid Futures • Dative of Means

Introduction to Contract Verbs

In chapter 4 you were introduced to the largest category of verbs: omega verbs, whose model verb is λύω. You were told that there were two other categories of verbs, contract verbs and μι verbs. This chapter will introduce you to contract verbs. You have seen many of them already. Contract verbs are actually omega verbs, but it is easiest to memorize the forms of a few model contract verbs, just like you did with λύω. The good news is that contract verbs differ from omega verbs only in the present and imperfect tenses. They are just like omega verbs in all the other tenses. There are three types of contract verbs: epsilon contract verbs, alpha contract verbs, and omicron contract verbs (some New Testament grammarians will instead use the terms epsilon-omega verbs, alpha-omega verbs, and omicron-omega verbs). This chapter will focus on the first and most common type of contract verb, the epsilon contract verb.

Epsilon Contract Verbs

You can tell if a verb is an epsilon contract verb by the epsilon before the omega in the first principal part.

φιλέω = to love

δοκέω = to seem

ποιέω = to make, do

You have already encountered quite a few contract verbs in the previous chapters when their forms did not differ from omega verbs. Your model epsilon contract verb will be φιλέω.

φιλέω = To Love

φιλέω, φιλήσω, ἐφίλησα, [   ], [   ], ἐφιλήθην = to love

As you can see, the only principal part ending that is different from λύω is the first principal part. For this reason only the present and imperfect tenses will be given below. In the following chart, you will see the forms of your model verb λύω, the uncontracted forms of φιλέω, and the contracted forms. Memorize the forms on the right. λύω and the uncontracted forms are given only so that you can see the contractions. The uncontracted first principal part is given so that you will know it is a contract verb. You will never see φιλέω in a sentence, only φιλῶ. If this is not helpful, ignore the forms on the left and focus only on the contracted forms.

φιλέω = to love

	Present Active Indicative			Present Middle/Passive Indicative		
Singular						
1st	λύ–ω	(φιλέ–ω)	φιλ–ῶ	λύ–ομαι	(φιλέ–ομαι)	φιλ–οῦμαι
2nd	λύ–εις	(φιλέ–εις)	φιλ–εῖς	λύ–ῃ/ει	(φιλέ–ῃ/ει)	φιλ–ῇ/εῖ
3rd	λύ–ει	(φιλέ–ει)	φιλ–εῖ	λύ–εται	(φιλέ–εται)	φιλ–εῖται
Plural						
1st	λύ–ομεν	(φιλέ–ομεν)	φιλ–οῦμεν	λυ–όμεθα	(φιλε–όμεθα)	φιλ–ούμεθα
2nd	λύ–ετε	(φιλέ–ετε)	φιλ–εῖτε	λύ–εσθε	(φιλέ–εσθε)	φιλ–εῖσθε
3rd	λύ–ουσι(ν)	(φιλέ–ουσι(ν))	φιλ–οῦσι(ν)	λύ–ονται	(φιλέ–ονται)	φιλ–οῦνται

φιλέω = to love

	Present Active Infinitive			Present Middle/Passive Infinitive		
	λύ–ειν	(φιλέ–ειν)	**φιλ–εῖν**	λύ–εσθαι	(φιλέ–εσθαι)	**φιλ–εῖσθαι**
	Present Active Imperative			*Present Middle/Passive Imperative*		
Singular						
2nd	λῦ–ε	(φίλε–ε)	**φίλ–ει**	λύ–ου	(φιλέ–ου)	**φιλ–οῦ**
3rd	λυ–έτω	(φιλε–έτω)	**φιλ–είτω**	λυ–έσθω	(φιλε–έσθω)	**φιλ–είσθω**
Plural						
2nd	λύ–ετε	(φιλέ–ετε)	**φιλ–εῖτε**	λύ–εσθε	(φιλέ–εσθε)	**φιλ–εῖσθε**
3rd	λυ–όντων	(φιλε–όντων)	**φιλ–ούντων**	λυ–έσθων	(φιλε–έσθων)	**φιλ–είσθων**
	Imperfect Active Indicative			*Imperfect Middle/Passive Indicative*		
Singular						
1st	ἔλυ–ον	(ἐφίλε–ον)	**ἐφίλ–ουν**	ἐλυ–όμην	(ἐφιλε–όμην)	**ἐφιλ–ούμην**
2nd	ἔλυ–ες	(ἐφίλε–ες)	**ἐφίλ–εις**	ἐλύ–ου	(ἐφιλέ–ου)	**ἐφιλ–οῦ**
3rd	ἔλυ–ε(ν)	(ἐφίλε–ε)	**ἐφίλ–ει**	ἐλύ–ετο	(ἐφιλέ–ετο)	**ἐφιλ–εῖτο**
Plural						
1st	ἐλύ–ομεν	(ἐφιλέ–ομεν)	**ἐφιλ–οῦμεν**	ἐλυ–όμεθα	(ἐφιλε–όμεθα)	**ἐφιλ–ούμεθα**
2nd	ἐλύ–ετε	(ἐφιλέ–ετε)	**ἐφιλ–εῖτε**	ἐλύ–εσθε	(ἐφιλέ–εσθε)	**ἐφιλ–εῖσθε**
3rd	ἔλυ–ον	(ἐφίλε–ον)	**ἐφίλ–ουν**	ἐλύ–οντο	(ἐφιλέ–οντο)	**ἐφιλ–οῦντο**

It is easier to simply memorize the contracted forms, but the following table of contractions might be helpful. Notice how the epsilon is always absorbed by long vowels and diphthongs.

ε contracted	ε absorbed
ε + ε = ει	ε + ου = ου
ε + ο = ου	ε + ω = ω
	ε + η = η

Liquid Futures

There are a few verbs which have what are called "liquid futures," whose stems end in λ, ρ, μ, ω, or ζ. You do not need to memorize these letters, as liquid futures are identifiable by the circumflex on the final letter of the second principal part.

μένω, μενῶ = to remain

βάλλω, βαλῶ = to throw

These "liquid futures" have future forms that look exactly like the present tense of φιλέω above, i.e., βαλῶ, βαλεῖς, βαλεῖ, etc.

Dative of Means

Greek uses the dative to express that *by means of which* something is done.

> ¶ πρεσβυτικός, –ή, –όν (adj.) = old-fashioned | κάλαμος, –ου, ὁ = a reed-pen

ὁ πρεσβυτικὸς διδάσκαλος τῷ καλάμῳ γράφει τὰ γράμματα.

The old-fashioned teacher writes the letters *with a reed-pen*.

Koine/Classical Distinction

In classical Greek, the dative of means does not require a preposition. You will, however, often see the proposition ἐν + dative used in the New Testament and in other Koine Greek texts where classical Greek would use a dative of means without the preposition.

Summary of Case Uses Learned Thus Far

Nominative	*Genitive*	*Dative*	*Accusative*
Subject	Genitive of Possession	Dative of Indirect Object	Direct Object
Predicate Nominative	Objective Genitive	Dative of Respect	Accusative of Duration of Time
	Partitive Genitive	Dative of Time When	
	Genitive of Time within Which	Dative of Degree of Difference	
	Genitive of Agent (with ὑπό)	Dative of Means	
	Genitive Absolute		
	Genitive of Comparison		

Vocabulary

αἷμα, –ατος, τό = blood

ναός, –οῦ, ὁ = temple

στρατιώτης, –ου, ὁ = soldier

ὕδωρ, ὕδατος, τό = water

εὐθύς (adv.) = at once, immediately

αἰτέω, αἰτήσω, ᾔτησα, [   ], [   ], ᾐτήθην = to ask

ἀποκρίνω, ἀποκρινῶ, ἀπέκρινα, —, [   ], ἀπεκρίθην = to set apart; (middle and passive) to answer, respond

▸ βαπτίζω, βαπτίσω, ἐβάπτισα, [   ], [   ], ἐβαπτίσθην = to submerge; to baptize

εὑρίσκω, εὑρήσω, εὗρον, [   ], [   ], εὑρέθην = to find

ζητέω, ζητήσω, ἐζήτησα, [   ], [   ], ἐζητήθην = to seek

▸ μισέω, μισήσω, ἐμίσησα, [   ], [   ], ἐμισήθην = to hate

νοέω, νοήσω, ἐνόησα, [   ], [   ], ἐνοήθην = to think; to know

▸ φιλέω, φιλήσω, ἐφίλησα, [   ], [   ], ἐφιλήθην = to love; see chap. 10 Etymology and Discussion Topics

φρονέω, φρονήσω, ἐφρόνησα, [   ], —, — = to think; to be prudent, wise

Sentences

1. σοφία γάρ ἐστι καὶ μαθεῖν ὃ μὴ νοεῖς. (Menander, *Fragments*)

> ¶ μαθεῖν: aorist infinitive of μανθάνω
>
> καὶ: here adverbial "also"
>
> μὴ: here = οὐ

2. ὁ δὲ Ἰησοῦς κάτω κύψας τῷ δακτύλῳ κατέγραφεν εἰς τὴν γῆν. (John 8:6)

> ¶ κάτω (adv.) = downward
>
> κύψας: aorist participle of κύπτω = to stoop, bend forward
>
> ▸ δάκτυλος, –ου, ὁ = finger
>
> καταγράφω = to inscribe, write down

3. ἰδοὺ γὰρ ἀπὸ τοῦ νῦν μακαριοῦσίν με πᾶσαι αἱ γενεαί. (Luke 1:48)

> ¶ ἰδού = behold
>
> τοῦ νῦν = from now on: literally
> "from the now," the definite
> article is sometimes attached to
> adverbs to make a noun.
>
> μακαρίζω, μακαριῶ = to call
> blessed
>
> γενεά, –ᾶς, ἡ = generation
>
> με: the "me" is Mary. This line
> forms part of her "Magnificat" in
> Luke's gospel.

4. πολλοὶ μὲν εὐτυχοῦσιν, οὐ φρονοῦσι δέ. (Menander, *Fragments*)

> ¶ εὐτυχέω = to be lucky, fortunate

5. ἀνὴρ δὲ χρηστὸς χρηστὸν οὐ μισεῖ ποτε. (Euripides, *Fragments*)

> ¶ ποτε = ever

6. ἀλλ᾽ εἷς τῶν στρατιωτῶν λόγχῃ αὐτοῦ τὴν πλευρὰν ἔνυξεν, καὶ ἐξῆλθεν εὐθὺς αἷμα καὶ ὕδωρ. (John 19:34)

> ¶ λόγχη, –ης, ἡ = spear
>
> αὐτοῦ: Jesus, who has been
> crucified
>
> πλευρά, –ᾶς, ἡ = side
>
> νύσσω, νύξω, ἔνυξα = to pierce
>
> ἐξέρχομαι, ἐξελεύσομαι, ἐξῆλθον =
> to go or come out of

7. ἀπεκρίθη Ἰησοῦς καὶ εἶπεν αὐτοῖς, "Λύσατε τὸν ναὸν τοῦτον καὶ ἐν τρισὶν ἡμέραις ἐγερῶ αὐτόν." (John 2:19)

> ¶ Λύσατε: your model verb λύω
> can also mean "to destroy," in the
> sense that loosening or taking
> something apart can destroy
> something.
>
> τοῦτον: "this" temple is the tem-
> ple in Jerusalem.
>
> ἐγείρω, ἐγερῶ = to raise up

8. κἀγὼ ὑμῖν λέγω, αἰτεῖτε, καὶ δοθήσεται ὑμῖν· ζητεῖτε, καὶ εὑρήσετε· κρούετε, καὶ ἀνοιγήσεται ὑμῖν. (Luke 11:9)

> ¶ κἀγὼ = καὶ ἐγὼ. The speaker is Jesus.
>
> δοθήσεται = will be given: future passive of the μι verb δίδωμι = to give
>
> κρούω = to knock
>
> ἀνοιγήσεται = it will be opened: future passive of ἀνοίγω = to open

9. νὺξ μὲν ἀναπαύει, ἡμέρα δ' ἔργον ποιεῖ. (Menander, *Fragments*)

> ¶ ἀναπαύω = to make to stop or cease

▶ 10. καὶ ἐκήρυσσεν λέγων, "Ἔρχεται ὁ ἰσχυρότερός μου ὀπίσω μου, οὗ οὐκ εἰμὶ ἱκανὸς κύψας λῦσαι τὸν ἱμάντα τῶν ὑποδημάτων αὐτοῦ· ἐγὼ ἐβάπτισα ὑμᾶς ὕδατι, αὐτὸς δὲ βαπτίσει ὑμᾶς ἐν πνεύματι ἁγίῳ." (Mark 1:7–8)

> ¶ The speaker is John the Baptist.
>
> κηρύσσω = to proclaim, preach
>
> ἰσχυρός, –ά, –όν = strong
>
> ὀπίσω (adv.) = back; after (+gen.)
>
> ἱκανός, –ή, –όν (adj.) = sufficient; worthy (+ inf.)
>
> κύπτω = to stoop, bend forward
>
> ἱμάς, –άντος, ὁ = strap
>
> ὑπόδημα, –ατος, τό = sandal

Etymology and Discussion Topics

φιλέω and μισέω

English has numerous compounds formed from these antonyms. A philanthropist loves ἄνθρωποι, while a misanthrope hates them. Misogyny is a hatred of γυνή, while misandry is a hatred of ἀνήρ.

βαπτίζω, βαπτίσω, ἐβάπτισα, [   ], [   ], ἐβαπτίσθην = to submerge in water; to baptize

This word means literally "to dip or submerge." As they did for many words in Christianity, the Romans decided against using a Latin word to translate this verb and simply transliterated it instead.

δάκτυλος, –ου, ὁ = finger

This word meant "finger," and the dinosaur pterodactyl is so called because it is thought to have had winged (πτέρυξ) fingers. This word was also used to signify a metrical foot consisting of one long and two short syllables. The dactylic hexameter, the epic meter of the *Iliad* and *Odyssey*, thus consists of six (ἕξ) dactyls.

ἐκήρυσσεν λέγων

Greek is very fond of using a circumstantial participle where English would prefer to use two finite verbs. Instead of saying "The professor saw that there was no coffee and began to lament," Greek would say, "The professor, having seen that there was no coffee, lamented." Instead of saying "he was preaching and saying," the New Testament in particular prefers "ἐκήρυσσεν λέγων." Although it can sound awkward in your translations, try translating it literally until you become comfortable with this construction, at which time you can translate the participle as a finite verb if you wish.

Chapter 25 ⟨⟩

Alpha Contract Verbs • Interrogative Pronouns •
Indefinite Pronouns

Alpha Contract Verbs

You can tell if a verb is an alpha contract verb by the alpha before the omega in the first principal part. For example:

νικάω = to conquer, win

τιμάω = to honor

ἀγαπάω = to love

νικάω = To Conquer

Your model alpha contract verb will be νικάω.

νικάω, νικήσω, ἐνίκησα, [   ], [   ], ἐνικήθην = to conquer, win

Like all contract verbs, νικάω differs from the endings of λύω only in the present and imperfect tenses.

νικάω = to conquer, win

	Present Active Indicative			*Present Middle/Passive Indicative*		
Singular						
1st	λύ–ω	(νικά–ω)	νικ–ῶ	λύ–ομαι	(νικά–ομαι)	νικ–ῶμαι
2nd	λύ–εις	(νικά–εις)	νικ–ᾷς	λύ–η/ει	(νικά–η/ει)	νικ–ᾷ
3rd	λύ–ει	(νικά–ει)	νικ–ᾷ	λύ–εται	(νικά–εται)	νικ–ᾶται
Plural						
1st	λύ–ομεν	(νικά–ομεν)	νικ–ῶμεν	λυ–όμεθα	(νικα–όμεθα)	νικ–ώμεθα
2nd	λύ–ετε	(νικά–ετε)	νικ–ᾶτε	λύ–εσθε	(νικά–εσθε)	νικ–ᾶσθε
3rd	λύ–ουσι(ν)	(νικά–ουσι(ν))	νικ–ῶσι(ν)	λύ–ονται	(νικά–ονται)	νικ–ῶνται

	Present Active Infinitive			*Present Middle/Passive Infinitive*		
	λύ–ειν	(νικά–ειν)	νικ–ᾶν	λύ–εσθαι	(νικά–εσθαι)	νικ–ᾶσθαι

	Present Active Imperative			*Present Middle/Passive Imperative*		
Singular						
2nd	λῦ–ε	(νίκα–ε)	νίκ–α	λύ–ου	(νικά–ου)	νικ–ῶ
3rd	λυ–έτω	(νικα–έτω)	νικ–άτω	λυ–έσθω	(νικα–έσθω)	νικ–άσθω
Plural						
2nd	λύ–ετε	(νικά–ετε)	νικ–ᾶτε	λύ–εσθε	(νικά–εσθε)	νικ–ᾶσθε
3rd	λυ–όντων	(νικα–όντων)	νικ–ώντων	λυ–έσθων	(νικα–έσθων)	νικ–άσθων

	Imperfect Active Indicative			*Imperfect Middle/Passive Indicative*		
Singular						
1st	ἔλυ–ον	(ἐνίκα–ον)	ἐνίκ–ων	ἐλυ–όμην	(ἐνικα–όμην)	ἐνικ–ώμην
2nd	ἔλυ–ες	(ἐνίκα–ες)	ἐνίκ–ας	ἐλύ–ου	(ἐνικά–ου)	ἐνικ–ῶ
3rd	ἔλυ–ε(ν)	(ἐνίκα–ε)	ἐνίκ–α	ἐλύ–ετο	(ἐνικά–ετο)	ἐνικ–ᾶτο
Plural						
1st	ἐλύ–ομεν	(ἐνίκά–ομεν)	ἐνικ–ῶμεν	ἐλυ–όμεθα	(ἐνικα–όμεθα)	ἐνικ–ώμεθα
2nd	ἐλύ–ετε	(ἐνίκά–ετε)	ἐνικ–ᾶτε	ἐλύ–εσθε	(ἐνικά–εσθε)	ἐνικ–ᾶσθε
3rd	ἔλυ–ον	(ἐνίκα–ον)	ἐνίκ–ων	ἐλύ–οντο	(ἐνικά–οντο)	ἐνικ–ῶντο

Once again, it is easier to simply memorize the contracted forms, but the following table of contractions might be helpful. Notice how the alpha usually dominates the epsilon/eta sounds, but becomes omega when it meets omicron/omega sounds.

ε/η sounds	o/ω sounds
α + ε = α	α + ου = ω
α + ει = ᾳ	α + ω = ω
α + η = ᾳ	α + ο = ω

One oddball alpha contract verb is **ζάω = to live**. It is technically an alpha contract verb, but it has an eta everywhere νικάω has an alpha, e.g., ζῇ instead of ζᾷ, ζῆν instead of ζᾶν.

Interrogative Pronouns

As its name implies, the interrogative pronoun "who," "what" is used to ask questions. A question can be either *direct*, "What are you reading?" or *indirect*, "I know what you are reading."

	τίς, τί (interrogative pronoun) = who, what	
	m/f	n
Singular		
Nom.	τίς	τί
Gen.	τίνος (τοῦ)	τίνος (τοῦ)
Dat.	τίνι (τῷ)	τίνι (τῷ)
Acc.	τίνα	τί
Plural		
Nom.	τίνες	τίνα
Gen.	τίνων	τίνων
Dat.	τίσι(ν)	τίσι(ν)
Acc.	τίνας	τίνα

The alternate forms for the genitive and dative singular look exactly like the definite article, but they will not cause you too much confusion. If it is next to a noun, it is most likely the definite article. Since the definite article is so common, always assume τοῦ and τῷ are definite articles; only when they do not make sense should you try and translate them as interrogatives.

τί θέλεις;

What do you want?

τίνες λέγουσιν;

Who is speaking?

In addition to being a pronoun, the interrogative can also function as an adjective and modify nouns in gender, number, and case.

τί βιβλίον γράφεις;

What book are you writing?

Finally, τί is also an adverb meaning "why" in questions. Context will allow you to distinguish this adverbial usage from the interrogative pronoun.

τί ὑπάγετε;

Why are you leaving?

Indefinite Pronouns

The indefinite pronoun "someone," "something" is quite common in Greek. With the exception of the alternate neuter nominative and accusative plural forms, *the forms of the indefinite are exactly the same as the interrogative pronoun;* the only way you can tell the difference is to look at the accent. Generally speaking, the interrogative pronoun will always have the accent on its first syllable; the indefinite will either have an accent on the last syllable (the ultima) or none at all since they are enclitics (see appendix C).

	τις, τι *(indefinite pronoun)* = *a certain, some*	
	m/f	*n*
Singular		
Nom.	τις	τι
Gen.	τινός (του)	τινός (του)
Dat.	τινί (τῳ)	τινί (τῳ)
Acc.	τινά	τι
Plural		
Nom.	τινές	τινά (ἄττα)
Gen.	τινῶν	τινῶν
Dat.	τισί(ν)	τισί(ν)
Acc.	τινάς	τινά (ἄττα)

Just like the interrogative, the indefinite can also act as an adjective when it modifies a noun in gender, number, and case. When it acts thus, the best translation is usually "a certain…" or "some…". The idea is that the author does not consider the identity of the noun particularly important, or he does not wish to specify, e.g., "A *certain* Athenian once asked Socrates why he asked so many questions."

The preferred place for the indefinite when it acts as an adjective is right after the noun in the predicate position.

The story of the prodigal son begins with just such an indefinite adjective: ἄνθρωπός τις εἶχεν δύο υἱούς. "A certain man had two sons." (Luke 15:11).

Vocabulary

▸ κύκλος, –ου, ὁ – circle, wheel

πρᾶγμα, –ατος, τό = matter, thing

οὔτε (adv.) = "and not," but almost always used in pairs οὔτε…οὔτε "neither…nor." Where μή is appropriate, μήτε replaces οὔτε.

τίς, τί (interrogative pronoun) = who, what

τις, τι (indefinite pronoun) = a certain, some

τί (adv.) = why?

ἀποθνῄσκω, ἀποθανοῦμαι, ἀπέθανον, [   ], —, — = to die

διαφέρω, διοίσω, διήνεγκα (διήνεγκον), [   ], [   ], διενέχθην = to carry across; to differ; differ from (+ gen.)

ἐάω, ἐάσω, εἴασα, [   ], [   ], εἰάθην = to allow

ἐρωτάω, ἐρωτήσω, ἠρώτησα, [   ], [   ], ἠρωτήθην = to ask, question

εὐτυχέω, εὐτυχήσω, εὐτύχησα, [   ], [   ], εὐτυχήθην = to prosper

ζάω, ζήσω, ἔζησα, —, —, — = to live

▸ μέλλω, μελλήσω, ἐμέλλησα, —, —, — = to be likely to (+ pres. inf.) be about to (+ future inf.); to hesitate to (+ pres. inf.)

νικάω, νικήσω, ἐνίκησα, [   ], [   ], ἐνικήθην = to conquer, win

φιλοσοφέω, φιλοσοφήσω, ἐφιλοσόφησα, [   ], [   ], ἐφιλοσόφηθην = to philosophize

Sentences

1. ζῶ δὲ οὐκέτι ἐγώ, ζῇ δὲ ἐν ἐμοὶ Χριστός. (Gal 2:20)

> ¶ ζῇ: the oddball alpha contract verb mentioned above. You might have expected ζᾷ.

2. μὴ νικῶ ὑπὸ τοῦ κακοῦ, ἀλλὰ νίκα ἐν τῷ ἀγαθῷ τὸ κακόν. (Rom 12:21)

> ¶ νικῶ: not indicative, but imperative
>
> ἐν: an example of the Koine use of ἐν with the dative of means

3. ἐρωτηθεὶς ποῖον οἶνον ἡδέως πίνει, ὁ Διογένης ἔφη, "τὸν ἀλλότριον." (Diogenes the Cynic, in Diogenes Laertius, *Lives of Eminent Philosophers*)

> ¶ ποῖος, –α, –ον (adj.) = what sort, what kind
>
> ἡδέως πίνει; i.e., what his favorite wine was
>
> Διογένης, –ους, ὁ = Diogenes (the cynic)
>
> ἀλλότριος, –α, –ον (adj.) = belonging to another

► 4. λέγει αὐτῷ ὁ Πιλᾶτος, "Τί ἐστιν ἀλήθεια;" (John 18:38)

> ¶ αὐτῷ: Jesus
>
> Πιλᾶτος, –ου, ὁ = Pontius Pilate, the Roman prefect of Judaea

5. τίς ἡμᾶς χωρίσει ἀπὸ τῆς ἀγάπης τοῦ Χριστοῦ; (Rom 8:35)

6. οὐδὲν ὁ Θαλῆς ἔφη τὸν θάνατον διαφέρειν τοῦ ζῆν. "σὺ," ἔφη τις, "διὰ τί οὐκ ἀποθνήσκεις;" "ὅτι," ἔφη, "οὐδὲν διαφέρει." (Thales, in Diogenes Laertius, *Lives of Eminent Philosophers*)

> ¶ Θαλῆς, –οῦ, ὁ = Thales
>
> οὐδὲν: here adverbial, "in no way"
>
> ὅτι: here "because"

7. ὧν ἕνεκα ζῆν ἐθέλεις, τούτων χάριν καὶ ἀποθανεῖν μὴ κατόκνει. (Pythagoras, in Stobaeus, *Anthology*)

> ❡ ζῆν = to live: present infinitive of ζάω
>
> τούτων χάριν: when the accusative of χάρις is preceded by a genitive, it means "for the sake of."
>
> κατοκνέω = to shrink back from

8. μήτε νέος μελλέτω φιλοσοφεῖν, μήτε γέρων κοπιάτω φιλοσοφῶν. (Epicurus, *Letter to Menoeceus*)

> ❡ γέρων, –οντος, ὁ = old man
>
> κοπιάω = to grow tired of (+ part.)

▶ 9. ὡς κύκλος τῶν ἀνθρώπων ἐστὶ πράγματα, περιφερόμενος δὲ οὐκ ἐᾷ ἀεὶ τοὺς αὐτοὺς εὐτυχεῖν. (Herodotus, *Histories*)

> ❡ περιφέρω = to carry around; (middle) to revolve, go around

10. εἶπεν δὲ αὐτοῖς, "Ὑμεῖς δὲ τίνα με λέγετε εἶναι;" Πέτρος δὲ ἀποκριθεὶς εἶπεν, "Τὸν Χριστὸν τοῦ θεοῦ." (Luke 9:20)

> ❡ εἶπεν: the speaker is Jesus
>
> αὐτοῖς: his disciples
>
> Πέτρος, –ου, ὁ = Peter; see chapter 11, Etymology and Discussion Topics

Etymology and Discussion Topics

κύκλος, –ου, ὁ = circle, wheel

From this word come our compounds with "cycle" such as "tricycle," "bicycle," and "unicycle" (three, two, and one wheels respectively). The mythical Cyclops was so named from a combination of κύκλος and ὄψ "eye."

μέλλω, μελλήσω, ἐμέλλησα, —, —, — = to be likely to (+ pres. inf.) be about to (+ future inf.); to hesitate to (+ pres. inf.)

This verb can be confusing to beginning students. The idea behind the verb is "going to." When it takes a future infinitive it means "about to." When it takes a present infinitive it can mean "about to / likely to" or "hesitate to." How can the same words mean two different things? When a student adamantly tells himself "I am going to start writing that paper!" this is frequently a sign of procrastination. If one hesitates, he is always "going to" do it. Context will make it clear which meaning is meant when μέλλω takes the present infinitive. If it takes the future infinitive, it cannot mean "hesitate."

Τί ἐστιν ἀλήθεια

One might have expected τίς since ἀλήθεια is feminine, but Greek will frequently use the neuter in the sense of "What (kind of thing) is so and so." As you will come to see, the indefinite often has a slightly condescending nature to it.

ὡς κύκλος τῶν ἀνθρώπων ἐστὶ πράγματα, περιφερόμενος δὲ οὐκ ἐᾷ αεὶ τοὺς αὐτοὺς εὐτυχεῖν.

The original "Wheel of Fortune," this famous line is uttered by the Lydian king Croesus as a warning to Cyrus the Great, who had had a particularly good run of luck. Croesus himself had previously learned this lesson from his own bitter experience, having recently suffered a downfall after a sting of good luck.

Chapter 26 ~

Omicron Contract Verbs • Contract Adjectives • Dative of Possession •
Participles of Contract Verbs

Omicron Contract Verbs

You can tell if a verb is an omicron contract verb by the omicron before the omega in the first principal part. Some examples:

δηλόω = to reveal, make known

πληρόω = to fill

χαριτόω = to show grace or favor

δηλόω = To Reveal

Your model omicron contract verb will be δηλόω.

δηλόω, δηλώσω, ἐδήλωσα, [   ], [   ], ἐδηλώθην = to reveal, make known

Like all contract verbs, δηλόω differs from the endings of λύω only in the present and imperfect tenses.

δηλόω = *to reveal, make known*

	Present Active Indicative			Present Middle/Passive Indicative		
Singluar						
1st	λύ–ω	(δηλό–ω)	δηλ–**ῶ**	λύ–ομαι	(δηλόομαι)	δηλ–**οῦμαι**
2nd	λύ–εις	(δηλό–εις)	δηλ–**οῖς**	λύ–ῃ/ει	(δηλόῃ/δηλόει)	δηλ–**οῖ**
3rd	λύ–ει	(δηλό–ει)	δηλ–**οῖ**	λύ–εται	(δηλό–εται)	δηλ–**οῦται**
Plural						
1st	λύ–ομεν	(δηλό–ομεν)	δηλ–**οῦμεν**	λυ–όμεθα	(δηλο–όμεθα)	δηλ–**ούμεθα**
2nd	λύ–ετε	(δηλό–ετε)	δηλ–**οῦτε**	λύ–εσθε	(δηλό–εσθε)	δηλ–**οῦσθε**
3rd	λύ–ουσι(ν)	(δηλό–ουσι(ν))	δηλ–**οῦσι(ν)**	λύ–ονται	(δηλό–ονται)	δηλ–**οῦνται**

	Present Active Infinitive			Present Middle/Passive Infinitive		
	λύ–ειν	(δηλό–ειν)	δηλ–**οῦν**	λύ–εσθαι	(δηλό–εσθαι)	δηλ–**οῦσθαι**

	Present Active Imperative			Present Middle/Passive Imperative		
Singular						
2nd	λῦ–ε	(δήλο–ε)	δήλ–**ου**	λύ–ου	(δηλό–ου)	δηλ–**οῦ**
3rd	λυ–έτω	(δηλο–έτω)	δηλ–**ούτω**	λυ–έσθω	(δηλο–έσθω)	δηλ–**ούσθω**
Plural						
2nd	λύ–ετε	(δηλό–ετε)	δηλ–**οῦτε**	λύ–εσθε	(δηλό–εσθε)	δηλ–**οῦσθε**
3rd	λυ–όντων	(δηλο–όντων)	δηλ–**ούντων**	λυ–έσθων	(δηλο–έσθων)	δηλ–**ούσθων**

	Imperfect Active Indicative			Imperfect Middle/Passive Indicative		
Singular						
1st	ἔλυ–ον	(ἐδήλο–ον)	ἐδήλ–**ουν**	ἐλυ–όμην	(ἐδηλο–όμην)	ἐδηλ–**ούμην**
2nd	ἔλυ–ες	(ἐδήλο–ες)	ἐδήλ–**ους**	ἐλύ–ου	(ἐδηλό–ου)	ἐδηλ–**οῦ**
3rd	ἔλυ–ε(ν)	(ἐδήλο–ε)	ἐδήλ–**ου**	ἐλύ–ετο	(ἐδηλό–ετο)	ἐδηλ–**οῦτο**
Plural						
1st	ἐλύ–ομεν	(ἐδηλό–ομεν)	ἐδηλ–**οῦμεν**	ἐλυ–όμεθα	(ἐδηλο–όμεθα)	ἐδηλ–**ούμεθα**
2nd	ἐλύ–ετε	(ἐδηλό–ετε)	ἐδηλ–**οῦτε**	ἐλύ–εσθε	(ἐδηλό–εσθε)	ἐδηλ–**οῦσθε**
3rd	ἔλυ–ον	(ἐδήλο–ον)	ἐδήλ–**ουν**	ἐλύ–οντο	(ἐδηλό–οντο)	ἐδηλ–**οῦντο**

Once again, it is easier to simply memorize the contracted forms, but the following table of contractions might be helpful.

o + o = ου   o + ει = οι

o + ε = ου   o + η = οι

o + ου = ου   o + ω = ω

Contract Adjectives

A few adjectives of the 1st and 2nd declension contract, but the spelling of the endings will differ only in the masculine nominative and accusative singular and neuter nominative and accusative singular. Instead of –ος you will see –ους and instead of –ον you will see –οῦν. All other forms will be like normal adjectives of the 1st and 2nd declension. When you see an adjective with the endings of –οῦς, –ᾶ, –οῦν or –οῦς, –ῆ, –οῦν, it is a contract adjective.

χρυσοῦς, –ῆ, –οῦν (adj.) = golden

φοινικοῦς, –ῆ, –οῦν (adj.) = purple, crimson

σιδηροῦς, –ᾶ, –οῦν (adj.) = iron

διπλοῦς, –ῆ, –οῦν (adj.) = double

Dative of Possession

In addition to the genitive of possession, Greek often uses the dative to signify the possessor.

τῷ Σωκράτει υἱός ἐστιν.

Socrates has a son. (Literally: There is a son to Socrates.)

Summary of Case Uses Learned Thus Far

Nominative	*Genitive*	*Dative*	*Accusative*
Subject	Genitive of Possession	Dative of Indirect Object	Direct Object
Predicate Nominative	Objective Genitive	Dative of Respect	Accusative of Duration of Time
	Partitive Genitive	Dative of Time When	
	Genitive of Time within Which	Dative of Degree of Difference	
	Genitive of Agent (with ὑπό)	Dative of Means	
	Genitive Absolute	Dative of Possession	
	Genitive of Comparison		

Participles of Contract Verbs

The same rules of contraction apply to the participles of contract verbs. Since, however, the endings will be the same, such contractions will cause little confusion. Instead of νικαόμενος, you will see νικώμενος, instead of φιλεόντος, you will see φιλοῦντος, and instead of δηλόον, you will see δηλοῦν, etc.

Vocabulary

γνῶσις, –εως, ἡ = knowledge

ἀργυροῦς, –ᾶ, –οῦν (adj.) = silver
ἐχθρός, –ή, –όν (adj.) = hostile;
ἐχθρός, –οῦ, ὁ = enemy
μικρός, –ά, –όν (adj.) = small
ὅλος, –η, –ον (adj.) = whole, entire
χρυσοῦς, –ῆ, –οῦν (adj.) = golden

▸ ἀγαπάω, ἀγαπήσω, ἠγάπησα, [   ], [   ], ἠγαπήθην = to love
δηλόω, δηλώσω, ἐδήλωσα, [   ], [   ], ἐδηλώθην = to reveal, make known
οἰκοδομέω, οἰκοδομήσω, ᾠκοδόμησα, [   ], [   ], ᾠκοδομήθην = to build up
οἴομαι (sometimes spelled οἶμαι), οἰήσομαι, —, —, —, ᾠήθην = to think, suppose

Sentences

1. ἡ γνῶσις φυσιοῖ, ἡ δὲ ἀγάπη οἰκοδομεῖ. (1 Cor 8:1)

> ⁋ φυσιόω = to puff up

2. μικρὰ ζύμη ὅλον τὸ φύραμα ζυμοῖ. (Gal 5:9)

> ⁋ ζύμη, –ης, ἡ = leaven
> φύραμα, –ατος, τό = dough
> ζυμόω = to leaven

3. φίλτατος εἶ καὶ ἀληθῶς χρυσοῦς, ὦ Φαῖδρε, εἴ με οἴει λέγειν ὡς Λυσίας. (Socrates, in Plato, *Phaedrus*)

> ⁋ φίλτατος, –η, –ον (adj.) = dearest:
> used as a term of affection in
> conversation
> Ψαιδρος, –ου, ὁ = Phaedrus
> Λυσίας, –ου, ὁ = Lysias, a famous
> orator

▶ 4. ὁ θάνατος οὐδὲν πρὸς ἡμᾶς· τὸ γὰρ διαλυθὲν ἀναισθητεῖ, τὸ δ᾽ ἀναισθητοῦν οὐδὲν πρὸς ἡμᾶς. (Epicurus, in Diogenes Laertius, *Lives of Eminent Philosophers*)

> ⁋ διαλυθὲν: aorist passive participle
> of διαλύω = to dissolve, destroy
> ἀναισθητέω = to lack perception

▶ 5. διπλῶς ὁρῶσιν οἱ μαθόντες γράμματα. (Menander, *Fragments*)

> ⁋ διπλῶς (adv.) = double

6. ἀλλὰ ὑμῖν λέγω τοῖς ἀκούουσιν, ἀγαπᾶτε τοὺς ἐχθροὺς ὑμῶν, καλῶς ποιεῖτε τοῖς μισοῦσιν ὑμᾶς. (Luke 6:27)

> ⁋ The speaker is Jesus. The context
> makes it clear that the verbs are
> imperative, not indicative.

7. καὶ εἰ ἀγαπᾶτε τοὺς ἀγαπῶντας ὑμᾶς, ποία ὑμῖν χάρις ἐστίν; καὶ γὰρ οἱ ἁμαρτωλοὶ τοὺς ἀγαπῶντας αὐτοὺς ἀγαπῶσιν. (Luke 6:32)

> ⁋ ποῖος, –α, –ον (adj.) = of what
> kind?
> καὶ γὰρ = for even

8. ἀεὶ τὸ λυποῦν ἐκδίωκε τοῦ βίου. (Menander, *Fragments*)

> ⁋ λυπέω = to cause grief or pain
> ἐκδιώκω = to banish; banish from
> (+ gen.)

9. Βίων ἔλεγε κατὰ Ἡσίοδον τρία γένη εἶναι μαθητῶν: χρυσοῦν, ἀργυροῦν, χαλκοῦν· χρυσοῦν μὲν τὸ γένος τῶν διδόντων καὶ μανθανόντων· ἀργυροῦν δὲ τὸ γένος τῶν διδόντων καὶ μὴ μανθανόντων· χαλκοῦν δὲ τὸ γένος τῶν μανθανόντων μέν, οὐ διδόντων δέ.

(Bion, in Diogenes Laertius, *Lives of Eminent Philosophers*)

❡ Βίων, –ωνος, ὁ = Bion of Borysthenes, a philosopher and teacher

▶ κατὰ Ἡσίοδον = in accordance with Hesiod, in the manner of Hesiod: see Etymology and Discussion Topics below

χαλκοῦς, –ῆ, –οῦν (adj.) = bronze

τῶν διδόντων: present active participle of δίδωμι, a μι verb, "those giving," i.e., "those who pay"

τὸ γένος τῶν = the type of those who

10. καὶ ἰδοὺ ἄνθρωπος ἦν ἐν Ἰερουσαλὴμ ᾧ ὄνομα Συμεών, καὶ ὁ ἄνθρωπος οὗτος δίκαιος καὶ εὐλαβής, προσδεχόμενος παράκλησιν τοῦ Ἰσραήλ, καὶ πνεῦμα ἦν ἅγιον ἐπ᾽ αὐτόν. (Luke 2:25)

❡ ἰδοὺ: aorist middle imperative of ὁράω. The middle technically has the sense of "see for yourself," but ἰδοὺ and the active imperative ἴδε are used without distinction, especially in the New Testament.

Ἱεροσόλυμα, –ων, τά = Jerusalem (here indeclinable)

Συμεών, –ῶνος, ὁ = Symeon

εὐλαβής, –ές (adj.) = prudent; pious

προσδέχομαι = to accept; await

παράκλησις, –εως, ἡ = exhortation; consolation

Ἰσραήλ = Israel

Etymology and Discussion Topics

ἀγαπάω, ἀγαπήσω, ἠγάπησα, —, —, ἠγαπήθην = **to love**

This verb originally meant "to have affection for/ be fond of." It is with the translation of the Septuagint and the especially the New Testament that this verb and the noun *ἀγάπη* come to represent divine love. See also chapter 10 Etymology and Discussion Topic.

ὁ θάνατος οὐδὲν πρὸς ἡμᾶς· τὸ γὰρ διαλυθὲν ἀναισθητεῖ, τὸ δ' ἀναισθητοῦν οὐδὲν πρὸς ἡμᾶς.

For Epicurus, the afterlife did not exist, nor did the soul exist apart from the body. The above statement explains why the philosopher should not fear death.

διπλῶς ὁρῶσιν οἱ μαθόντες γράμματα

How can those who have learned to read see *διπλῶς*?

κατὰ Ἡσίοδον τρία γένη εἶναι

In Hesiod's *Works and Days*, he describes five ages/races (*γένη*) of men: gold, silver, bronze, the age of heroes, and our present age. According to Hesiod, each age is significantly worse than the previous age, and he laments, "If only I did not live among the fifth age!" Bion is here alluding to this Hesiodic passage. How serious do you think Bion's description of the bronze type of student is?

Chapter 27 ∽

The Perfect Tense • οἶδα = To Know • Indirect Questions

The Perfect Tense

The perfect tense (from the Latin *perficere*, "to carry out, complete") describes an action that is completed. In English we form the perfect by combining "have" and the past participle.

The time *has arrived*.

I *have fought* the good fight.

Rome *has spoken*.

While the idea of a completed action is a good description, you might find it more useful to think of the perfect as an action that has occurred in the past, but has *bearing upon the present*. As you can see in the above examples, the completion of the action in the past has bearing upon the present. If "the time has arrived," the speaker presumably wants some action or recognition of this event to occur at the present. When St. Paul states, "I have fought the good fight," he is expressing his present readiness to accept death. When someone says, "Rome has spoken," they are implying that a question should not continue to be debated. The perfect can almost always be translated with "have/has" in English.

The perfect is also the third *aspect* in Greek. As you might expect, it expresses completed action. This is the rarest aspect in Greek.

The perfect active is the 4th principal part. Below are the perfect active forms for your model omega verb λύω. Contract verbs form their perfect in the same way as omega verbs.

Perfect Active Indicative

	Singular		Plural	
1st	λέλυ–**κα**	I have loosened	λελύ–**καμεν**	we have loosened
2nd	λέλυ–**κας**	you have loosened	λελύ–**κατε**	you have loosened
3rd	λέλυ–**κε(ν)**	he/she/it has loosened	λελύ–**κασι(ν)**	they have loosened

Just when you were getting used to the idea of augmentation in the imperfect and aorist tenses, the perfect takes it one step further and introduces you to *reduplication*. Simply speaking, augment the verb and then repeat the first letter of the stem before the augment, e.g., παιδεύω → πεπαίδευκα. If the verb starts with a vowel or diphthong, simply augment the verb, e.g., ἁμαρτάνω → ἡμάρτηκα. Some verbs that begin with a vowel or diphthong won't be augmented, but you can tell that they are perfect by the endings, e.g., εὐτυχέω → εὐτύχηκα. Finally, one further exception to the "repeat the first letter before the augment" rule occurs when the verb starts with a φ, θ, or χ.

φ changes to π	φιλέω → πεφίληκα
θ changes to τ	θαυμάζω → τεθαύμακα
χ changes to κ	χαίρω → κεχάρηκα

The kappa is characteristic of the perfect active endings and is therefore best memorized as part of the ending. However, technically the kappa is part of the perfect stem, and the endings are what follows, e.g., α, ας, ε(ν), etc. Just as you were encouraged to memorize the sigma as part of the aorist endings, even though it was technically part of the aorist stem, so too it is helpful to memorize the kappa as part of the perfect endings. In chapter 12 you learned that after certain consonants the sigma disappears in the aorist tense, e.g., μένω → ἔμεινα, so too the kappa is often absent from the perfect endings, e.g., γίγνομαι → γέγονα. How then do you tell if a perfect has the kappa? You look at the 4th principal part.

Perfect Infinitive Active

The perfect active infinitive is λελυ–**κέναι**.

The perfect infinitive expresses perfective aspect. For a review of aspect, see chapter 12. Perfective aspect expresses an action that was completed in the past, but has bearing on the present. Keep this in mind when you find the perfect infinitive in indirect statements.

ὁ Σωκράτης φησὶν πεπαιδευκέναι οὐδένα.

Socrates says that he has educated no one.

Perfect Imperative Active

The perfect imperative is extremely rare will not be used in this book, although its forms can be found in Appendix A.

Perfect Active Participle

While the perfect active participle is rare, it is important to be familiar with its forms. The distinguishing kappa in the endings should alert you to the presence of a perfect participle. Just like other active participles, you can see how the perfect participle is a mix of third declension (m & n) and second declension (f) adjective endings.

	Perfect Active Participle		
	m	*f*	*n*
Singular			
Nom.	λελυ–**κώς**	λελυ–**κυῖα**	λελυ–**κός**
Gen.	λελυ–**κότος**	λελυ–**κυίας**	λελυ–**κότος**
Dat.	λελυ–**κότι**	λελυ–**κυίᾳ**	λελυ–**κότι**
Acc.	λελυ–**κότα**	λελυ–**κυῖαν**	λελυ–**κός**
Plural			
Nom.	λελυ–**κότες**	λελυ–**κυῖαι**	λελυ–**κότα**
Gen.	λελυ–**κότων**	λελυ–**κυιῶν**	λελυ–**κότων**
Dat.	λελυ–**κόσι(ν)**	λελυ–**κυίαις**	λελυ–**κόσι(ν)**
Acc.	λελυ–**κότας**	λελυ–**κυίας**	λελυ–**κότα**

ὁ πεπαιδευκὼς τὸ μάθημα ἄνθρωπος οὐκ ἀεὶ σοφός ἐστιν.

The person having taught the lesson is not always wise.

οἶδα = To Know

This extremely important verb occurs only in the perfect and pluperfect tenses, and so is traditionally called a "defective verb" (a little harsh don't you think). Verbs like οἶδα exist only in the perfect tenses. Below are the perfect indicative and infinitive forms of οἶδα. The full declension of οἶδα can be found in appendix A.

	Perfect Active Indicative			
	Singular		*Plural*	
1st	οἶδα	I know	ἴσμεν	we know
2nd	οἶσθα	you know	ἴστε	you know
3rd	οἶδε(ν)	he/she/it knows	ἴσασι(ν)	they know

	Perfect Active Imperative			
	Singular		*Plural*	
2nd	ἴσθι	know	ἴστε	know
3rd	ἴστω	let him/her know	ἴστων	let them know

Perfect Active Infinitive

The perfect infinitive active is εἰδ–**έναι.**

❡ ἔλεγχος, –οῦ, ὁ = test

οἱ μαθηταὶ ἀεὶ βουλόμεθα εἰδέναι περὶ τίνος ὁ ἔλεγχός ἐστιν.

The students always want to know what is on the test. (Literally "about what the test is")

Indirect Questions

An *indirect* question is a *direct* question expressed indirectly.

Example	*Type of question*
What is the answer?	direct
The student said, "*What is the answer?*"	direct
Professors dislike always having to state *what the answer is.*	indirect
Where are you going?	direct
Socrates asked, "*Where are you going?*"	direct
Socrates constantly asked travelers *where they were going.*	indirect

Indirect questions are introduced by interrogative pronouns, adjectives, and adverbs. With one exception you will learn in chapter 40, the mood and tense of the verb in the direct question remain unchanged in the indirect question.

τί ἐστιν ἀλήθεια;

What is truth? (direct question)

Σωκράτης οἶδε τί ἐστιν ἀλήθεια.

Socrates knows *what truth is*. (indirect question)

τίνας ἀνθρώπους βλέπεις;

What people do you see? (direct question)

λέγε με τίνας ἀνθρώπους βλέπεις.

Tell me *what people you see*. (indirect question)

Vocabulary

εἰρήνη, –ης, ἡ = peace

▸ εὐδαιμονία, –ας, ἡ = happiness; prosperity

ὥρα, –ας, ἡ = hour; season

▸ θνητός, –ή, –όν (adj.) = mortal;

θνητός, –οῦ, ὁ = a mortal

▸ ὅμοιος, –α, –ον (adj.) = like, similar to (+dat.)

ἐγγίζω, ἐγγιῶ, ἤγγισα, ἤγγικα, —, ἠγγίσθην = to bring near; approach, be imminent

▸ λαλέω, λαλήσω, ἐλάλησα, λελάληκα, [   ], ἐλαλήθην = to chatter; say

λογίζομαι, λογιοῦμαι, ἐλογισάμην, —, [   ], ἐλογίσθην = to calculate; reflect, think

▸ μαρτυρέω, μαρτυρήσω, ἐμαρτύρησα, μεμαρτύρηκα, [   ], ἐμαρτυρήθην = to testify

μετανοέω, μετανοήσω, μετενόησα, μετανενόηκα, —, — = to change one's mind; repent

οἰκέω, οἰκήσω, ᾤκησα, ᾤκηκα, [   ], ᾠκήθην = to live, dwell

Sentences

▶ 1. μετανοεῖτε, ἤγγικεν γὰρ ἡ βασιλεία τῶν οὐρανῶν. (Matthew 3:2)

> ¶ The speaker is John the Baptist.

2. οὐδεὶς ὃ νοεῖς μὲν οἶδεν, ὃ δὲ ποιεῖς βλέπει. (Menander, *Fragments*)

> ¶ βλέπει: the implied subject is "everyone."

3. ἐν τῷ κόσμῳ θλῖψιν ἔχετε, ἀλλὰ θαρσεῖτε, ἐγὼ νενίκηκα τὸν κόσμον.
(John 16:33)

> ¶ θλῖψις, –εως, ἡ = affliction
>
> θαρσεῖτε: imperative, not indicative, of θαρσέω = to have courage, be bold
>
> ἐγώ: Jesus

4. εἶπεν δὲ πρὸς τὴν γυναῖκα, "Ἡ πίστις σου σέσωκέν σε· πορεύου εἰς εἰρήνην."
(Luke 7:50)

> ¶ εἶπεν: aorist of λέγω = he said: the grammatical subject is Jesus.

5. κἀγὼ ἑώρακα, καὶ μεμαρτύρηκα ὅτι οὗτός ἐστιν ὁ υἱὸς τοῦ θεοῦ. (John 1:34)

> ¶ κἀγώ = καὶ ἐγώ: John the Baptist
>
> ἑώρακα: see ὁράω

6. θνητὸς γεγονώς, ἄνθρωπε, μὴ φρόνει μέγα. (Menander, *Fragments*)

> ¶ γεγονώς: perfect participle of γίγνομαι. Often γίγνομαι must be translated like εἰμί, i.e., "being mortal," or "since you are mortal," instead of literally translating it "having become mortal."

7. ὁ δὲ λέγων ἢ μήπω τοῦ φιλοσοφεῖν ὑπάρχειν ὥραν ἢ παρεληλυθέναι τὴν ὥραν ὅμοιός ἐστι τῷ λέγοντι πρὸς εὐδαιμονίαν ἢ μὴ παρεῖναι τὴν ὥραν ἢ μηκέτι εἶναι. (Epicurus, *Letter to Menoeceus*)

> ¶ ἢ...ἢ = either...or
>
> μήπω (adv.) = not yet
>
> ὑπάρχω = to begin (+ gen.)
>
> παρεληλυθέναι = perfect infinitive of παρέρχομαι = to pass by
>
> ὅμοιός ἐστι τῷ λέγοντι = is like one saying that
>
> πρὸς εὐδαιμονίαν = for happiness, with respect to happiness
>
> πάρειμι = to be present, at hand
>
> μηκέτι (adv.) = no longer

8. ἄνδρες Ἀθηναῖοι, τῶν μὲν σοφώτερος, τῶν δὲ ἀνδρειότερός εἰμι· σοφώτερος μὲν τῶν τὴν ἀπάτην Πεισιστράτου μὴ συνιέντων, ἀνδρειότερος δὲ τῶν ἐπισταμένων μέν, διὰ δέος δὲ σιωπώντων. (Solon, in Diogenes Laertius, *Lives of Eminent Philosophers*)

> ¶ These words were reportedly spoken by the famous Athenian Solon about the future dictator Peisistratus.
>
> τῶν μὲν...τῶν δὲ: remember that Greek often uses the definite article in the sense of "some... others."
>
> ἀνδρεῖος, –α, –ον (adj.) = brave
>
> ἀπάτη, –ης, ἡ = trick, deceit
>
> Πεισίστρατος, –ου, ὁ = Peisistratus
>
> τῶν...μὴ συνιέντων = than those who do not perceive
>
> συνιέντων: present participle of the μι verb συνίημι = to perceive
>
> δέος, –ους, τό = fear
>
> σιωπάω = to remain silent

9. οὐκ οἴδατε ὅτι ναὸς θεοῦ ἐστε καὶ τὸ πνεῦμα τοῦ θεοῦ οἰκεῖ ἐν ὑμῖν;
(1 Cor 3:16)

> ¶ οὐκ οἴδατε = do you not know?: expects the answer "yes."

10. ὅτε ἤμην νήπιος, ἐλάλουν ὡς νήπιος, ἐφρόνουν ὡς νήπιος, ἐλογιζόμην ὡς νήπιος· ὅτε γέγονα ἀνήρ, κατήργηκα τὰ τοῦ νηπίου. (1 Cor 13:11)

¶ ἤμην = I was: alternate Koine form of ἤ, 1st person singular imperfect of εἰμί

νήπιος, –α, –ον (adj.) = infant, child: technically an adjective, νήπιος frequently functions as a substantive

γέγονα: see γίγνομαι

καταργέω = to leave idle, put aside

ὅτε = when; since

Etymology and Discussion Topics

εὐδαιμονία, –ας, ἡ = happiness; prosperity

This word for happiness literally means "having a good daemon." As you can see, this word contains the ancient notion that happiness depended to a large extent on forces outside of one's control. It therefore often meant "prosperous." It is Aristotle who further defines and clarifies what is true εὐδαιμονία.

θνητός, –οῦ, ὁ = a mortal

As a substantive adjective, θνητός is often used when comparing human beings to the gods, οἱ ἀθάνατοι. For the ancient Greeks, humans were literally "those who die" while the gods were "those who do not die." Mortality loomed as a great unbridgeable chasm that separated the human and divine realms. Small wonder then that so many Greeks had a hard time accepting a god who would chose to suffer and die.

ὅμοιος, –α, –ον (adj.) = like, similar to (+ dat.)

While some early Christians held that Jesus was ὁμοιούσιος to the Father (of like substance) and thus not in fact God, others held that Jesus was ὁμοούσις (of the same substance) as the Father, a view which would prevail at the first Council of Nicaea. The smallest of Greek letters, the iota, could thus make all the difference in meaning.

λαλέω, λαλήσω, ἐλάλησα, λελάληκα, [   ], ἐλαλήθην = **to chatter; say**

This verb undergoes a change in meaning from classical to Koine. In the classical sense, it means "to chatter," or "to prattle." It is used of birds and other animals as well as human nonsense. It would be a mistake to translate it as "babble" in the New Testament. By the time of the gospels, it is simply another word for λέγω.

μαρτυρέω, μαρτυρήσω, ἐμαρτύρησα, μεμαρτύρηκα, [   ], ἐμαρτυρήθην = **to testify**

We get our word "martyr" from this word. To "witness" does not simply mean that someone sees or observes something. It means that someone sees and then puts their credibility (and often their lives) on the line. It is like the difference between seeing a crime and testifying under oath about what you saw. When the New Testament speaks of "bearing witness" or "testifying," words often used to translate this verb, something far more serious than simple passive observation is signified.

μετανοεῖτε, ἤγγικεν γὰρ ἡ βασιλεία τῶν οὐρανῶν. (Matthew 3:2)

Often translated as "repent," μετανοεῖτε literally means "change your thinking." The call for repentance entails far more than "crying uncle." Not only does this admonition demand a change in action, but a change in how one views the world. This sentence also illustrates the sense of the perfect. "Has come near" implies something quite pertinent for the present.

Chapter 28 ⌒

Perfect Middle/Passive • Dative of Agent

Perfect Middle/Passive

The perfect middle/passive consists of the reduplicated perfect stem and the primary middle/passive endings you learned in chapter 14. Unlike the present middle/passive endings, the primary endings are added directly to the stem without a thematic vowel.

<table>
<tr><th colspan="5" align="center">Perfect Middle/Passive Indicative</th></tr>
<tr><th></th><th colspan="2" align="center">λύω</th><th colspan="2" align="center">Ending</th></tr>
<tr><th></th><th>Singular</th><th>Plural</th><th>Singular</th><th>Plural</th></tr>
<tr><td>1st</td><td>λέλυ–μαι</td><td>λελύ–μεθα</td><td>μαι</td><td>μεθα</td></tr>
<tr><td>2nd</td><td>λέλυ–σαι</td><td>λέλυ–σθε</td><td>σαι</td><td>σθε</td></tr>
<tr><td>3rd</td><td>λέλυ–ται</td><td>λέλυ–νται</td><td>ται</td><td>νται</td></tr>
</table>

Perfect Middle/Passive Infinitive: λελύ–**σθαι**
Perfect Middle/Passive Participle: λελυ–**μένος, –η, –ον**

The perfect middle/passive participle is formed with the endings of the present middle/passive participle added to the perfect stem. You have now learned all of the participles in Greek. See appendix A for a summary of participle endings.

When the perfect verb stem ends in a vowel, attaching the primary endings is straightforward. When the perfect stem ends in a consonant, unfortunately, the same rules that caused letter changes in the aorist and future—e.g., πέμψω, not πέμπσω and ἕλξω, not ἕλκσω—apply in the case of the perfect middle/passive endings. Below is a chart of common contractions. This chart should be referred to if you encounter a form that you do not recognize, but that you suspect is perfect middle/passive.

The ending…	…when attached to a stem ending in…		
	π, β, φ	κ, γ, χ	τ, δ, θ, ζ, ν
	…becomes:		
–μαι	–μμαι	–γμαι	–σμαι
–σαι	–ψαι	–ξαι	–σαι
–ται	–πται	–κται	–σται
–μεθα	–μμεθα	–γμεθα	–σμεθα
–σθε	–φθε	–χθε	–σθε
–νται	Formed periphrastically (see below)		

Verbs whose perfect stems end in a consonant form the 3rd person plural periphrastically, with the perfect middle/passive participle + εἰσί. Other verb forms can be performed periphrastically as well. The term "periphrastic" comes from περί and φράζω, so literally "to speak in a roundabout way." It usually means using a participle and the word "to be" instead of a single verb form. For example, English express the imperfect tense periphrastically with "was reading" in the sentence "The student was reading Homer."

The 1st person singular perfect middle/passive form is also the 5th principal part. You have now been introduced to all the principal parts. To review: all principal parts are 1st person singular indicative.

Principal Parts of the Greek Verb

1	2	3	4	5	6
present active	future active	aorist active	perfect active	perfect m/p	aorist passive

The complete principal parts of your model verb are as follows:

λύω, λύσω, ἔλυσα, λέλυκα, λέλυμαι, ἐλύθην

From this point on, if you see a verb listed with a missing principal part, it either does not exist or is extremely rare.

Dative of Agent

When the perfect (or pluperfect) passive is used, Greek prefers to use the *dative of agent* without a preposition rather than ὑπό + the *genitive of agent*.

ἡ ἀλήθεια μεμαρτύρηται τοῖς σοφοῖς.

The truth has been witnessed by the wise.

Summary of Case Uses Learned Thus Far

Nominative	Genitive	Dative	Accusative
Subject	Genitive of Possession	Dative of Indirect Object	Direct Object
Predicate Nominative	Objective Genitive	Dative of Respect	Accusative of Duration of Time
	Partitive Genitive	Dative of Time When	
	Genitive of Time within Which	Dative of Degree of Difference	
	Genitive of Agent (with ὑπό)	Dative of Means	
	Genitive Absolute	Dative of Possession	
	Genitive of Comparison	Dative of Agent	

Vocabulary

▸ ἀγών, –ῶνος, ὁ = contest, struggle

κεφαλή, –ῆς, ἡ = head

▸ ὕβρις, –εως, ἡ = violence; arrogance

φύσις, –εως, ἡ = nature

ἄπειρος, –ον (adj.) = without experience of (+gen.); unlimited, infinite

ἀγωνίζομαι, ἀγωνιοῦμαι, ἠγωνισάμην, ἠγώνισμαι, ἠγωνίσθην = to compete, fight, struggle

γελάω, γελάσομαι, ἐγέλασα, —,—, ἐγελάσθην = to laugh; to mock

τελέω, τελέσω, ἐτέλεσα, τετέλεκα, τετέλεσμαι, ἐτελέσθην = to complete, fulfill τηρέω, τηρήσω, ἐτήρησα, τετήρηκα, τετήρημαι, ἐτηρήθην = to observe, keep; protect

φοβέω, φοβήσω, ἐφόβησα, πεφόβηκα, πεφόβημαι, ἐφοβήθην = to put to flight; (middle and passive) to be afraid, fear

▶ φύω, φύσω, ἔφυσα/ ἔφυν, πέφυκα, —, — = to produce, grow. This verb is transitive in the present, future, and 1st aorist; intransitive in the 2nd aorist, perfect, and pluperfect.

Sentences

1. τὸν καλὸν ἀγῶνα ἠγώνισμαι, τὸν δρόμον τετέλεκα, τὴν πίστιν τετήρηκα. (2 Tim. 4:7)

¶ δρόμος, –ου, ὁ = course, race

2. βλέπων πεπαίδευμ᾽ εἰς τὰ τῶν πολλῶν κακά. (Menander, *Fragments*)

¶ πεπαίδευμ᾽ = πεπαίδευμαι, "I have become educated," perfect passive of παιδεύω

εἰς: take with βλέπων = looking at

3. Λάζαρος ὁ φίλος ἡμῶν κεκοίμηται. (John 11:11)

¶ Λάζαρος, –ου, ὁ = Lazarus, a proper name

κοιμάω = to put to sleep; (middle) fall asleep; die

4. θνητὸς πεφυκὼς μὴ γέλα τεθνηκότα. (Menander, *Fragments*)

¶ πεφυκὼς = having been born: perfect active participle of φύω

τεθνηκότα: masculine accusative singular perfect active participle of θνήσκω = to die: here the object of γέλα

▶ 5. ἡ εὐτραπελία πεπαιδευμένη ὕβρις ἐστίν. (Aristotle, *Rhetoric*)

¶ εὐτραπελία, –ας, ἡ = wit; a witty remark

πεπαιδευμένη: modifies ὕβρις

6. τῇ γὰρ χάριτί ἐστε σεσῳσμένοι διὰ πίστεως· καὶ τοῦτο οὐκ ἐξ ὑμῶν, θεοῦ τὸ δῶρον. (Eph 2:8)

❡ σεσῳσμένοι: perfect passive participle of σῴζω = to save

Remember that the perfect passive can be formed periphrastically, i.e., participle + εἰμί.

▶ 7. ὁ τῆς φύσεως πλοῦτος καὶ ὥρισται καὶ εὐπόριστός ἐστιν, ὁ δὲ τῶν κενῶν δοξῶν εἰς ἄπειρον ἐκπίπτει. (Epicurus, in Diogenes Laertius, *Lives of Eminent Philosophers*)

❡ ὥρισται: perfect passive of ὁρίζω = to limit; define

εὐπόριστος, –ον (adj.) = easy to secure

ὁ δὲ: supply πλοῦτος.

ἐκπίπτω = to fall; rush out, issue forth

8. ἀλλὰ καὶ αἱ τρίχες τῆς κεφαλῆς ὑμῶν πᾶσαι ἠρίθμηνται. μὴ φοβεῖσθε. (Luke 12:7)

❡ θρίξ, τριχός, ἡ = hair

ἠρίθμηνται: perfect passive of ἀριθμέω = to number

9. εἰ γὰρ ἐχθροὶ ὄντες κατηλλάγημεν τῷ θεῷ διὰ τοῦ θανάτου τοῦ υἱοῦ αὐτοῦ, πολλῷ μᾶλλον καταλλαγέντες σωθησόμεθα ἐν τῇ ζωῇ αὐτοῦ. (Rom 5:10)

❡ κατηλλάγημεν: perfect passive of καταλλάσσω = to change; reconcile

καταλλαγέντες: aorist passive participle of καταλλάσσω

σωθησόμεθα: future passive of σῴζω

10. ἐρωτηθεὶς τίνι διαφέρουσιν οἱ πεπαιδευμένοι τῶν ἀπαιδεύτων, "ὅσῳ," εἶπεν, "οἱ ζῶντες τῶν τεθνεώτων." (Aristotle, in Diogenes Laertius, *Lives of Eminent Philosophers*)

❡ ἐρωτηθεὶς: aorist passive participle of ἐρωτάω = to ask

εἶπεν = Aristotle is the grammatical subject

ἀπαίδευτος, –ον (adj.) = uneducated

ὅσῳ = by as much as: the correlative to τίνι above

ζῶντες: present active participle of ζάω = to live

τεθνεώτων: perfect participle of θνήσκω = to die

Etymology and Discussion Topics

ἀγών, –ῶνος, ὁ = contest, struggle

The ancient Greeks loved contests. Derived from the verb ἄγω, the noun ἀγών originally referred to a meeting place, whether for the gods or humans. One use was for gatherings where athletic games were held, i.e., an arena or field. Eventually ἀγών came to be used for any contest, whether physical, such as racing or wrestling, or verbal, such as a debate.

ὕβρις, –εως, ἡ = violence; arrogance

The basic meaning of ὕβρις is insolence. When we say "hubris," we usually mean pride or arrogance. While this meaning is found in the ancient word ὕβρις, very often it signifies violence, especially when a person abuses or mistreats someone who cannot defend themselves. Ancient "hubris" thus concerns not only a person's attitude towards the divine, but the way he treats his fellow man.

φύω, φύσω, ἔφυσα/ ἔφυν, πέφυκα, —, — = to produce, grow

The intransitive tenses of this verb (2nd aorist, perfect, pluperfect) can often be translated like εἰμί. "You have been born mortal" is another way of saying "you are mortal."

ἡ εὐτραπελία πεπαιδευμένη ὕβρις ἐστίν.

What do you think the meaning of this sentence is? Does Aristotle's use of πεπαιδευμένη soften ὕβρις or is he being facetious?

ὁ τῆς φύσεως πλοῦτος καὶ ὥρισται καὶ εὐπόριστός ἐστιν, ὁ δὲ τῶν κενῶν δοξῶν εἰς ἄπειρον ἐκπίπτει.

Notice the paradoxical way that Epicurus contrasts φύσις and δόξα. That which is limited is easy to obtain, while that which is limitless is as fleeting as air.

Chapter 29 ⟼

Pluperfect and Future Perfect • Reflexive Pronoun

Pluperfect and Future Perfect

The pluperfect describes an action that has already been completed when another action occurred in the past. It is in a sense "more past." We usually express the pluperfect in English by "had" and the past participle.

Although the teacher *had finished* the lecture, he kept on talking.

When the student came to class, she *had read* the assigned readings.

The future perfect describes an action that *will have* already been completed when another action occurs in the future. We usually express the future perfect in English by "will have" and the past participle.

When you finish this book, you *will have read* many beautiful lines of Greek.

To form the pluperfect, add the pluperfect endings to the augmented perfect stem (yes, Greek can add three letters to the beginning of a verb). If the perfect stem begins with a vowel, the beginning of the stem cannot be augmented again and will remain the same.

		Pluperfect Active Indicative		
		λύω		Endings
Singular				
1st	ἐλελύ–**κη**	I had loosened		**κη**
2nd	ἐλελύ–**κης**	you had loosened		**κης**
3rd	ἐλελύ–**κει(ν)**	he/she/it had loosened		**κει(ν)**
Plural				
1st	ἐλελύ–**κεμεν**	we had loosened		**κεμεν**
2nd	ἐλελύ–**κετε**	you had loosened		**κετε**
3rd	ἐλελύ–**κεσαν**	they had loosened		**κεσαν**

To form the pluperfect middle/passive, add the secondary endings you learned in chapter 14 to the augmented perfect stem. For clarity, the passive translations have been given below.

		Pluperfect Middle/Passive Indicative		
		λύω		Endings
Singular				
1st	ἐλελύ–**μην**	I had been loosened		**μην**
2nd	ἐλέλυ–**σο**	you had been loosened		**σο**
3rd	ἐλέλυ–**το**	he/she/it had been loosened		**το**
Plural				
1st	ἐλελύ–**μεθα**	we had been loosened		**μεθα**
2nd	ἐλέλυ–**σθε**	you had been loosened		**σθε**
3rd	ἐλέλυ–**ντο**	they had been loosened		**ντο**

¶ κώνειον, –ου, τό = hemlock (a type of poison) | πίνω, πίομαι, ἔπιον, πέπωκα, πέπομαι, ἐπόθην = to drink

ὅτε ὁ Σωκράτης ἀπέθανεν, ἐπεπώκει τὸ κώνειον.

When Socrates died, he had drunk the hemlock.

ὅτε ὁ Σωκράτης ἀπέθανεν, ἡ πόλις οὐκ ἐβέβλαπτο ὑπ᾽ αὐτοῦ.

When Socrates died, the city had not been harmed by him.

The future perfect is extremely rare and with few exceptions is expressed periphrastically with the perfect participle + future tense of εἰμί.

¶ ᾄδω, ᾄσω = to sing, recite | θρασύς, –εῖα, –ύ (adj.) = bold, brave

ὅτε ὁ μαθητὴς ᾄσει τὸν Ὅμηρον, γεγονὼς ἔσται θρασύς.

When the student will recite Homer, he will have become brave.

Congratulations, you have now learned all seven of Greek's tenses: present, future, imperfect, aorist, perfect, pluperfect, and future perfect.

Reflexive Pronoun

The reflexive pronoun (from the Latin *reflectere* "to turn back") points back to the subject of the verb. Since it is not the subject, but points back to it, there are no nominative forms.

Reflexive Pronouns

	1st Person		2nd Person	
Singular				
Gen.	ἐμαυτοῦ, –ῆς	of myself	σεαυτοῦ (σαυτοῦ), –ῆς	of yourself
Dat.	ἐμαυτῷ, –ῇ	to/for myself	σεαυτῷ (σαυτῷ), –ῇ	to/for yourself
Acc.	ἐμαυτόν, –ήν	myself	σεαυτόν (σαυτόν), –ήν	yourself
Plural				
Gen.	ἡμῶν αὐτῶν	of ourselves	ὑμῶν αὐτῶν	of yourselves
Dat.	ἡμῖν αὐτοῖς, –αῖς	to/for ourselves	ὑμῖν αὐτοῖς, –αῖς	to/for yourselves
Acc.	ἡμᾶς αὐτούς, –άς	ourselves	ὑμᾶς αὐτούς, –άς	yourselves

For the 1st person singular reflexive pronoun, simply add ἐμ to the forms of αὐτός. For the 2nd person singular reflexive pronoun, add σε to the forms of αὐτός. There are no neuter forms for pronouns of the 1st and 2nd person. The plural of both the 1st and 2nd person reflexive pronouns is formed by adding the corresponding form of αὐτός after the personal pronoun. Sometimes you will see shortened forms of the 2nd person singular where the ε drops out, i.e., σαυτοῦ, σαυτῷ, σαυτόν instead of σεαυτοῦ, σεαυτῷ, σεαυτόν.

The 3rd person reflexive pronoun is formed by adding ἑ to αὐτός. Like the 2nd person singular, the 3rd person singular reflexive pronoun is often shorted by removing the ε and keeping the breathing. The rough breathing is thus the only thing that will sometimes distinguish the personal pronoun from the reflexive pronoun.

	3rd Person Reflexive Pronoun			
	m	*f*	*n*	*Translation*
Singular				
Gen.	ἑαυτοῦ (αὑτοῦ)	ἑαυτῆς (αὑτῆς)	ἑαυτοῦ (αὑτοῦ)	of him/her/itself
Dat.	ἑαυτῷ (αὑτῷ)	ἑαυτῇ (αὑτῇ)	ἑαυτῷ (αὑτῷ)	to/for him/her/itself
Acc.	ἑαυτόν (αὑτόν)	ἑαυτήν (αὑτήν)	ἑαυτό (αὑτό)	him/her/itself
Plural				
Gen.	ἑαυτῶν (αὑτῶν)	ἑαυτῶν (αὑτῶν)	ἑαυτῶν (αὑτῶν)	of themselves
Dat.	ἑαυτοῖς (αὑτοῖς)	ἑαυταῖς (αὑταῖς)	ἑαυτοῖς (αὑτοῖς)	to/for themselves
Acc.	ἑαυτούς (αὑτούς)	ἑαυτάς (αὑτάς)	ἑαυτά (αὑτά)	themselves

❡ πολλάκις (adv.) = often | ἐπαινέω = to praise

ἄνθρωπος πολλάκις ἑαυτὸν βλάπτει.

Man often harms himself.

τί δ᾽ ἐπαινεῖτε ὑμᾶς αὐτούς;

But why do you praise yourselves?

Vocabulary

δένδρον, –ου, τό = tree

ἐσθής, ἐσθῆτος, ἡ = clothing, garment

▸ οὐσία, –ας, ἡ = substance, being; property, riches

ἄλλος, –η, –ο (adj.) = other, another

λαμπρός, –ά, –όν (adj.) = shining, splendid

▸ οἷος, οἵα, οἷον (adj.) = such as; of what sort

▸ ὅσος, –η, –ον (adj.) = how much, how big; as much as

πλησίος, –α, –ον (adj.) = neighboring; as substantive πλησίος, –ου, ὁ = a neighbor

ἡνίκα (adv.) = when; while

δέω, δήσω, ἔδησα, δέδεκα, δέδεμαι, ἐδέθην = to bind

πληρόω, πληρώσω, ἐπλήρωσα, πεπλήρωκα, πεπλήρωμαι, ἐπληρώθην = to fill, fulfill

προέρχομαι, προελεύσομαι, προῆλθον, προελήλυθα, —, — = to go out, present oneself

Sentences

▶ 1. γνῶθι σαυτόν. (Oracle at Delphi)

¶ These words were reportedly inscribed above the temple at Delphi.

γνῶθι = aorist imperative of γιγνώσκω

2. καὶ οὐδεὶς ἐπίασεν αὐτόν, ὅτι οὔπω ἐληλύθει ἡ ὥρα αὐτοῦ. (John 8:20)

¶ αὐτόν: Jesus

ἐπίασεν: Koine spelling of ἐπίεσεν, aorist active of πιέζω = to press; arrest

ὅτι: here "because"

οὔπω (adv.) = not yet

ἐληλύθει: pluperfect of ἔρχομαι

3. ὁ σοφὸς ἐν αὑτῷ περιφέρει τὴν οὐσίαν. (Menander, *Fragments*)

¶ περιφέρω = to carry around

οὐσίαν: here "wealth" or "riches"

▶ 4. Ῥαδάμανθυς ἀγαθὸς ἦν ἀνήρ· ἐπεπαίδευτο γὰρ ὑπὸ τοῦ Μίνωος. (Plato, *Minos*)

¶ Ῥαδάμανθυς, –υος, ὁ = Rhadamanthus, one of the three judges in Hades

Μίνως, –ωος, ὁ = Minos, a mythical king of Crete

▶ 5. ἡνίκα δὲ Φίλιππος ἐτεθνήκει, ὁ Δημοσθένης λαμπρὰν ἐσθῆτα προῆλθεν
ἔχων. (Plutarch, *Lives of the Ten Orators*)

    ¶ Φίλιππος, –ου, ὁ = Phillip, here Phillip II of Macedon, Alexander's father.

    ἐτεθνήκει: pluperfect of θνήσκω = to die

    Δημοσθένης, –ους, ὁ = Demosthenes, the famous Athenian orator, was an outspoken opponent of Philip II. When Philip died, Demosthenes was still in mourning for his daughter, and thus wore dark clothes in public. His choice of attire upon hearing the news of Philip's death gives some insight into the depth of his hatred for Philip.

    ἔχων: here "wearing"

6. ὁ γὰρ πᾶς νόμος ἐν ἑνὶ λόγῳ πεπλήρωται, ἐν τῷ "Ἀγαπήσεις τὸν πλησίον σου
ὡς σεαυτόν." (Gal 5:14)

    ¶ τῷ: this definite article modifies the clause that follows. "in the [commandment] 'You will love…'"

7. πρᾶττε τὰ σαυτοῦ, μὴ τὰ τῶν ἄλλων φρόνει. (Menander, *Fragments*)

    ¶ φρόνει: imperative, not indicative

▶ 8. ἀμὴν λέγω ὑμῖν, ὅσα ἐὰν δήσητε ἐπὶ τῆς γῆς ἔσται δεδεμένα ἐν οὐρανῷ καὶ
ὅσα ἐὰν λύσητε ἐπὶ τῆς γῆς ἔσται λελυμένα ἐν οὐρανῷ. (Matthew 18:18)

    ¶ ὅσα ἐὰν δήσητε = as many things as you bind, whatever you bind: ἐὰν δήσητε is a subjunctive clause that will be introduced in chapter 35.

    ἔσται δεδεμένα: future perfect passive of δέω

    ὅσα ἐὰν λύσητε = whatever you loosen: another subjunctive clause you will learn in chapter 35

    ἔσται λελυμένα: future perfect passive of λύω

    See Etymology and Discussion Topics below for another interpretation of these future perfect passives.

9. ἔλεγεν οὖν, "Τίνι ὁμοία ἐστὶν ἡ βασιλεία τοῦ θεοῦ, καὶ τίνι ὁμοιώσω
αὐτήν; ὁμοία ἐστὶν κόκκῳ σινάπεως, ὃν λαβὼν ἄνθρωπος ἔβαλεν εἰς κῆπον
ἑαυτοῦ, καὶ ηὔξησεν καὶ ἐγένετο εἰς δένδρον, καὶ τὰ πετεινὰ τοῦ οὐρανοῦ
κατεσκήνωσεν ἐν τοῖς κλάδοις αὐτοῦ." (Luke 13:18–19)

¶ ἔλεγεν: the grammatical subject
is Jesus; note the imperfect tense,
which implies that this parable
was repeatedly spoken

ὁμοιόω = to liken, compare
(+ dat.)

κόκκος, –ου, ὁ = grain, seed

σίναπι, –εως, τό = mustard

κῆπος, –ου, τό = garden

ηὔξησεν: aorist of αὐξάνω

πετεινός, –ή, –όν (adj.) = winged;
τὰ πετεινὰ = winged things: i.e.,
birds

κατασκηνόω = to settle

κλάδος, –ου, ὁ = branch

10. τὸ γνῶθι σαυτὸν πᾶσίν ἐστι χρήσιμον. (Menander, *Fragments*)

¶ τὸ γνῶθι σαυτὸν: literally "the
know thyself," i.e., the saying or
admonition "Know thyself."

χρήσιμος, –η, –ον (adj.) = useful

Etymology and Discussion Topics

οὐσία, –ας, ἡ = substance, being; property, riches

Formed from the feminine participle of εἰμί, this noun could mean substance or being and was therefore an important word in philosophy and theology. It could also, however, refer to material wealth or property. Context is
key when translating this word.

οἷος and ὅσος

These words can be tricky to translate. Generally speaking, οἷος denotes
quality while ὅσος denotes quantity. In practice, however, they will often best
be translated like simple relatives. While your English translation will often
be the same, it is important to keep the difference between these two words
in mind.

γνῶθι σαυτόν.

This admonition was reportedly placed above the entrance to the temple of Delphi. For the ancients, "knowing yourself" was not the same thing as our modern notion of "finding yourself." It involved not personal self-discovery but self-awareness and knowledge of what a human is (anthropology in the classical sense), specifically the importance of knowing your mortal limitations as a remedy against hubris.

Ῥαδάμανθυς ἀγαθὸς ἦν ἀνήρ· ἐπεπαίδευτο γὰρ ὑπὸ τοῦ Μίνωος.

Rhadamanthus and Minos were two famous lawgivers renowned for their judgment. There is a story that after their death they were tasked (along with Aeacus) with judging those who journey to the underworld after death.

ἡνίκα δὲ Φίλιππος ἐτεθνήκει, ὁ Δημοσθένης λαμπρὰν ἐσθῆτα προῆλθεν ἔχων.

When Philip II of Macedon began to expand his territory, the independent Greek city states were divided on his intentions. Many people viewed his expansion benignly, and some even welcomed his interest in Greece as a whole. Others, however, believed that Philip was scheming to conquer all of Greece. Foremost among them was Demosthenes, who wrote a series of speeches warning Athens, and all of Greece, to take Philip seriously. In the end the Athenians did not pay attention to Demosthenes until it was too late. Cicero's speeches warning Rome against the designs of Marc Antony are therefore called the *Philippics* on this account. If you read the speeches of Winston Churchill in which he tries to warn the world about the designs of Hitler, you can see many of the same arguments as those used by Demosthenes, as Churchill knew his Demosthenes quite well.

ἀμὴν λέγω ὑμῖν, ὅσα ἐὰν δήσητε ἐπὶ τῆς γῆς ἔσται δεδεμένα ἐν οὐρανῷ καὶ ὅσα ἐὰν λύσητε ἐπὶ τῆς γῆς ἔσται λελυμένα ἐν οὐρανῷ. (Matthew 18:18)

Some believe that ἔσται δεδεμένα and ἔσται λελυμένα should not be treated as future perfect passives but as periphrastic future passives. You will, therefore, often see this translated not with future perfects, but with futures. How does the future perfect change the meaning of this passage? What does it mean that the binding and loosening will have already happened in heaven as opposed to happening as the same time or after the actions on earth?

Chapter 30 〜

μι Verbs • Present Tense and Imperfect Tense

μι Verbs: Present Tense and Imperfect Tense

You are already familiar with omega verbs and their offshoot contract verbs. This chapter will introduce you to the remaining verb type, μι verbs. The number of μι verbs is quite small, but those few are extremely important, whether in their absolute form or in compound verbs. It is therefore important that you memorize three model μι verbs. The good news is that, for the most part, μι verbs differ from omega verbs only in the present, imperfect, and aorist tenses. Your three model μι verbs will be δίδωμι = to give, τίθημι = to put, place, and ἵστημι = to stand.

	Present Active Indicative			
	δίδωμι = to give	*τίθημι = to put, place*	*ἵστημι = to stand*	*Endings*
Singluar				
1st	δίδω–**μι**	τίθη–**μι**	ἵστη–**μι**	μι
2nd	δίδω–**ς**	τίθη–**ς**	ἵστη–**ς**	ς
3rd	δίδω–**σι(ν)**	τίθη–**σι(ν)**	ἵστη–**σι(ν)**	σι(ν)
Plural				
1st	δίδο–**μεν**	τίθε–**μεν**	ἵστα–**μεν**	μεν
2nd	δίδο–**τε**	τίθε–**τε**	ἵστα–**τε**	τε
3rd	διδό–**ασι(ν)**	τιθέ–**ασι(ν)**	ἱστ–**ᾶσι(ν)**	ασι(ν)

Present Middle/Passive Indicative

	δίδωμι	τίθημι	ἵστημι	Endings
Singular				
1st	δίδο–μαι	τίθε–μαι	ἵστα–μαι	μαι
2nd	δίδο–σαι	τίθε–σαι	ἵστα–σαι	σαι
3rd	δίδο–ται	τίθε–ται	ἵστα–ται	ται
Plural				
1st	διδό–μεθα	τιθέ–μεθα	ἱστά–μεθα	μεθα
2nd	δίδο–σθε	τίθε–σθε	ἵστα–σθε	σθε
3rd	δίδο–νται	τίθε–νται	ἵστα–νται	νται

As you can see, in the present active there is a vowel shift from the singular to the plural. The present middle/passive endings are the same as the present middle/passive of omega verbs and thus they use the primary middle/passive endings you learned in chapter 14.

Imperfect Active Indicative

	δίδωμι	τίθημι	ἵστημι	Ending
Singular				
1st	ἐδίδου–ν	ἐτίθη–ν	ἵστη–ν	ν
2nd	ἐδίδου–ς	ἐτίθει–ς	ἵστη–ς	ς
3rd	ἐδίδου	ἐτίθει	ἵστη	–
Plural				
1st	ἐδίδο–μεν	ἐτίθε–μεν	ἵστα–μεν	μεν
2nd	ἐδίδο–τε	ἐτίθε–τε	ἵστα–τε	τε
3rd	ἐδίδο–σαν	ἐτίθε–σαν	ἵστα–σαν	σαν

Imperfect Middle/Passive Indicative

	δίδωμι	τίθημι	ἵστημι	Endings
Singular				
1st	ἐδιδό–μην	ἐτιθέ–μην	ἱστά–μην	μην
2nd	ἐδίδο–σο	ἐτίθε–σο	ἵστα–σο	σο
3rd	ἐδίδο–το	ἐτίθε–το	ἵστα–το	το
Plural				
1st	ἐδιδό–μεθα	ἐτιθέ–μεθα	ἱστά–μεθα	μεθα
2nd	ἐδίδο–σθε	ἐτίθε–σθε	ἵστα–σθε	σθε
3rd	ἐδίδο–ντο	ἐτίθε–ντο	ἵστα–ντο	ντο

The imperfect active endings are the same as the endings of the irregular aorists (like βαίνω's ἔβην) you learned in chapter 17. The imperfect middle/passive endings are the same as the imperfect middle/passive of omega verbs and thus they use the secondary middle/passive endings you learned in chapter 14.

Present Active Infinitive

δίδωμι	τίθημι	ἵστημι	Ending
διδό–**ναι**	τιθέ–**ναι**	ἱστά–**ναι**	**ναι**

Present Middle/Passive Infinitive

δίδωμι	τίθημι	ἵστημι	Ending
δίδο–**σθαι**	τίθε–**σθαι**	ἵστα–**σθαι**	**σθαι**

Present Active Imperative

	δίδωμι	τίθημι	ἵστημι	Endings
Singular				
2nd	δίδου	τίθει	ἵστη	–
3rd	διδό–**τω**	τιθέ–**τω**	ἱστά–**τω**	**τω**
Plural				
2nd	δίδο–**τε**	τίθε–**τε**	ἵστα–**τε**	**τε**
3rd	διδό–**ντων**	τιθέ–**ντων**	ἱστά–**ντων**	**ντων**

Present Middle/Passive Imperative

	δίδωμι	τίθημι	ἵστημι	Endings
Singular				
2nd	δίδο–**σο**	τίθε–**σο**	ἵστα–**σο**	**σο**
3rd	διδό–**σθω**	τιθέ–**σθω**	ἱστά–**σθω**	**σθω**
Plural				
2nd	δίδο–**σθε**	τίθε–**σθε**	ἵστα–**σθε**	**σθε**
3rd	διδό–**σθων**	τιθέ–**σθων**	ἱστά–**σθων**	**σθων**

μι verbs use the same imperative endings as omega verbs. Keep in mind the variability of the 2nd person singular active imperatives.

Present Participles of μι Verbs

The present participles for μι verbs closely resemble endings you have already learned. For a review of all the participle endings, see appendix A.

Present Active Participle

διδούς, διδοῦσα, διδόν	ἱστάς, ἱστᾶσα, ἱστάν	τιθείς, τιθεῖσα, τιθέν
¶ The endings of δίδωμι are the same as λύω with the exception of the masculine nominative singular, which has –ους instead of –ων.	¶ The endings of ἵστημι are the same as the aorist active participle of λύω.	¶ The endings of τίθημι are the same as the aorist passive participle of λύω.

Present Middle/Passive Participle

διδόμενος, –η, –ον	ἱστάμενος, –η, –ον	τιθέμενος, –η, –ον

Vocabulary

▸ αἰτία, –ας, ἡ = cause, blame

ἐντολή, –ῆς, ἡ = order, commandment

κλέος, –ου τό = glory

▸ μωρία, –ας, ἡ = foolishness, stupidity

ποιμήν, –ένος, ὁ = shepherd

▸ φυσικός, –ή, –όν (adj.) = natural, physical

ἀποδίδωμι, ἀποδώσω, ἀπέδωκα, ἀποδέδωκα, ἀποδέδομαι, ἀπεδόθην = to return, render; to define, explain

δίδωμι, δώσω, ἔδωκα, δέδωκα, δέδομαι, ἐδόθην = to give

ἵημι, ἥσω, ἧκα, εἷκα, εἷμια, εἵθην = to throw

▸ ἵστημι, στήσω, ἔστησα/ἔστην, ἕστηκα, ἕσταμαι, ἐστάθην = to set; to stand

παραδίδωμι, παραδώσω, παρέδωκα, παραδέδωκα, παραδέδομαι, παρεδόθην = to hand over, to betray

τίθημι, θήσω, ἔθηκα, τέθηκα, τέθειμαι, ἐτέθην = to put, place

Sentences

1. ὁ Ἀριστοτέλης ἔν τοῖς φυσικοῖς αἰτιολογικώτατος πάντων ἐγένετο ὥστε καὶ περὶ τῶν ἐλαχίστων τὰς αἰτίας ἀποδιδόναι. (Diogenes Laertius, *Lives of Eminent Philosophers*)

> ❡ Ἀριστοτέλης, –ους, ὁ = Aristotle
>
> τοῖς φυσικοῖς: the title of the work commonly translated as *Physics*
>
> αἰτιολογικός, –ή, –όν (adj.) = inquisitive of causes
>
> ἐγένετο = was: γίγνομαι is often best translated like εἰμί rather than "became."
>
> καὶ: here adverbial "even"
>
> ἐλάχιστος, –η, –ον (adj.) = smallest

2. ἐγώ εἰμι ὁ ποιμὴν ὁ καλός, ὁ ποιμὴν ὁ καλὸς τὴν ψυχὴν αὐτοῦ τίθησιν ὑπὲρ τῶν προβάτων. (John 10:11)

> ❡ τίθησιν: literally "places," here the meaning is "puts down" or "lays down."
>
> πρόβατον, –ου, τό = sheep

3. ὁ Ἰησοῦς ἐταράχθη τῷ πνεύματι καὶ ἐμαρτύρησεν καὶ εἶπεν, " Ἀμὴν ἀμὴν λέγω ὑμῖν ὅτι εἷς ἐξ ὑμῶν παραδώσει με." (John 13:21)

> ❡ ἐταράχθη: aorist passive of ταράσσω.

4. ἐντολὴν καινὴν δίδωμι ὑμῖν, ἵνα ἀγαπᾶτε ἀλλήλους. (John 13:34)

> ❡ ἵνα: here "that"
>
> ἀλλήλους = each other

5. εἰρήνην ἀφίημι ὑμῖν, εἰρήνην τὴν ἐμὴν δίδωμι ὑμῖν· οὐ καθὼς ὁ κόσμος δίδωσιν ἐγὼ δίδωμι ὑμῖν. μὴ ταρασσέσθω ὑμῶν ἡ καρδία μηδὲ δειλιάτω. (John 14:27)

> ❡ ἀφίημι = to let go; dismiss: here "give" or "release."
>
> δειλιάω = to be afraid

6. ἀναστήσω αὐτὸν ἐν τῇ ἐσχάτῃ ἡμέρᾳ. (John 6:44)

> ❡ ἀνίστημι = to raise up, resurrect
>
> αὐτὸν: the one who believes.

7. θεὸς δὲ τοῖς ἀργοῖσιν οὐ παρίσταται. (Menander, *Fragments*)

¶ παρίστημι = to stand by; (middle) assist (+ dat.)

ἀργός, –ή, –όν (adj.) = not working, lazy

8. ἡ μωρία δίδωσιν ἀνθρώποις κακά. (Menander, *Fragments*)

9. καίτοι τί κλέος εὐκλεέστερόν ἐστιν ἢ τὸν αὐτάδελφον ἐν τάφῳ τιθεῖσα; (Sophocles, *Antigone*)

¶ The speaker is Antigone, hence the feminine participle τιθεῖσα.

καίτοι (adv.) = certainly, indeed

εὐκλεής, –ές (adj.) = glorious, famous

αὐτάδελφος, –ου, ὁ = brother, here Polynices, who had been killed (by his and Antigone's brother Eteocles) fighting against his own city of Thebes

τάφος, –ου, ὁ = grave, tomb

10. φῶς ἱλαρὸν ἁγίας δόξης ἀθανάτου Πατρός, οὐρανίου, ἁγίου, μάκαρος, Ἰησοῦ Χριστέ, ἐλθόντες ἐπὶ τὴν ἡλίου δύσιν, ἰδόντες φῶς ἑσπερινόν, ὑμνοῦμεν Πατέρα, Υἱόν, καὶ ἅγιον Πνεῦμα, Θεόν. ἄξιόν σε ἐν πᾶσι καιροῖς ὑμνεῖσθαι φωναῖς αἰσίαις, Υἱὲ Θεοῦ, ζωὴν ὁ διδούς· διὸ ὁ κόσμος σὲ δοξάζει.

(early Christian hymn)

¶ The *Phos Hilaron* is the earliest Christian hymn recorded outside the bible.

ἱλαρός, –ά, –όν (adj.) = cheerful, merry

οὐράνιος, –ον (adj.) = heavenly

μάκαρ, –αρος (adj) = blessed, happy

οὐρανίου, ἁγίου, μάκαρος: these three adjectives modify Πατρός.

ἐλθόντες: aorist participle of ἔρχομαι

ἥλιος, –ου, ὁ = the sun

δύσις, –εως, ἡ = setting of the sun or stars

ἰδόντες: aorist participle of ὁράω

ἑσπερινός, ή, όν = evening, western

ὑμνέω = to hymn, sing praise of (+ acc.)

ἄξιόν = it is right (+ acc. and infinitive)

αἴσιος, –ον = auspicious

δοξάζω = think, imagine; to magnify, extol (+ acc.)

διό = διὰ ὅ: for which reason, wherefore

Etymology and Discussion Topics

αἰτία, –ας, ἡ = cause, blame

The study of causation is called etiology (sometimes spelled aetiology) and comes from this noun. It is also used in a legal context and means "blame."

μωρία, –ας, ἡ = foolishness, stupidity

Our derogatory term "moron" comes from this Greek word, and stupidity is an acceptable translation in many circumstances. It is often, however, better translated as "foolishness," especially in the New Testament. It can denote the folly or foolishness of otherwise "intelligent" people.

φυσικός, –ή, –όν (adj.) = natural, physical

Many of our academic nouns that end in "–ics" were originally Greek adjectives like φυσικός ending in –ικος. Examples include physics, rhetoric, politics, and economics.

ἵστημι, στήσω, ἔστησα/ἔστην, ἕστηκα, ἕσταμαι, ἐστάθην = to set; to stand

This verb, long the bane of beginning Greek students, causes confusion because it has both a 1st and a 2nd aorist with different meanings. Hopefully by now you remember the distinction between transitive and intransitive verbs. If you need to review, see chapter 4. The 1st aorist ἔστησα is transitive, while the 2nd aorist ἔστην (conjugated like the irregular aorists in chapter 17) is intransitive. In addition, the perfect active and aorist passive are intransitive. It can be a bit confusing, but this chart should help. There are a couple of rare exceptions, but in general this chart holds true.

Transitivity of ἴστημι = to set; to stand	
Transitive	*Intransitive*
Present Active	2nd Aorist Active
Future Active	Perfect Active
1st Aorist Active	Aorist Passive
Other middles and passives can be intransitive	

Chapter 31 ⌒

μι Verbs: Aorist Tense

μι Verbs: Aorist Tense

δίδωμι and τίθημι have one set of forms for the aorist active, while ἵστημι is notable for having two aorists with two different meanings (see prev. chapter's Etymology and Discussion Topics). The first aorist of ἵστημι (formed like the aorist of λύω) is *transitive*, while the second aorist (formed like the aorist of βαίνω in chapter 17) is *intransitive*.

				Aorist Active Indicative	
					ἵστημι
	δίδωμι	*τίθημι*	*Endings*	*1st Aorist*	*2nd Aorist*
Singular					
1st	ἔδω‑κα	ἔθη‑κα	κα	ἔστη‑σα	ἔστη‑ν
2nd	ἔδω‑κας	ἔθη‑κας	κας	ἔστη‑σας	ἔστη‑ς
3rd	ἔδω‑κε(ν)	ἔθη‑κε(ν)	κε(ν)	ἔστη‑σε(ν)	ἔστη
Plural					
1st	ἔδο‑μεν	ἔθε‑μεν	μεν	ἐστή‑σαμεν	ἔστη‑μεν
2nd	ἔδο‑τε	ἔθε‑τε	τε	ἐστή‑σατε	ἔστη‑τε
3rd	ἔδο‑σαν	ἔθε‑σαν	σαν	ἔστη‑σαν	ἔστη‑σαν

¶ κώνειον, –ου, τό = hemlock (a type of poison)

ὁ Σωκράτης ἔστησε τὸν ποτήριον.

Socrates stood up/placed the cup.

ὁ Σωκράτης ἔστη.

Socrates stood up.

ὁ ἄνθρωπος ἔδωκε τὸ κώνειον τῷ Σωκράτει.

A person gave the hemlock to Socrates.

The aorist middle is formed by attaching the secondary endings you learned in chapter 14 to the aorist stem with a shortened stem vowel.

	Aorist Middle Indicative		
	δίδωμι	*τίθημι*	*Endings*
Singular			
1st	ἐδό–**μην**	ἐθέ–**μην**	μην
2nd	ἔδ–**ου**	ἔθ–**ου**	σο → ου
3rd	ἔδο–**το**	ἔθε–**το**	το
Plural			
1st	ἐδό–**μεθα**	ἐθέ–**μεθα**	μεθα
2nd	ἔδο–**σθε**	ἔθε–**σθε**	σθε
3rd	ἔδο–**ντο**	ἔθε–**ντο**	νται

ἵστημι does not have a 2nd aorist middle since the 2nd aorist active is intransitive. Remember that the sigma of the second person singular drops out and the omicron contracts.

As you learned in the last chapter, with few exceptions μι verbs differ from omega verbs only in the present, imperfect, and aorist tenses. The aorist passive of μι verbs is formed exactly like the aorist passive of omega verbs, i.e., ἐδόθην, ἐτέθην, ἐστάθην.

τὸ κώνειον ἐδόθη τῷ Σωκράτει.

The hemlock was given to Socrates.

For the infinitives, imperatives, and participles of μι verbs, the aorist active and middle have the same endings as the present tense, but they are added to the aorist stem. It is helpful to compare the following forms with those of chapter 30, as the endings are the same.

Aorist Active Infinitive

δίδωμι	τίθημι	ἵστημι	Ending
δοῦ–**ναι**	θεῖ–**ναι**	στῆ–**ναι**	ναι

Aorist Middle Infinitive

δίδωμι	τίθημι	ἵστημι	Ending
δό–**σθαι**	θέ–**σθαι**	none	σθαι

Aorist Active Imperative

	δίδωμι	τίθημι	ἵστημι 2nd Aorist	Endings
Singular				
2nd	δός	θές	στῆθι	—
3rd	δό–**τω**	θέ–**τω**	στή–**τω**	τω
Plural				
2nd	δό–**τε**	θέ–**τε**	στῆ–**τε**	τε
3rd	δό–**ντων**	θέ–**ντων**	στά–**ντων**	ντων

Aorist Middle Imperative

	δίδωμι	τίθημι	ἵστημι	Endings
Singular				
2nd	δοῦ	θοῦ	—	σο → ου
3rd	δό–**σθω**	θέ–**σθω**	—	σθω
Plural				
2nd	δό–**σθε**	θέ–**σθε**	—	σθε
3rd	δό–**σθων**	θέ–**σθων**	—	σθων

Remember that the second person singular middle imperative endings contract after the sigma drops out, hence the change from σο to ου.

❡ φύλαξ, –ακος, ὁ = guard

μὴ δότω ὁ φύλαξ τὸ κώνειον τῷ Σωκράτει.

Let the guard not give the hemlock to Socrates.

στάντων καὶ ἐλθόντων οἱ διδάσκαλοι τοῦ Σωκράτους.

Let the students of Socrates stand and depart.

Aorist Participles of μι Verbs

The aorist participles for μι verbs closely resemble endings you have already learned. For a review of all the participle endings, see appendix A.

Aorist Active Participle

δούς, δοῦσα, δόν	θείς, θεῖσα, θέν	στάς, στᾶσα, στάν
¶ The forms are identical to the present active participle (διδούς, διδοῦσα, διδόν) without the initial δι.	¶ The forms are identical to the present active participle (τιθείς, τιθεῖσα, τιθέν) without the initial τι.	¶ The forms are identical to the present active participle (ἱστάς, ἱστᾶσα, ἱστάν) without the initial ἱ.

Aorist Middle Participle

δόμενος, –η, –ον	θέμενος, –η, –ον	στάμενος, –η, –ον (1st Aorist)
¶ The forms are identical to the present middle participle (διδόμενος, –η, –ον) without the initial δι.	¶ The forms are identical to the present middle participle (τιθέμενος, –η, –ον) without the initial τι.	¶ There is no 2nd aorist middle participle for ἵστημι. The 1st aorist forms are identical to the present participle (ἱστάμενος, –η, –ον) without the initial ἱ.

¶ κατατίθημι = to put down

καταθεὶς τὸ κώνειον ὁ φύλαξ ἦλθεν.

Having put down the hemlock, the guard left.

δοὺς τὸ κώνειον τῷ Σωκράτει, ὁ φύλαξ ἦλθεν.

Having given the hemlock to Socrates, the guard left.

Vocabulary

παῖς, παιδός, ὁ or ἡ = child

πούς, ποδός, ὁ = foot

στρατός, –οῦ, ὁ = army

▸ συμφορά, –ᾶς, ἡ = occurrence; misfortune

▸ φρήν, φρενός, ἡ = heart, mind

ἀφίημι, ἀφήσω, ἀφῆκα, ἀφεῖκα, ἀφεῖμαι, ἀφείθην = to cast off, release; pardon (+ dat.)

▸ πάσχω, πείσομαι, ἔπαθον, πέπονθα, —, — = to experience; suffer

ὑποτίθημι, ὑποθήσω, ὑπέθηκα, ὑποτέθεικα, ὑποτέθειμαι, ὑπετέθην = place under, offer; (middle) to give advice to (+ dat.)

Sentences

1. ὁ νόμος διὰ Μωϋσέως ἐδόθη, ἡ χάρις καὶ ἡ ἀλήθεια διὰ Ἰησοῦ Χριστοῦ.
(John 1:17)

> ❡ Μωϋσῆς, Μωϋσέως, ὁ = Moses
>
> ἐδόθη: aorist passive of δίδωμι

2. Ἰησοῦς εἴπεν, "Τετέλεσται," καὶ κλίνας τὴν κεφαλὴν παρέδωκεν τὸ πνεῦμα.
(John 19:30)

> ❡ κλίνας: aorist active participle of κλίνω = to bend, bow
>
> παρέδωκεν: aorist of παραδίδωμι

3. θοῦ δ' ἐν φρενὸς δέλτοισι τοὺς ἐμοὺς λόγους. (Sophocles, *Fragments*)

> ❡ θοῦ: aorist middle imperative of τίθημι. This is one of those instances where the active could have been used. You can, however, see how the middle captures the sense of doing this for one's advantage.
>
> δ' = δὲ
>
> δέλτοισι = δέλτοις
>
> δέλτος, –ου, ἡ = tablet (for writing)
>
> φρενὸς: supply "your."

4. ἡ δὲ τὰ σφυρὰ τοῦ παιδὸς θεραπεύσασα, Οἰδίπουν αὐτὸν καλεῖ· τοῦτο
θεμένη τὸ ὄνομα διὰ τὸ τοὺς πόδας ἀνοιδῆσαι. (Zenobius, *Proverbs*)

    ¶ This passage describes the origin of the name Oedipus: Οἰδίπους = οἶδος "swelling" + πούς "foot."

    ἡ δὲ = and she: the wife of the cowherd who found the baby exposed and left to die.

    σφυρόν, –οῦ, τό = ankle. The baby's ankles had been pierced.

    θεραπεύσασα: aorist active participle of θεραπεύω = to serve; treat medically

    ἀνοιδῆσαι: aorist active infinitive of ἀνοιδέω = to swell, be swollen.

5. ἐς γῆν δ᾽ Ἀτρεῖδαι πᾶς στρατός τ᾽ ἔστη βλέπων. (Euripides, *Iphigenia in Aulis*)

    ¶ This play recounts how Agamemnon sacrificed his daughter in order to appease Artemis, who was preventing the fleet from sailing to Troy. This line depicts the shame of those viewing the imminent sacrifice.

    ἐς = εἰς

    Ἀτρεῖδαι: the Atreidae, or sons of Atreus, were Agamemnon and Menelaus.

    τ᾽ = τε, here linking the two subjects Ἀτρεῖδαι and στρατός.

    ἔστη: the subject is both the Atreidae and the army.

6. ἀνὰ δ᾽ ὁ πτολίπορθος Ὀδυσσεὺς ἔστη σκῆπτρον ἔχων. (Homer, *Iliad*)

    ¶ πτολίπορθος, –ον (adj.) = city-destroying

    Ὀδυσσεύς, έως, ὁ = Odysseus

    σκῆπτρον, –ου, τό = scepter. In Homeric assemblies, the holding of the royal scepter signified the person's right to speak and so (theoretically) prevented everyone from shouting at once.

    ἀνὰ … ἔστη = ἀνέστη = stood up: in Homer compound verbs are often broken up and their parts separated, a phenomenon called "tmesis," from the verb τέμνω "to cut."

7. καὶ νῦν προσελθὼν στῆθι πλησίον πατρός, σκέψαι δ' ὁποίας συμφορὰς

πέπονθα. (Sophocles, *Women of Trachis*)

¶ The speaker is a dying Heracles addressing his son Hyllus.

προσελθών: aorist active participle of προσέρχομαι = to approach

πλησίον (adv.) = near (+ gen.)

πατρός: supply "your"

σκέψαι: aorist middle imperative of σκέπτομαι "to look, examine"

ὁποῖος, –α, –ον (adj.) = of what kind or sort

πέπονθα: see πάσχω in vocabulary above.

8. ἐρωτηθεὶς "τί δύσκολον," ἔφη, "τὸ ἑαυτὸν γνῶναι." "τί δὲ εὔκολον," "τὸ ἄλλῳ

ὑποθέσθαι." (Thales, in Diogenes Laertius, *Lives of Eminent Philosophers*)

¶ ἔφη = he said: the speaker is Thales.

ἐρωτηθεὶς = having been asked: aorist passive participle of ἐρωτάω.

τί δύσκολον = what is hard?: δύσκολος, –ον (adj.) = difficult

τί δὲ εὔκολον: supply another ἐρωτηθεὶς before this question and an ἔφη after it.

εὔκολος, –ον (adj.) = easy

ὑποθέσθαι: aorist middle infinitive of ὑποτίθημι

9. τοίνυν ἀπόδοτε τὰ Καίσαρος Καίσαρι καὶ τὰ τοῦ θεοῦ τῷ θεῷ. (Luke 20:25)

¶ τοίνυν (part.) = τοι + νῦν = therefore, accordingly

ἀπόδοτε: aorist active imperative of ἀποδίδωμι.

Καῖσαρ, –αρος, ὁ = Caesar

▸ 10. πάτερ ἡμῶν ὁ ἐν τοῖς οὐρανοῖς, ἁγιασθήτω τὸ ὄνομά σου, ἐλθέτω ἡ βασιλεία σου, γενηθήτω τὸ θέλημά σου, ὡς ἐν οὐρανῷ καὶ ἐπὶ γῆς. τὸν ἄρτον ἡμῶν τὸν ἐπιούσιον δὸς ἡμῖν σήμερον· καὶ ἄφες ἡμῖν τὰ ὀφειλήματα ἡμῶν, ὡς καὶ ἡμεῖς ἀφήκαμεν τοῖς ὀφειλέταις ἡμῶν· καὶ μὴ εἰσενέγκῃς ἡμᾶς εἰς πειρασμόν, ἀλλὰ ῥῦσαι ἡμᾶς ἀπὸ τοῦ πονηροῦ. (Matthew 6: 9–13)

¶ ἁγιασθήτω: aorist passive imperative of ἁγιάζω = to make or treat as holy

ἐλθέτω: aorist active imperative of ἔρχομαι

ὡς...καὶ = just as...so also

ἐπιούσιος, –ον (adj.): an obscure adjective occurring only here, meaning "daily," or perhaps "supernatural"

σήμερον (adv.) = today, now

ἄφες: aorist active imperative of ἀφίημι

ὀφείλημα, –ατος, τό = debt (used as a metaphor for "transgression" in Hebrew.)

ὡς καὶ = just as

ὀφειλέτης, –ου, ὁ = debtor; sinner

μὴ εἰσενέγκῃς = don't lead us: a prohibitive subjunctive you will learn in chapter 32

πειρασμός, –οῦ, ὁ = test; temptation

ῥῦσαι: aorist imperative of ῥύομαι = to protect, deliver from

Etymology and Discussion Topics

συμφορά, –ᾶς, ἡ = occurrence; misfortune

The verb συμφορέω literally means "to gather together." It normally means to come together for good or beneficial purposes. The adjective συμφορός, –όν means "useful" or "advantageous." Things that come together, however, can also be bad. The noun συμφορά can mean "misfortune." To make things even more confusing, συμφορός, –όν can be used substantively to mean advantage or benefits. Consequently, τὰ συμφορά "benefits" and ἡ συμφορά "misfortune" look very similar, but have opposite meanings.

φρήν, φρενός, ἡ = heart, mind

If you have ever encountered the odd word "midriff" (an old word for diaphragm) in a translation of an ancient Greek poem, it is probably a translation of φρήν. This word is notoriously difficult to translate. Separating the chest from the belly, the diaphragm is that spot where you might feel a sudden pang of emotion. It was therefore used to refer to the seat of the feelings and passions and is translated as "heart," "mind," or even "soul." Before we laugh too much at this mistaken anatomy, let us remember how often we point to our intestines and erroneously call it a "stomach" ache.

πάσχω, πείσομαι, ἔπαθον, πέπονθα, —, — = to experience; suffer

This word means principally "to experience." For the most part, the "experience" signified is bad, hence our translation "to suffer." It can also, however, be used of the experience of falling in love. The chorus in Aeschylus's *Agamemnon* states that Zeus has laid it down for human beings that "πάθει μάθος" (understanding [comes] through suffering/experience).

The Lord's Prayer (Matthew 6: 9–13)

Most people are familiar with this most famous of Christian prayers. Most English translations, however, are a combination of this version and the shorter one found in Luke's gospel. There are several fascinating things to observe about this version.

τὸν ἄρτον ἡμῶν τὸν ἐπιούσιον. Normally translated as "our daily bread," the adjective ἐπιούσιον occurs in Greek literature only here (or Luke's version of the prayer) or in later Christian citations of this passage. A uniquely attested word is called a hapax legomenon (literally "said once," from ἅπαξ "once" and the passive participle of λέγω). The only way to tell its meaning is from context and by breaking down the word. The first part of the adjective is from the preposition ἐπί. The second part is a participle from either the verb εἰμί "to be" or εἶμι "to go." One possibility is that it means "for the present" (ἐπί + εἰμί), hence "daily." Another possibility is that is means "for the future" (ἐπί + εἶμι). Finally, another intriguing possibility is that ἐπί is not used in the sense of "for," but rather "upon." The meaning of ἐπιούσιον would therefore be "supernatural" (ἐπί + εἰμί). In fact, St. Jerome translates ἐπιούσιον as *panem supersubstantialem* in the Vulgate.

ἀφήκαμεν. Often translated as a present, the tense is aorist. The person praying is therefore asking to be forgiven in the same way as he has forgiven others. If one has not forgiven others, this is perhaps not a prayer that one would wish to pray. The use of the present in our English translation comes from the version in Luke, which uses the present tense.

τοῦ πονηροῦ. One of the names of the devil in the New Testament is the substantive ὁ πονηρός "the evil one." Is this line asking God to deliver us from evil (the genitive of the neuter τὸ πονηρόν) or the devil (the genitive of the masculine ὁ πονηρός)?

Chapter 32

The Subjunctive • Independent Uses of the Subjunctive

The Subjunctive

As opposed to the indicative mood, which *indicates,* or makes claims, the subjunctive mood roughly communicates possibilities or ideals. The subjunctive mood in Greek is often difficult for English speakers because the use of the subjunctive is disappearing in English. In the tables below, you will not see a translation beside any of the subjunctive forms. This is because there is no single translation for the subjunctive in Greek. You must identify what type of subjunctive it is before you can translate it.

The uses of the subjunctive are divided into two categories, independent uses and dependent uses. Independent uses are subjunctives that serve as the main verb in an independent clause (see chapter 10 for a review of the difference between independent and dependent clauses). Dependent uses are subjunctives that serve as the verb in a dependent clause. This chapter will introduce you to the independent uses of the subjunctive. The dependent uses of the subjunctive will be spread out over the remaining chapters.

The word *subjunctive* (from the Latin *subjungere* "to subordinate") was chosen to describe this mood since many subjunctives you will see occur in dependent clauses. Below is a chart of the subjunctives you will encounter in this book. This is by no means an exhaustive list. A knowledge of these subjunctives will enable you to deal with the most common subjunctives as you begin reading Greek texts. You can learn the remaining subjunctives from Greek grammar books as you progress in your study of Greek.

Uses of the Subjunctive	
Independent	*Dependent*
Hortatory Subjunctive	Purpose Clause (chapter 33)
Deliberative Subjunctive	Fear Clause (chapter 38)
Prohibitive Subjunctive	Effort Clause (chapter 38)

Tenses of the Subjunctive

The subjunctive exists only in the present, aorist, and perfect tenses. Since the perfect subjunctive, which expresses completed aspect, is very rare, the forms of the perfect subjunctive will not be given in this chapter, but placed in Appendix A for reference. Just like the imperative, *the subjunctive tenses do not express time, but aspect.* Present subjunctives have imperfect aspect while aorist subjunctives have aoristic aspect. Subjunctives do not have infinitives or participles. As you will see, the subjunctive mood largely uses the same endings as the indicative with a lengthening of the thematic vowel. This lengthening of the thematic vowel is thus the marker for the subjunctive.

Omega Verbs				
Present Active	*Present M/P*	*Aorist Active*	*Aorist Middle*	*Aorist Passive*
λύ–ω	λύ–ωμαι	λύ–σω	λύ–σωμαι	λυθ–ῶ
λύ–ῃς	λύ–ῃ	λύ–σῃς	λύ–σῃ	λυθ–ῇς
λύ–ῃ	λύ–ηται	λύ–σῃ	λύ–σηται	λυθ–ῇ
Plural				
λύ–ωμεν	λυ–ώμεθα	λύ–σωμεν	λυ–σώμεθα	λυθ–ῶμεν
λύ–ητε	λύ–ησθε	λύ–σητε	λύ–σησθε	λυθ–ῆτε
λύ–ωσι(ν)	λύ–ωνται	λύ–σωσι(ν)	λύ–σωνται	λυθ–ῶσι(ν)

As you can see, the aorist active and middle subjunctive forms consist simply of a sigma in front of the present forms (technically the present forms are added to the aorist stem without the augment). Don't confuse these for future subjunctives, as there is no future subjunctive. Remember that only the indicative mood is augmented. The aorist passive subjunctive consists of the present subjunctive endings added to the aorist passive stem (6th principal part) without the augment.

Although it is best to memorize these endings as new endings, the following chart illustrates the lengthening of the thematic vowel.

Present Active Indicative	Vowel Lengthening	Present Active Subjunctive	Present M/P Indicative	Vowel Lengthening	Present M/P Subjunctive
		Singular			
λύ–ω	ω can't be lengthened	λύ–ω	λύ–ομαι	ο → ω	λύ–ωμαι
λύ–εις	ει → η	λύ–ῃς	λύ–ῃ/ λύ–ει	η, ει → η	λύ–ῃ
λύ–ει	ει → η	λύ–ῃ	λύ–εται	ε → η	λύ–ηται
		Plural			
λύ–ομεν	ο → ω	λύ–ωμεν	λυ–όμεθα	ο → ω	λυ–ώμεθα
λύ–ετε	ε → η	λύ–ητε	λύ–εσθε	ε → η	λύ–ησθε
λύ–ουσι(ν)	ου → ω	λύ–ωσι(ν)	λύ–ονται	ο → ω	λύ–ωνται

The subjunctives of 2nd aorists use the endings of the present subjunctive, e.g., ἔλθω (from ἦλθον, 2nd aorist of ἔρχομαι), βάλω (from ἔβαλον, 2nd aorist of βάλλω).

Subjunctive of εἰμί

The present (and only) subjunctive of εἰμί is quite simple, as the forms are the subjunctive endings of λύω, i.e., ὦ, ᾖς, ᾖ, ὦμεν, ἦτε, ὦσι(ν).

Contract Verbs (Present Subjunctive)

	νικάω		φιλέω		δηλόω
Present Active	Present M/P	Present Active	Present M/P	Present Active	Present M/P
		Singular			
νικ–ῶ	νικ–ῶμαι	φιλ–ῶ	φιλ–ῶμαι	δηλ–ῶ	δηλ–ῶμαι
νικ–ᾷς	νικ–ᾷ	φιλ–ῇς	φιλ–ῇ	δηλ–οῖς	δηλ–οῖ
νικ–ᾷ	νικ–ᾶται	φιλ–ῇ	φιλ–ῆται	δηλ–οῖ	δηλ–ῶται
		Plural			
νικ–ῶμεν	νικ–ώμεθα	φιλ–ῶμεν	φιλ–ώμεθα	δηλ–ῶμεν	δηλ–ώμεθα
νικ–ᾶτε	νικ–ᾶσθε	φιλ–ῆτε	φιλ–ῆσθε	δηλ–ῶτε	δηλ–ῶσθε
νικ–ῶσι(ν)	νικ–ῶνται	φιλ–ῶσι(ν)	φιλ–ῶνται	δηλ–ῶσι(ν)	δηλ–ῶνται

Only the present subjunctive endings are given above since the aorist subjunctive is identical to the aorist subjunctive of omega verbs. The present subjunctive endings of alpha contract verbs are identical in the present indicative and present subjunctive. Only context will enable you to tell the difference. The endings of epsilon contract verbs are identical to the subjunctive of omega verbs. The chart below summarizes the subjunctive for contract verbs.

	Contract Verb Subjunctives		
	α Contract (νικάω)	*ε Contract (φιλέω)*	*ο Contract (δηλόω)*
Present Active Subjunctive	Same as indicative for alpha contract verbs	Same as subjunctive for omega verbs	ῶ, οῖς, οῖ, ῶμεν, ῶτε, ῶσι(ν)
Present M/P Subjunctive	Same as indicative for alpha contract verbs	Same as subjunctive for omega verbs	ῶμαι, οῖ, ῶται, ώμεθα, ῶσθε, ῶνται
Aorist A/M/P Subjunctive	Same as subjunctive for omega verbs	Same as subjunctive for omega verbs	Same as subjunctive for omega verbs

μι Verb Subjunctive Forms

Subjunctive of μι Verbs: δίδωμι

Present Active	*Present M/P*	*Aorist Active*	*Aorist Middle*	*Aorist Passive*
διδ–ῶ	διδ–ῶμαι	δ–ῶ	δ–ῶμαι	δοθ–ῶ
διδ–ῷς	διδ–ῷ	δ–ῷς	δ–ῷ	δοθ–ῇς
διδ–ῷ	διδ–ῶται	δ–ῷ	δ–ῶται	δοθ–ῇ
		Plural		
διδ–ῶμεν	διδ–ώμεθα	δ–ῶμεν	δ–ώμεθα	δοθ–ῶμεν
διδ–ῶτε	διδ–ῶσθε	δ–ῶτε	δ–ῶσθε	δοθ–ῇτε
διδ–ῶσι(ν)	διδ–ῶνται	δ–ῶσι(ν)	δ–ῶνται	δοθ–ῶσι(ν)

Subjunctive of μι Verbs: τίθημι

Present Active	*Present M/P*	*Aorist Active*	*Aorist Middle*	*Aorist Passive*
τιθ–ῶ	τιθ–ῶμαι	θ–ῶ	θ–ῶμαι	τεθ–ῶ
τιθ–ῇς	τιθ–ῇ	θ–ῇς	θ–ῇ	τεθ–ῇς
τιθ–ῇ	τιθ–ῆται	θ–ῇ	θ–ῆται	τεθ–ῇ
		Plural		
τιθ–ῶμεν	τιθ–ώμεθα	θ–ῶμεν	θ–ώμεθα	τεθ–ῶμεν
τιθ–ῆτε	τιθ–ῆσθε	θ–ῆτε	θ–ῆσθε	τεθ–ῆτε
τιθ–ῶσι(ν)	τιθ–ῶνται	θ–ῶσι(ν)	θ–ῶνται	τεθ–ῶσι(ν)

Subjunctive of μι Verbs: ἵστημι

Present Active	Present M/P	Aorist Active	Aorist Middle	Aorist Passive
ἱστ–ῶ	ἱστ–ῶμαι	στ–ῶ	—	σταθ–ῶ
ἱστ–ῇς	ἱστ–ῇ	στ–ῇς	—	σταθ–ῇς
ἱστ–ῇ	ἱστ–ῆται	στ–ῇ	—	σταθ–ῇ
		Plural		
ἱστ–ῶμεν	ἱστ–ώμεθα	στ–ῶμεν	—	σταθ–ῶμεν
ἱστ–ῆτε	ἱστ–ῆσθε	στ–ῆτε	—	σταθ–ῆτε
ἱστ–ῶσι(ν)	ἱστ–ῶνται	στ–ῶσι(ν)	—	σταθ–ῶσι(ν)

Independent Uses of the Subjunctive

Hortatory Subjunctive

The hortatory subjunctive (from the Latin *hortari*, "to urge") is used in the 1st person to urge or command an action. Since Greek does not have a 1st person imperative, the hortatory subjunctive performs that function. While the 1st person singular does exist, the 1st person plural is more common. The negative for hortatory subjunctives (and most subjunctives) is μή.

λέγωμεν τὴν ἀλήθειαν.

Let us speak the truth.

δῶ ἀεὶ τὴν δόξαν τῷ ἀγαθῷ μαθητῇ.

May I always give glory to the good student.

μὴ μέλλωμεν ζητεῖν τὴν ἀλήθειαν.

Let us not hesitate to seek the truth.

Deliberative Subjunctive

Occasionally you will see the subjunctive in the first person used in a question to express doubt or indecision on the part of the speaker. This use is called a deliberative subjunctive.

λέγωμεν τὴν ἀλήθειαν;

Shall we speak the truth?

δῶ ἀεὶ τὴν δόξαν τῷ ἀγαθῷ μαθητῇ;

Am I to always give glory to the good student?

Prohibitive Subjunctive

Greek uses μή + subjunctive in the 2nd person (and sometimes the 3rd person) to express a negative command. It can be translated the same as a negative imperative.

❡ κώνειον, –ου, τό = hemlock (a type of poison)

μὴ πίνῃς τὸ κώνειον.

Don't drink the hemlock.

μὴ δῶτε τὴν δόξαν τῷ κακῷ μαθητῇ.

Don't give glory to the bad student.

Vocabulary

ἐγκώμιον, –ου, τό = encomium, eulogy

ὄχλος, –ου, ὁ = crowd, multitude

ἀσθενής, –ές (adj.) = weak

ἄφρων, –ονος (adj.) = senseless; silent

▸ δή (particle) = so, then; indeed

ὁμοίως (adv.) = similarly, in the same way

δοκέω, δόξω, ἔδοξα, δέδοχα, δέδογμαι, ἐδόχθην = to think, deem; to seem

δοξάζω, δοξάσω, ἐδόξασα, δεδόξακα, δεδόξασμαι, ἐδοξάσθην = to think; believe, judge

ἐλεέω, ἐλεήσω, ἠλέησα, ἠλέηκα, ἠλέημαι, ἠλεήθην = to have compassion or pity for one

μάχομαι, μαχήσομαι, ἐμαχεσάμην, —, μεμάχημαι, ἐμαχέσθην = to fight, battle

▸ μιμέομαι, μιμήσομαι, ἐμιμησάμην, μεμίμημαι, — = to imitate, reproduce

φράζω, φράσω, ἔφρασα, πέφρακα, πέφρασμαι, ἐφράσθην = to explain; declare; devise

ψέγω, ψέξω, ἔψεξα, —, ἔψεγμαι, ἐψέχθην = to criticize, reproach

Sentences

1. νῦν μαχώμεθα φαίδιμ' Ἀχιλλεῦ. (Homer, *Iliad*)

> ¶ These words are uttered by Aster-
> opaeus shortly before his death at
> the hands of Achilles in the *Iliad*.
>
> φαίδιμ' = φαίδιμε, vocative of
> φαίδιμος, –ον (adj.) = shining,
> famous
>
> Ἀχιλλεῦ: vocative of Ἀχιλλεῦς,
> –εως, ὁ = Achilles

2. διέλθωμεν δὴ ἕως Βηθλέεμ καὶ ἴδωμεν τὸ ῥῆμα τοῦτο τὸ γεγονὸς ὃ ὁ κύριος

   ἐγνώρισεν ἡμῖν. (Luke 2:15)

> ¶ These words are uttered by
> the shepherds after the angels
> announced the birth of Christ to
> them.
>
> διέλθωμεν: aorist subjunctive of
> διέρχομαι "go through"
>
> ἕως Βηθλέεμ = unto Bethlehem:
> i.e., go through the countryside
> until they reach Bethlehem
>
> ἴδωμεν: aorist subjunctive of ὁράω
>
> γεγονὸς = thing that has hap-
> pened: perfect neuter participle
> of γίγνομαι
>
> γνωρίζω = to make known

3. ἡμεῖς ἀγαπῶμεν, ὅτι αὐτὸς πρῶτος ἠγάπησεν ἡμᾶς. (1 John 4:19)

> ¶ ὅτι: here "because"
>
> αὐτὸς: God

▶ 4. ὑπὲρ σεαυτοῦ μὴ φράσῃς ἐγκώμιον. (Menander, *Fragments*)

5. ἴωμεν καὶ ἀκούσωμεν τοῦ ἀνδρός. (Socrates, in Plato, *Protagoras*)

> ¶ ἴωμεν: present subjunctive of εἶμι
> (not εἰμί)
>
> τοῦ ἀνδρός: the famous sophist
> Protagoras
>
> Remember that ἀκούω takes the
> genitive of the person listened to.

6. καὶ μὴ εἰσενέγκῃς ἡμᾶς εἰς πειρασμόν. (Luke 11:4)

> ¶ This line is from Luke's version of the Lord's prayer. The subject in this case is God.
>
> εἰσενέγκῃς: aorist subjunctive of εἰσφέρω = to carry in/into
>
> πειρασμός, –οῦ, ὁ = test; temptation

7. ἃ ψέγομεν ἡμεῖς, ταῦτα μὴ μιμώμεθα. (Menander, *Fragments*)

> ¶ ἃ = the things which

8. κύριε, μὴ τῷ θυμῷ σου ἐλέγξῃς με μηδὲ τῇ ὀργῇ σου παιδεύσῃς με. ἐλέησόν με, κύριε, ὅτι ἀσθενής εἰμι. (Psalms 6:1)

> ¶ ἐλέγξῃς: aorist subjunctive of ἐλέγχω = to cross-examine; test
>
> ἐλέησόν: aorist imperative of ἐλεέω.
>
> ὅτι = because

▶ 9. πάλιν λέγω, μή τίς με δόξῃ ἄφρονα εἶναι. (2 Cor 11:16)

> ¶ τίς: the indefinite τις, not the interrogative τίς. The enclitic με has thrown the accent backward.
>
> δόξῃ: aorist subjunctive of δοκέω.

10. καὶ ἐπηρώτων αὐτὸν οἱ ὄχλοι λέγοντες, "Τί οὖν ποιήσωμεν;" ἀποκριθεὶς δὲ ἔλεγεν αὐτοῖς, "Ὁ ἔχων δύο χιτῶνας μεταδότω τῷ μὴ ἔχοντι, καὶ ὁ ἔχων βρώματα ὁμοίως ποιείτω." (Luke 3:10–11)

> ¶ ἐπηρώτων: imperfect indicative of ἐπερωτάω = to question
>
> χιτών, –νος, ὁ = a tunic, cloak
>
> μεταδότω: aorist imperative of μεταδίδωμι = to give part of. This verb is used since one would be "part" of two.
>
> βρῶμα, –ατος, τό = food

Etymology and Discussion Topics

δή and Other Particles

In addition to the traditional eight parts of speech (nouns, adjectives, pronouns, verbs, adverbs, prepositions, conjunctions, and interjections) employed by English, Greek has a class of words called particles, as first mentioned in chapter 6. Particles are incredibly subtle and often untranslatable. They add nuance and tone to a sentence and are one of the things that make ancient Greek such a rich language. When you see a definition for a particle, take it with a grain of salt. Particles can rarely be reduced to simple English equivalents. Take the particle δή that you learned in the vocabulary of this chapter. Among its many uses, δή can be emphatic and is sometimes translated as "indeed." δή can also be used as a connective "then, therefore." Only context will tell you which meaning is required. In sentence #2, the δή is connective in the sense that the shepherds have just been told of the birth of Christ. Therefore they wish to go see him.

μιμέομαι, μιμήσομαι, ἐμιμησάμην, μεμίμημαι, —, — = to imitate, reproduce

From this verb and the noun μίμησις (imitation: many –σις nouns are translated by English –tion nouns) comes our English verb "to mimic." The concept of μίμησις and its power is of crucial importance in Plato's philosophy.

ὑπὲρ σεαυτοῦ μὴ φράσῃς ἐγκώμιον.

An encomium is a speech of praise, usually for someone that is still alive, whereas a eulogy is typically a speech of praise for someone who is deceased.

πάλιν λέγω, μή τίς με δόξῃ ἄφρονα εἶναι. (2 Cor 11:16)

The adjective ἄφρων is a combination of the privative alpha and φρήν. One who does not have a φρήν is therefore "senseless."

Chapter 33 ～

Purpose Clauses

Purpose Clauses

In chapter 32 you learned about independent uses of the subjunctive (hortatory, deliberative, and prohibitive). This chapter will introduce you to one of the three dependent uses of the subjunctive you will learn in this book, the purpose clause.

A purpose clause expresses the purpose or reason for an action. In English we usually express purpose with such words as "in order to," "so that," or simply "to."

I am memorizing all these verb forms *in order to* read Greek.

We are studying *to* get good grades.

The student sat in the front row *so that* she could hear the lecture better.

English expresses negative purpose with such words as "so that . . . not," and "lest."

I am studying *so that* I do *not* fail the class.

The student laughed at the professor's bad joke *lest* there be an awkward silence.

A purpose clause is a *dependent* clause, and so it can never be a complete sentence on its own. It *depends* upon an independent clause to make sense.

"We are studying" is an independent clause, while "to get good grades" cannot be a sentence.

Greek purpose clauses are introduced by ἵνα, ὡς, or ὅπως, with ἵνα being the most common. Negative purpose clauses are introduced by ἵνα μή, ὡς μή, ὅπως μή, or μή. Your translation will not be affected by which of the above Greek words introduces the purpose clause. The verb in the purpose clause is put into the *subjunctive* mood. Remember that a purpose clause is not the only way Greek can express purpose. We have seen that Greek can also use the infinitive (chapter 16) and the future participle (chapter 21).

Vocabulary

▸ ὁδός, –οῦ, ἡ = road, way

στόμα, –ατος, τό = mouth

χρεία, –ας, ἡ = need, want

ἥττων (Koine ἥσσων), –ονος (adj.) = inferior, less

πένης, –ητος (adj.) = poor

πλείων, –ον (adj.) = greater, more

πλούσιος, –α, –ον (adj.) = rich

φαῦλος, –η, –ον (adj.) = cheap, base; evil

ὅπως, ἵνα, ὡς (used to introduce purpose clauses) = in order to, so that, to

ἐσθίω, ἔδομαι, ἔφαγον, ἐδήδοκα, ἐδήδεσμαι, ἠδέσθην = to eat

▸ κρίνω, κρινῶ, ἔκρινα, κέκρικα, κέκριμαι, ἐκρίθην = to separate; judge, condemn

σπεύδω, σπεύσω, ἔσπευσα, ἔσπευκα, ἔσπευσμαι, — = to hasten; be eager to, strive to (+ inf.)

Sentences

▶ 1. τούτου χάριν πάντα πράττομεν, ὅπως μήτε ἀλγῶμεν μήτε ταρβῶμεν.

(Epicurus, *Letter to Menoeceus*)

❡ τούτου: points to the following clause

τούτου χάριν when proceeded by a genitive, the accusative of χάρις means "for the sake of," so here "for the sake of this…"

μήτε…μήτε = neither…nor

ἀλγέω = to suffer

ταρβέω = to be afraid

2. πᾶς γὰρ ὁ φαῦλα πράσσων μισεῖ τὸ φῶς καὶ οὐκ ἔρχεται πρὸς τὸ φῶς, ἵνα μὴ ἐλεγχθῇ τὰ ἔργα αὐτοῦ. (John 3:20)

❡ πᾶς…ὁ…πράσσων = everyone doing

ἐλεγχθῇ: aorist passive subjunctive of ἐλέγχω

3. οὐ γὰρ ἦλθον ἵνα κρίνω τὸν κόσμον ἀλλ᾽ ἵνα σώσω τὸν κόσμον. (John 12:47)

❡ ἦλθον: aorist of ἔρχομαι; the grammatical subject is Jesus.

σώσω: remember that there is no future subjunctive. Although the spelling is the same as the future indicative, the ἵνα tells you that it is an aorist subjunctive in a purpose clause.

4. μὴ κρίνετε, ἵνα μὴ κριθῆτε. (Matthew 7:1)

5. διὰ τοῦτο δύο ὦτα ἔχομεν, στόμα δὲ ἕν, ἵνα πλείονα μὲν ἀκούωμεν, ἥττονα δὲ λέγωμεν. (Zeno of Citium, in Diogenes Laertius, *Lives of Eminent Philosophers*)

❡ οὖς, ὠτός, τό = ear

▶ 6. μὴ σπεῦδε πλουτεῖν, μὴ ταχὺς πένης γένῃ. (Menander, *Fragments*)

❡ γένῃ: aorist subjunctive of γίγνομαι

ταχύς, –εῖα, –ύ (adj.) = swift

7. κἀγὼ τὴν δόξαν ἣν δέδωκάς μοι δέδωκα αὐτοῖς, ἵνα ὦσιν ἓν καθὼς ἡμεῖς ἕν.

   (John 17:22)

> ¶ Here Jesus speaks to God.
>
> κἀγὼ = καὶ ἐγὼ
>
> δέδωκάς: perfect of δίδωμι
>
> αὐτοῖς: i.e., the disciples
>
> ὦσιν: present subjunctive of εἰμί

8. σύ τ᾽, Ἰνάχειον σπέρμα, τοὺς ἐμοὺς λόγους θυμῷ βάλ᾽, ὡς τέρματ᾽ ἐκμάθῃς

   ὁδοῦ. (Aeschylus, *Prometheus Bound*)

> ¶ The speaker is Prometheus, who will prophesy to Io the end of her ordeal.
>
> Ἰνάχειον σπέρμα: the "Inachean seed" or "seed of Inachus" is Io, who was turned into a cow by a jealous Hera and forced to flee her home.
>
> βάλ᾽ = βάλε: aorist imperative of βάλλω
>
> τέρματ᾽ = τέρματα = end: direct object of ἐκμάθῃς: aorist subjunctive of ἐκμανθάνω = to learn

9. ὁ Σωκράτης δ᾽ ἔλεγεν τῶν ἄλλων ἀνθρώπων διαφέρειν καθ᾽ ὅσον οἱ μὲν ζῶσιν

   ἵν᾽ ἐσθίωσιν, αὐτὸς δ᾽ ἐσθίει ἵνα ζῇ. (Athenaeus, *Deinosophistae*)

> ¶ διαφέρειν: supply "he" as the subject of this infinitive in indirect statement.
>
> καθ᾽ ὅσον = in as much as
>
> ἵν᾽ = ἵνα
>
> ζῇ: 3rd person singular present subjunctive of ζάω

10. καὶ ἀποκριθεὶς ὁ Ἰησοῦς εἶπεν πρὸς αὐτούς, "Οὐ χρείαν ἔχουσιν οἱ
ὑγιαίνοντες ἰατροῦ ἀλλὰ οἱ κακῶς ἔχοντες. οὐκ ἐλήλυθα καλέσαι δικαίους
ἀλλὰ ἁμαρτωλοὺς εἰς μετάνοιαν." (Luke 5:31–32)

¶ αὐτούς: the Pharisees

ὑγιαίνω = to be healthy

ἔχω κακῶς = to be sick. Similar
to the English expression "to fare
well," Greek uses the verb ἔχειν
and the adverb εὖ for "to be well"
and ἔχειν and the adverb κακῶς
for "to be sick."

ἐλήλυθα: perfect of ἔρχομαι

μετάνοια, –ας, ἡ = repentance,
conversion

Etymology and Discussion Topics

ὁδός, –οῦ, ἡ = road, way

Although this noun belongs to the 2nd declension and is declined exactly like λόγος, it is nevertheless feminine. ὁδός can refer to a physical road or the abstract notion of "way." In the ancient Christian text *The Didachē*, ὁ ὁδός "the way" is a term for Christianity.

κρίνω, κρινῶ, ἔκρινα, κέκρικα, κέκριμαι, ἐκρίθην = to separate; judge

This verb literally means "to separate." If you separate things, you can distinguish between them. From this comes the meaning of "to judge," whether it be an intellectual judging or a legal one. You have already encountered the compound verb ἀποκρίνω, especially its middle and passive meaning "to respond," in your examples.

τούτου χάριν πάντα πράττομεν, ὅπως μήτε ἀλγῶμεν μήτε ταρβῶμεν.

This sentence of Epicurus encapsulates his view of the greatest good in life: pleasure. For Epicurus, pleasure is not a possession of something, but rather the absence of pain.

μὴ σπεῦδε πλουτεῖν, μὴ ταχὺς πένης γένῃ.

Greek often uses an adjective where English would use an adverb, as in the above example. We would prefer to say "lest you quickly become poor," whereas Greek uses an adjective. In such cases it is best to translate those adjectives as adverbs.

Chapter 34 ∽

The Optative • Independent Uses of the Optative

The Optative

Independent Uses of the Optative

The optative is the fourth and final mood in Greek. Like the subjunctive, the optative does not indicate or make claims, but rather expresses hope or possibility. It can be helpful to think of the optative as an even less certain, or more remote, subjunctive. Like the subjunctive, the optative has independent uses and dependent uses. This chapter will introduce you to the two most common independent uses of the optative.

Forms of the Optative

The optative exists in the present, aorist, future, and perfect tenses. Like the perfect subjunctive, the perfect optative, which expresses perfective aspect, is very rare and will not be included in this chapter. You can find the forms in appendix A at the back of your book. The future optative is reserved for one use that you will learn in chapter 39. Therefore, just like the subjunctive, you will for the most part encounter the optative in either the present or the aorist and these will denote *aspect, not time*. The present optative expresses imperfect aspect while the aorist optative expresses aoristic aspect. There is no optative infinitive or participle.

Omega Verbs

Present Active Optative	Present M/P Optative	Future Active Optative	Future Middle Optative	Future Passive Optative
		Singular		
λύ–οιμι	λυ–οίμην	λύ–σοιμι	λυ–σοίμην	λυ–θησοίμην
λύ–οις	λύ–οιο	λύ–σοις	λύ–σοιο	λυ–θήσοιο
λύ–οι	λύ–οιτο	λύ–σοι	λύ–σοιτο	λυ–θήσοιτο
		Plural		
λύ–οιμεν	λυ–οίμεθα	λύ–σοιμεν	λυ–σοίμεθα	λυ–θησοίμεθα
λύ–οιτε	λύ–οισθε	λύ–σοιτε	λυ–σοισθε	λυ–θήσοισθε
λύ–οιεν	λύ–οιντο	λύ–σοιεν	λυ–σοιντο	λυ–θήσοιντο

Omega Verbs

Aorist Active Optative	Aorist Middle Optative	Aorist Passive Optative
	Singular	
λύ–σαιμι	λυ–σαίμην	λυ–θείην
λύ–σειας (λύ–σαις)	λύ–σαιο	λυ–θείης
λύ–σειε(ν) (λύ–σαι)	λύ–σαιτο	λυ–θείη
	Plural	
λύ–σαιμεν	λυ–σαίμεθα	λυ–θείημεν (λυθεῖμεν)
λύ–σαιτε	λύ–σαισθε	λυ–θείητε (λυθεῖτε)
λύ–σειαν (λύ–σαιεν)	λύ–σαιντο	λυ–θείησαν (λυθεῖεν)

Just like the subjunctive, the optative of 2nd aorists uses the endings of the present optative, e.g., ἔλθοιμι (from ἦλθον, 2nd aorist of ἔρχομαι), βάλοιμι (from ἔβαλον, 2nd aorist of βάλλω).

The marker for the optative is the iota: οι in the present and future, αι in the aorist active and middle, and ειη in the aorist passive.

Just like the indicative, the future merely adds a sigma to the present endings in the active and middle optative.

In the aorist active and middle, the ο of οι is replaced by α, giving αι instead of οι. In a perfect world, the aorist active forms in parentheses would be the most common, as they are more regular in form, but in real Greek texts you will find the εια forms are more common.

Once again, contract verbs contract in the present optative. The good news is that contract verbs are the same as omega verbs in the aorist and future. Therefore only the present forms will differ and are listed below.

Contract Verbs					
Present Active Optative	Present M/P Optative	Present Active Optative	Present M/P Optative	Present Active Optative	Present M/P Optative
Contraction: α + οι → ῳ		Contraction: ε + οι → οι		Contraction: ο + οι → οι	
Singular					
νικ–ῴην	νικ–ῴμην	φιλ–οίην	φιλ–οίμην	δηλ–οίην	δηλ–οίμην
νικ–ῴης	νικ–ῷο	φιλ–οίης	φιλ–οῖο	δηλ–οίης	δηλ–οῖο
νικ–ῴη	νικ–ῷτο	φιλ–οίη	φιλ–οῖτο	δηλ–οίη	δηλ–οῖτο
Plural					
νικ–ῷμεν	νικ–ῴμεθα	φιλ–οῖμεν	φιλ–οίμεθα	δηλ–οῖμεν	δηλ–οίμεθα
νικ–ῷτε	νικ–ῷσθε	φιλ–οῖτε	φιλ–οῖσθε	δηλ–οῖτε	δηλ–οῖσθε
νικ–ῷεν	νικ–ῷντο	φιλ–οῖεν	φιλ–οῖντο	δηλ–οῖεν	δηλ–οῖντο

Alternate forms for the optative are listed in Appendix A.

The optative endings of μ verbs are similar to the optative of omega verbs. Below are given the endings for δίδωμι, τίθημι, and ἵστημι.

δίδωμι			
Present Active Optative	Present M/P Optative	Aorist Active Optative	Aorist Middle Optative
Singular			
διδ–οίην	διδ–οίμην	δ–οίην	δ–οίμην
διδ–οίης	διδ–οῖο	δ–οίης	δ–οῖο
διδ–οίη	διδ–οῖτο	δ–οίη	δ–οῖτο
Plural			
διδ–οῖμεν	διδ–οίμεθα	δ–οῖμεν	δ–οίμεθα
διδ–οῖτε	διδ–οῖσθε	δ–οῖτε	δ–οῖσθε
διδ–οῖεν	διδ–οῖντο	δ–οῖεν	δ–οῖντο

τίθημι			
Present Active Optative	Present M/P Optative	Aorist Active Optative	Aorist Middle Optative
Singular			
τιθ–είην	τιθ–είμην	θ–είην	θ–είμην
τιθ–είης	τιθ–εῖο	θ–είης	θ–εῖο
τιθ–είη	τιθ–εῖτο	θ–είη	θ–εῖτο
Plural			
τιθ–εῖμεν	τιθ–είμεθα	θ–εῖμεν	θ–είμεθα
τιθ–εῖτε	τιθ–εῖσθε	θ–εῖτε	θ–εῖσθε
τιθ–εῖεν	τιθ–εῖντο	θ–εῖεν	θ–εῖντο

ἵστημι			
Present Active Optative	*Present M/P Optative*	*Aorist Active Optative*	*Aorist Middle Optative*
Singular			
ἱστ–*αίην*	ἱστ–*αίμην*	στ–*αίην*	—
ἱστ–*αίης*	ἱστ–*αῖο*	στ–*αίης*	—
ἱστ–*αίη*	ἱστ–*αῖτο*	στ–*αίη*	—
Plural			
ἱστ–*αῖμεν*	ἱστ–*αίμεθα*	στ–*αῖμεν*	—
ἱστ–*αῖτε*	ἱστ–*αῖσθε*	στ–*αῖτε*	—
ἱστ–*αῖεν*	ἱστ–*αῖντο*	στ–*αῖεν*	—

The aorist forms are merely the present forms without the initial δι, τι, and ἱ.

The future optative endings of μι verbs are identical to those of omega verbs, which consist of the 2nd principal part and the future optative endings, e.g., δώσοιμι, δώσοις, δώσοι, etc.

The aorist passive optative endings of μι verbs are identical to those of omega verbs, which consist of the 6th principal part without the augment and the aorist passive optative endings, e.g., δοθείην, δοθείης, δοθείη, etc.

The 1st aorist optative of ἵστημι is identical to the aorist optative of omega verbs.

Finally, presented below are the optative forms of the verb εἰμί.

εἰμί	
Present	*Future*
Singular	
εἴ–*ην*	ἐσ–*οίμην*
εἴ–*ης*	ἔσ–*οιο*
εἴ–*η*	ἔσ–*οιτο*
Plural	
εἴ–*μεν* or εἴημεν	ἐσ–*οίμεθα*
εἴ–*τε* or εἴητε	ἔσ–*οισθε*
εἴ–*εν* or εἴησαν	ἔσ–*οιντο*

Independent Uses of the Optative

Just like the subjunctive, the optative occurs in independent and dependent clauses. This chapter will introduce you to the two most common uses of the optative, the Optative of Wish and the Potential Optative.

	Uses of the Optative	
Independent	*Dependent*
Optative of Wish	Sequence of Moods (chapter 39)
Potential Optative	

Optative of Wish

The word "optative" comes from a usage connoting desire, as the Latin word *optare* means "to wish." The optative of wish consists of a verb in the optative mood, sometimes introduced by εἴθε or εἰ γάρ. Traditionally the optative of wish is translated by "Would that…" or "If only…," but other wording is appropriate as long as the idea of a wish is expressed. The negative μή makes the wish a negative.

¶ ἀοιδή, –ῆς, ἡ = song | Σειρήν, –ῆνος, ἡ = Siren

εἰ γὰρ ἀκούοιμι τὴν ἀοιδὴν τῶν Σειρήνων.

If only I could hear the song of the Sirens. / Would that I could hear the song of the Sirens. / I wish that I could hear the song of the Sirens.

μὴ νῦν παύοιτο ἡ ἀοιδὴ τῶν Σειρήνων.

Would that the song of the Sirens not cease now. / May the song of the Sirens not cease now.

Potential Optative

The potential optative consists of the optative and the particle ἄν. The particle ἄν (usually placed after the optative) cannot be translated by itself. The potential optative states that something might possibly happen (or not happen). The negative οὐ is used for a negative potential optative.

ἡ ἀοιδὴ τῶν Σειρήνων βλάπτοι ἂν τοὺς ἀνθρώπους.

The song of the Sirens might harm the men.

ἡ ἀοιδὴ τῶν Σειρήνων οὐ βλάπτοι ἂν τοὺς ἀνθρώπους.

The song of the Sirens might not harm the men.

The Optative in New Testament Greek

The optative mood, while quite common in classical Greek, is rare in the New Testament. Does this mean that if you are primarily interested in New Testament Greek you need not learn the optative? In the words of St. Paul, μὴ γένοιτο "May it not happen!" While the optative in the New Testament is rare, it occurs in some very important passages.

Vocabulary

ἐπίγνωσις, –εως, ἡ = recognition; knowledge

▸ μορφή, –ῆς, ἡ = form, shape

πῆμα, –ατος, τό = adversity, misfortune

τέρμα, –ατος, τό = end, limit

ἄρα (part.) = then, next
ἔτι (adv.) = still
πῶς (adv.) = how?

▸ τε (conj.) = and

ὦ (interj.) = O!, Oh! (always precedes a vocative)

ἥδομαι, ἡσθήσομαι, —, —, ἥσθην, — = to feel pleasure, be pleased

μαίνομαι, μανοῦμαι, ἐμηνάμην, —, μεμάνημαι, ἐμάνην = to rage; be mad, crazy

πλεονάζω, πλεονάσω, ἐπλεόνασα, πεπλεόνακα, πεπλεόνασμαι, ἐπλεονάσθην = to be superabundant; increase

συμφέρω, συνοίσω, συνήνεγκα/συνήνεγκον, —, —, — = to bring together, benefit; be useful

Sentences

1. ὦ δύσποτμ᾽, εἴθε μήποτε γνοίης ὃς εἶ. (Sophocles, *Oedipus Tyrannus*)

> ¶ This line is from Sophocles' *Oedipus Tyrannus*. The words are spoken to Oedipus by Jocasta, who knows the true identity Oedipus.
>
> δύσποτμ᾽ = δύσποτμε
>
> δύσποτμος, –ον (adj.) = unlucky
>
> γνοίης: aorist optative of γιγνώσκω

▶ 2. ἀστέρας εἰσαθρεῖς, ἀστὴρ ἐμός· εἴθε γενοίμην οὐρανός, ὡς πολλοῖσ᾽ ὄμμασιν εἰς σὲ βλέπω.

(Plato, *Epigrams*)

> ¶ ἀστήρ, –έρος, ὁ – star
>
> εἰσαθρέω = to look upon
>
> ὡς: introduces a purpose clause here
>
> πολλοῖσ᾽ = πολλοῖσι = πολλοῖς. See Etymology and Discussion section for this alternate dative plural.
>
> ὄμμα, –ατος, τό = eye
>
> βλέπω: subjunctive, not indicative

3. εἶπεν δὲ Μαριάμ, "Ἰδοὺ ἡ δούλη κυρίου· γένοιτό μοι κατὰ τὸ ῥῆμά σου." καὶ ἀπῆλθεν ἀπ᾽ αὐτῆς ὁ ἄγγελος. (Luke 1:38)

> ¶ This passage follows the angel's message to Mary that she would bear the child of God.
>
> εἶπεν: aorist of λέγω
>
> Ἰδοὺ: aorist imperative of ὁράω.
>
> ἀπῆλθεν: aorist of ἀπέρχομαι = to depart

4. εἰ ἄρα ὁ Ἔρως τῶν καλῶν ἐνδεής ἐστι, τὰ δὲ ἀγαθὰ καλά, κἂν τῶν ἀγαθῶν ἐνδεὴς εἴη. (Plato, *Symposium*)

> ¶ ἐνδεής, –ές (adj.) = lacking (+ gen.)
>
> τὰ δὲ ἀγαθὰ καλά: supply "are." Remember that the subject gets the definite article and the predicate does not.
>
> κἂν = καὶ ἂν: καὶ is an adverbial "also."

5. μή μοι γένοιθ᾽, ἃ βούλομ᾽, ἀλλ᾽ ἃ συμφέρει. (Menander, *Fragments*)

> ¶ γένοιθ᾽ = γένοιτο
>
> βούλομ᾽ = βούλομαι
>
> ἀλλ᾽ = ἀλλά

▶ 6. τί οὖν ἐροῦμεν; ἐπιμένωμεν τῇ ἁμαρτίᾳ ἵνα ἡ χάρις πλεονάσῃ; μὴ γένοιτο· οἵτινες ἀπεθάνομεν τῇ ἁμαρτίᾳ, πῶς ἔτι ζήσομεν ἐν αὐτῇ; (Rom 6:1–2)

> ¶ ἐροῦμεν: future of λέγω
>
> ἐπιμένω = to remain in (+ dat.)
>
> οἵτινες = ἡμεῖς οἵ. You will learn about ὅστις in chapter 35.
>
> ἀπεθάνομεν: aorist of ἀποθνῄσκω
>
> ζήσομεν: future of ζάω

7. σοῦ γὰρ φθιμένης οὐκέτ᾽ ἂν εἴην. (Euripides, *Alcestis*)

> ¶ This line is taken from Euripides' *Alcestis*. The speaker is Admetus and the words are addressed to his wife Alcestis, who is about to die.
>
> φθίω = to perish, here part of a genitive absolute with conditional force, i.e., "if you should perish"
>
> οὐκέτ᾽ = οὐκέτι

8. μανείην μᾶλλον ἢ ἡσθείην. (Antisthenes, in Diogenes Laertius, *Lives of Eminent Philosophers*)

> ¶ μανείην: see μαίνομαι
>
> ἡσθείην: see ἥδομαι

9. φεῦ φεῦ, βροτείων πημάτων ὅσαι τύχαι
ὅσαι τε μορφαί· τέρμα δ᾽ οὐκ εἴποι τις ἄν.
(Euripides, *Antiope*)

> ¶ φεῦ (interjection) = alas
>
> βρότειος, –α, –ον (adj.) = mortal, human
>
> ὅσαι: here "how many [are] the…"
>
> ▶ τε: translate before the second ὅσαι
>
> εἴποι: aorist optative of λέγω

10. χάρις ὑμῖν καὶ εἰρήνη πληθυνθείη ἐν ἐπιγνώσει τοῦ θεοῦ καὶ Ἰησοῦ τοῦ κυρίου ἡμῶν. (2 Peter 1:2)

¶ πληθυνθείη: aorist optative passive of πληθύνω = to increase, multiply

Etymology and Discussion Topics

μορφή, –ῆς, ἡ = form

From this word come many English words such as "to morph," "morphology," "metamorphosis," and "polymorph."

τε (conj.) = and

This conjunction is usually translated before the word that it follows, as in #9. For more on postpositives, see Chapter 6, Etymology and Discussion Topics.

ἀστέρας εἰσαθρεῖς, ἀστὴρ ἐμός· εἴθε γενοίμην οὐρανός, ὡς πολλοῖσ' ὄμμασιν εἰς σὲ βλέπω.

This epigram is attributed to Plato, but many have their doubts about whether he actually composed it or not. The author plays off the image of the stars as the eyes of the heavens. Notice the alternate dative plural form of πολλοῖσι(ν). You will often find these poetic forms ending in –οισι(ν) for the masculine and neuter dative plural and –αισι(ν) for the feminine dative plural. In this book, however, you will always be given the normal forms in the notes.

τί οὖν ἐροῦμεν; ἐπιμένωμεν τῇ ἁμαρτίᾳ, ἵνα ἡ χάρις πλεονάσῃ; μὴ γένοιτο· οἵτινες ἀπεθάνομεν τῇ ἁμαρτίᾳ, πῶς ἔτι ζήσομεν ἐν αὐτῇ; (Rom 6:1–2)

What do you think St. Paul is arguing against in this sentence?

Chapter 35 ～

Introduction to Conditions • Simple Conditions • Future Conditions •
Substitutions for εἰ • Mixed Conditions

Introduction to Conditions

Roughly speaking, a conditional sentence is an "if…then" sentence and is traditionally divided into a protasis and an apodosis. While the terms *protasis* and *apodosis* are very helpful, you can use the term "if clause" for protasis and "then clause" for apodosis if you choose. The protasis, or "if clause," is always a dependent clause while the apodosis, or "then clause," is always an independent clause.

Protasis (if clause) = dependent clause

Apodosis (then clause) = independent clause

If the student learns Greek, *his life will be blessed.*
If the professor doesn't know the time, *he will not stop talking.*

As you can see, the word "then" need not always appear in the sentence, but the use of the term "then clause" nevertheless communicates that the apodosis is contingent upon the protasis.

Simple Conditions

Simple conditions use the indicative in both the protasis (if clause) and the apodosis (then clause). The protasis (if clause) is usually introduced by the word εἰ "if." There is no "then" to mark the apodosis (then clause). The negative of the protasis (if clause) is μή, while the negative of the apodosis (then clause) is οὐ. You will see a variety of tenses.

¶ ταπεινοφροσύνη, –ης, ἡ = humility

εἰ γὰρ ἔχομεν τὴν ταπεινοφροσύνην, ἔχομεν τὴν ἀρχὴν τῆς σοφίας.

For if we have humility, we have the beginning of wisdom.

εἰ γὰρ εἴχομεν τὴν ταπεινοφροσύνην, εἴχομεν τὴν ἀρχὴν τῆς σοφίας.

For if we had humility, we had the beginning of wisdom.

εἰ γὰρ ἕξομεν τὴν ταπεινοφροσύνην, ἕξομεν τὴν ἀρχὴν τῆς σοφίας.

For if we will have humility, we will have the beginning of wisdom.

If all Greek conditions were simple conditions, learning Greek would be easier, but the richness and subtlety of Greek conditions would be lost. Most conditions are not simple. Far more common are the future conditions you will learn in this chapter and the general conditions you will learn in chapter 36.

Future Conditions

Greek has two conditions that are employed for future conditions, the *future more vivid* and the *future less vivid*. As you might have guessed, the future more vivid presents conditions that are probable, while the future less vivid expresses conditions that are less probable or merely possible. More correctly, the future more vivid condition expresses a protasis (if clause) that is probable, while the future less vivid expresses a protasis (if clause) that is less probable or merely possible. The apodosis (then clause) of any condition follows if the protasis (if clause) of that condition is true. Just like simple conditions, the negative of the protasis (if clause) is μή, while the negative of the apodosis (then clause) is οὐ.

Future More Vivid

Future more vivid conditions are introduced by ἐάν (ἤν or ἄν) and the subjunctive in the protasis (if clause) and have the future indicative in the apodosis (then clause). ἐάν, ἤν, and ἄν can all be translated as "if" with no difference in meaning. All three (ἐάν, ἤν, and ἄν) are actually combinations of εἰ "if" and the untranslatable particle ἄν, but it is easiest to think of all three as meaning "if." Remember that the tense of the subjunctive denotes aspect, not time.

<table>
<tr><td></td><td colspan="2" align="center">Future More Vivid Conditional</td></tr>
<tr><td></td><td>Protasis</td><td>Apodosis</td></tr>
<tr><td>grammar</td><td>ἐάν (ἤν, ἄν) + subjunctive</td><td>future indicative</td></tr>
<tr><td>nuance</td><td colspan="2">Speaker regards the protasis as probable.</td></tr>
<tr><td>example</td><td>ἐὰν οἱ ἄνθρωποι τὸν Σωκράτην ἀποκτείνωσιν</td><td>τοὺς μαθητὰς βλάψουσιν.</td></tr>
<tr><td></td><td>If the people kill Socrates</td><td>then they will harm the students.</td></tr>
</table>

The easiest way to translate future more vivid conditions is to translate the protasis (if clause) with a present or future and the apodosis (then clause) with a future. The reason why the present or future can be used to translate the protasis (if clause) is that English is inconsistent with the tense of the protasis (if clause). Notice how we always seem to use the present tense when we mean the future tense. When we say "If the students read Pindar tomorrow, they will despair," we use the present tense "read" when we mean the future tense. We could say "if we will read…," but English prefers the present tense, even though we are talking about the future.

Future Less Vivid

As opposed to the future *more* vivid condition, in a future *less* vivid condition the speaker views the protasis (if clause) as less than likely or merely possible. Future less vivid conditions are introduced by εἰ and the optative in the protasis (if clause) and have the optative and the untranslatable particle ἄν in the apodosis (then clause). Remember that the tense of the optative denotes aspect, not time.

<table>
<tr><td></td><td colspan="2" align="center">Future Less Vivid Conditional</td></tr>
<tr><td></td><td>Protasis</td><td>Apodosis</td></tr>
<tr><td>grammar</td><td>εἰ + optative</td><td>optative + ἄν</td></tr>
<tr><td>nuance</td><td colspan="2">Speaker regards the protasis as merely possible.</td></tr>
<tr><td>example</td><td>εἰ οἱ ἄνθρωποι τὸν Σωκράτην ἀποκτείνειαν</td><td>τοὺς μαθητὰς βλάπτοιεν ἄν.</td></tr>
<tr><td></td><td>If the people should kill Socrates</td><td>then they would harm the students.</td></tr>
</table>

The easiest way to translate a future less vivid condition is by "should...
would."

Substitutions for εἰ

Relative Pronouns and Adverbs

For all conditions, the εἰ "if" of the protasis (if clause) can be replaced
by relative pronouns or adverbs. "If you learn Greek, you will be happy" is
the equivalent of "Whoever learns Greek will be happy." Likewise, "If Aristophanes is read, there will be laughter" is the equivalent of "When Aristophanes is read, there will be laughter." In such cases the εἰ is left out, but
the ἄν must be retained if the protasis (if clause) started with ἐάν, ἤν, or ἄν.
One such pronoun is the indefinite relative pronoun ὅστις, ἥτις, ὅ τι, which is
declined as follows. As you can see, it is simply a combination of the relative
pronoun and the indefinite pronoun τις.

	ὅστις, ἥτις, ὅ τι = whoever, whatever		
	m	*f*	*n*
Singular			
Nom.	ὅστις	ἥτις	ὅ τι
Gen.	οὗτινος (ὅτου)	ἧστινος	οὗτινος (ὅτου)
Dat.	ᾧτινι (ὅτῳ)	ᾗτινι	ᾧτινι (ὅτῳ)
Acc.	ὅντινα	ἥντινα	ὅ τι
Plural			
Nom.	οἵτινες	αἵτινες	ἅτινα (ἅττα)
Gen.	ὧντινων (ὅτων)	ὧντινων	ὧντινων (ὅτων)
Dat.	οἷστισι(ν) (ὅτοις)	αἷστισι(ν)	οἷστισι(ν) (ὅτοις)
Acc.	οὕστινας	ἅστινας	ἅτινα (ἅττα)

The shortened forms listed in the parentheses are common. The neuter is traditionally written as two words so as to avoid confusion with ὅτι.

¶ ἀποκτείνω, ἀποκτενῶ, ἀπέκτεινα = to kill | ὅπου (adv.) = where, wherever

ἐὰν οἱ ἄνθρωποι τὸν Σωκράτην ἀποκτείνωσιν, τοὺς μαθητὰς βλάψουσιν.

If the people kill Socrates, they will harm the students.

ὅστις ἂν τὸν Σωκράτην ἀποκτείνῃ, τοὺς μαθητὰς βλάψει.

Whoever kills Socrates will harm the students.

ὅπου ἂν οἱ ἄνθρωποι τὸν Σωκράτην ἀποκτείνωσιν, τοὺς μαθητὰς βλάψουσιν.

Wherever the people kill Socrates, they will harm the students.

εἰ οἱ ἄνθρωποι τὸν Σωκράτην ἀποκτείνειαν, τοὺς μαθητὰς βλάπτοιεν ἄν.

If the people should kill Socrates, they would harm the students.

ὅπου οἱ ἄνθρωποι τὸν Σωκράτην ἀποκτείνειαν, τοὺς μαθητὰς βλάπτοιεν ἄν.

Wherever the people should kill Socrates, they would harm the students.

Sometimes the ἄν is combined with the relative adverb. One such adverb is ὅταν (ὅτε "when" + ἄν).

ὅταν ὁ Σωκράτης παιδεύῃ, τοὺς μαθητὰς οὐ βλάψει.

Whenever Socrates teaches, he will not harm the students.

Conditional participle

In chapter 20 you learned about the conditional participle. We examined the temporal (when), causal (since), and concessive (although) uses of the circumstantial participle. The circumstantial participle can also have *conditional* force. In such cases both εἰ and ἄν are omitted.

ἐὰν οἱ ἄνθρωποι τὸν Σωκράτην ἀποκτείνωσιν, τοὺς μαθητὰς βλάψουσιν.

If the people kill Socrates, they will harm the students.

οἱ ἄνθρωποι τὸν Σωκράτην ἀποκτείνοντες, τοὺς μαθητὰς βλάψουσιν.

If the people kill Socrates, they will harm the students.

εἰ οἱ ἄνθρωποι τὸν Σωκράτην ἀποκτείνειαν, τοὺς μαθητὰς βλάπτοιεν ἄν.

If the people should kill Socrates, they would harm the students.

οἱ ἄνθρωποι τὸν Σωκράτην ἀποκτείνοντες, τοὺς μαθητὰς βλάπτοιεν ἄν.

If the people should kill Socrates, they would harm the students.

Mixed Conditions

Sometimes conditions don't fall neatly into one category. Sometimes the author might begin with one condition in mind and then change his mind and finish with the apodosis of a different condition. Suppose someone intended to say the following future less vivid condition about Socrates:

¶ οἴκαδε (adv.) = towards home

εἰ ὁ Σωκράτης λέγοι περὶ τῆς ἀληθείας, οὔποτε ἔλθοιμεν ἄν οἴκαδε.

If Socrates should speak about the truth, we would never go home.

Now suppose halfway through the statement the speaker realizes that Socrates wanting to speak about the truth is not less vivid at all, but a certainty. The author realizes that the conversation will never end and that they will not be able to go home. He might then switch to the apodosis of a future more vivid condition with a future indicative.

εἰ ὁ Σωκράτης λέγοι περὶ τῆς ἀληθείας, οὔποτε ἐλευσόμεθα οἴκαδε.

If Socrates should speak about the truth, we *will* never go home.

Such mixed conditions are not the norm, but it is important to realize that not all conditions fit neatly into a category.

Imperatives in the Apodosis

Occasionally you will see an imperative in the apodosis of a condition.

¶ τρέχω = to run

εἰ βλέπεις τὸν Σωκράτην, τρέχε.

If you see Socrates, run!

ἐὰν βλέπῃς τὸν Σωκράτην, τρέχε.

If you see Socrates, run!

εἰ βλέποις τὸν Σωκράτην, τρέχε.

If you should see Socrates, run!

Vocabulary

ἱερόν, –οῦ, τό = temple

χρῆμα, –ατος, τό = thing; in plural "wealth"

θεῖος, –α, –ον (adj.) = divine

ἱερός, –ά, –όν (adj.) = sacred, holy

ὅστις, ἥτις, ὅ τι (adj. and pron.) = whoever, whatever

πολιτικός, –ή, –όν (adj.) = civic, political

ὁπότε (adv.) = when

τότε (adv.) = then, at that time

ἀπόλλυμι, ἀπολῶ, ἀπώλεσα, ἀπολώλεκα, —, — = to destroy, lose

▸ κρύπτω, κρύψω, ἔκρυψα, κέκρυφα, κέκρυμμαι, ἐκρύφθην = to hide, conceal

▸ ὁμιλέω, ὁμιλήσω, ὡμίλησα, ὡμίληκα, ὡμίλημαι, ὡμιλήθην = to gather, unite; to associate with (+ dat.)

Sentences

▸ 1. ἡμεῖς γὰρ ὁπότ' ἀρχόμεθα ζῆν, τότ' ἀποθνήσκομεν. (Theophrastus, Diogenes Laertius, *Lives of Eminent Philosophers*)

> ¶ ὁπότ' = ὁπότε
>
> ζῆν: infinitive of ζάω

2. ἤγαγεν δὲ αὐτὸν εἰς Ἰερουσαλὴμ καὶ ἔστησεν ἐπὶ τὸ πτερύγιον τοῦ ἱεροῦ, καὶ εἶπεν αὐτῷ, "Εἰ υἱὸς εἶ τοῦ θεοῦ, βάλε σεαυτὸν ἐντεῦθεν κάτω. (Luke 4:9)

> ¶ ἤγαγεν: aorist of ἄγω. The subject is the Devil.
>
> αὐτὸν: Jesus
>
> Ἰερουσαλὴμ = Jerusalem
>
> ἔστησεν: 1st (not 2nd) aorist of ἵστημι. The implied direct object is Jesus.
>
> πτερύγιον, –ου, τό = turret, peak
>
> ἐντεῦθεν (adv.) = from here
>
> κάτω (adv.) = down, downward

▸ 3. ἐὰν δ' ἔχωμεν χρήμαθ', ἔξομεν φίλους. (Menander, *Fragments*)

> ¶ χρήμαθ' = χρήματα
>
> ἔξομεν: future of ἔχω

4. ἐγώ εἰμι ὁ ἄρτος ὁ ζῶν ὁ ἐκ τοῦ οὐρανοῦ καταβάς· ἐάν τις φάγῃ ἐκ τούτου τοῦ ἄρτου ζήσει εἰς τὸν αἰῶνα. (John 6:51)

> ¶ ζῶν: present participle of ζάω
>
> καταβάς: aorist participle of καταβαίνω = to descend
>
> φάγῃ: aorist subjunctive of ἐσθίω.
>
> ζήσει: future of ζάω

5. ἄν τι αἰτήσητε τὸν πατέρα ἐν τῷ ὀνόματί μου δώσει ὑμῖν. (John 16:23)

> ¶ δώσει: future of δίδωμι
>
> αἰτέω takes an accusative of the thing asked for and an accusative of the person from whom something is asked.

6. ὃς γὰρ ἂν θέλῃ τὴν ψυχὴν αὐτοῦ σῶσαι, ἀπολέσει αὐτήν· ὃς δ' ἂν ἀπολέσῃ τὴν ψυχὴν αὐτοῦ ἕνεκεν ἐμοῦ, οὗτος σώσει αὐτήν. (Luke 9:24)

> ¶ θέλῃ = ἐθέλῃ
>
> ψυχὴν: here "life," not "soul"
>
> σῶσαι: aorist infinitive of σῴζω
>
> ἀπολέσει: ἀπολέσω is an alternate future for ἀπόλλυμι.

7. κακοῖς ὁμιλῶν καὐτὸς ἐκβήσῃ κακός. (Menander, *Fragments*)

> ¶ καὐτὸς = καὶ αὐτὸς
>
> ἐκβήσῃ: 2nd person singular future middle of ἐκβαίνω = to step off; come out, turn out

8. οὐκ ἔστιν οὐδείς, ὅστις οὐχ αὑτῷ φίλος. (Menander, *Fragments*)

9. ἀλλ’ οὐ τὰ θεῖα κρυπτόντων θεῶν μάθοις ἄν, οὐδ’ εἰ πάντ’ ἐπεξέλθοις σκοπῶν.

(Sophocles, *Fragments*)

¶ The apodosis (then clause) can preceed the protasis (if clause), as in this sentence and the next.

κρυπτόντων: the active of κρύπτω can sometimes be intransitive.

οὐδ’ = οὐδέ (adv.) = not even

πάντ’ = πάντα

ἐπεξέλθοις: aorist optative of ἐπεξέρχομαι = to go out

σκοπῶν: present participle of σκοπέω = to see, look at

10. μᾶλλον ἂν τὰ πολιτικὰ πράττοιμι, εἰ μόνος αὐτὰ πράττοιμι. (Socrates, in Xenophon, *Memorabilia*)

Etymology and Discussion Topics

κρύπτω, κρύψω, ἔκρυψα, κέκρυφα, κέκρυμμαι, ἐκρύφθην = to hide, conceal

From this verb come the words "crypt," where a body is concealed, and "cryptology," the study of secret codes, i.e., encryption.

ὁμιλέω, ὁμιλήσω, ὡμίλησα, ὡμίληκα, ὡμίλημαι, ὡμιλήθην = to gather, unite

The homily delivered at Mass is derived from this word since it is given to those assembled for the liturgy.

ἡμεῖς γὰρ ὁπότ’ ἀρχόμεθα ζῆν, τότ’ ἀποθνήσκομεν.

Simple conditions tend to be common in shorter conditions such as this one.

οὐκ ἔστιν οὐδείς, ὅστις οὐχ αὐτῷ φίλος.

What do you think the meaning of this sentence is?

Chapter 36 ∾

General Conditions

General Conditions

In chapter 35 you learned about future conditions, which state that if X occurs in the future, Y will follow. General conditions state a general truth, i.e., *whenever* X occurs, Y occurs. The difference is subtle. Future conditions tend to be used for single occurrences, while general conditions tend to be used for repeated circumstances. There are two general conditions in Greek, the *present general* and the *past general*. The present general is by far the more common of the two.

> If the teacher reads Homer aloud, he will become very animated.
> *Future More Vivid*

> If the teacher should read Homer aloud, he would become very animated. *Future Less Vivid*

> If the teacher reads Homer aloud, he becomes very animated.
> *Present General*

> If the teacher read Homer aloud, he became very animated.
> *Past General*

Present General

A present general condition begins like a future more vivid construction with ἐάν (ἤν, ἄν) + subjunctive in the protasis (if clause), but instead of a future indicative, a present general has a present indicative in the apodosis (then clause).

	Present General Conditional	
	Protasis	*Apodosis*
grammar	ἐάν (ἤν, ἄν) + subjunctive	present indicative
example	ἐὰν ὁ Διογένης πίνῃ τὸν οἶνον	πίνει τὸν ἀλλότριον οἶνον.
	If Diogenes drinks wine	then he drinks someone else's wine.

If you see a condition that starts with ἐάν (ἤν, ἄν) + subjunctive, you must look to the apodosis (then clause) to see what kind of condition it is.

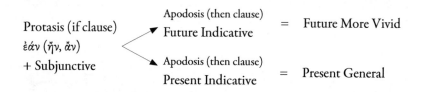

Protasis (if clause)
ἐάν (ἤν, ἄν)
+ Subjunctive

Apodosis (then clause)
Future Indicative   =   Future More Vivid

Apodosis (then clause)
Present Indicative   =   Present General

Past General

A past general condition expresses the same "If X, then Y" relationship as the present general, but places the condition in the past.

	Past General Conditional	
	Protasis	*Apodosis*
grammar	εἰ + optative	imperfect indicative
example	εἰ ὁ Διογένης πίνοι τὸν οἶνον	ἔπινε τὸν ἀλλότριον οἶνον.
	If Diogenes drank wine	then he drank someone else's wine.

If you see a condition that starts with εἰ + optative, you must look to the apodosis (then clause) to see what kind of condition it is.

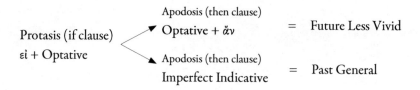

Protasis (if clause)
εἰ + Optative

Apodosis (then clause)
Optative + ἄν   =   Future Less Vivid

Apodosis (then clause)
Imperfect Indicative   =   Past General

That being said, past general conditions are very rare, so if you see εἰ + optative in the protasis (if clause), try it as a future less vivid condition first.

Just like future conditions, general conditions can substitute a relative pronoun or adverb for the εἰ of the protasis (if clause). For future more vivid and present general conditions, the ἄν must be retained.

¶ ταπεινοφροσύνη, –ης, ἡ = humility

ἐὰν ἄνθρωπος ἔχῃ τὴν ταπεινοφροσύνην, ἔχει τὴν ἀρχὴν τῆς σοφίας.

If a man has humility, he has the beginning of wisdom.

ὅστις ἂν ἔχῃ τὴν ταπεινοφροσύνην ἔχει τὴν ἀρχὴν τῆς σοφίας.

Whoever has humility has the beginning of wisdom.

Vocabulary

► ἀνάγκη, –ης, ἡ = necessity

► διάκονος, –ου, ὁ = servant

οἰκία, οἰκίας, ἡ = house

σῖτος, –ου, ὁ = grain, bread

διό (διὰ ὅ) = on account of which, wherefore

ὅτε (adv.) = when; ὅταν (ὅτε + ἄν) whenever

► περ (part.) = indeed, truly; although; at least (See Etymology and Discussion Topics below for more on περ)

ποτε (adv.) = ever

ἀσθενέω, ἀσθενήσω, ἠσθένησα, ἠσθένηκα, —, — = to be weak

δέχομαι, δέξομαι, ἐδεξάμην, —, ἐδεδέγμην, ἐδέχθην = to receive

πάρειμι, παρέσομαι = to be present

Sentences

1. ἀνὴρ πονηρὸς δυστυχεῖ, κἂν εὐτυχῇ. (Menander, *Fragments*)

> ¶ δυστυχέω = to be unhappy, unfortunate
>
> κἂν = καὶ ἄν = even if

2. ἀμὴν ἀμὴν λέγω ὑμῖν, ἐὰν μὴ ὁ κόκκος τοῦ σίτου πεσὼν εἰς τὴν γῆν ἀποθάνῃ, αὐτὸς μόνος μένει· ἐὰν δὲ ἀποθάνῃ, πολὺν καρπὸν φέρει. (John 12:24)

> ¶ κόκκος, –ου, ὁ = grain, seed
>
> πεσὼν: aorist participle of πίπτω
>
> ἀποθάνῃ: aorist subjunctive of ἀποθνήσκω

3. λέγει ἡ μήτηρ αὐτοῦ τοῖς διακόνοις, "Ὅ τι ἂν λέγῃ ὑμῖν ποιήσατε." (John 2:5)

> ¶ αὐτοῦ: Jesus

4. ἀλλ᾽ εἴ τι μὴ φέροιμεν ὤτρυνεν φέρειν. (Euripides, *Alcestis*)

> ¶ This line is from the *Alcestis*. The speaker is a servant who is exasperated at the house guest, the Greek hero Heracles. Heracles was often presented as having a voracious appetite.
>
> ὤτρυνεν: imperfect of ὀτρύνω = to urge. The subject is Heracles. Here supply the direct object "us" + the infinitive φέρειν "to bring" + "it."

5. τὸ φρικωδέστατον οὖν τῶν κακῶν ὁ θάνατος οὐδὲν πρὸς ἡμᾶς, ὅταν περ μὲν ἡμεῖς ὦμεν, ὁ θάνατος οὐ πάρεστιν. (Epicurus, in Diogenes Laertius, *Lives of Eminent Philosophers*)

> ¶ φρικώδης, –ες (adj.) = that which causes shuddering, horrible
>
> ὁ θάνατος: here in apposition to τὸ φρικωδέστατον
>
> ὦμεν: subjunctive of εἰμί

6. εἴ ποτε βουλεύσαιμι φίλῳ κακόν, αὐτὸς ἔχοιμι. (Theognis, *Elegies*)

> ¶ ἔχοιμι: supply "it," i.e., κακόν
>
> This is another example of a mixed condition. It begins as a future less vivid, but in place of an apodosis with ἄν + optative you have what kind of clause?

▶ 7. διὸ εὐδοκῶ ἐν ἀσθενείαις, ἐν ὕβρεσιν, ἐν ἀνάγκαις, ἐν διωγμοῖς καὶ στενοχωρίαις, ὑπὲρ Χριστοῦ· ὅταν γὰρ ἀσθενῶ, τότε δυνατός εἰμι. (2 Cor 12:10)

¶ εὐδοκέω = to be pleased; pleased with (+ ἐν)

διωγμός, –οῦ, ὁ = persecution

στενοχωρία, –ας, ἡ = narrowness, difficulty

8. καὶ ὅταν τις ἐξίῃ τῆς οἰκίας, ζητείτω πρότερον τί μέλλει πράσσειν· καὶ ὅταν εἰσέλθῃ πάλιν, ζητείτω τί ἔπραξε. (Cleobulus, in Diogenes Laertius, *Lives of Eminent Philosophers*)

¶ ἐξίῃ: present subjunctive of ἔξειμι = to go out.

πρότερον (adv.) = first

πράσσειν = πράττειν

εἰσέλθῃ: aorist subjunctive of εἰσέρχομαι = to go in

ἔπραξε: aorist of πράττω

9. ὃς ἂν δέξηται τοῦτο τὸ παιδίον ἐπὶ τῷ ὀνόματί μου ἐμὲ δέχεται, καὶ ὃς ἂν ἐμὲ δέξηται δέχεται τὸν ἀποστείλαντά με. (Luke 9:48)

¶ ἀποστείλαντά: aorist participle of ἀποστέλλω = to send, dispatch

10. τότε γὰρ ἡδονῆς χρείαν ἔχομεν ὅταν ἐκ τοῦ μὴ παρεῖναι τὴν ἡδονὴν ἀλγῶμεν· ὅταν δὲ μὴ ἀλγῶμεν, οὐκέτι τῆς ἡδονῆς δεόμεθα. καὶ διὰ τοῦτο τὴν ἡδονὴν ἀρχὴν καὶ τέλος λέγομεν εἶναι τοῦ μακαρίως ζῆν. (Epicurus, *Letter to Menoeceus*)

¶ ἐκ: here "out of," i.e., "on account of" + gen.

τοῦ … ἡδονὴν: an articular infinitive

ἀλγέω = to suffer

ζῆν: infinitive of ζάω = to live

Etymology and Discussion Topics

ἀνάγκη, –ης, ἡ = necessity

This word for necessity is rarely used in a positive sense. It usually has the connotation of "compulsion." It can also serve as a word for fate.

διάκονος, –ου, ὁ = servant

From this word comes our word "deacon." Deacons are members of the clergy in the Catholic and other Christian churches. As their name suggests, their charge is to assist or serve.

περ (part.) = indeed, truly

This particle is used by itself or attached to the end of certain words, usually with the purpose of strengthening them. Confusingly, it can also add concessive "although" or limited "at least" force. Context will provide you with the correct translation.

ὅταν γὰρ ἀσθενῶ, τότε δυνατός εἰμι.

What do you think Paul means by this seemingly paradoxical statement?

Chapter 37 ∽

Unreal Conditions

Often referred to as "contrary to fact" or "counterfactual" conditions, unreal conditions express a situation that has no chance of becoming a reality. The following chart, though extremely simplified, can be helpful in understanding the relationship between future and unreal conditions.

The condition…	*…expresses a situation that is…*
Future More Vivid	probable
Future Less Vivid	possible
Unreal	impossible

Unreal conditions are either present or past. The present is handled by present unreal conditions and the past by past unreal conditions. All unreal conditions must have the untranslatable particle ἄν in the apodosis (then clause).

If other people did not exist, I would be holy.
   Present Unreal

If Socrates would have fled, he would not have died.
   Past Unreal

Present Unreal

	Present Unreal Conditional	
	Protasis	Apodosis
grammar	εἰ + imperfect indicative	imperfect indicative + ἄν
example	εἰ ἄλλοι ἄνθρωποι οὐκ ἦσαν	ἐγὼ ἅγιος ἦν ἄν.
	If other people did not exist	I would be holy.

At first glance it might seem odd that Greek uses the indicative mood for unreal conditions. After all, the indicative mood is the mood of fact. The reason seems to be that since the condition has no chance of coming true, its unreality is therefore a fact.

Past Unreal

	Past Unreal Conditional	
	Protasis	Apodosis
grammar	εἰ + aorist indicative	aorist indicative + ἄν
example	εἰ ὁ Σωκράτης ἔφυγεν,	οὐκ ἀπέθανεν ἄν.
	If Socrates would have fled,	then he would not have died.

It is important to note that English translations of unreal conditions will vary. The above example (εἰ ὁ Σωκράτης ἔφυγεν, οὐκ ἀπέθανεν ἄν) could also be translated as "If Socrates had fled, he would not have died." The important thing is that you express the unreality of the condition.

If the time of the unreal condition is obvious from the context, and the aorist or imperfect doesn't seem to make sense, then the verbs are emphasizing aspect, not time. You will therefore see imperfect indicatives in unreal conditions that seem to talk about the past; the author simply wants to stress imperfect aspect. Likewise you may find aorist indicatives in unreal conditions that seem to have an impact on the present, in which case the author simply wants to express aoristic aspect. Context will tell you when this occurs.

Unattainable Wish

In chapter 34 you learned about the optative of wish, which uses the optative. If the wish is considered unattainable, Greek uses εἴθε or εἰ γάρ + imperfect indicative for an unattainable wish in the present and εἴθε or εἰ γάρ

+ aorist indicative for an unattainable wish in the past. A negative unattainable wish takes μή.

> εἴθε ὁ Σωκράτης ἔζων ἔτι.
>
> Would that Socrates were still living.
>
> εἴθε ὁ Σωκράτης μὴ ἀπέθανεν.
>
> Would that Socrates had not died.

In the first sentence, the imperfect of ζάω "to live" is used. In the second example the aorist of ἀποθνῄσκω "to die" is used. Both wishes are impossible, but one of them is present and the other is past.

Now that you have learned all of the different conditions, refer to appendix A in the back of your book for a complete list.

Vocabulary

κρήνη, –ης, ἡ = spring, well

ὅρκος, –ου, τό = oath

τέκνον, –ου, τό = child

▶ δεινός, –ή, –όν (adj.) = terrible, dreadful

▶ ξένος, –η, –ον (adj.) = foreign, strange; as substantive ξένος, –ου ὁ = stranger, foreigner

ἐπί + dative = for

μήποτε (adv.) = never

ποῦ (adv.) = where

ὧδε (adv.) = thus; here

αἱρέω, αἱρήσω, εἷλον, ᾕρηκα, ᾕρημαι, ᾑρέθην = to hold; to snatch, seize

εἰσοράω, εἰσόψομαι, εἰσεῖδον, —, —, — = to look at, see

Sentences

1. εἰ γὰρ ἐπιστεύετε Μωϋσεῖ, ἐπιστεύετε ἂν ἐμοί, περὶ γὰρ ἐμοῦ ἐκεῖνος
ἔγραψεν. (John 5:46)

> ¶ The speaker is Jesus.
>
> Μωϋσεῖ: dative of Μωϋσῆς, –οῦ,
> ὁ = Moses

2. εἰ μὴ γὰρ ὅρκοις θεῶν ἄφαρκτος ἡρέθην, οὐκ ἂν ποτ᾽ ἔσχον μὴ οὐ τάδ᾽
ἐξειπεῖν πατρί. (Euripides, *Hippolytus*)

> ¶ This line is spoken by Hippoly-
> tus, who has been falsely accused
> of seducing his stepmother. He
> has information that will prove
> his innocence to his father, but
> he had previously sworn an oath
> not to divulge such information.
>
> ὅρκοις: here a dative of agent
>
> ἄφαρκτος, –ον (adj.) = defenseless
>
> ποτ᾽ = ποτε
>
> ἔσχον: aorist of ἔχω
>
> ἔχω + infinitive can mean "to be
> able to," so here with the negative
> οὐκ…ἔσχον μὴ οὐ ἐξειπεῖν "I
> would not have been able to not
> speak out…"
>
> μὴ οὐ: Greek will often have a
> redundant negative
>
> τάδ᾽ = τάδε: accusative plural
> of ὅδε
>
> ἐξειπεῖν: aorist infinitive of
> ἐκλέγω "to speak out," here +
> dative.

3. ἔλεγον οὖν αὐτῷ, "Ποῦ ἐστιν ὁ πατήρ σου;" ἀπεκρίθη Ἰησοῦς, "Οὔτε ἐμὲ
οἴδατε οὔτε τὸν πατέρα μου· εἰ ἐμὲ ᾔδειτε, καὶ τὸν πατέρα μου ἂν ᾔδειτε."
(John 8:19)

> ¶ ἔλεγον: the "they" here are the
> Pharisees; the "him" is Jesus.
>
> οἴδατε: 2nd person plural of οἶδα
> "to know." ᾔδειτε is pluperfect,
> but it is acting as an imperfect
> here since οἶδα is a defective verb.
> See Chapter 27 for more on οἶδα.

4. εἶπεν οὖν ἡ Μάρθα πρὸς τὸν Ἰησοῦν, "Κύριε, εἰ ἦς ὧδε οὐκ ἂν ἀπέθανεν ὁ ἀδελφός μου." (John 11:21)

¶ These words are spoken after Martha learns that her brother Lazarus has died.

ἦς: since εἰμί does not have an aorist, the imperfect is used instead. The context, however, makes it clear that this is what kind of condition?

5. Orestes: εἴθ' ἦν Ὀρέστης πλησίον κλύων τάδε.
   Electra: ἀλλ', ὦ ξέν', οὐ γνοίην ἂν εἰσιδοῦσά νιν.

(Euripides, *Electra*)

¶ These words are spoken at the grave of Agamemnon. The exiled Orestes has snuck back into the city posing as someone else lest he be killed by his mother. He knows that Electra is his sister, but she does not recognize him, as the last time she saw him he was a small child.

πλησίον: adverbial here "near"

κλύων: present participle of κλύω = to hear; perceive

ξέν' = ξένε

γνοίην: aorist optative of γιγνώσκω

νιν = αὐτόν: Orestes

6. ἰὼ Λάϊειον τέκνον, εἴθε σ' εἴθε σε μήποτ' εἶδον. (Sophocles, *Oedipus Tyrannus*)

¶ The speaker here is Jocasta, the mother and wife of Oedipus.

ἰὼ (interjection) = alas, woe: a cry of anguish

Λάϊειος, –ον (adj.) = of Laius: Laius was Oedipus's father.

εἶδον: aorist of ὁράω

▶ 7. οὐ γὰρ ἄν ποτε θνῄσκων ἐσώθην, μὴ 'πί τῳ δεινῷ κακῷ. (Sophocles, *Oedipus Tyrannus*)

❡ The speaker is Oedipus. He is referring to his rescue from death as a baby.

ἐσώθην: aorist passive of σῴζω

μὴ: supply "if I was not saved for…" or "if it were not for…"

'πί = ἐπί + dative = for

τῳ = τινί

8. εἴθε γὰρ αἱ κρῆναι καὶ ἄρτους ἔφερον. (Crates, in Diogenes, *Lives of Eminent Philosophers*)

9. εἰ γὰρ κατιδεῖν βιοῦ τέλος ἦν. (Theognis, *Elegies*)

❡ κατιδεῖν: aorist infinitive of καθοράω = to observe, perceive distinctly

κατιδεῖν…ἦν: ἔστι + infinitive = it is possible to

▶ 10. εἰ μὴ πατὴρ ἦσθ', εἶπον ἄν σ' οὐκ εὖ φρονεῖν. (Sophocles, *Antigone*)

❡ These words are spoken by Haimon to his father Creon in Sophocles' *Antigone*.

πατήρ: supply "my" before πατὴρ.

ἦσθ' = ἦσθα, 2nd person imperfect of εἰμί.

εἶπον: aorist of λέγω.

σ' = σε

Notice the mixed unreal condition here.

Etymology and Discussion Topics

δεινός, –ή, –όν (adj.) = terrible, dreadful

Dinosaur is derived from this adjective and σαύρα, –ας, ἡ = lizard, thus "terrible lizard." The adjective can also mean "clever," and can function as a sort of backhanded compliment. In the trial of Socrates, his accusers warn the jury against being charmed by Socrates, who they claim is δεινός at speaking, a charge Socrates vehemently denies.

ξένος, –η, –ον (adj.) = foreign, stranger

From this adjective is derived our word "xenophobia," a combination of ξένος and φόβος "fear." This adjective was not always used in a negative sense. Hospitality was a vitally important concept in classical Greece. In addition to hospitality shown to strangers, many Greek families from different cities maintained a pact of friendship called ξενία. In the *Iliad* a memorable exchange occurs between Diomedes and Glaucus, two warriors who are about to fight in battle before they realize that their families share such a bond.

οὐ γὰρ ἄν ποτε θνήσκων ἐσώθην, μὴ 'πί τῳ δεινῷ κακῷ.

These words are spoken by Oedipus at the end of the play *Oedipus Tyrannus*. The rescue he speaks of is his rescue as a baby by the shepherd. The evil he speaks of is that he unknowingly killed his father and married his mother.

εἰ μὴ πατὴρ ἦσθ', εἶπον ἄν σ' οὐκ εὖ φρονεῖν.

This is an example of the rhetorical device *praeteritio*, whereby the speaker says something while saying that he will not say something. Another example would be a politician stating, "It is beneath me to call my opponent a liar, so I refuse to spell out his many lies."

Chapter 38 ⁓

Object Clauses of Effort, Fear, and Caution • Accusative Absolute •
Accusative of Respect

Object Clauses of Effort, Fear, and Caution

We have seen that most verbs take an accusative as a direct object (chapter 3).

¶ μισέω = to hate | τῦφος, –ου, ὁ = vanity

ὁ Διογένης μισεῖ τὸν τῦφον.

Diogenes hates vanity.

ἡ σοφία τρέφει τὴν ψυχήν.

Wisdom feeds the soul.

We have also seen that some verbs take a complimentary infinitive to complete their meaning (chapter 7).

ὁ Σωκράτης οὐκ ἐθέλει φυγεῖν.

Socrates does not wish to flee.

δύναμαι βλέπειν.

I am able to see.

Sometimes a verb takes as a direct object not a noun or an infinitive, but a whole clause. These are called *object clauses*. The two major object clauses are *fear clauses* and *effort clauses*.

The children fear *broccoli*.

Direct Object

The children fear that broccoli will be served for dinner.

Object Clause (Fear Clause)

The children see to it that the broccoli disappears.

Object Clause (Effort Clause)

Fear Clauses

Fear clauses are introduced by verbs such as φοβοῦμαι (the middle of φοβέω) and δέδοικα, both of which mean "to fear." Fear clauses can also be introduced by verbs of suspicion or anxiety such as ὀκνέω "to hesitate" or "to shrink from doing." If the author fears that something will happen, is happening, or has already happened, the clause is introduced by μή. If the author fears that something will not happen, is not happening, or did not happen, the clause is introduced by μὴ οὐ. If the thing feared has not happened yet, the verb of the fear clause is put into the subjunctive. If the thing feared has already happened or is presently happening, the verb is put into the indicative.

Type of Fear	Main Verb	Fear Clause
The subject fears that something *will* happen.	verb of fearing	μή + subjunctive
The subject fears that something *will not* happen.	verb of fearing	μὴ οὐ + subjunctive
The subject fears that something *has* happened or *is* happening.	verb of fearing	μή + indicative
The subject fears that something *has not* happened or *is not* happening.	verb of fearing	μὴ οὐ + indicative

¶ πίπτω, πεσοῦμαι, ἔπεσον = to fall; fail

φοβοῦμαι μὴ ἡ ἀλήθεια πίπτῃ.

I fear that the truth will fail.

φοβοῦμαι μὴ οὐ ἡ μωρία πίπτῃ.

I fear that foolishness will not fail.

φοβοῦμαι μὴ ἡ ἀλήθεια πίπτει.

I fear that the truth is failing.

φοβοῦμαι μὴ οὐ ἡ μωρία πίπτει.

I fear that foolishness is not failing.

φοβοῦμαι μὴ ἡ ἀλήθεια ἔπεσεν.

I fear that the truth failed.

φοβοῦμαι μὴ οὐ ἡ μωρία ἔπεσεν.

I fear that foolishness did not fail.

Effort Clauses

Effort clauses are introduced by verbs such as πράττω "to do" and ὁράω "to see." Effort clauses introduced by πράττω have the sense of "make it so that." Effort clauses introduced by ὁράω have the sense of "see to it that." Positive effort clauses take ὅπως + future indicative (sometimes ὡς + future indicative) while negative effort clauses take ὅπως μή + future indicative (sometimes ὡς μή + future indicative).

Type of Effort	Main Verb	Effort Clause
The subject makes the effort that something happen.	verb of effort	ὅπως + future indicative or ὡς + future indicative
The subject makes the effort that something not happen.	verb of effort	ὅπως μή + future indicative or ὡς μή + future indicative

οἱ ἀγαθοὶ φιλόσοφοι πράττουσιν ὅπως ἡ ἀλήθεια νικήσει τὴν μωρίαν.

The good philosophers make it so that the truth will conquer foolishness.

οἱ ἀγαθοὶ φιλόσοφοι πράττουσιν ὅπως μὴ ἡ μωρία νικήσει τὴν ἀλήθειαν.

The good philosophers make it so that foolishness will not conquer the truth.

Imperatives frequently introduce effort clauses.

ὅρα ὅπως ἡ ἀλήθεια νικήσει τὴν μωρίαν.

See to it that the truth conquers foolishness.

ὅρα ὅπως μὴ ἡ μωρία νικήσει τὴν ἀλήθειαν.

See to it lest foolishness conquer the truth.

As you can see, the exact wording of an effort clause will depend on the context. Sometimes it is preferable to translate the future indicative of the effort clause as a present.

Object Clauses of Caution

Verbs of caution stand somewhere between fear and effort clauses and can thus take either μή or ὅπως μή + subjunctive or ὅπως μή + future indicative. Both of the following sentences can be translated as "See to that you do not speak foolishness."

βλέπετε ὅπως μή λέξετε τὴν μωρίαν.

βλέπετε μή λέγητε τὴν μωρίαν.

Accusative Absolute

In chapter 21 you learned the genitive absolute, a construction in which a noun and a participle, separated from the rest of the sentence, are put into the genitive case to describe the circumstances under which the action of the sentence takes place. When the participle is from an impersonal verb such as ἐξόν (from ἔξεστιν), Greek prefers the *accusative absolute*, which consists of the participle and an infinitive.

❡ ὑπομένω = to persevere | λείπω = to leave, quit

μαθήματος ὄντος χαλεποῦ, ὁ μαθητὴς ὑπέμενεν. (genitive absolute)

The lesson being difficult, the student persevered.

ἐξὸν λείπειν, ὁ μαθητὴς ὑπέμενεν. (accusative absolute)

It being possible to quit, the student persevered.

Accusative of Respect

In chapter 5 you learned the dative of respect. Similar in meaning is the accusative of respect. The accusative of respect is common with adjectives and verbs that describe qualities or traits.

❡ μέγεθος, –εος, τό = stature

ὁ Σωκράτης ἦν μικρὸς τὸ μέγεθος.

Socrates was small in stature (literally "small with respect to stature").

One of the most famous accusatives of respect is the epithet of Achilles usually translated as "swift-footed Achilles."

❡ πούς, ποδός, ὁ = foot | ὠκύς, –εῖα, –ύ (adj.) = swift

πόδας ὠκὺς Ἀχιλλεύς

Literally "Achilles swift with respect to feet." It is of course, not necessary to translate accusatives of respect literally.

Vocabulary

ὄμμα, –ατος, τό = eye

οὖς, ὠτός, τό = ear

ἀνδρεῖος, –α, –ον (adj.) = manly, courageous

▸ στενός, –ή, –όν (adj.) = narrow, confined

συνετός, –ή, –όν (adj.) = intelligent

ὅπως (adv. and conj.) = how, as (adv.); that (conj.), used to introduce purpose and effort clauses.

δεῖ (impersonal verb) = it is necessary (+ inf.)

δέδοικα, plupf. ἐδεδοίκη = to fear (defective verb whose perfect = present and whose pluperfect = aorist or imperfect).

εἰσέρχομαι, εἰσελεύσομαι, εἰσῆλθον, εἰσελήλυθα, —, — = to enter

ἔξεστιν (impersonal verb) = it is possible (+ inf.)

ἐπαινέω, ἐπαινέσω, ἐπήνεσα, ἐπηνεσάμην, ἐπήνεκα, ἐπήνημαι, ἐπῃνέθην = to praise, approve

ὀκνέω, ὀκνήσω, ὤκνησα, —, —, — = to hesitate, shrink from

Sentences

1. εἰ μέν τις φοβεῖται μὴ ἀποβάλλῃ τὴν οὐσίαν, οὗτος δειλός, εἰ δέ τις θαρσεῖ περὶ ταῦτα, ἀνδρεῖος; (Aristotle, *Magna Moralia*)

> ¶ ἀποβάλλω = to throw off; lose
>
> οὐσίαν: here "property," or "possessions"
>
> θαρσέω = to be courageous

▶ 2. ὑμεῖς, ὦ Λακεδαιμόνιοι, ἡ μόνη ἐλπίς, δέδιμεν μὴ οὐ βέβαιοι ἦτε. (Thucydides, *History of the Peloponnesian War*)

❡ Taken from Thucydides' *History of the Peloponnesian War*, the speakers are the Plataeans, who are asking for Spartan protection against Thebes. Their fears will turn out to be well founded.

δέδιμεν: 1st person plural of δέδοικα

βέβαιος, –α, –ον (adj.) = steadfast, dependable

ἦτε: 2nd person plural subjunctive of εἰμί

3. ἐπαινούμενός ποτε ὑπὸ πονηρῶν, ἔφη, "ἀγωνιῶ μή τι κακὸν εἴργασμαι." (Antisthenes, in Diogenes Laertius, *Lives of Eminent Philosophers*)

❡ ἔφη = [Antisthenes] said

ἀγωνιάω = to be distressed

εἴργασμαι: perfect of ἐργάζομαι

4. εἰ δὲ ἀλλήλους δάκνετε καὶ κατεσθίετε, βλέπετε μὴ ὑπ' ἀλλήλων ἀναλωθῆτε. (Gal 5:15)

❡ ἀλλήλων, ἀλλήλοις, ἀλλήλους = each other. Not found in the nominative or singular.

δάκνω = to bite

κατεσθίω = to consume, devour

ἀναλωθῆτε: aorist passive subjunctive of ἀναλίσκω = to consume

5. ἀγωνίζεσθε εἰσελθεῖν διὰ τῆς στενῆς θύρας, ὅτι πολλοί, λέγω ὑμῖν, ζητήσουσιν εἰσελθεῖν καὶ οὐκ ἰσχύσουσιν. (Luke 13:24)

❡ ἀγωνίζεσθε εἰσελθεῖν: in addition to effort clauses, the infinitive can be used to express effort.

θύρα, –ας, ἡ = door, gate

ὅτι: here "because"

ἰσχύω = to be strong; to be able to

6. ἔλεγε συνετῶν μὲν ἀνδρῶν, πρὶν γενέσθαι τὰ δυσχερῆ, προνοῆσαι ὅπως μὴ

γένηται. (Pittacus, in Diogenes Laertius, *Lives of Eminent Philosophers*)

¶ ἔλεγε: the speaker is Pittacus, one of the ancient seven sages of Greece.

συνετῶν = [it is a mark] of intelligent men. The genitive is often used in such constructions with an infinitive (here προνοῆσαι) to express the mark or characteristic of a class of people.

πρὶν (adv. and conj.) = before (+ inf.); until. See chapter 39 for more on πρίν.

δυσχερής, –ές (adj.) = hard to manage, difficult

προνοέω = to foresee; to take thought for, plan how

γένηται: aorist subjunctive of γίγνομαι, a rare case where an effort clause takes a subjunctive

7. ὁ δὲ εἶπεν, "Βλέπετε μὴ πλανηθῆτε· πολλοὶ γὰρ ἐλεύσονται ἐπὶ τῷ ὀνόματί μου

λέγοντες, Ἐγώ εἰμι· καί, Ὁ καιρὸς ἤγγικεν· μὴ πορευθῆτε ὀπίσω αὐτῶν."

(Luke 21:8)

¶ The speaker is Jesus.

πλανάω = to lead astray

ἐλεύσονται: future of ἔρχομαι

ἐπὶ: here "in"

▶ ὀπίσω (adv. or prep.) = (adv.) back; (prep.) after (+ gen.)

8. ὦ μέγ᾽ εὔδαιμον κόρη, τί παρθενεύῃ δαρόν, ἐξόν σοι γάμου τυχεῖν μεγίστου.

(Aeschylus, *Prometheus Bound*)

¶ In the play *Prometheus Bound*, Io relates how spirits haunted her dreams trying to convince her to yield to the lustful demands of Zeus.

μέγ᾽ = μέγα: adverbial, here "very"

εὔδαιμον: here vocative

κόρη, –ης, ἡ = maiden, girl

παρθενεύω = to raise unmarried; (middle) = to remain unmarried

δαρόν (adv.) = so long

ἐξόν: from ἔξεστιν

μέγιστος, –η, –ον (adj.) = the superlative of μέγας

γάμος, –ου, ὁ = wedding, the term being used as a euphemism here, as Zeus would never marry a mortal

τυχεῖν: aorist infinitive of τυγχάνω, here + gen. "to obtain"

9. τίς εὐδαίμων, "ὁ τὸ μὲν σῶμα ὑγιής, τὴν δὲ ψυχὴν εὔπορος, τὴν δὲ φύσιν εὐπαίδευτος." (Thales, in Diogenes Laertius, *Lives of Eminent Philosophers*)

¶ τίς εὐδαίμων = who is happy? What follows is Thales' answer to this question.

ὑγιής, ές (adj.) = healthy

εὔπορος, –ον (adj.) = resourceful

εὐπαίδευτος, –ον (adj.) = well educated; quick to learn

▶ 10. τυφλὸς τά τ᾽ ὦτα τόν τε νοῦν τά τ᾽ ὄμματ᾽ εἶ. (Sophocles, *Oedipus Tyrannus*)

¶ The speaker is Oedipus and these words are addressed to Tiresias, the blind seer.

τυφλός, –ή, –όν (adj.) = blind

Etymology and Discussion Topics

στενός, –ή, –όν (adj.) = narrow, confined

From this word come our words stenographer and stenography (στενός + γραφή "writing"), which involves the use of abbreviations to facilitate the quick recording of information.

ὑμεῖς, ὦ Λακεδαιμόνιοι, ἡ μόνη ἐλπίς, δέδιμεν μὴ οὐ βέβαιοι ἦτε.

In this speech, the citizens of Plataea are pleading with the Spartans for their lives. When war broke out, the Plataeans sided with Athens, their ally. After the city was taken by the Spartans and their allies the Thebans, the Thebans demanded that the Plataeans be executed. The Plataeans cited their care for the Spartan dead who fell at the battle of Plataea in the Persian War (a war in which the Thebans sided with the Persians, as the Plataeans point out). The plea of the Plataeans was ignored by the Spartans and all the remaining Plataeans were executed.

ὦ μέγ᾽ εὔδαιμον κόρη, τί παρθενεύῃ δαρόν, ἐξόν σοι γάμου τυχεῖν μεγίστου.

The play Prometheus Bound has traditionally been ascribed to Aeschylus, although many now doubt that Aeschylus was the author. Whoever the author, this dark play focuses on the consequences of refusing to bow to Zeus's power. Io's reward for resisting the advances of Zeus is to be thrown out of her house by her father. In this play, Zeus himself turns her into a cow. In other versions a jealous Hera turns her into a cow. In her wanderings she crossed from Europe into Asia. The Bosporus (βόσπορος), which connects Europe and Asia, was explained by the Greeks (probably incorrectly) as being derived from βοῦς "cow" and πόρος "passage."

τυφλὸς τά τ᾽ ὦτα τόν τε νοῦν τά τ᾽ ὄμματ᾽ εἶ.

At this moment in the play Oedipus Tyrannus, Oedipus thinks that Tiresias, the blind prophet, is a liar or a fool at best. Sophocles plays off the irony that it is in fact Oedipus who is blind to the truth although he has sight (for the moment), while Tiresias, although physically blind, knows the truth.

Chapter 39 ⌒

Verbal Adjectives in −τέος, −τέα, −τέον • *Cautious Assertions and Cautious Denials* • *Emphatic Denials and Prohibitions*

Verbal Adjectives in −τέος, −τέα, −τέον

Greek has a verbal adjective (sometimes called a *verbal*) that does not have an easy English equivalent. These verbal adjectives add −τέος, −τέα, −τέον to the aorist passive stem. The formation of these verbal adjectives can be a bit complicated, but for the most part they are formed from the aorist passive stem without the theta, e.g., λυτέος, −α, −ον, or παιδευτέος, −α, −ον. Some spelling changes can occur and in a few cases −τέος, −τέα, −τέον is added to a stem other than the aorist passive. Two things, however, will help you to identify these verbal adjectives. The first is that the distinctive −τέος, −τέα, −τέον endings tend to stand out. Second, many dictionaries will simply list verbal adjectives as an entry separate from the verb.

Verbal adjectives in −τέος, −τέα, −τέον have the sense of necessity or obligation. λυτέος, −α, −ον means "to be loosened" or "to be destroyed." παιδευτέος, −α, −ον means "to be educated." Since they don't have an equivalent in English (they are similar to the gerundive in Latin), translations of verbal adjectives in −τέος, −τέα, −τέον can vary.

When verbal adjectives in −τέος, −τέα, −τέον modify a noun, they are placed in the predicate position and are passive. Sometimes a form of the verb εἰμί is present, sometimes it is implied.

¶ παιδεύω = to teach | διώκω = to pursue, hunt | φήμι = to say, speak

ὁ παῖς παιδευτέος ἐστίν.

The child must be taught.

ὁ παῖς παιδευτέος.

The child must be taught.

ἡ μωρία οὐ διωκτέα ἐστίν.

Foolishness must not be pursued.

ἡ μωρία οὐ διωκτέα.

Foolishness must not be pursued.

Verbal adjectives in –τέος, –τέα, –τέον always take a *dative of agent* rather than a genitive of agent.

ὁ παῖς τῷ διδασκάλῳ παιδευτέος ἐστίν.

The child must be taught by the teacher.

ἡ μωρία τοῖς διδασκάλοις οὐ διωκτέα.

Foolishness must not be pursued by teachers.

As odd as it sounds, the neuter singular of a verbal adjective in –τέον can be used *actively* and take a direct object. In such cases it is usually best to translate the verbal adjective in –τέον as "we must…" or "one must," even though it is technically passive. These verbal adjectives can function as the main verb in an independent clause.

φατέον τὴν ἀλήθειαν.

We must speak the truth. / One must speak the truth.

οὐ φατέον τὴν μωρίαν.

We must not speak foolishness. / One must not speak foolishness.

Finally, verbal adjectives can be placed in the attributive position and used as substantive adjectives.

τὰ λεκτέα

things to be said / things that must be said

τὰ πρακτέα

things to be done / things that must be done

Verbal adjectives in –τός, –τή, –τόν

Formed from the same stem as those ending in –τέος, –τέα, –τέον, verbal adjectives that end in –τός, –τή, –τόν do not have the notion of necessity, but rather possibility or simply the perfect passive meaning. The good news is that all adjectives that end in –τός, –τή, –τόν will be listed as adjectives in dictionaries. You have already encountered quite a few such as ἀγαπητός, –τή, –τόν "beloved" and δυνατός, –ή, –όν "possible, powerful." They have been listed like other adjectives with –ός, –ή, –όν. They are introduced in this chapter not because you need to translate them differently than other adjectives, but so that you do not confuse them with verbal adjectives in –τέος, –τέα, –τέον. If you don't see the *e*, there is no necessity.

Cautious Assertions and Cautious Denials

Greek will often use an indicative or subjunctive with μή to make a cautious assertion and μὴ οὐ to make a cautious denial. Just like fear clauses, if the author makes a cautions assertion or denial about the present or past, the indicative is used. If the author makes a cautions assertion or denial about the future, the subjunctive is used.

Cautious assertion that something *is* or *was* the case.	μή + indicative
Cautious denial that something *is* or *was* the case.	μὴ οὐ + indicative
Cautious assertion that something *will be* the case.	μή + subjunctive
Cautious denial that something *will be* the case.	μὴ οὐ + subjunctive

The use of "perhaps" is often the best way to translate cautious assertions and "perhaps not" the best way to translate cautions denials.

μὴ ὁ φιλόσοφος χαλεπός ἐστιν.

Perhaps the philosopher is difficult.

μὴ ὁ φιλόσοφος χαλεπός ᾖ.

Perhaps the philosopher will be difficult.

μὴ οὐ τὸ μάθημα χαλεπόν ἐστιν.

Perhaps the lesson is not difficult.

μὴ οὐ τὸ μάθημα χαλεπὸν ᾖ.

Perhaps the lesson will not be difficult.

This can be very confusing for beginning students, for whom "yes, but this adds to the remarkable subtlety of Greek" is seldom comforting. See the section "Hints to Avoid Confusion" below.

Emphatic Denials and Prohibitions

Greek uses οὐ μή with either the future indicative or subjunctive to express an emphatic denial. If your teacher promises you that there is nothing more to memorize, you might respond:

οὐ μὴ πιστεύσω τῷ διδασκάλῳ.

I *will not trust* the teacher!

However, οὐ μή can be used with a prohibitive subjunctive to make it even more emphatic. If your fellow student tells you that the teacher promised there would be nothing more to memorize, you might respond:

οὐ μὴ πιστεύσῃς τῷ διδασκάλῳ.

Do not trust the teacher!

Hints to Avoid Confusion

Hint #1: How to tell the difference between a cautious denial and an emphatic denial.

As we have seen, οὐ is primarily the negative of the indicative, which states facts, while μή negates the subjunctive, which deals with possibilities. To remember the difference between οὐ μή and μὴ οὐ, look to the first of the two negatives. If the first negative is οὐ (οὐ μή), it is a fact and therefore an emphatic denial. If the first negative is μὴ (μὴ οὐ), it is a possibility and therefore a cautions denial.

Hint #2: How to recognize cautious assertions.

The good news is that cautions assertions (and denials) are not very common, and you should only try translating μή as a cautious assertion if the context demands it. Second, if you see μή and an indicative acting as the verb in an independent clause, it is probably a cautious assertion, as unattainable wishes are distinguished by εἴθε and εἰ γάρ. Cautious assertions with the subjunctive are less difficult to spot if they occur in the 3rd person, as the hortatory and deliberate subjunctives are most common in the 1st person. Once again, context will tell you if a 2nd person subjunctive is a prohibitive subjunctive, emphatic prohibition, or a cautions assertion.

Vocabulary

ἀνάστασις, –εως, ἡ = a raising; resurrection

αἱρετός, –ή, –όν (adj.) = to be chosen; preferable

διδακτός, –ή, –όν (adj.) = able to be taught, teachable

ἡμέτερος, –α, –ον (adj.) = our

ἔξω (adv.) = out, outside

πάντως (adv.) = in all ways, completely

▸ παρά (prep.) = from (+ gen.); beside (+ dat.); to, contrary to (+ acc.)

ἐκφεύγω, ἐκφεύξω, ἐξέφυγον, ἐκπέφευγα, —, — = to escape, avoid

θεραπεύω, θεραπεύσω, ἐθεράπευσα, τεθεράπευκα, τεθεράπευμαι, ἐθεραπεύθην = to care for, respect; (middle) to serve

μνημονεύω, μνημονεύσω, ἐμνημόνευσα, ἐμνημόνευκα, ἐμνημόνευμαι = to remember

▸ περιπατέω, περιπατήσω, περιεπάτησα, —, —, — = to walk around

ὠφελέω, ὠφελήσω, ὠφέλησα, ὠφέληκα, ὠφέλημαι, ὠφελήθην = to help, assist

Sentences

1. τὰ μὲν διδακτὰ μανθάνω, τὰ δ᾽ εὑρετὰ ζητῶ, τὰ δ᾽ εὐκτὰ παρὰ θεῶν ἠτησάμην.
(Sophocles, *Fragments*)

> ❡ εὑρετός, –ή, –όν (adj.) = able to be found, discoverable
>
> εὐκτός, –ή, –όν (adj.) = wished for, desired
>
> ἠτησάμην: aorist middle of αἰτέω

2. καλῶν οὐδὲν ἄνευ πόνου καὶ ἐπιμελείας οἱ θεοὶ διδόασιν ἀνθρώποις, ἀλλ᾽ εἴτε τοὺς θεοὺς ἵλεως εἶναί σοι βούλει, θεραπευτέον τοὺς θεούς, εἴτε ὑπὸ φίλων ἐθέλεις ἀγαπᾶσθαι, τοὺς φίλους εὐεργετητέον, εἴτε ὑπό τινος πόλεως ἐπιθυμεῖς τιμᾶσθαι, τὴν πόλιν ὠφελητέον. (Prodicus, in Stobaeus, *Anthology*)

> ❡ ἄνευ (prep.) = without (+ gen.)
>
> ἐπιμέλεια, –ας, ἡ = care, attention
>
> εἴτε…εἴτε…εἴτε = if…and if…and if…
>
> βούλει: 2nd person singular indicative
>
> ἵλεως (adv.) = kindly, in a well-disposed manner. Here it modifies εἶναί.
>
> θεραπευτέον: as you can see, the translation of impersonal verbal adjectives in –τέον often can't be translated simply as "we must" or "one must." Here "you must" is probably the best translation.
>
> εὐεργετητέον = you must show kindness to
>
> ἐπιθυμέω = to desire
>
> τιμάω = to honor

3. πᾶν ἀγαθὸν αἱρετόν ἐστιν. (Musonius, in Stobaeus, *Anthology*)

> ❡ πᾶν: here "every"

▸ 4. μνημονευτέον δὲ ὡς τὸ μέλλον οὔτε ἡμέτερον οὔτε πάντως οὐχ ἡμέτερον,
ἵνα μήτε πάντως προσμένωμεν ὡς ἐσόμενον μήτε ἀπελπίζωμεν ὡς πάντως οὐκ
ἐσόμενον. (Epicurus, in Diogenes Laertius, *Lives of Eminent Philosophers*)

> ¶ ὡς: "that" introduces indirect statement here.
>
> τὸ μέλλον: literally, "the about to be," i.e., the future
>
> προσμένω = to wait; wait for (+ acc.)
>
> ὡς ἐσόμενον = as though it will be: i.e., as though the future or some event in the future will happen
>
> ἀπελπίζω = to have no hope, despair

5. ἀλλὰ οἶνον νέον εἰς ἀσκοὺς καινοὺς βλητέον. (Luke 5:38)

> ¶ ἀσκός, –οῦ, ὁ = skin (animal skins were used to hold liquids in the ancient world.)
>
> βλητέον: verbal adjective from βάλλω

6. καλὸν οὖν τὸ ἅλας· ἐὰν δὲ καὶ τὸ ἅλας μωρανθῇ, ἐν τίνι ἀρτυθήσεται; οὔτε
εἰς γῆν οὔτε εἰς κοπρίαν εὔθετόν ἐστιν· ἔξω βάλλουσιν αὐτό. ὁ ἔχων ὦτα
ἀκούειν ἀκουέτω. (Luke 14:34–35)

> ¶ ἅλας,–ατος, τό = salt
>
> μωραίνω = to be foolish. The passive sense here is "to lose its flavor."
>
> ἀρτύω = to prepare; season
>
> ἐν τίνι ἀρτυθήσεται = what shall it flavor?
>
> κοπρία, –ας, ἡ = trash pile
>
> εὔθετος, –ον (adj.) = well-placed; suitable

▸ 7. μὴ ἀγροικότερον ᾖ τὸ ἀληθὲς εἰπεῖν. (Socrates, in Plato, *Gorgias*)

> ¶ ἄγροικος, –ον (adj.) = rustic,
>
> τὸ: introduces an articular infinitive

8. ἀλλὰ μὴ οὐ τοῦτ' ᾖ χαλεπόν, ὦ ἄνδρες, θάνατον ἐκφυγεῖν, ἀλλὰ πολὺ
χαλεπώτερον πονηρίαν. (Socrates, in Plato, *Apology*)

> ❡ τοῦτ' = τοῦτο
>
> ὦ ἄνδρες = oh men [of the jury].
> This line was spoken at his trial.
>
> πολὺ: here adverbial, "much"
>
> πονηρίαν: direct object of the
> implied ἐκφυγεῖν

9. ἐγώ εἰμι ἡ ἀνάστασις καὶ ἡ ζωή· ὁ πιστεύων εἰς ἐμὲ κἂν ἀποθάνῃ ζήσεται, καὶ
πᾶς ὁ ζῶν καὶ πιστεύων εἰς ἐμὲ οὐ μὴ ἀποθάνῃ εἰς τὸν αἰῶνα. (John 11:25–26)

> ❡ εἰς ἐμὲ = in me
>
> κἂν = καὶ ἂν = even if
>
> ζήσεται: the middle is used intran-
> sitively here, "will live."
>
> εἰς τὸν αἰῶνα = into the age: i.e.,
> "forever"

10. λέγω δέ, πνεύματι περιπατεῖτε καὶ ἐπιθυμίαν σαρκὸς οὐ μὴ τελέσητε.
(Gal 5:16)

> ❡ τελέσητε: here "fulfill"

Etymology and Discussion Topics

παρά (prep.) = from (+ gen.); beside (+ dat.); to, contrary to (+ acc.)

This preposition is often used with the accusative to mean "contrary to,"
while κατά is used with the accusative to mean "in accordance with." Two
English words derived from παρά are "paranormal" (παρά + νόμος) and "pa-
ralysis" (παρά + λύσις "loose, free").

περιπατέω, περιπατήσω, περιεπάτησα, —, —, — = to walk around

There is a strong link between walking and philosophy in Plato and Aristotle. The platonic dialogue *Phaedrus* begins on a walk. Aristotle and his
followers were known as Peripatetics, and the lectures of Plato and Aristotle
are sometimes referred to as "walks." What might be the benefits of learning
while walking?

μνημονευτέον δὲ ὡς τὸ μέλλον οὔτε ἡμέτερον οὔτε πάντως οὐχ ἡμέτερον, ἵνα μήτε πάντως προσμένωμεν ὡς ἐσόμενον μήτε ἀπελπίζωμεν ὡς πάντως οὐκ ἐσόμενον.

What is Epicurus saying about the relationship between fate and free-will?

μὴ ἀγροικότερον ᾖ τό ἀληθὲς εἰπεῖν.

Considering Socrates' contempt of sophistic rhetoric, why might he refer to speaking the truth as ἀγροικότερον?

Chapter 40 ～

Sequence of Moods • Temporal Clauses

Sequence of Moods

Greek divides the tenses of verbs in the indicative mood into two categories, primary and secondary.

Primary Tenses	*Secondary Tenses*
present	imperfect
future	aorist
perfect	pluperfect
future perfect	

The easiest way to remember primary and secondary tenses is the following: secondary tenses are past tenses and primary tenses are not. Notice that secondary tenses have the augment, while primary tenses do not. It might seem odd that the perfect is treated as a primary and not a secondary tense. Remember that the perfect tense indicates something that has happened in the past (is completed) but *has bearing upon the present*.

We have seen that verbs in *dependent clauses* can be indicative (relative clause, indirect statement with ὅτι/ὡς, indirect question, effort clause, actual result clause, fear clause), subjunctive (purpose clause, fear clause, protasis "if clause" of a condition), or optative (protasis "if clause" of a condition).

If a dependent clause is introduced by a verb in a secondary tense, the dependent clause is said to be in secondary sequence, and its verb *can be changed from the indicative or subjunctive into the optative.* Notice the word "can." It is an option that not all authors choose to take. You can get a sense of why this is so from the following English example.[1]

I study Greek so that I can read Plato. (primary sequence)

I studied Greek so that I could read Plato. (secondary sequence)

In the first example, the independent clause is "I study Greek." The verb "study" is present and therefore the dependent clause that it introduces "so that I can read Plato" is in *primary sequence*. If this were Greek, the verb of the dependent clause would be in the subjunctive mood. In the second example the dependent clause is introduced by a verb in the past tense "studied" and therefore the dependent clause is in *secondary sequence*. If this were Greek, the author would have the *option* of changing the verb into the optative.

ὁ Σωκράτης λέγει ἵνα παιδεύῃ ἀνθρώπους. (λέγει = primary sequence)

Socrates speaks in order to educate men.

ὁ Σωκράτης ἔλεγεν ἵνα παιδεύοι ἀνθρώπους.(ἔλεγεν = secondary sequence)

Or the verb in the dependent clause can remain unchanged:

ὁ Σωκράτης ἔλεγεν ἵνα παιδεύῃ ἀνθρώπους.

Both sentences would be translated "Socrates spoke in order to educate men." As you can see, it is an option to change the subjunctive παιδεύῃ to the optative παιδεύοι in secondary sequence. The English translation, however, stays the same.

When indirect statement is in secondary sequence, the tense of the indicative is changed (if it is changed) to the corresponding tense of the optative.

ὁ Σωκράτης λέγει ὅτι ἡ πόλις ἀδικήσει τὸν φιλόσοφον. (λέγει = primary sequence)

Socrates says that the city will harm the philosopher.

---

1. It is of course not a perfect example, as the use of "can" and "could" is determined by tense and not mood. Nevertheless, it approximates what is happening in Greek.

ὁ Σωκράτης ἔλεγεν ὅτι ἡ πόλις ἀδικήσοι τὸν φιλόσοφον. (ἔλεγεν = secondary sequence)

Or the verb in the dependent clause can remain unchanged:

ὁ Σωκράτης ἔλεγεν ὅτι ἡ πόλις ἀδικήσει τὸν φιλόσοφον.

Both sentences would be translated "Socrates said that the city would harm the philosopher."

If the dependent clause in secondary sequence contains a subjunctive and ἄν, the ἄν is eliminated.

¶ ἀποθνήσκω, ἀποθανοῦμαι, ἀπέθανον = to die

ὁ φιλόσοφος λέγει ὅτι ἐὰν ἡ φιλοσοφία ἀποθάνῃ, ἡ σοφία ἀποθανεῖται.

The philosopher says that if philosophy dies, wisdom will die.

ὁ φιλόσοφος ἔλεγεν ὅτι εἰ ἡ φιλοσοφία ἀποθάνοι, ἡ σοφία ἀποθανεῖται.

Or the verb in the dependent clause can remain unchanged:

ὁ φιλόσοφος ἔλεγεν ὅτι ἐὰν ἡ φιλοσοφία ἀποθάνῃ, ἡ σοφία ἀποθανεῖται.

Both sentences would be translated "The philosopher said that if philosophy dies, wisdom will die." Once again, whether or not the author changes the verb of a dependent clause in secondary sequence has no impact on your English translation.

If a dependent clause is introduced by a verb in the subjunctive, it is in primary sequence. If a dependent clause is introduced by a verb in the optative, it is sometimes treated as being in primary sequence and sometimes as being in secondary sequence.

There are a couple of instances where the verb of a dependent clause in secondary sequence cannot be changed into the corresponding tense of optative. In indirect statement and indirect questions, a verb in a secondary tense of the indicative cannot be changed into the optative. In addition, the indicative + ἄν cannot be changed into the optative. If, however, you do not plan on composing Greek, you do not need to worry about these exceptions.

Temporal Clauses

As the name suggests, temporal clauses express time. All temporal clauses are dependent clauses. For the most part temporal clauses refer to either definite time in the present or past, or indefinite time in the future. When referring to definite time in the present or past, the verb in the temporal clause is indicative. When referring to future time, the verb is placed in either the subjunctive (with ἄν) or the optative. In such cases it is helpful to think of temporal clauses as the equivalent of the protasis in a future condition. If a subjunctive is used, the author is fairly confident that it will occur, if the optative is used, he is less confident.

¶ ὁπότε = when

λέγε μοι ὁπότ᾽ ἄν ὁ Πλάτων ἀποθάνῃ.

Tell me when Plato dies.

λέγε μοι ὁπότε ὁ Πλάτων ἀποθάνοι.

Tell me when Plato should die.

λέγε μοι ὁπότε ὁ Πλάτων ἀπέθανεν.

Tell me when Plato died.

πρίν

The conjunction πρίν has two meanings. When πρίν precedes an infinitive, it means "before." In such cases the verb will take a subject in the accusative as though it were in indirect statement. It can also mean "until." When it refers to a time in the future it takes the subjunctive and ἄν. When it refers to a time in the past it takes the indicative.

πρίν + infinitive	before
πρίν + subjunctive and ἄν	until (future time)
πρίν + indicative	until (past time)

ὁ Πλάτων ἦν εὐδαίμων πρὶν τὸν Σωκράτη ἀποθανεῖν.

Plato was happy before Socrates died.

ὁ Πλάτων ἦν εὐδαίμων πρὶν ὁ Σωκράτης ἀπέθανεν.

Plato was happy until Socrates died.

ὁ φιλόσοφος ἔσται εὐδαίμων πρὶν ἡ σοφία ἂν ἀποθάνῃ.

The philosopher will be happy until wisdom dies.

Vocabulary

θύρα, –ας, ἡ = door, entrance

κίνησις, –εως, ἡ = motion

▶ παραβολή, –ῆς, ἡ = analogy, parable

ποτήριον, –ου, τό = cup

ἕως (conj.) = while, as long as; until

ὁσάκις (adv.) = as many times as, whenever

πρίν (conj.) = before (+ inf.); until (+ subj. or past tense of indic.)

ἐπιθυμέω , ἐπιθυμήσω, ἐπεθύμησα, —, —, — = to desire (+ gen.)

ἐπιτυγχάνω, ἐπιτεύξομαι, ἐπέτυχον, ἐπιτετύχηκα, —, — = to happen upon (+ gen.); obtain (+ gen.); meet (+ dat.)

Sentences

1. ἐπηρώτων δὲ αὐτὸν οἱ μαθηταὶ αὐτοῦ τίς αὕτη εἴη ἡ παραβολή. (Luke 8:9)

> ¶ ἐπηρώτων: imperfect of ἐρωτάω. The disciples are the subject.
>
> αὐτὸν: Jesus

2. καί ποτέ τινος ἀκούσας ὡς μέγιστον ἀγαθὸν εἴη τὸ πάντων ἐπιτυγχάνειν ὧν τις ἐπιθυμεῖ, εἶπε, "πολὺ δὲ μεῖζον τὸ ἐπιθυμεῖν ὧν δεῖ." (Menedemus, in Diogenes Laertius, *Lives of Eminent Philosophers*)

> ¶ ἀκούσας: aorist participle of ἀκούω. The subject of this participle and the verb εἶπε is Menedemus.
>
> ὡς = that: introducing indirect statement
>
> πολὺ: here adverbial "much"
>
> μεῖζον = better
>
> ὧν δεῖ = which things are necessary: Greek will often attract the case of the relative to its antecedent. Here the antecedent is the implied "things," which would be in the genitive because of ἐπιθυμεῖν.

3. εἰπόντος τινὸς ὡς ἀεὶ τοὺς φιλοσόφους βλέποι παρὰ ταῖς τῶν πλουσίων
θύραις, "καὶ γὰρ οἱ ἰατροί," φησί, "παρὰ ταῖς τῶν νοσούντων· ἀλλ᾽ οὐ παρὰ
τοῦτό τις ἂν ἕλοιτο νοσεῖν ἢ ἰατρεύειν." (Aristippus, in Diogenes Laertius, *Lives of
Eminent Philosophers*)

> ¶ φησί: the subject is Aristippus
>
> εἰπόντος: aorist participle of λέγω.
>
> ὡς = that: introducing indirect
> statement
>
> βλέποι: the subject is the "some-
> one" just mentioned
>
> παρὰ ταῖς...θύραις = at the
> doors: i.e., to ask for money
>
> καὶ γὰρ: this combination can
> mean "for indeed," or "yes, also."
> The sense here is probably the
> latter, "Yes, but you also [see]..."
>
> νοσούντων: present participle of
> νοσέω = to be sick
>
> παρὰ τοῦτό = for this reason
>
> ἕλοιτο: aorist optative of αἱρέω
>
> νοσέω = to be sick
>
> ἰατρεύω = to be a physician

4. ὁμοίως καὶ πρὸς τὸν εἰπόντα ὅτι κίνησις οὐκ ἔστιν, ἀναστὰς περιεπάτει.
(Diogenes Laertius, *Lives of Eminent Philosophers*)

> ¶ The subject is the cynic Dio-
> genes.
>
> πρὸς τὸν εἰπόντα = against some-
> one saying
>
> κίνησις οὐκ ἔστιν: i.e., some think-
> ers like Parmenides believed that
> change was an illusion
>
> ἀναστὰς: 2nd aorist participle of
> ἀνίστημι = to raise up. Remember
> that the 2nd aorist of ἵστημι and
> its compounds are intransitive.

5. ὁ δὲ εἶπεν, "Λέγω σοι, Πέτρε, οὐ φωνήσει σήμερον ἀλέκτωρ ἕως τρίς με ἀπαρνήσῃ εἰδέναι." (Luke 22:34)

> ❡ εἶπεν: the grammatical subject is Jesus.
>
> Πέτρε: vocative of Πέτρος, –ου, ὁ = Peter
>
> φωνέω = to make a sound
>
> σήμερον (adv.) = today
>
> ἀλέκτωρ, –ορος, ὁ = cock, rooster
>
> τρίς (adv.) = three times, thrice
>
> ἀπαρνέομαι = to deny
>
> εἰδέναι: infinitive of οἶδα

6. αὐτός, ὦ Φαίδων, παρεγένου Σωκράτει ἐκείνῃ τῇ ἡμέρᾳ ᾗ τὸ φάρμακον ἔπιεν ἐν τῷ δεσμωτηρίῳ; (Plato, Phaedo)

> ❡ This is the opening line of the Phaedo. The speaker is Echecrates, who wants to learn from Phaedo what transpired on the day that Socrates died.
>
> Φαίδων, –ωνος, ὁ = Phaedo
>
> παρεγένου: 2nd person singular aorist of παραγίγνομαι = to be beside or near (+ dat.)
>
> φάρμακον, –ου, τό = drug; poison
>
> δεσμωτηρίον, –ου, τό = prison

7. Χαιρεφῶν ποτε καὶ εἰς Δελφοὺς ἐλθὼν ἐτόλμησε τοῦτο μαντεύσασθαι—καί, ὅπερ λέγω, μὴ θορυβεῖτε, ὦ ἄνδρες—ἤρετο γὰρ δὴ εἴ τις ἐμοῦ εἴη σοφώτερος. ἀνεῖλεν οὖν ἡ Πυθία μηδένα σοφώτερον εἶναι. (Socrates, in Plato, *Apology*)

❡ Χαιρεφῶν, –ωνος, ὁ = Chaerephon, a friend of Socrates

εἰς Δελφοὺς = to [the oracle at] Delphi

ἐλθὼν: aorist participle of ἔρχομαι.

τολμάω = to dare (+ inf.)

μαντεύομαι = to prophesy; to ask an oracle

ὅπερ λέγω = what I am about to say

θορυβέω = to make a disturbance

καί, ὅπερ λέγω, μὴ θορυβεῖτε, ὦ ἄνδρες: Socrates, at his trial, suspects that his next statement might cause considerable consternation on the part of the jury.

ἤρετο: aorist of ἔρομαι = to ask

ἀνεῖλεν: aorist of ἀναιρέω = to ordain (used of an oracular response)

Πυθία, –ας, ἡ = the Pythia, the priestess of Apollo at Delphi

8. ὁσάκις γὰρ ἐὰν ἐσθίητε τὸν ἄρτον τοῦτον καὶ τὸ ποτήριον πίνητε, τὸν θάνατον τοῦ κυρίου καταγγέλλετε, ἄχρις οὗ ἔλθῃ. (1 Cor 11:26)

❡ ὁσάκις γὰρ ἐὰν: It is impossible to translate the ἐὰν here, but you should be aware of what condition it is signifying.

καταγγέλω = to proclaim

ἄχρις (conj.) = until (+ gen.)

οὗ = which: another case of the relative being attracted into the case of an implied antecedent, here "time"

ἔλθῃ: aorist subjunctive of ἔρχομαι; the implied subject is Jesus.

▶ 9. μήπω μέγαν εἴπῃς πρὶν τελευτήσαντ᾽ ἴδῃς. (Sophocles, in Stobaeus, *Anthology*)

❡ μήπω (adv.) = not yet: here "don't…until…"

εἴπῃς: aorist subjunctive of λέγω

μέγαν εἴπῃς = say [a man] is great

τελευτήσαντ᾽ = τελευτήσαντα, aorist participle of τελευτάω = to finish; to die

ἴδῃς: aorist subjunctive of ὁράω

▶ 10. οὐ μὲν γάρ ποτ᾽ ἔφασκε γῆς καρπὸν ἀνήσειν, πρὶν ἴδοι ὀφθαλμοῖσιν ἑὴν εὐώπιδα κούρην. (*Homeric Hymn to Demeter*)

❡ The subject is the goddess Demeter, who, as the goddess of grain, went "on strike" after her daughter Persephone was abducted by Hades.

ἔφασκε: imperfect of φημί. οὐ + φημί = deny. Here "she denied that she would," or "she said that she would never" (+ inf.)

ἀνήσειν: future infinitive of ἀνίημι = to send up

ἴδοι: aorist optative of ὁράω

ὀφθαλμοῖσιν = ὀφθαλμοῖς

ὀφθαλμός, –οῦ, ὁ = eye

ἑός, –ή, –όν (adj.) = his/her own

εὐῶπις, –ιδος (adj.) = fair-eyed

κούρη = κόρη, –ης, ἡ = girl

Etymology and Discussion Topics

παραβολή, –ῆς, ἡ = analogy, parable

A parable is a way of explaining or describing something by analogy. παραβολή is a combination of παρά and βάλλω (which in addition to "throw" can mean "put"), thus "to put beside."

μήπω μέγαν εἴπῃς πρὶν τελευτήσαντ᾽ ἴδῃς.

This admonition not to pronounce anyone happy until they are dead is also found in Herodotus's story of Solon and Croesus. Solon gave Croesus similar advice, which turned out to be prophetic.

οὐ μὲν γάρ ποτ᾽ ἔφασκε γῆς καρπὸν ἀνήσειν, πρὶν ἴδοι ὀφθαλμοῖσιν ἑὴν εὐώπιδα κούρην.

The *Homeric Hymn to Demeter*, while almost certainly not composed by Homer, is a masterpiece of archaic Greek poetry. It tells the story of the abduction of Persephone and her mother Demeter's determined quest to win her back. In the end she only partially succeeds, agreeing to a deal whereby Persephone stays with Hades for part of the year (winter), consequently a season in which nothing grows. Persephone is often referred to simply as ἡ κόρη "the girl."

Appendix A. Morphology

Noun Endings and the Definite Article

	1st Declension	2nd Declension	3rd Declension	Definite Article		
	f *f* *m*	*m* *n*	*m/f* *n*	*m*	*f*	*n*
Singular						
Nominative	η (α) (ης)	ος ον	ς / — —	ὁ	ἡ	τό
Genitive	ης (ας) (ου)	ου ου	ος ος	τοῦ	τῆς	τοῦ
Dative	ῃ (ᾳ) (ῃ)	ῳ ῳ	ι ι	τῷ	τῇ	τῷ
Accusative	ην (αν) (ην)	ον ον	α/ν —	τόν	τήν	τό
Plural						
Nominative	αι	οι α	ες α	οἱ	αἱ	τά
Genitive	ων	ων ων	ων ων	τῶν	τῶν	τῶν
Dative	αις	οις οις	σι(ν) σι(ν)	τοῖς	ταῖς	τοῖς
Accusative	ας	ους α	ας α	τούς	τάς	τά

Model Nouns

	1st Declension		2nd Declension		3rd Declension
	f (soul)	*f (joy)*	*m (word)*	*n (book)*	*m (divinity)*
Singular					
Nominative	ψυχ–ή	χαρ–ά	λόγ–ος	βιβλί–ον	δαίμων
Genitive	ψυχ–ῆς	χαρ–ᾶς	λόγ–ου	βιβλί–ου	δαίμον–ος
Dative	ψυχ–ῇ	χαρ–ᾷ	λόγ–ῳ	βιβλί–ῳ	δαίμον–ι
Accusative	ψυχ–ήν	χαρ–άν	λόγ–ον	βιβλί–ον	δαίμον–α
(Vocative)	(ψυχή)	(χαρά)	(λόγε)	(βιβλίον)	(δαῖμον)
Plural					
Nominative	ψυχ–αί	χαρ–αί	λόγ–οι	βιβλί–α	δαίμον–ες
Genitive	ψυχ–ῶν	χαρ–ῶν	λόγ–ων	βιβλί–ων	δαιμόν–ων
Dative	ψυχ–αῖς	χαρ–αῖς	λόγ–οις	βιβλί–οις	δαίμο–σι(ν)
Accusative	ψυχ–άς	χαρ–άς	λόγ–ους	βιβλί–α	δαίμον–ας

	3rd Declension					
	n (body)	*f (grace)*	*f (city)*	*n (race)*	*m (Socrates)*	*m (king)*
Singular						
Nominative	σῶμα	χάρι–ς	πόλι–ς	γένος	Σωκράτ–ης	βασιλ–εύς
Genitive	σώματ–ος	χάριτ–ος	πόλ–εως	γέν–ους	Σωκράτ–ους	βασιλ–έως
Dative	σώματ–ι	χάριτ–ι	πόλ–ει	γέν–ει	Σωκράτ–ει	βασιλ–εῖ
Accusative	σῶμα	χάρι–ν	πόλι–ν	γένος	Σωκράτ–η	βασιλ–έα
(Vocative)	(σῶμα)	(χάρι)	(πόλι)	(γένος)	(Σώκρατες)	(βασιλεῦ)
Plural						
Nominative	σώματ–α	χάριτ–ες	πόλ–εις	γέν–η		βασιλ–εῖς
Genitive	σωμάτ–ων	χαρίτ–ων	πόλε–ων	γεν–ῶν		βασιλ–έων
Dative	σώμα–σι(ν)	χάρι–σι(ν)	πόλε–σι(ν)	γένε–σι(ν)		βασιλεῦ–σι(ν)
Accusative	σώματ–α	χάριτ–ας	πόλ–εις	γέν–η		βασιλέ–ας

Model Adjectives

	Adjectives of the 1st and 2nd Declension			Mixed Declension Adjectives		
	m	f	n	m	f	n
Singular						
Nominative	καλ–ός	καλ–ή	καλ–όν	ἡδ–ύς	ἡδεῖ–α	ἡδ–ύ
Genitive	καλ–οῦ	καλ–ῆς	καλ–οῦ	ἡδ–έος	ἡδεί–ας	ἡδ–έος
Dative	καλ–ῷ	καλ–ῇ	καλ–ῷ	ἡδ–εῖ	ἡδεί–ᾳ	ἡδ–εῖ
Accusative	καλ–όν	καλ–ήν	καλ–όν	ἡδ–ύν	ἡδεῖ–αν	ἡδ–ύ
(Vocative)	(καλέ)	(καλή)	(καλόν)	(ἡδύ)	(ἡδεῖα)	(ἡδύ)
Plural						
Nominative	καλ–οί	καλ–αί	καλ–ά	ἡδ–εῖς	ἡδεῖ–αι	ἡδ–έα
Genitive	καλ–ῶν	καλ–ῶν	καλ–ῶν	ἡδ–έων	ἡδει–ῶν	ἡδ–έων
Dative	καλ–οῖς	καλ–αῖς	καλ–οῖς	ἡδ–έσι	ἡδεί–αις	ἡδ–έσι
Accusative	καλ–ούς	καλ–άς	καλ–ά	ἡδ–εῖς	ἡδεί–ας	ἡδ–έα

*When the stem ends in (ε, ι, or ρ), α replaces η in feminine singular endings.

	3rd Declension Adjectives			
	m/f	n	m/f	n
Singluar				
Nominative	εὐδαίμων	εὔδαιμον	ἀληθ–ής	ἀληθ–ές
Genitive	εὐδαίμον–ος	εὐδαίμον–ος	ἀληθ–οῦς	ἀληθ–οῦς
Dative	εὐδαίμον–ι	εὐδαίμον–ι	ἀληθ–εῖ	ἀληθ–εῖ
Accusative	εὐδαίμον–α	εὔδαιμον	ἀληθ–ῆ	ἀληθ–ές
(Vocative)	(εὔδαιμ-ον)	(εὔδαιμ-ον)	(ἀληθές)	(ἀληθές)
Plural				
Nominative	εὐδαίμον–ες	εὐδαίμον–α	ἀληθ–εῖς	ἀληθ–ῆ
Genitive	εὐδαιμόν–ων	εὐδαιμόν–ων	ἀληθ–ῶν	ἀληθ–ῶν
Dative	εὐδαίμο–σι(ν)	εὐδαίμο–σι(ν)	ἀληθέ–σι(ν)	ἀληθέ–σι(ν)
Accusative	εὐδαίμον–ας	εὐδαίμον–α	ἀληθ–εῖς	ἀληθ–ῆ

Irregular Adjectives

	πᾶς, πᾶσα, πᾶν (adj.) = all			μέγας, μεγάλη, μέγα (adj.) = great, large		
	m	f	n	m	f	n
Singular						
Nominative	πᾶ–ς	πᾶσ–α	πᾶν	μέγας	μεγάλ–η	μέγα
Genitive	παντ–ός	πάσ–ης	παντ–ός	μεγάλ–ου	μεγάλ–ης	μεγάλ–ου
Dative	παντ–ί	πάσ–η	παντ–ί	μεγάλ–ῳ	μεγάλ–η	μεγάλ–ῳ
Accusative	πάντ–α	πᾶσ–αν	πᾶν	μεγάν	μεγάλ–ην	μέγα
Plural						
Nominative	πάντ–ες	πᾶσ–αι	πάντ–α	μεγάλ–οι	μεγάλ–αι	μεγάλ–α
Genitive	πάντ–ων	πασ–ῶν	πάντ–ων	μεγάλ–ων	μεγάλ–ων	μεγάλ–ων
Dative	πᾶ–σι(ν)	πάσ–αις	πᾶ–σι(ν)	μεγάλ–οις	μεγάλ–αις	μεγάλ–οις
Accusative	πάντ–ας	πάσ–ας	πάντ–α	μεγάλ–ους	μεγάλ–ας	μεγάλ–α

	πολύς, πολλή, πολύ (adj.) = much, many		
	m	f	n
Singular			
Nominative	πολ–ύς	πολλ–ή	πολ–ύ
Genitive	πολλ–οῦ	πολλ–ῆς	πολλ–οῦ
Dative	πολλ–ῷ	πολλ–η	πολλ–ῷ
Accusative	πολ–ύν	πολλ–ήν	πολ–ύ
Plural			
Nominative	πολλ–οί	πολλ–αί	πολλ–ά
Genitive	πολλ–ῶν	πολλ–ῶν	πολλ–ῶν
Dative	πολλ–οῖς	πολλ–αῖς	πολλ–οῖς
Accusative	πολλ–ούς	πολλ–άς	πολλ–ά

Comparatives and Superlatives

	σοφώτερος, –τερα, –τερον = wiser			καλλίων, –ιον = more beautiful	
	m	*f*	*n*	*m/f*	*n*
Singular					
Nominative	σοφώ–τερος	σοφω–τέρα	σοφώ–τερον	καλλ–ίων	κάλλ–ιον
Genitive	σοφω–τέρου	σοφω–τέρας	σοφω–τέρου	καλλ–ίονος	καλλ–ίονος
Dative	σοφω–τέρῳ	σοφω–τέρᾳ	σοφω–τέρῳ	καλλ–ίονι	καλλ–ίονι
Accusative	σοφώ–τερον	σοφω–τέραν	σοφώ–τερον	καλλ–ίονα (καλλ–ίω)	κάλλ–ιον
(Vocative)	(σοφώτερε)	(σοφωτέρα)	(σοφώτερον)	(κάλλιον)	(κάλλιον)
Plural					
Nominative	σοφώ–τεροι	σοφώ–τεραι	σοφώ–τερα	καλλ–ίονες	καλλ–ίονα (καλλ–ίω)
Genitive	σοφω–τέρων	σοφω–τέρων	σοφω–τέρων	καλλ–ιόνων	καλλ–ιόνων
Dative	σοφω–τέροις	σοφω–τέραις	σοφω–τέροις	καλλ–ίοσι(ν)	καλλ–ίοσι(ν)
Accusative	σοφω–τέρους	σοφω–τέρας	σοφώ–τερα	καλλ–ίονας	καλλ–ίονα (καλλ–ίω)

	σοφώτατος, –τατη, –τατον = wisest			κάλλιστος, –ιστη, –ιστον = most beautiful		
	m	*f*	*n*	*m*	*f*	*n*
Singular						
Nominative	σοφώ–τατος	σοφω–τάτη	σοφώ–τατον	κάλλ–ιστος	καλλ–ίστη	κάλλ–ιστον
Genitive	σοφω–τάτου	σοφω–τάτης	σοφω–τάτου	καλλ–ίστου	καλλ–ίστης	καλλ–ίστου
Dative	σοφω–τάτῳ	σοφω–τάτῃ	σοφω–τάτῳ	καλλ–ίστῳ	καλλ–ίστῃ	καλλ–ίστῳ
Accusative	σοφώ–τατον	σοφω–τάτην	σοφώ–τατον	κάλλ–ιστον	καλλ–ίστην	κάλλ–ιστον
(Vocative)	(σοφώτατε)	(σοφωτάτη)	(σοφώτατον)	(κάλλιστε)	(καλλίστη)	(κάλλιστον)
Plural						
Nominative	σοφώ–τατοι	σοφώ–ταται	σοφώ–τατα	κάλλ–ιστοι	κάλλ–ισται	κάλλ–ιστα
Genitive	σοφω–τάτων	σοφω–τάτων	σοφω–τάτων	καλλ–ίστων	καλλ–ίστων	καλλ–ίστων
Dative	σοφω–τάτοις	σοφω–τάταις	σοφω–τάτοις	καλλ–ίστοις	καλλ–ίσταις	καλλ–ίστοις
Accusative	σοφω–τάτους	σοφω–τάτας	σοφώ–τατα	καλλ–ίστους	καλλ–ίστας	κάλλ–ιστα

Participles

| Present Active |||| 1st Aorist Active |||| Perfect Active |||
m	f	n	m	f	n	m	f	n
ων	ουσα	ον	σας	σασα	σαν	κως	κυια	κος
οντος	ουσης	οντος	σαντος	σασης	σαντος	κοτος	κυιας	κοτος
οντι	ουση	οντι	σαντι	σαση	σαντι	κοτι	κυιᾳ	κοτι
οντα	ουσαν	ον	σαντα	σασαν	σαν	κοτα	κυιαν	κος
οντες	ουσαι	οντα	σαντες	σασαι	σαντα	κοτες	κυιαι	κοτα
οντων	ουσων	οντων	σαντων	σασων	σαντων	κοτων	κυιων	κοτων
ουσι(ν)	ουσαις	ουσι(ν)	σασι(ν)	σασαις	σασι(ν)	κοσι(ν)	κυιαις	κοσι(ν)
οντας	ουσας	οντα	σαντας	σασας	σαντα	κοτας	κυιας	κοτα

| Present Middle/Passive |||| 1st Aorist Middle |||| 1st Aorist Passive |||
m	f	n	m	f	n	m	f	n
ομενος	ομενη	ομενον	σαμενος	σαμενη	σαμενον	θεις	θεισα	θεν
ομενου	ομενης	ομενου	σαμενου	σαμενης	σαμενου	θεντος	θεισης	θεντος
ομενῳ	ομενη	ομενῳ	σαμενῳ	σαμενη	σαμενῳ	θεντι	θειση	θεντι
ομενον	ομενην	ομενον	σαμενον	σαμενην	σαμενον	θεντα	θεισαν	θεν
ομενοι	ομεναι	ομενα	σαμενοι	σαμεναι	σαμενα	θεντες	θεισαι	θεντα
ομενων	ομενων	ομενων	σαμενων	σαμενων	σαμενων	θεντων	θεισων	θεντων
ομενοις	ομεναις	ομενοις	σαμενοις	σαμεναις	σαμενοις	θεισι(ν)	θεισαις	θεισι(ν)
ομενους	ομενας	ομενα	σαμενους	σαμενας	σαμενα	θεντας	θεισας	θεντα

Future Active Participle	add σ to present active endings, i.e., σων, σουσα, σον, etc.
Future Middle Participle	add σ to present middle/passive endings, i.e., σομενος, σομενη, σομενον, etc.
Future Passive Participle	add θησ to present middle/passive endings, i.e., θησομενος, etc.
Perfect Middle/Passive	add present middle/passive endings to the perfect stem, i.e., λελυμένος, etc.
2nd Aorist Participle	active and middle = aorist stem + present endings
μι verbs	ἵστημι: uses the aorist active endings without the sigma for the present active participle (ἱστάς, ἱστᾶσα, ἱστάν). For the aorist active, take away the ἱ (στάς, στᾶσα, στάν). τίθημι: uses the aorist passive endings for the present participle (τιθείς, τιθεῖσα, τιθὲν). For the aorist active, take way the τι (θείς, θεῖσα, θέν). δίδωμι: uses regular endings except that the masculine nominative ending is διδούς rather than διδών. For the aorist, take away the δι-.

Pronouns

| | Personal Pronouns | | | Interrogative Pronoun | | Relative Pronoun | | |
	1st	2nd	3rd	m/f	n	m	f	n
Singular								
Nominative	ἐγώ	σύ	αὐτός	τίς	τί	ὅς	ἥ	ὅ
Genitive	ἐμοῦ (μου)	σοῦ	performs the	τίνος (τοῦ)	τίνος (τοῦ)	οὗ	ἧς	οὗ
Dative	ἐμοί (μοι)	σοί	functions	τίνι (τῷ)	τίνι (τῷ)	ᾧ	ᾗ	ᾧ
Accusative	ἐμέ (με)	σέ	of the 3rd	τίνα	τί	ὅν	ἥν	ὅ
Plural			person					
Nominative	ἡμεῖς	ὑμεῖς	personal pronoun	τίνες	τίνα	οἵ	αἵ	ἅ
Genitive	ἡμῶν	ὑμῶν		τίνων	τίνων	ὧν	ὧν	ὧν
Dative	ἡμῖν	ὑμῖν		τίσι(ν)	τίσι(ν)	οἷς	αἷς	οἷς
Accusative	ἡμᾶς	ὑμᾶς		τίνας	τίνα	οὕς	ἅς	ἅ

*The indefinite pronoun is identical to the interrogative, but without the accent on the first syllable.

| | Reflexive Pronoun | | | | |
| | 1st Person | 2nd Person | 3rd Person | | |
	m/f	m/f	m	f	n
Singular					
Genitive	ἐμαυτοῦ, –ῆς	σεαυτοῦ, –ῆς	ἑαυτοῦ (αὐτοῦ)	ἑαυτῆς (αὐτῆς)	ἑαυτοῦ (αὐτοῦ)
Dative	ἐμαυτῷ, –ῇ	σεαυτῷ, –ῇ	ἑαυτῷ (αὐτῷ)	ἑαυτῇ (αὐτῇ)	ἑαυτῷ (αὐτῷ)
Accusative	ἐμαυτόν, –ήν	σεαυτόν, –ήν	ἑαυτόν (αὐτόν)	ἑαυτήν (αὐτήν)	ἑαυτό (αὐτό)
Plural					
Genitive	ἡμῶν αὐτῶν	ὑμῶν αὐτῶν	ἑαυτῶν	ἑαυτῶν	ἑαυτῶν
Dative	ἡμῖν αὐτοῖς, –αῖς	ὑμῖν αὐτοῖς, –αῖς	ἑαυτοῖς	ἑαυταῖς	ἑαυτοῖς
Accusative	ἡμᾶς αὐτούς, –άς	ὑμᾶς αὐτούς, –άς	ἑαυτούς	ἑαυτάς	ἑαυτά

Demonstratives

	οὗτος, αὕτη, τοῦτο = *this*			ἐκεῖνος, ἐκείνη, ἐκεῖνο = *that*		
	m	*f*	*n*	*m*	*f*	*n*
Singular						
Nominative	οὗτ–ος	αὕτ–η	τοῦτ–ο	ἐκεῖν–ος	ἐκείν–η	ἐκεῖν–ο
Genitive	τούτ–ου	ταύτ–ης	τούτ–ου	ἐκείν–ου	ἐκείν–ης	ἐκείν–ου
Dative	τούτ–ῳ	ταύτ–ῃ	τούτ–ῳ	ἐκείν–ῳ	ἐκείν–ῃ	ἐκείν–ῳ
Accusative	τοῦτ–ον	ταύτ–ην	τοῦτ–ο	ἐκεῖν–ον	ἐκείν–ην	ἐκεῖν–ο
Plural						
Nominative	οὗτ–οι	αὕτ–αι	ταῦτ–α	ἐκεῖν–οι	ἐκεῖν–αι	ἐκεῖν–α
Genitive	τούτ–ων	τούτ–ων	τούτ–ων	ἐκείν–ων	ἐκείν–ων	ἐκείν–ων
Dative	τούτ–οις	ταύτ–αις	τούτ–οις	ἐκείν–οις	ἐκείν–αις	ἐκείν–οις
Accusative	τούτ–ους	ταύτ–ας	ταῦτ–α	ἐκείν–ους	ἐκείν–ας	ἐκεῖν–α

	ὅδε = *this*		
	m	*f*	*n*
Singular			
Nominative	ὅδε	ἥδε	τόδε
Genitive	τοῦδε	τῆσδε	τοῦδε
Dative	τῷδε	τῆδε	τῷδε
Accusative	τόνδε	τήνδε	τόδε
Plural			
Nominative	οἵδε	αἵδε	τάδε
Genitive	τῶνδε	τῶνδε	τῶνδε
Dative	τοῖσδε	ταῖσδε	τοῖσδε
Accusative	τούσδε	τάσδε	τάδε

Adverbs

	Positive	Comparative	Superlative
Most adverbs	σοφῶς	σοφώτερον	σοφώτατα
Some adverbs	καλῶς	κάλλιον	κάλλιστα
Alternate way	καλῶς	μᾶλλον καλῶς	μάλιστα καλῶς

Numbers

	One			Two	Three		Four	
	m	f	n	m/f/n	m/f	n	m/f	n
Nominative	εἷς	μία	ἕν	δύο	τρεῖς	τρία	τέτταρες	τέτταρα
Genitive	ἑνός	μιᾶς	ἑνός	δυοῖν	τριῶν	τριῶν	τεττάρων	τεττάρων
Dative	ἑνί	μιᾷ	ἑνί	δυοῖν	τρισί(ν)	τρισί(ν)	τέτταρσι(ν)	τέτταρσι(ν)
Accusative	ἕνα	μίαν	ἕν	δύο	τρεῖς	τρία	τέτταρας	τέτταρα

Important Numbers

Cardinal		Ordinal	
εἷς, μία, ἕν	1	πρῶτος, −η, −ον	1st
δύο	2	δεύτερος, −α, −ον	2nd
τρεῖς, τρία	3	τρίτος, −η, −ον	3rd
τέτταρες, τέτταρα	4	τέταρτος, −η, −ον	4th
πέντε	5	πέμπτος, −η, −ον	5th
δέκα	10	δέκατος, −η, −ον	10th
εἴκοσι(ν)	20	εἰκοστός, −ή, −όν	20th
πεντήκοντα	50	πεντηκοστός, −ή, −όν	50th
ἑκατόν	100	ἑκατοστός, −ή, −όν	100th
χίλιοι, −αι, −α	1000	χιλιοστός,−ή, −όν	1,000th

Omega Verb

		Present		Future		Imperfect		Aorist	
		sg	*pl*	*sg*	*pl*	*sg*	*pl*	*sg*	*pl*
					Indicative				
Active	1	ω	ομεν	σω	σομεν	ον	ομεν	σα	σαμεν
	2	εις	ετε	σεις	σετε	ες	ετε	σας	σατε
	3	ει	ουσι(ν)	σει	σουσι(ν)	ε(ν)	ον	σε(ν)	σαν
Middle	1	ομαι	ομεθα	σομαι	σομεθα	ομην	ομεθα	σαμην	σαμεθα
	2	η (ει)	εσθε	ση (σει)	σεσθε	ου	εσθε	σω	σασθε
	3	εται	ονται	σεται	σονται	ετο	οντο	σατο	σαντο
Passive	1	ομαι	ομεθα	θησομαι	θησομεθα	ομην	ομεθα	θην	θημεν
	2	η (ει)	εσθε	θηση (ει)	θησεσθε	ου	εσθε	θης	θητε
	3	εται	ονται	θησεται	θησονται	ετο	οντο	θη	θησαν
					Subjunctive				
Active	1	ω	ωμεν					σω	σωμεν
	2	ης	ητε					σης	σητε
	3	η	ωσι(ν)					ση	σωσι(ν)
Middle	1	ωμαι	ωμεθα					σωμαι	σωμεθα
	2	η	ησθε					ση	σησθε
	3	ηται	ωνται					σηται	σωνται
Passive	1	ωμαι	ωμεθα					θω	θωμεν
	2	η	ησθε					θης	θητε
	3	ηται	ωνται					θη	θωσι(ν)
					Optative				
Active	1	οιμι	οιμεν	σοιμι	σοιμεν			σαιμι	σαιμεν
	2	οις	οιτε	σοις	σοιτε			σειας (σαις)	σαιτε
	3	οι	οιεν	σοι	σοιε			σειε(ν) (σαι)	σειαν (σαιεν)
Middle	1	οιμην	οιμεθα	σοιμην	σοιμεθα			σαιμην	σαιμεθα
	2	οιο	οισθε	σοιο	σοισθε			σαιο	σαισθε
	3	οιτο	οιντο	σοιτο	σοιντο			σαιτο	σαιντο
Passive	1	οιμην	οιμεθα	θησοιμην	θησοιμεθα			θειην	θειημεν (θειμεν)
	2	οιο	οισθε	θησοιο	θησοισθε			θειης	θειητε (θειτε)
	3	οιτο	οιντο	θησοιτο	θησοιντο			θειη	θειησαν (θειεν)

		Perfect		Pluperfect		Future Perfect
		sg	pl	sg	pl	
		Indicative				
Active	1	κα	καμεν	κη	κεμεν	periphrastic
	2	κας	κατε	κης	κετε	
	3	κε(ν)	κασι(ν)	κει(ν)	κεσαν	
Middle	1	μαι	μεθα	μην	μεθα	periphrastic
	2	σαι	σθε	σο	σθε	or perfect stem
	3	ται	νται	το	ντο	+ future middle endings
Passive	1	μαι	μεθα	μην	μεθα	periphrastic
	2	σαι	σθε	σο	σθε	or perfect stem
	3	ται	νται	το	ντο	ǀ future middle endings
		Subjunctive				
Active		periphrastic or				
	1	κω	κωμεν			
	2	κης	κητε			
	3	κη	κωσι(ν)			
Middle	1	periphrastic				
	2					
	3					
Passive	1	periphrastic				
	2					
	3					
		Optative				
Active		periphrastic or				
	1	κοιμι	κοιμεν			
	2	κοις	κοιτε			
	3	κοι	κοιεν			
Middle	1	periphrastic				
	2					
	3					
Passive	1	periphrastic				
	2					
	3					

Imperatives

		Omega Verbs		α Contract		ε Contract		o Contract	
		sg	pl	sg	pl	sg	pl	sg	pl
Present Active	2	ε	ετε	α	ατε	ει	ειτε	ου	ου
	3	ετω	οντων	ατω	ωντων	ειτω	ουντων	ουτω	ου
Present M/P	2	ου	εσθε	ω	ασθε	ου	εισθε	ου	ου
	3	εσθω	εσθων	ασθω	ασθων	εισθω	εισθων	ουσθω	ου
Aorist Active	2	σον	σατε						
	3	σατω	σαντων						
Aorist Middle	2	σαι	σασθε						
	3	σασθω	σασθων						
Aorist Passive	2	θητι	θητε						
	3	θητω	θεντων						
Perfect Active		periphrastic or				Same as Omega Verbs			
	2	κε	κετε						
	3	κετω							
Perfect M/P		periphrastic or							
	2	σο	σθε						
	3	σθω	σθων						

Infinitives

	Omega Verbs	α Contract	ε Contract	o Contract
Present Active	ειν	ᾶν	εῖν	οῦν
Present M/P	εσθαι	ᾶσθαι	εῖσθαι	οῦσθαι
Future Active	σειν			
Future Middle	σεσθαι			
Future Passive	θησεσθαι			
Aorist Active	σαι		Same as Omega Verbs	
Aorist Middle	σασθαι			
Aorist Passive	θηναι			
Perfect Active	κεναι			
Perfect M/P	σθαι			

Contract Verbs

Present Tense

		α Contract		ε Contract		o Contract	
Indicative	Present Active	ῶ	ῶμεν	ῶ	οῦμεν	ῶ	οῦμεν
		ᾷς	ᾶτε	εῖς	εῖτε	οῖς	οῦτε
		ᾷ	ῶσι(ν)	εῖ	οῦσι(ν)	οῖ	οῦσι(ν)
	Present M/P	ῶμαι	ωμεθα	οῦμαι	ουμεθα	οῦμαι	οῦμεθα
		ᾷ	ᾶσθε	ῇ (ει)	εῖσθε	οῖ	οῦσθε
		ᾶται	ῶνται	εῖται	οῦνται	οῦται	οῦνται
Subjunctive	Present Active	ῶ	ῶμεν	ῶ	ῶμεν	ῶ	ῶμεν
		ᾷς	ᾶτε	ῇς	ῆτε	οῖς	ῶτε
		ᾷ	ῶσι(ν)	ῇ	ῶσι(ν)	οῖ	ῶσι(ν)
	Present M/P	ῶμαι	ώμεθα	ῶμαι	ώμεθα	ῶμαι	ωμεθα
		ᾷ	ᾶσθαι	ῇ	ῆσθε	οῖ	ῶσθε
		ᾶται	ῶνται	ῆται	ῶνται	ῶται	ῶνται
Optative	Present Active	ῴην (ῷμι)	ῷμεν (ῴημεν)	οίην (οῖμι)	οῖμεν (οίημεν)		
		ῴης (ῷς)	ῷτε (ῴητε)	οίης (οῖς)	οῖτε (οίητε)	Same as ε Contract	
		ῴη (ῷ)	ῷεν (ῴησαν)	οίη (οῖ)	οῖεν (οίησαν)		
	Present M/P	ῴμην	ῴμεθα	οίμην	οίμεθα	οίμην	οίμεθα
		ῷο	ῷσθε	οῖο	οῖσθε	οῖο	οῖσθε
		ῷτο	ῷντο	οῖτο	οῖντο	οῖτο	οῖντο

Imperfect Tense

		α Contract		ε Contract		o Contract	
Indicative	Imperfect Active	ων	ῶμεν	ουν	οῦμεν	ουν	οῦμεν
		ας	ᾶτε	εις	εῖτε	ους	οῦτε
		α	ων	ει	ουν	ου	ουν
	Imperfect M/P	ώμην	ώμεθα	ούμην	ούμεθα	ούμην	ούμεθα
		ῶ	ᾶσθε	οῦ	εῖσθε	οῦ	οῦσθε
		ᾶτο	ῶντο	εῖτο	οῦντο	οῦτο	οῦντο

μι Verbs

The endings of δίδωμι are identical to omega verbs in the future, perfect, and aorist passive. These endings will therefore not be given. Alternate forms are given in parentheses.

δίδωμι, δώσω, ἔδωκα, δέδωκα, δέδομαι, ἐδόθην = *to give*

		Present Active	Present M/P	Imperfect Active	Imperfect M/P	Aorist Active	Aorist Middle
Indicative sg	1	δίδωμι	δίδομαι	ἐδίδουν	ἐδιδόμην	ἔδωκα	ἐδόμην
	2	δίδως	δίδοσαι	ἐδίδους	ἐδίδοσο	ἔδωκας	ἔδου
	3	δίδωσι(ν)	δίδοται	ἐδίδου	ἐδίδοτο	ἔδωκε(ν)	ἔδοτο
pl	1	δίδομεν	διδόμεθα	ἐδίδομεν	ἐδιδόμεθα	ἔδομεν	ἐδόμεθα
	2	δίδοτε	δίδοσθε	ἐδίδοτε	ἐδίδοσθε	ἔδοτε	ἔδοσθε
	3	διδόασι(ν)	δίδονται	ἐδίδοσαν	ἐδίδοντο	ἔδοσαν	ἔδοντο
Subjunctive sg	1	διδῶ	διδῶμαι			δῶ	δῶμαι
	2	διδῷς	διδῷ			δῷς	δῷ
	3	διδῷ	διδῶται			δῷ	δῶται
pl	1	διδῶμεν	διδώμεθα			δῶμεν	δώμεθα
	2	διδῶτε	διδῶσθε			δῶτε	δῶσθε
	3	διδῶσι(ν)	διδῶνται			δῶσι(ν)	δῶνται
Optative sg	1	διδοίην	διδοίμην			δοίην	δοίμην
	2	διδοίης	διδοῖο			δοίης	δοῖο
	3	διδοίη	διδοῖτο			δοίη	δοῖτο
pl	1	διδοῖμεν (διδοίημεν)	διδοίμεθα			δοῖμεν (δοίημεν)	δοίμεθα
	2	διδοῖτε (διδοίητε)	διδοῖσθε			δοῖτε (δοίητε)	δοῖσθε
	3	διδοῖεν (διδοίησαν)	διδοῖντο			δοῖεν (δοίησαν)	δοῖντο
Imperative sg	2	δίδου	δίδο-σο			δός	δοῦ
	3	διδότω	διδόσθω			δότω	δόσθω
pl	2	δίδοτε	δίδοσθε			δότε	δόσθε
	3	διδόντων	διδόσθων			δόντων	δόσθων
Infinitive		διδόναι	δίδοσθαι			δοῦναι	δόσθαι

The endings of τίθημι are identical to omega verbs in the future, perfect, and aorist passive. These endings will therefore not be given. Alternate forms are given in parentheses.

τίθημι, θήσω, ἔθηκα, τέθηκα, τέθειμαι, ἐτέθην = to put, place

			Present		Imperfect		Aorist	
			Active	M/P	Active	M/P	Active	Middle
Indicative	sg	1	τίθημι	τίθεμαι	ἐτίθην	ἐτιθέμην	ἔθηκα	ἐθέμην
		2	τίθης	τίθεσαι	ἐτίθεις	ἐτίθεσο	ἔθηκας	ἔθου
		3	τίθησι(ν)	τίθεται	ἐτίθει	ἐτίθετο	ἔθηκε(ν)	ἔθετο
	pl	1	τίθεμεν	τιθέμεθα	ἐτίθεμεν	ἐτιθέμεθα	ἔθεμεν	ἐθέμεθα
		2	τίθετε	τίθεσθε	ἐτίθετε	ἐτίθεσθε	ἔθετε	ἔθεσθε
		3	τιθέασι(ν)	τίθενται	ἐτίθεσαν	ἐτίθεντο	ἔθεσαν	ἔθεντο
Subjunctive	sg	1	τιθῶ	τιθῶμαι			θῶ	θῶμαι
		2	τιθῇς	τιθῇ			θῇς	θῇ
		3	τιθῇ	τιθῆται			θῇ	θῆται
	pl	1	τιθῶμεν	τιθώμεθα			θῶμεν	θώμεθα
		2	τιθῆτε	τιθῆσθε			θῆτε	θῆσθε
		3	τιθῶσι(ν)	τιθῶνται			θῶσι(ν)	θῶνται
Optative	sg	1	τιθείην	τιθείμην			θείην	θείμην
		2	τιθείης	τιθεῖο			θείης	θεῖο
		3	τιθείη	τιθεῖτο			θείη	θεῖτο
	pl	1	τιθεῖμεν (τιθείημεν)	τιθείμεθα			θεῖμεν (θείημεν)	θείμεθα
		2	τιθεῖτε (τιθείητε)	τιθεῖσθα			θεῖτε (θείητε)	θεῖσθα
		3	τιθεῖεν (τιθείησαν)	τιθεῖντο			θεῖεν (θείησαν)	θεῖντο
Imperative	sg	2	τίθει	τίθεσο			θές	θοῦ
		3	τιθέτω	τιθέσθω			θέτω	θέσθω
	pl	2	τίθετε	τίθεσθε			θέτε	θέσθε
		3	τιθέντων	τιθέσθων			θέντων	θέσθων
Infinitive			τιθέναι	τίθεσθαι			θεῖναι	θέσθαι

The endings of ἵστημι are identical to omega verbs in all but the present, imperfect, 2nd aorist, and perfect. These endings will therefore not be given. Alternate forms are given in parentheses. Since the 2nd aorist is intransitive, aorist middle forms do not exist.

ἵστημι, στήσω, ἔστησα/ἔστην, ἕστηκα, ἕσταμαι, ἐστάθην = to set; to stand

			Present		Imperfect		2nd Aorist	Perfect
			Active	M/P	Active	M/P	Active	Active
Indicative	sg	1	ἵστημι	ἵσταμαι	ἵστην	ἱστάμην	ἔστην	ἕστηκα
		2	ἵστης	ἵστασαι	ἵστης	ἵστασο	ἔστης	ἕστηκας
		3	ἵστησι(ν)	ἵσταται	ἵστη	ἵστατο	ἔστη	ἕστηκε(ν)
	pl	1	ἵσταμεν	ἱστάμεθα	ἵσταμεν	ἱστάμεθα	ἔστημεν	ἕσταμεν
		2	ἵστατε	ἵστασθε	ἵστατε	ἵστασθε	ἔστητε	ἕστατε
		3	ἱστᾶσι(ν)	ἵστανται	ἵστασαν	ἵσταντο	ἔστησαν	ἑστᾶσι(ν)
Subjunctive	sg	1	ἱστῶ	ἱστῶμαι			στῶ	ἑστῶ
		2	ἱστῇς	ἱστῇ			στῇς	ἑστῇς
		3	ἱστῇ	ἱστῆται			στῇ	ἑστῇ
	pl	1	ἱστῶμεν	ἱστώμεθα			στῶμεν.	ἑστῶμεν
		2	ἱστῆτε	ἱστῆσθε			στῆτε	ἑστῆτε
		3	ἱστῶσι(ν)	ἱστῶνται			στῶσι(ν)	ἑστῶσι(ν)
Optative	sg	1	ἱσταίην	ἱσταίμην			σταίην	ἑσταίην
		2	ἱσταίης	ἱσταῖο			σταίης	ἑσταίης
		3	ἱσταίη	ἱσταῖτο			σταίη	ἑσταίη
	pl	1	ἱσταῖμεν (ἱσταίημεν)	ἱσταίμεθα			σταῖμεν (σταίημεν)	ἑσταῖμεν (ἑσταίημεν)
		2	ἱσταῖτε (ἱσταίητε)	ἱσταῖσθε			σταῖτε (σταίητε)	ἑσταῖτε (ἑσταίητε)
		3	ἱσταῖεν (ἱσταίησαν)	ἱσταῖντο			σταῖεν (σταίησαν)	ἑσταῖεν (ἑσταίησαν)
Imperative	sg	2	ἵστη	ἵστασο			στῆθι	ἕσταθι
		3	ἱστάτω	ἱστάσθω			στήτω	ἑστάτω
	pl	2	ἵστατε	ἵστασθε			στῆτε	ἕστατε
		3	ἱστάντων	ἱστάσθων			στάντων	ἑστάντων
Infinitive			ἱστάναι	ἵστασθαι			στῆναι	ἑστάναι

Important Irregular Verbs

			εἰμί = to be			εἶμι = to go	
			Present	Imperfect	Future	Present	Imperfect
Indicative	sg	1	εἰμί	ἦ (ἦν)	ἔσομαι	εἶμι	ἦα (ἤειν)
		2	εἶ	ἦσθα	ἔσῃ (ἔσει)	εἶ	ἤεισθα (ἤεις)
		3	ἐστί(ν)	ἦν	ἔσται	εἶσι(ν)	ἤειν (ἤει)
	pl	1	ἐσμέν	ἦμεν	ἐσόμεθα	ἴμεν	ᾖμεν
		2	ἐστέ	ἦστε (ἦτε)	ἔσεσθε	ἴτε	ᾖτε
		3	εἰσί(ν)	ἦσαν	ἔσονται	ἴασι(ν)	ᾖσαν (ᾔεσαν)
Subjunctive	sg	1	ὦ			ἴω	
		2	ᾖς			ἴῃς	
		3	ᾖ			ἴῃ	
	pl	1	ὦμεν			ἴωμεν	
		2	ἦτε			ἴητε	
		3	ὦσι(ν)			ἴωσι(ν)	
Optative	sg	1	εἴην		ἐσοίμην	ἴοιμι (ἰοίην)	
		2	εἴης		ἔσοιο	ἴοις	
		3	εἴη		ἔσοιτο	ἴοι	
	pl	1	εἶμεν (εἴημεν)		ἐσοίμεθα	ἴοιμεν	
		2	εἶτε (εἴητε)		ἔσοισθε	ἴοιτε	
		3	εἶεν (εἴησαν)		ἔσοιντο	ἴοιεν	
Imperative	sg	2	ἴσθι			ἴθι	
		3	ἔστω			ἴτω	
	pl	2	ἔστε			ἴτε	
		3	ἔστων			ἰόντων	
Infinitive			εἶναι		ἔσεσθαι	ἰέναι	

οἶδα = to know

			Perfect (acts as present)	Future Perfect (acts as future)	Pluperfect (acts as aorist or imperfect)
Indicative	sg	1	οἶδα	εἴσομαι	ἤδη (ἤδειν)
		2	οἶσθα	εἴσῃ (εἴσει)	ἤδησθα (ἤδεις)
		3	οἶδε(ν)	εἴσεται	ἤδει(ν)
	pl	1	ἴσμεν	εἰσόμεθα	ἤσμεν (ἤδεμεν)
		2	ἴστε	εἴσεσθε	ἤστε (ἤδετε)
		3	ἴσασι(ν)	εἴσονται	ἤσαν (ἤδεσαν)
Subjunctive	sg	1	εἰδῶ		
		2	εἰδῇς		
		3	εἰδῇ		
	pl	1	εἰδῶμεν		
		2	εἰδῆτε		
		3	εἰδῶσι(ν)		
Optative	sg	1	εἰδείην		
		2	εἰδείης		
		3	εἰδείη		
	pl	1	εἰδεῖμεν (εἰδείημεν)		
		2	εἰδεῖτε (εἰδείητε)		
		3	εἰδεῖεν (εἰδείησαν)		
Imperative	sg	2	ἴσθι		
		3	ἴστω		
	pl	2	ἴστε		
		3	ἴστων		
Infinitive			εἰδέναι		

φημί = *to say*

			Present	Imperfect
			Active	Active
Indicative	sg	1	φημί	ἔφην
		2	φής	ἔφησθα (ἔφης)
		3	φησί(ν)	ἔφη
	pl	1	φαμέν	ἔφαμεν
		2	φατέ	ἔφατε
		3	φασί(ν)	ἔφασαν
Subjunctive	sg	1	φῶ	
		2	φῇς	
		3	φῇ	
	pl	1	φῶμεν	
		2	φῆτε	
		3	φῶσι(ν)	
Optative	sg	1	φαίην	
		2	φαίης	
		3	φαίη	
	pl	1	φαῖμεν (φαίημεν)	
		2	φαῖτε (φαίητε)	
		3	φαῖεν (φαίησαν)	
Imperative	sg	2	φάθι	
		3	φάτω	
	pl	2	φάτε	
		3	φάντων	
Imperative			φάναι	

Appendix B. Important Notes on Greek Grammar

A number in parentheses indicates the chapter in which a grammatical concept is discussed.

Nouns

Vocative (3)

The case of direct address. It often follows ὦ or accompanies a verb in the imperative.

ὦ ἄνθρωπε
O man.

Nominative

Subject (3)

The grammatical subject of a sentence.

ὁ Σωκράτης ἐπαίδευσε τὸν Πλάτωνα.
Socrates taught Plato.

Predicate Nominative (3)

Part of a predicate, oftentimes accompanying εἰμι = to be.

ὁ Σωκράτης ἐστὶν ἀνήρ.
Socrates is a man.

Genitive

Genitive of Possession (5)

Says who or what possesses something. ἡ ἀγάπη τοῦ θεοῦ "the love **of God**" refers to the love God has for someone else. Most of the time the thing possessed is physical, but often it is not. This genitive can be in either the predicate or the attributive position. ἡ ἀγάπη τοῦ θεοῦ, ἡ τοῦ θεοῦ ἀγάπη, and τοῦ θεοῦ ἡ ἀγάπη all mean "the love **of God**."

Objective Genitive (5)

Indicates the object of some verbal idea implied in another noun. In ὁ φόβος τοῦ θεοῦ, "the fear **of God**," the genitive refers to the object of the fear, i.e., the fear someone has of God, not God's fear (which would be a genitive of possession).

Partitive Genitive (7)

Signifies the whole from which a *part* is taken, e.g., μόριον τῆς ψυχῆς "a piece **of the soul**."

Genitive of Time within Which (13)

Signifies a span of time during part of which an action takes place (unlike the accusative of duration of time, when the action takes place during the entire span).

νυκτὸς ὁ διδάσκαλος ἀπέθανεν.
The teacher died **at night**.

Genitive of Agent (+ ὑπό) (14)

With ὑπό designates the agent of passively constructed verbs. The genitive of agent is used primarily with persons.

παιδεύομαι ὑπὸ τοῦ φιλοσόφου.
I am taught by **the philosopher**.

Genitive Absolute (21)

Describes the circumstances under which the main action occurs. Usually consists of a noun (normally not the grammatical subject) and a participle in the genitive case.

μαθήματος ὄντος χαλεποῦ, ὁ μαθητὴς ὑπέμενεν.
The lesson being difficult, the student persevered.

Genitive of Comparison (23)

Indicates the Z in a sentence like "X is Y-er than Z." Equivalent to the comparative plus ἤ.

ὁ Ὀδυσσεύς ἐστι σοφώτερος Πολυφήμου.
Odysseus is wiser **than Polyphemus**.

Dative

Dative of Indirect Object (5)

Signifies the indirect object of a verb.

ὁ Πέτρος νέμει τὰ βιβλία τῷ Παύλῳ.
Peter gives the scrolls **to Paul**.

Dative of Respect (5)

Indicates the person or thing for whom something is true or is done.

ἡ ἀμαθία θάνατός ἐστι τοῖς ἀνθρώποις.
Ignorance is death **for humans**.

Dative of Time When (13)

Specifies the point at which an action takes place.

τῇ ἀρχῇ τῆς ἡμέρας ἐφώνησεν ἀλέκτωρ.
At the beginning of the day a rooster crowed.

Dative of Degree of Difference (23)

Expresses the degree to which a comparison or superlative is true.

ὁ Σωκράτης ἐστὶ πολλῷ σοφώτατος τῶν Ἑλλήνων.
Socrates is **by far** (lit. by much) the wisest of the Greeks.

Dative of Means (24)

Signifies the means or instrument by which something is done. No preposition is needed.

ὁ πρεσβυτικὸς διδάσκαλος τῷ καλάμῳ γράφει τὰ γράμματα.
The old-fashioned teacher writes the letters **with a reed pen**.

Dative of Possession (26)

Indicates possession, often with the 3rd person of εἰμί. The thing possessed is put into the nominative case.

τῷ Σωκράτει υἱός ἐστιν.
Socrates has a son.

Dative of Agent (28)

Specifies agency. Has no preposition and comes only with perfect and pluperfect passive verbs. The genitive of personal agent (see above) is used elsewhere.

ἡ ἀλήθεια μεμαρτύρηται τοῖς σοφοῖς.
The truth has been witnessed **by the wise**.

Accusative

Direct Object (4)

Specifies the direct object of a verb. This is the most common use of the accusative.

οἱ ἄνθρωποι τὸν δεσμὸν λύουσιν.
The people loosen **the chain**.

Accusative of Duration of Time (13)

Indicates the time throughout which an action takes place. Unlike the genitive of time within which, this construction indicates that the action takes place the entire time. Normally found with intransitive verbs.

οἱ μαθηταὶ ἐκαθεύδησαν τὸ μάθημα τοῦ διδασκάλου.
The students slept **through the lesson** of the teacher.

Accusative of Respect (38)

Indicates the respect to which a statement is true. This accusative is common with adjectives and verbs that describe qualities or traits.

ὁ Σωκράτης ἦν μικρὸς τὸ μέγεθος.
Socrates was small **in stature** (literally "small with respect to stature").

Accusative Absolute (38)

Similar to the genitive absolute, but used with impersonal verbs.

ἐξὸν λείπειν, ὁ μαθητὴς ὑπέμενεν.
It being possible to quit, the student persevered.

Clauses and Phrases

Participles

A participle is a verbal adjective, and as such shares properties of both adjectives and verbs. All participles agree with their nouns in gender, number, and case. The Greek participle is capable of several functions. It can be *attributive*, *circumstantial*, or *supplementary*.

Attributive Participle (19)

Stands in the *attributive* position and functions just like an adjective. It may take an object as well.

ὁ ἀείδων ἄνθρωπός ἐστι βαρύς.
The singing man is tiresome.

Circumstantial Participle (20)

Stands in the *predicate* position. It describes the circumstances under which the main action of the sentence takes place:

Temporal. The participial phrase indicates the time in which the action in the independent clause takes place.

λέγων τὴν ἀλήθειαν, ὁ διδάσκαλος ἐπαίδευε τοὺς μαθητάς.
When he was speaking the truth, the teacher was educating the students.

Concessive. The participial phrase indicates an action in spite of which the independent clause takes place.

λέγων τὴν ἀλήθειαν, ὁ διδάσκαλος οὐκ ἐπαίδευε τοὺς μαθητάς.
Although he was speaking the truth, the teacher was not educating the students.

Causal. The participial phrase indicates that on account of which the action in the independent clause takes place.

θελχθέντες ὑπὸ τοῦ δημαγωγοῦ, οἱ πολῖται ἥμαρτον.
Having been charmed by the demagogue, the citizens erred.

Conditional (35). The participial phrase indicates the condition under which the action in the independent clause takes place. Replaces the protasis of any condition, omitting εἰ and ἄν. The negative is μή.

οἱ ἄνθρωποι τὸν Σωκράτην ἀποκτείνοντες, τοὺς μαθητὰς βλάψουσιν.
If the people kill Socrates, they will harm the students.

Supplementary Participle (21)

Stands in the *predicate* position, like a circumstantial participle, but completes the meaning of certain verbs.

ὁ φιλόσοφος οὐ παύεται λέγων.
The philosopher doesn't stop **speaking**.

Conditions (35–37)

Protasis (if clause)	Apodosis (then clause)
Conditionals	
Simple	
εἰ + indicative	indicative
Speaker is neutral about the possibility of the outcome.	
εἰ γὰρ ἔχομεν τὴν ταπεινοφροσύνην,	ἔχομεν τὴν ἀρχὴν τῆς σοφίας.
For if we have humility	*then we have the beginning of wisdom.*
Future	
Future More Vivid	
ἐάν (ἤν, ἄν) + subjunctive	future indicative
Speaker regards the protasis as probable.	
ἐὰν οἱ ἄνθρωποι τὸν Σωκράτην ἀποκτείνωσιν	τοὺς μαθητὰς βλάψουσιν.
If the people kill Socrates	*then they will harm the students.*
Future Less Vivid	
εἰ + optative	*optative +ἄν*
Speaker regards the protasis as merely possible.	
εἰ οἱ ἄνθρωποι τὸν Σωκράτην ἀποκτείνειαν	τοὺς μαθητὰς βλάπτοιεν ἄν.
If the people should kill Socrates	*then they would harm the students.*
General	
Present General	
ἐάν (ἤν, ἄν) + subjunctive	*present indicative*
ἐὰν ὁ Διογένης πίνῃ τὸν οἶνον	πίνει τὸν ἀλλότριον οἶνον.
If Diogenes drinks wine	*then he drinks someone else's wine.*
Past General	
εἰ + optative	*imperfect indicative*
εἰ ὁ Διογένης πίνοι τὸν οἶνον	ἔπινε τὸν ἀλλότριον οἶνον.
If Diogenes drank wine	*then he drank someone else's wine.*
Unreal[a]	
Present Unreal	
εἰ + imperfect indicative	*imperfect indicative + ἄν*
εἰ ἄλλοι ἄνθρωποι οὐκ ἦσαν	ἐγὼ ἅγιος ἦν ἄν.
If other people did not exist	*then I would be holy.*
Past Unreal	
εἰ + aorist indicative	*aorist indicative + ἄν*
εἰ ὁ Σωκράτης ἔφυγεν,	οὐκ ἀπέθανεν ἄν.
If Socrates would have fled,	*then he would not have died.*

a Often the distinction between the two unreal conditionals is aspectual not temporal.

The negative of the protasis is μή, the negative of the apodosis is οὐ, unless the apodosis contains an imperative or another expression that requires μή.

Independent Uses of the Subjunctive

Hortatory Subjunctive (32)

Restricted to the 1st person (usually plural), behaves like an imperative. The negative is μή.

> λέγωμεν τὴν ἀλήθειαν.
> **Let us speak** the truth.

Deliberative Subjunctive (32)

Occasionally you will see the subjunctive in the first person used in a question to express doubt or indecision on the part of the speaker.

> λέγωμεν τὴν ἀλήθειαν;
> **Shall we speak** the truth?

Prohibitive Subjunctive (32)

Expresses a negative command, with μή and the subjunctive in the 2nd person (and sometimes the 3rd person). It can be translated the same as a negative imperative.

> μὴ πίνῃς τὸ κώνειον.
> **Don't drink** the hemlock.

Independent Uses of the Optative

Optative of Wish (34)

Expresses a wish, used either with or without εἴθε or εἰ γάρ.

> εἰ γὰρ ἀκούοιμι τὴν ἀοιδὴν τῶν Σειρήνων.
> **If only I could hear** the song of the Sirens.

Potential Optative (34)

With ἄν expresses a possibility. The negative is οὐ.

> ἡ ἀοιδὴ τῶν Σειρήνων βλάπτοι ἂν τοὺς ἀνθρώπους.
> The song of the Sirens **might harm** the men.

Dependent Clauses

Purpose Clause (33)

Expresses the reason behind an action. Purpose clauses are introduced by ἵνα, ὡς, or ὅπως, with ἵνα being the most common. Negative purpose clauses are introduced by ἵνα μή, ὡς μή, ὅπως μή, or μή.

μὴ κρίνετε, ἵνα μὴ κριθῆτε.
Do not judge, **in order that you not be judged**.

Result Clause (22)

Expresses the result of an action, whether *actual* or *natural/expected*.
Actual Result Clause. With ὥστε governing a clause with an indicative verb, expresses what occurred as a result of the events in the main clause.

ὁ Σωκράτης οὕτως ἀληθῶς εἶπεν ὥστε βαρὺς ἦν τοῖς πολλοῖς.
Socrates spoke so truthfully **that he was tiresome to many**.

Natural Result Clause. With ὥστε governing a clause with the infinitive (and the subject of the result clause changed into the accusative case), specifies the natural result of the main action. Whereas an actual result clause says that a particular result actually happened, a natural result clause does not stress that it did happen, only that it would naturally follow from that action. The negative is μή.

τὸ παιδίον ἔχει τὴν σοφίαν ὥστε τοὺς φιλοσόφους θαυμάσαι.
The child has wisdom **so as to make the philosophers marvel**.

Direct versus Indirect Questions (27)

An *indirect* question is a *direct* question expressed indirectly. A direct question normally needs to be translated with a question mark and stands on its own, whereas an indirect question is embedded in a larger sentence and may not be translated with a question mark.

τί ἐστιν ἀλήθεια;
What is truth? = direct question

Σωκράτης οἶδε τί ἐστιν ἀλήθεια.
Socrates knows **what truth is**. = indirect question

Fear Clause (38)

Expresses that the author fears that something will happen, is happening, or has happened. The clause is introduced by μή. If the author fears that something will not happen, is not happening, or has not happened, the clause is introduced by μὴ οὐ. If the thing feared has not happened, the verb of the fear clause is put into the subjunctive. If the thing feared has already happened or is presently happening, the verb is put into the indicative.

φοβοῦμαι μὴ ἡ ἀλήθεια πίπτῃ.
I fear **that the truth will fail**.

Effort Clause (38)

Indicates an intended result from the main clause. Positive effort clauses take ὅπως + future indicative (sometimes ὡς + future indicative) while negative effort clauses take ὅπως μή + future indicative (sometimes ὡς + future indicative).

οἱ ἀγαθοὶ φιλόσοφοι πράττουσιν ὅπως ἡ ἀλήθεια νικήσει τὴν μωρίαν.
The good philosophers make it **so that the truth will conquer foolishness**.

Clause of Caution (38)

Describes an action or circumstance aginst which the author is cautioning. Verbs of caution stand somewhere between fear and effort clauses and can thus take either μή or ὅπως μή + subjunctive or ὅπως μή + future indicative.

βλέπετε μὴ λέγητε τὴν μωρίαν.
See to that you do not speak foolishness

βλέπετε ὅπως μὴ λέξετε τὴν μωρίαν.
See to that you do not speak foolishness.

Unattainable Wish (37)

Expresses an impossible desire. Uses εἴθε or εἰ γάρ + imperfect indicative for an unattainable wish in the present and εἴθε or εἰ γάρ + aorist indicative for an unattainable wish in the past. A negative unattainable wish takes μή.

εἴθε ὁ Σωκράτης ἔζων ἔτι.
Would that Socrates were still living.

Direct and Indirect Statement

An *indirect* statement is a *direct* statement expressed indirectly. A direct statement normally needs to be translated with quotation marks and stands on its own, whereas an indirect statement is embedded in a larger sentence and is not translated with quotation marks.

An indirect statement can be expressed in one of three ways.

ὅτι/ὡς (11). After verbs of speaking, ὅτι (less frequently ὡς) is used to introduce the indirect statement and can be translated as "that."

ὁ διδάσκαλος λέγει ὅτι ἡ ἀρετή ἐστι χαλεπή.
The teacher says **that excellence is difficult**.

Accusative and Infinitive (11). Used primarily with verbs of thinking and believing, Greek changes what would have been the nominative of the direct statement to the accusative case, and it changes what would have been the verb of the direct statement into the corresponding case of the infinitive.

ὁ διδάσκαλός φασι τὴν ἀρετὴν εἶναι χαλεπήν.
The teacher says **that excellence is difficult**.

Accusative and Participle (21). Used primarily with verbs of perception, the construction is like the accusative and infinitive construction, but with a participle instead of the infinitive. The tense of the participle in indirect statement indicates both time and aspect.

> αἰσθάνομαι τὸν φιλόσοφον ὄντα σοφόν.
> I perceive **that the philosopher is wise**.

Sequence of Moods (40)

When a subjunctive or indicative is used in a dependent clause, it *may* be changed to an *optative* if the verb that introduces the dependent clause is in a secondary tense (imperfect, aorist, pluperfect).

> ὁ Σωκράτης ἔλεγεν ἵνα παιδεύοι ἀνθρώπους.
> Socrates spoke **in order to educate men**. (changed to the optative)

> ὁ Σωκράτης ἔλεγεν ἵνα παιδεύῃ ἀνθρώπους.
> Socrates spoke **in order to educate men**. (subjunctive retained)

Appendix C. Rules of Accentuation

Below are the most important rules, or more accurately tendencies, of accentuation. This is by no means an exhaustive list and there are of course exceptions.

In a Greek word, the accent falls on one of the last three syllables: the antepenult, the penult, or the ultima.

syllable before the next-to-last syllable	next-to-last syllable	last syllable
antepenult	penult	ultima

There are three accents: the acute (´), the circumflex (῀), and the grave (`). The *grave* accent can go *only* on the ultima.

The *circumflex* can go only on the ultima or penult, over only long syllables—i.e., those with long vowels or diphthongs.[1] It can go on the penult only if the ultima is short.

The *acute* accent can go on any of the last three syllables, but on the antepenult only if the ultima is short.

The grave accent is found only on the ultima because when a word that ends with an acute on the ultima is followed by another word (i.e., when it is neither the last word of a sentence nor followed by punctuation), the acute becomes a grave. Thus ψυχή becomes ψυχὴ in ψυχὴ πόλεως "the soul of a polis."

Recessive and Persistent Accent

Recessive Accent

Most verbs have recessive accent. This means that the accent wants to stay as far away from the ultima as possible. Remember that whether the ultima is long or short determines how far back the accent can go. Look at the present tense of your model verb λύω.

---

1. Exception: final αι and οι are treated as short (except in the optative), even though they are diphthongs.

	Singular	Plural
1st	λύω	λύομεν
2nd	λύεις	λύετε
3rd	λύει	λύουσι(ν)

Notice how the accent gets to stay on the antepenult of the plural forms because the ultima is short. Now look at the aorist active forms of λύω. The accent stays on the antepenult in the first and second person plural. Since the accent cannot go before the antepenult, it cannot stay on the epsilon in the 1st and 2nd person plural forms.

	Singular	Plural
1st	ἔλυον	ἐλύομεν
2nd	ἔλυες	ἐλύετε
3rd	ἔλυε(ν)	ἔλυον

Persistent Accent

Most, but not all, nouns, adjectives, and participles have persistent accent. This means that the accent will try and stay on the syllable that it is on in the nominative. It will not try and move back. Remember your model noun βιβλίον.

	Singular	Plural
Nom.	βιβλίον	βιβλία
Gen.	βιβλίου	βιβλίων
Dat.	βιβλίῳ	βιβλίοις
Acc.	βιβλίον	βιβλία
(Voc.)	(βιβλίον)	

Notice how the accent stays on the iota. Sometimes, however, the ultima forces the accent to be moved, even though it is persistent. The noun ἄνθρωπος has an accent on its antepenult, but when it declines and the ultima becomes long, e.g., ἀνθρώπου, the accent has to be pulled to the penult since a long ultima will not allow the antepenult to be accented. Likewise, the 3rd declension noun δῶρον has a circumflex on its penult, but it must change to δώρου since a circumflex can be on the penult only if the ultima is short.

Sadly, many words have neither persistent nor recessive accent and their patterns must be learned over time.

Words with No Accent

Some short words have no accent. These are classified as proclitic (meaning "leaning forward"—they are thought to be pronounced with the following word) or enclitics ("leaning backward," thought to be pronounced with the preceding word).

Proclitics: The nominative masculine and feminine of the definite article (ὁ, ἡ, οἱ, αἱ), the prepositions ἐν, ἐκ, and εἰς, and the words εἰ, ὡς, and οὐ are proclitics and have no accent. An exception occurs when a proclitic is followed by an enclitic.

Enclitics: There are far more enclitics than proclitics. Included are personal pronouns, a couple of verbs, some particles, a couple of indefinite pronouns, and some indefinite adverbs. Enclitics are also different in that they can change the accent of a preceding word.

If the word before the enclitic…	then…	Example
has an acute on the antepenult	add another acute accent to the ultima of that word.	ἄνθρωπός τις
has an acute on the penult	don't change if the enclitic is one syllable; if two syllables, the enclitic will have an accent on the ultima.	λέγω τοι λόγος ἐστί
has a circumflex on the penult	add another acute accent to the ultima of that word.	σῶμά τι
has an acute or circumflex on the ultima	don't change anything.	νοῦς τις
has a grave on the ultima	change the grave accent to an acute accent.	θεός τις

As you can see, the only time an enclitic will have an accent is if it has two syllables and is preceded by a word with an acute on the penult, or if it is followed by another enclitic.

ἐστι is accented on the first syllable if it is the first word of a sentence and means "it is possible," and in a few other circumstances.

Appendix D. The Dual

In addition to the singular and the plural, Greek has a third number, the dual. The dual refers to two things that form a pair. Because it is such a rare number, the plural most often being used for pairs, the forms of the dual were not introduced in the main text of this book. It is used sparingly in Homer and is almost extinct in the classical era. Despite the rarity of the dual, it is a neat grammatical number in that it is used for two things which the author wishes to treat as a natural pair. For example, a pair of twins could be called δίδύμω (dual) as well as δίδυμοι (plural). For nouns and adjectives, the nominative, accusative, and vocative cases share endings and the genitive and dative cases share endings. The endings for the nominative, accusative, and vocative vary for the different declensions, but the endings of the genitive and dative end in -ιν. Below are given the dual for each of your model nouns (except for the singular Σωκράτης) and adjectives as well as the definite article.

	1st Declension		Endings	2nd Declension		Endings
Nom., Acc., Voc.	ψυχ–ά	χαρ–ά	–α	λόγ–ω	βιβλίω	–ω
Gen., Dat.	ψυχ–αῖν	χαρ–αῖν	–αιν	λόγ–οιν	βιβλί-οιν	–οιν

	3rd Declension					Endings
Nom., Acc., Voc.	δαίμον–ε	σώματ–ε	χάριτ–ε	πόλ–ει	βασιλ–ῆ	–ε, –ει, –η
Gen., Dat.	δαιμόν–οιν	σωμάτ–οιν	χαρίτ–οιν	πολέ–οιν	βασιλέ–οιν	–οιν

	καλός, –ή, –όν		
	m	f	n
Nom., Acc., Voc.	καλ–ώ	καλ–ά	καλ–ώ
Gen., Dat.	καλ–οῖν	καλ–αῖν	καλ–οῖν

367

	ἀληθής, –ές		*εὐδαίμων, –ον*	
	m/f	*n*	*m/f*	*n*
Nom., Acc., Voc.	ἀληθ–εῖ	ἀληθ–εῖ	εὐδαίμον–ε	εὐδαίμον–ε
Gen., Dat.	ἀληθ–οῖν	ἀληθ–οῖν	εὐδαιμόν–οιν	εὐδαιμόν–οιν

	Definite Article		
	m	*f*	*n*
Nom., Acc., Voc.	τώ	τώ	τώ
Gen., Dat.	τοῖν	τοῖν	τοῖν

The dual endings for verbs almost always end in –τον, –την, –σθον, or –σθην, making them rather easy to spot. In verbs, the dual is found only in the 2nd and 3rd person. There is no 1st person dual.

	λύω					
	Active Indicative					
	Present	*Imperfect*	*Future*	*Aorist*	*Perfect*	*Pluperfect*
2nd	λύ–ετον	ἐλύ–ετον	λύ–σετον	ἐλύ–σατον	λελύ–κατον	ἐλελύ–κετον
3rd	λύ–ετον	ἐλυ–έτην	λύ–σετον	ἐλυ–σάτην	λελύ–κατον	ἐλελυ–κέτην

	Middle/Passive Indicative					
			Fut. Middle	*Aor. Middle*		
2nd	λύ–εσθον	ἐλύ–εσθον	λύ–σεσθον	ἐλύ–σασθον	λέλυ–σθον	ἐλέλυ–σθον
3rd	λύ–εσθον	ἐλυ–έσθην	λύ–σεσθον	ἐλυ–σάσθην	λέλυ–σθον	ἐλέλυ–σθην
			Fut. Passive	*Aor. Passive*		
			λυ–θήσεσθον	ἐλύ–θητον		
			λυ–θήσεσθον	ἐλυ–θήτην		

	λύω					
	Subjunctive					
	Active			*Middle/Passive*		
	Present	*Aorist*	*Perfect*	*Present*	*Aorist M*	*Perfect*
2nd	λύ–ητον	λύ–σητον	λελύ–κητον	λύ–ησθον	λύ–σησθον	λελυμένω ἦτον
3rd	λύ–ητον	λύ–σητον	λελύ–κητον	λύ–ησθον	λύ–σησθον	λελυμένω ἦτον
					Aorist P	
					λυ–θῆτον	
					λυ–θῆτον	

		λύω		
		Active Optative		
	Present	*Future*	*Aorist*	*Perfect*
2nd	λύ–οιτον	λύ–σοιτον	λύ–σαιτον	λελυκότε εἴητον (εἶτον) or λελύκοιτον
3rd	λυ–οίτην	λυ–σοίτην	λυ–σαίτην	λελυκότε εἰήτην (εἴτην) or λελυκοίτην

		λύω		
		Middle/Passive Optative		
	Present	*Future M*	*Aorist M*	*Perfect*
2nd	λύ–οισθον	λύ–σοισθον	λύ–σαισθον	λελυμένω εἴητον (εἶτον)
3rd	λυ–οίσθην	λυ–σοίσθην	λυ–σαίσθην	λελυμένω εἰήτην (εἴτην)
		Future P	*Aorist P*	
		λυ–θήσοισθον	λυ–θεῖτον (λυθείητον)	
		λυ–θησοίσθην	λυ–θείτην (λυθειήτην)	

			λύω			
			Imperative			
		Active			*Middle/Passive*	
	Present	*Aorist*	*Perfect*	*Present*	*Aorist M*	*Perfect*
2nd	λύ–ετον	λύ–σατον	λελύ–κετον	λύ–εσθον	λύ–σασθον	λέλυ–σθον
3rd	λυ–έτων	λυ–σάτων	λελυ–κέτων	λυ–έσθων	λυ–σάσθων	λελύ–σθων
					Aorist P	
					λύ–θητον	
					λυ–θήτων	

Sentences

ἀλλὰ δῆλον ὅτι δύο ἐστὸν ψυχά, καὶ ὅταν μὲν ἡ ἀγαθὴ κρατῇ, τὰ καλὰ πράττεται,
ὅταν δὲ ἡ πονηρά, τὰ αἰσχρά. (Xenophon)
But it is clear that there are **two souls**, and whenever the good soul rules,
it does noble things, but whenever the wicked soul rules, it does shameful
things.

Helen: οἱ Τυνδάρειοι δ᾽ εἰσὶν ἢ οὐκ εἰσὶν κόροι;
Teucer: τεθνᾶσι κοὐ τεθνᾶσι· δύο δ᾽ ἐστὸν λόγω. (Euripides)

Helen: Are the sons of Tyndareus still alive or not?
Teucer: They have died and not died. There are **two accounts**.

μήτηρ τέθνηκε ταῖν ἀδελφαῖν ταῖν δυοῖν ταύταιν. (Menander)
The mother of **these two sisters** has died.

Appendix E. ὡς

The word ὡς can be a conjunction or adverb. Below is a summary of its most common uses.

		Uses of ὡς	
Chapter	*Function*	*Translation*	*Example*
11	start of indirect statement	that	ὁ διδάσκαλος λέγει ὡς ἡ ἀρετή ἐστι χαλεπή.
			The teacher says **that** excellence is difficult.
33	start of a purpose clause (equivalent to ἵνα and ὅπως) with the subjunctive	in order to	ἐσθίω ὡς ζῶ.
			I eat **in order to** live.
38	start of an effort clause (equivalent to ὅπως) with the future indicative	that	ὅρα ὡς ἡ ἀλήθεια νικήσει τὴν μωρίαν.
			See to it **that** the truth conquers foolishness.
	causal marker	since	πάσχω ὡς μανθάνω.
			I suffer **since** I understand
	superlative modifier	as … as possible	ὡς σοφώτατος
			as wise **as possible**
10 (vocab)	simile marker	as, like	μάχεται ὡς λέων.
			He fights **like** a lion.

Appendix F. How to Read a Greek Sentence

Step One: Read the passage aloud.

This first step is extremely important. Reading aloud is not done to practice your conversation skills, but it is a crucial aid in your understanding of Greek. You learn better the more senses that you employ. When you read a passage and try to translate it, you are using only your sight. When you read the passage aloud, you employ your ears and your mouth along with your sight.

Step Two: Read the sentence in order and guess the meaning.

You know more Greek than you think you do. When you begin a sentence by looking up each word you don't know, you waste time you might have saved if you had read through the entire sentence. The reason is that often the words you recognize at the end of a sentence will help you understand earlier words you might not have known.

Step Three: Find the main verb.

The verb is the most import word class. Failure to correctly translate sentences almost always comes from a misidentification or mistranslation of the main verb. If you can correctly identify and conjugate the verb, it will give you crucial information. First, it will tell you what is happening in the sentence. Second, it will tell you what kind of subject you need to look for. If the person is 1st or 2nd, you already have the subject. You don't need to look for a nominative. If the verb is in the 3rd person, you will need to look for a nominative subject. If it is singular, look for a nominative singular; if it is plural, look for a nominative plural. The one exception is the odd quirk about neuter plural subjects taking singular verbs. You will also occasionally see two singular nominatives, which collectively take a plural verb ("Jack and Jill go up the hill."). If you have the verb and the subject of a sentence, you are more than half way there. Next find a direct object if the verb is transitive. After you have the subject, the verb, and the object, try putting the rest of the sentence together.

Step Four: Reread the sentence in order.

Don't skip this last step. Not only will it reinforce what you have just translated, but these sentences should be read in the order in which they were composed. Just because Greek does not have a rigid word order, it does not follow that word order is unimportant. On the contrary, a lack of rigid word order frees the author to use word order to great effect, often providing key information about the sense of the sentence. The first and last words of a sentence are often placed there for emphasis.

Additional tips for reading sentences in this book

First, try and memorize the vocabulary from each chapter before you translate its sentences. It might not seem like it, but this will save you time in the long run. Second, and this is the most important tip, *always* read the notes. The material included in the notes consists primarily of things necessary for a proper translation that you would have no way of knowing otherwise.

Example Sentence

Let's take one example from your book, sentence 7 from chapter 8.

βουλὴ πονηρὰ χρηστὸν οὐκ ἔχει τέλος. (Menander)

After we have read the sentence aloud and guessed its meaning, we first look for the verb. There is only one verb in this sentence, ἔχει, which is 3rd person singular. We know that we need a singular subject in the nominative (or possibly in the neuter plural).

The only two nouns in the sentence are βουλή and τέλος. One looks like a 1st declension feminine like ψυχή and one looks like it could be a 2nd declension masculine like λόγος. Which one is the subject? We know that only one can be nominative. After looking up each word, we realize that τέλος is not a masculine 2nd declension noun but a neuter 3rd declension noun like γένος. Since all neuter nouns are identical in the nominative and accusative singular, we know that τέλος could be nominative or accusative. βουλή, however, can only be nominative. We know therefore that βουλή, which cannot be another case, is the nominative subject.

Since we see the negative οὐκ right before the verb, we know it is a negative. We now have "A plan does not have…" We now need to look for a direct object in the accusative. The only accusative noun (χρηστὸν is an adjective) is τέλος. We now have "A plan does not have an end…"

Now that we have the subject, verb, and direct object, we look at the remainder of the words. We know that πονηρὰ is an adjective, either feminine nominative singular or neuter nominative/accusative plural. Since we already have the subject and direct object, it only makes sense for πονηρὰ to be a feminine nominative singular adjective modifying our feminine nominative singular noun βουλὴ. We now have "A wicked plan does not have an end."

The only untranslated word is the adjective χρηστὸν, which by now is easily identified as a neuter accusative adjective modifying our neuter accusative noun τέλος. The final translation is therefore "A wicked plan does not have a useful end."

Now that we know the meaning, let us read it again in order. We see that the subject "a plan wicked" would be identifiable by the audience (this was originally a play) from the first two words. The next word to be heard, "useful," would be jarring right next to the word "wicked." Greek loves to juxtapose two contrasting words. The listener would then need to suspend this adjective "useful" while he heard the verb "does not have." The listener would know that the sentence means "A wicked plan does not have a useful…," but what exactly is useful is not heard until the final word, "end," which comes fittingly at the end of the sentence. This sentence is close to our "The end does not justify the means." As you read Greek sentences, prepare to be surprised at times by the final words of a sentence, and always pay attention to the subtle ways that composition can change the meaning and tone of a sentence.

Appendix G. Supplementary Exercises

Chapter 2

Change the following verbs into the plural.

a. εἰμί   _____

b. ἐστίν   _____

c. εἶ   _____

Change the following verbs into the singular.

a. ἐστέ   _____

b. εἰσίν   _____

c. ἐσμέν   _____

Write the corresponding definite article next to the following nouns.

_____ ἀγάπη   _____ λόγος

_____ ἀλήθεια   _____ νόμος

_____ ἀρετή   _____ σοφία

_____ βιβλίον   _____ χαρά

_____ ἔργον   _____ ψυχή

Translate the following sentences into Greek.

1. Wisdom is joy.

_____

2. The Spirit is life.

_____

3. Excellence and truth exist.

_____

4. A book is a gift.

_____

5. The law is a gift.

_____

Chapter 3

To which case do the following short descriptions apply?

"of" case   _____   "to/for" case   _____

"object" case   _____   "address" case   _____

"subject" case   _____

Give the case and number for each of the following noun forms. Some forms have more than one answer.

	Case	Number		Case	Number
ψυχῆς	_____	_____	λόγος	_____	_____
ψυχῶν	_____	_____	λόγε	_____	_____
ψυχάς	_____	_____	λόγοι	_____	_____
ψυχαί	_____	_____	λόγων	_____	_____
ψυχῇ	_____	_____	λόγον	_____	_____
χαρᾷ	_____	_____	βιβλίον	_____	_____

(continues)

	Case	Number		Case	Number
χαρά	_____	_____		_____	_____
χαραῖς	_____	_____	βιβλίου	_____	_____
χαράς	_____	_____	βιβλία	_____	_____
χαράν	_____	_____		_____	_____

For each of the following nouns, give the corresponding forms of the definite article and the adjective καλός.

Definite Article	Adjective		Definite Article	Adjective	
_____	_____	λόγος	_____	_____	βιβλία
_____	_____	λόγον	_____	_____	ψυχῇ
_____	_____	λόγους	_____	_____	ψυχῆς
_____	_____	βιβλίον	_____	_____	χαραῖς
_____	_____	βιβλίων	_____	_____	χαράν

Translate the following sentences into Greek.

1. Honor is immortal.

_____

2. Life is strange.

_____

3. The pleasure of anger is evil.

_____

4. Anger is bad for the good life.

_____

5. Base pleasure is not immortal.

_____

Chapter 4

Give the person, number, and mood for the following forms of λύω.

	Person	Number	Mood
λύω	1st person	singular	
λύομεν	1st person	plural	
λυόντων	3rd person	plural	
λύει	3rd person	singular	
λῦε	2nd person	singular	
λύουσι	3rd person	plural	
λύεις	2nd person	singular	
λυέτω	3rd person	singular	
λύετε	2nd person	plural	

Give the corresponding 2nd person personal pronoun for the following 1st person personal pronouns.

1st Person	2nd Person		1st Person	2nd Person
ἐγώ	σύ		ἡμᾶς	σύ
ἐμέ	σέ		ἐμοῦ	ἡμῶν
ἡμεῖς	ὑμεῖς			

Give the corresponding 1st person personal pronoun for the following 2nd person personal pronouns.

2nd Person	1st Person		2nd Person	1st Person
σοῦ	σύ or ἐμοῦ		σέ	ἐμέ
ὑμῖν	ἡμῖν		σοί	ἐμοί
ὑμῶν	ἡμῶν			

Translate the following sentences into Greek.

1. The Lord knows the heart of people.

Τοῦ κυρίου γιγνώσκω ἀ καρδίας ὁ ἄνθρωπος.

2. Don't (plural) throw stones.

βάλλω λίθος.

3. The blameless son knows the beloved father.

Ὀ ἀναμάρτητος οἶδεν ἀ ἀγαπητός πατήρ.

4. A stone does not bring forth fruit.

λίθος   προφέρω ὁ καρπός.

5. If you know the Lord, you know human beings.

εἰ   γινώσκω ὁ κύριός,   γινώσκω ἄνθρωποςου.

6. We know, but we do not speak.

γιγνώσκω, δέ   λέγω

Chapter 5

Would you use a dative of indirect object or a dative of respect to translate into Greek the following English sentences?

1. Writing is difficult for students.

χαλεπός

2. Give glory to God.

θεός.

3. Silence is difficult for teachers.

σιωπή   χαλεπός   for   διδάσκαλοςου.

4. The doctor gave advice to the patient.

ὁ ἰατρός

5. Patience is difficult for doctors.

χαλεπός   ἰατρόςου,

for

Would you use a genitive of possession or an objective genitive to translate the following English phrases?

1. The love of glory

ἡ ἀγάπη ___ δόξα. (of)

2. The glory of God

ἡ δόξανς ___ θεός. (of)

3. The kingdom of heaven

ἡ βασιλείας ___ ὁ οὐρανόςοῦ. (of)

4. Hatred of grief

μισέω ___ γυνή/ἀνήρ. (of) p203

Translate the following sentences into Greek.

¶ βάλλω = to throw | γιγνώσκω = to know | εἰμί = to be |
λέγω = to speak

1. Glory in grief speaks to the world.

δόξανς λύπης λέγω ___ ὁ κόσμοςου. (to)

2. Don't (singular) throw education to chance.

___ λέγω παιδείας ___ τύχης. (to)

3. The art of education knows moderation.

ἡ τέχνης (of) παιδεία γιγνώσκω τό μέτρουου.

4. Chance does not know moderation.

τύχη ___ γιγνώσκω μέτρουου.

5. Glory after grief is blessed.

___ εἰμί μακάριος.

6. Blessed are the doctors.

μακάριος εἰμί ὁ ἰατρόςοῦ.

Chapter 6

Give the case and number of the following nouns.

	Case	Number		Case	Number
μαθητής	nominative	singular	θαλάττης	genitive	singular
νεανίου	genitive	singular	θάλαττα	nominative	singular
νεανιῶν	genitive	plural	μαθητοῦ	genitive	singular
νεανίαι	nominative	plural	μαθητάς	accusative	plural
θαλάττας	accusative	plural			

Identify the function of αὐτός in the following sentences. Is it (1) a personal pronoun, (2) an intensive adjective, or (3) an adjective meaning "the same"?

¶ βάλλω = to throw | γιγνώσκω = to know | εἰμί = to be | λέγω = to speak

1. ὁ Ἰησοῦς αὐτὸς λέγει.

_____

2. γιγνώσκομεν τὸν αὐτὸν φίλον.

_____

3. τὰ ζῷα αὐτὰ οὐ λέγουσιν.

_____

4. μὴ λεγέτω αὐτῷ ὁ μαθητής.

_____

5. ὁ Ἰησοῦς λέγει αὐτοῖς.

_____

Translate the following sentences into Greek.

❡ βάλλω = to throw | γιγνώσκω = to know | εἰμί = to be |
λέγω = to speak

1. Wine is a difficult friend.

_____

2. The student has the same treasure.

_____

3. The animals themselves speak.

_____

4. Jesus speaks to her.

_____

5. We have the same common treasure.

_____

6. Don't (singular) throw the wine at wicked friends.

_____

7. I do not know an evil animal.

_____

Chapter 7

Indicate whether the infinitives in the following sentences are complementary infinitives or articular infinitives.

1. δεῖ τῷ διδασκάλῳ γράφειν.

_____

2. ὁ πόνος τοῦ γράφειν χρηστός ἐστιν.

_____

3. τὸ τὰ ἄδικα πράττειν ἐστὶ κενὸν τοῖς βροτοῖς.

_____

4. οἱ διδάσκαλοι οὐκ ἐθέλουσιν μανθάνειν.

_____

5. ἐθέλομεν πράττειν τὰ δίκαια.

_____

Translate the following sentences into Greek.

1. Don't (plural) deal out injustice to the teacher.

_____

2. It is useful to remain.

_____

3. Let the unjust men among us not increase.

_____

4. It is necessary to learn just things.

_____

5. The men want to write empty things.

_____

6. I don't understand.

_____

Chapter 8

To what declension do the following nouns belong?

1. τέλος _____   6. σῶμα _____

2. θάνατος _____   7. χαρά _____

3. γένος _____   8. δαίμων _____

4. μαθητής _____   9. ἐλπίς _____

5. Σωκράτης _____

Change the following singular nouns to the plural.

δαίμονος _____   γένει _____

σῶμα _____   βασιλεύς _____

πόλεως _____

Change the following plural nouns to the singular.

δαίμονες _____   γένη _____

σώματα _____   βασιλέας _____

πόλεων _____

Translate the following sentences into Greek.

1. The death of Socrates teaches generations.

_____

2. Do you (singular) see the hope of the city?

_____

3. Faith teaches wisdom.

_____

4. The divinities see the deaths of kings.

_____

5. Grace is not private.

_____

6. Mothers teach fathers.

_____

Chapter 9

Identify the declension of the following adjectives.

1. εὐδαίμων, –ον   _____

2. ἀληθής, –ές   _____

3. καλός, –ή, –όν   _____

4. ἄξιος, –α, –ον   _____

5. ἡδύς, ἡδεῖα, ἡδύ   _____

Give the corresponding forms of the definite article and adjective for each of the following nouns.

Definite Article	Adjective ἀληθής		Definite Article	Adjective εὐδαίμων	
_____	_____	λόγῳ	_____	_____	Σωκράτης
_____	_____	δαίμων	_____	_____	σώματα
_____	_____	βιβλίοις	_____	_____	ψυχάς
_____	_____	βασιλέως	_____	_____	δαίμονες
_____	_____	πόλιν	_____	_____	γένεσιν

Translate the following sentences into Greek.

¶ γιγνώσκω = to know | εἰμί = to be | ἔχω = to have, hold | λέγω = to speak | πράττω = to do

1. The wife trusts the worthy husband.

_____

2. The happy women speak true things.

_____

3. I know the great temper of the man.

_____

4. Let the women do great things.

_____

5. A great spirit does many things.

_____

6. All things are sweet to the happy man.

_____

7. We trust the woman worthy of great things.

_____

Chapter 10

Convert the following adjectives into adverbs.

1. αἰσχρός _____   4. ἀληθής _____

2. δυνατός _____   5. εὐδαίμων _____

3. καλός _____

Are the following words definite articles or relative pronouns?

1. οἵ _____   6. ὅ _____

2. οἱ _____   7. ὅς _____

3. αἱ _____   8. τά _____

4. αἵ _____   9. ἅ _____

5. τό _____   10. ὧν _____

Translate the following sentences into Greek.

¶ γιγνώσκω = to know | εἰμί = to be | λέγω = to speak

1. The beginning of love is strong.

_____

2. Let the church not do shameful things.

_____

3. The church is now young, but she is strong.

_____

4. Let each person who is young always know love.

_____

5. The young men are always speaking to the shameful man whom I know.

_____

6. You (singular) know the beginning of love, which has profit.

_____

7. We are all able to speak shameful things.

_____

8. Let the shameful man know love again.

_____

Chapter 11

Change the following present indicative forms into the corresponding forms of the future indicative.

λύω   _____   πέμπεις   _____

λύετε   _____   ἄγει   _____

πέμπουσιν   _____   ἀγομεν   _____

Change the following direct statements into indirect statements with ὅτι, introduced by Σωκράτης λέγει "Socrates says that…"

¶ εἰμί = to be | λέγω = to speak

1. ἡ γῆ ἐστι πέτρα.

_____

2. ὁ ἀδελφὸς οὐκ ἔστιν ἀληθινός.

_____

3. οἱ ἄλλοι ἄγουσι τοὺς ἀληθινοὺς ἀδελφούς.

_____

4. οἱ ἄλλοι οὐ λέγουσι τὰ ἀληθινά.

_____

Change the following direct statements into indirect statements with the accusative and infinitive, introduced by Σωκράτης φησὶ "Socrates says that…"

1. ἡ γῆ ἐστι πέτρα.

_____

2. ὁ ἀδελφὸς οὐκ ἔστιν ἀληθινός.

_____

3. οἱ ἄλλοι ἄγουσι τοὺς ἀληθινοὺς ἀδελφούς.

_____

4. οἱ ἄλλοι οὐ λέγουσι τὰ ἀληθινά.

_____

Translate the following sentences into Greek.

> ❡ ἄνθρωπος, –ου, ὁ = human being, person | γιγνώσκω = to know |
> εἰμί = to be | κακός, –ή, –όν (adj.) = bad, base, evil | λέγω = to speak

1. Socrates says that the bad people lead trustful people to Hades.

_____

2. Socrates thinks that the earth is a rock.

_____

3. The evil brother will send the trustful brother to the gate.

_____

4. Let the evil man know Hades.

_____

5. You (plural) will know the trustful brother.

_____

Chapter 12

Change the following present indicative forms into the corresponding forms of the imperfect and aorist indicative.

Present Indicative	Imperfect Indicative	Aorist Indicative
λύω	_____	_____
ἀποκρύπτεις	_____	_____
ἀκούει	_____	_____
ἀποκαλύπτομεν	_____	_____
λαμβάνετε	_____	_____
μερίζουσιν	_____	_____

Change the following forms of the present imperative into the corresponding forms of the aorist imperative.

λῦε	_____	λαμβάνετε	_____
λυόντων	_____	μεριζόντων	_____
ἀκουέτω	_____	ἀπόκρυπτε	_____

Change the following forms of the present indicative of εἰμί into the corresponding forms of the imperfect indicative.

εἰμί	_____	εἶ	_____
ἐστί	_____	ἐσμέν	_____
ἐστέ	_____	εἰσίν	_____

Translate the following sentences into Greek.

¶ ἄνθρωπος, –ου, ὁ = human being, person | κακός, –ή, –όν (adj.) = bad, base, evil

1. The spirit seized the person.

_____

2. The quick person was seizing the slow person.

_____

3. We do not hear the childish language.

_____

4. We do not hear the childish person.

_____

5. Seize (singular) the knees of the swift person.

_____

6. Seize (singular) the knees of the swift person (and don't let go).

_____

7. The heavens hear the language of the children.

_____

8. The heavens heard the children.

_____

9. Let the child reveal the spirit.

_____

Chapter 13

Change the present tense verb that introduces the following indirect statements into the future and translate.

¶ ἄνθρωπος, –ου, ὁ = human being | νομίζω, νομιῶ = to think, consider
(the 3rd singular future of νομίζω is νομιεῖ)

1. Σωκράτης λέγει ὅτι ἡ φιλοσοφία διδάσκει τοὺς ἀνθρώπους.

_____

2. Σωκράτης νομίζει τὸ φῶς εἶναι ἅγιον.

_____

Change the present tense verb that introduces the following indirect statements into the aorist and translate.

1. Σωκράτης λέγει ὅτι ἡ φιλοσοφία διδάσκει τοὺς ἀνθρώπους.

_____

2. Σωκράτης νομίζει τὸ φῶς εἶναι ἅγιον.

_____

Indicate whether each of the following English sentences would be expressed with a Greek (1) genitive of time within which, (2) accusative of duration of time, or (3) dative of time when.

1. The students slept throughout the lecture.   _____

2. The students laughed during the lecture.   _____

3. The students slept at the lecture.   _____

Translate the following sentences into Greek.

> ¶ ἄνθρωπος, –ου, ὁ = human being, person | κακός, –ή, –όν (adj.) = bad, base, evil | λέγω = to say, speak

1. We used to speak to the philosopher.

_____

2. We spoke to the philosopher.

_____

3. I used to call the counsel of the philosopher evil.

_____

4. I called the counsel of the philosopher evil.

_____

5. You (plural) said that you had taught the philosopher.

_____

6. You (plural) said that you were teaching the philosopher.

_____

7. The philosophers call the day night.

_____

8. I say that the philosophers will speak to the evil people.

_____

9. I said that the philosophers would speak to the evil people.

_____

Chapter 14

Give the corresponding middle/passive forms for the following active forms.

Active	Middle/Passive	Active	Middle/Passive
ἔλυον (1st person sing.)	_____	λύομεν	_____
ἔλυον (3rd person pl.)	_____	λῦε	_____
λύει	_____	λύειν	_____

Switch the following sentences from active constructions into passive constructions with a genitive of agent. For example, for ἡ δύναμις πείθει ἀσθένειαν "Power persuades weakness," write ἡ ἀσθένεια πείθεται ὑπὸ δυνάμεως "Weakness is persuaded by power."

¶ ἄνθρωπος, –ου, ὁ = human being, γιγνώσκω = to know

1. τὸ πλῆθος φυλάττει τὸ παιδίον.

_____

2. ὁ νοῦς γιγνώσκει δύναμιν.

_____

3. οἱ ἄνθρωποι ἔσῳζον τὸ παιδίον.

_____

4. ἐφυλάττομεν τὰ παιδία.

_____

5. ὁ πόλεμος ἄρχει τῶν ἀνθρώπων.

_____

Translate the following sentences into Greek.

¶ ἄνθρωπος, –ου, ὁ = human being, person | κακός, –ή, –όν (adj.) = bad, base, evil | πάλιν (adv.) = back, again

1. Don't (plural) turn back.

_____

2. The children did not obey the base people.

_____

3. The mind is on guard against weakness.

_____

4. The multitude obeys power.

_____

5. The multitude are persuaded by power.

_____

Chapter 15

Change the following aorist active imperatives into aorist middle imperatives.

Aorist Active Imperative	Aorist Middle Imperative	Aorist Active Imperative	Aorist Middle Imperative
λῦσον	_____	λυσάντων	_____
λύσατε	_____	λυσάτω	_____

Change the following present middle/passive imperatives into aorist middle imperatives.

Present Middle/ Passive Imperative	Aorist Middle Imperative	Present Middle/ Passive Imperative	Aorist Middle Imperative
λυέσθων	_____	λύεσθε	_____
λυέσθω	_____	λύου	_____

Change the following present indicative forms of εἰμί into future indicatives.

Present Indicative	Future Indicative	Present Indicative	Future Indicative
εἰμί	_____	ἐστέ	_____
ἐστίν	_____	ἐσμέν	_____
εἶ	_____	εἰσί	_____

Translate the following sentences into Greek.

¶ ἀνήρ, ανδρός, ὁ = man, husband | γυνή, γυναικός, ἡ = woman; wife | εὐδαίμων, –ον (adj.) = fortunate, happy

1. We don't want to go.

_____

2. Let your will come to be.

_____

3. Justice will come.

_____

4. The men will be able to marvel.

_____

5. The woman became happy.

_____

6. I did not make justice.

_____

Chapter 16

Change the following aorist middle forms into aorist passive forms.

Aorist Middle Indicative	Aorist Passive Indicative	Aorist Middle Indicative	Aorist Passive Indicative
ἐλυσάμεθα	_____	ἐλύσατο	_____
ἐλύσω	_____	ἐλύσαντο	_____
ἐλυσάμην	_____	ἐλύσασθε	_____

Change the following future middle forms into future passive forms.

Future Middle Indicative	Future Passive Indicative	Future Middle Indicative	Future Passive Indicative
λύσομαι	_____	λυσόμεθα	_____
λύσει	_____	λύσεσθε	_____
λύσονται	_____	λύσεται	_____

Write out the individual words constituting each of the following examples of crasis.

1. κἀγω   _____   3. κἀμοί   _____

2. ταὐτά   _____

Translate the following sentences into Greek.

        ¶ ἀνήρ, ανδρός, ὁ = man; husband

1. The merciful will be called pure.

_____

2. The gentle man was comforted.

_____

3. Merciful things were done by the pure alone.

_____

4. Our bravery was not seen.

_____

5. Serve (plural) the gentle.

_____

6. My bravery will be summoned.

_____

Chapter 17

Translate the following sentences into Greek.

❡ ἀνήρ, ανδρός, ὁ = man; husband | γυνή, γυναικός, ἡ = woman; wife |
εὐδαίμων, –ον (adj.) = fortunate, happy

1. Zeus knew the cowardly man.

_____

2. Zeus will go to the famous men.

_____

3. The husband was questioned by the wife.

_____

4. We denied that the riddle was famous.

_____

Chapter 18

Add the corresponding form of each demonstrative (οὗτος, ἐκεῖνος, ὅδε) to the
following nouns.

❡ γυνή, γυναικός, ἡ = woman; wife | παιδίον, –ου, τό = child

	οὗτος	ἐκεῖνος	ὅδε
ὁ ἁμαρτωλός	_____	_____	_____
τὰ παιδία	_____	_____	_____
τῇ γυναικί	_____	_____	_____
τοὺς στρατηγούς	_____	_____	_____
τῶν στρατηγῶν	_____	_____	_____

Translate the following sentences into Greek.

> ¶ γιγνώσκω, γνώσομαι, ἔγνων, —, —, ἐγνώσθην = to know | ἐλέγχω,
> ἐλέγξω, ἤλεγξα = to cross-examine, question | πράττω (Koine
> πράσσω), πράξω, ἔπραξα, πέπραγμα or (πέπραχα), πέπραγμαι, ἐπράχθην
> = to do

1. This sinner prays; that sinner does not pray.

_____

2. Those generals questioned the wise men.

_____

3. I know that this general is wise.

_____

4. I know this: the wise man does wise things.

_____

5. The wise men will know that opportunity.

_____

6. Let the wise man pray.

_____

7. These things will be known by those people.

_____

Chapter 19

Identify the gender, number, case, tense, and voice of the following participles.

	Gender	Number	Case	Tense	Voice
ὤν	_____	_____	_____	_____	_____
ὄν	_____	_____	_____	_____	_____
	_____	_____	_____	_____	_____
οὔσης	_____	_____	_____	_____	_____
ὄντων	_____	_____	_____	_____	_____
	_____	_____	_____	_____	_____
λύοντα	_____	_____	_____	_____	_____
	_____	_____	_____	_____	_____
	_____	_____	_____	_____	_____
λύοντας	_____	_____	_____	_____	_____
λυομένην	_____	_____	_____	_____	_____
λύσουσαι	_____	_____	_____	_____	_____
λυσόμενοι	_____	_____	_____	_____	_____
λύσαντος	_____	_____	_____	_____	_____
λυσομένῳ	_____	_____	_____	_____	_____
	_____	_____	_____	_____	_____
λυθησομένους	_____	_____	_____	_____	_____
λυθείς	_____	_____	_____	_____	_____
λυθεῖσιν	_____	_____	_____	_____	_____
	_____	_____	_____	_____	_____

Translate the following sentences into Greek.

¶ γιγνώσκω, γνώσομαι, ἔγνων, —, —, ἐγνώσθην = to know | εἰμί = to be |
λέγω = to speak | πράττω (Koine πράσσω) = to do

1. A harm done is eternal.

_____

2. The poets speaking eternal things are not servile.

_____

3. Let the slaves flee.

_____

4. We will need the poets.

_____

5. We do not need a poet speaking servile things.

_____

6. The harms of the poets were known.

_____

7. Eternal is the mistake of the poet.

_____

Chapter 20

Translate the following sentences into Greek. Next, state whether the sentence contains an attributive participle, a circumstantial participle, or both.

¶ ἄνθρωπος, –ου, ὁ = human being, person | κακός, –ή, –όν (adj.) = bad, base, evil | φεύγω, φεύξομαι, ἔφυγον, —, —, — = to flee

1. Having harmed the evil person, the angel fled.

_____

2. I fled the angel harming the evil person.

_____

3. Being disturbed, the dead will harm us.

_____

4. The disturbed dead will harm us.

_____

5. Let them not flee, having harmed the dead.

_____

6. Since mercy is not new, it is dead.

_____

7. When mercy is not new, it is dead.

_____

8. Although the angel was harmed, he (the angel) is not dead.

_____

Chapter 21

Translate the following sentences and identify whether each sentence contains an (1) attributive participle, a (2) circumstantial participle, or (3) a supplementary participle

> ¶ ἄνθρωπος, –ου, ὁ = human being, person | ἐπί (prep.) = on, upon (+ gen.), on, by, for (+ dat.), to, against (+ acc.) | ὑπό (prep.) = under, by (+ gen.) | ἐκεῖνος, ἐκείνη, ἐκεῖνο (demonstrative adj.) = that, the former.

1. ὁ σοφιστὴς τρέφων τὸν δόλον, ἥμαρτεν.

2. παῦε τρέφων τὸν δόλον.

3. ἔτυχον (1st person) πορεύεσθαι ἐπὶ ἐκεῖνον τόπον.

4. οὐκ ἀναγκάσομεν τοὺς ἀνθρώπους τοὺς ἀναγκασθέντας ὑπὸ τῶν σοφιστῶν.

5. ἐκεῖνος σοφιστὴς λανθάνει Ἑλλάδα ἁμαρτάνων.

Translate the following sentences into Greek.

> ¶ ἀκούω = to hear | ἄνθρωπος, –ου, ὁ = human being, person | ἐκεῖνος, ἐκείνη, ἐκεῖνο (demonstrative adj.) = that; the former | ἀκούω = to hear

1. Stop (singular) compelling Greece to err.

2. The Sophists erred without the knowledge of Greece.

3. I did not come to compel the Sophists to cease.

4. When treachery ceases, Greece does not err.

5. I hear that the Sophists were coming to that place.

_____

6. I heard that the Sophists would come to that place.

_____

7. I heard that the Sophists had come to that place.

_____

Chapter 22

Write the corresponding forms of ψυχή, ἄνθρωπος, and βιβλίον for each of the following numeric adjectives.

	ψυχή		ἄνθρωπος		βιβλίον
μία	_____	εἷς	_____	ἕν	_____
μίαν	_____	ἑνός	_____	ἑνί	_____
δυοῖν	_____	δυοῖν	_____	δυοῖν	_____
τρισίν	_____	τρισίν	_____	τρισίν	_____
τέτταρες	_____	τέτταρες	_____	τέτταρα	_____

Identify whether the following English sentences would be expressed by an actual result clause or a natural result clause.

1. Alcibiades drank so much wine that he became sick.

_____

2. Alcibiades drank enough wine to become sick.

_____

3. Alcibiades had the charisma to sway the people.

_____

4. Alcibiades had so much charisma that he swayed the people.

_____

Translate the following sentences into Greek.

> ¶ ἄνθρωπος, –ου, ὁ = human being, person | ἁμαρτάνω, ἁμαρτήσομαι,
> ἥμαρτον = to err, sin | ἔχω, ἕξω (or σχήσω), ἔσχον = to have | πλοῦτος,
> –ου, ὁ = wealth | οὐκέτι (adv.) = no longer

1. No one has so much knowledge that they know nothing.

_____

2. I know one thing. You know two things. We know three things.

_____

3. No one has knowledge so as to no longer sin.

_____

4. We had so much wealth that we divided the men.

_____

5. Don't (singular) separate knowledge.

_____

Chapter 23

Write the corresponding comparative and superlative forms for the following adjectives.

Positive Adjective	Comparative Adjective	Superlative Adjective	Positive Adjective	Comparative Adjective	Superlative Adjective
σοφός	_____	_____	καλά	_____	_____
σοφή	_____	_____	καλοῦ	_____	_____
σοφῷ	_____	_____	καλάς	_____	_____

Write the corresponding comparative and superlative forms for the following adverbs.

Positive Adverb	Comparative Adverb	Superlative Adverb
σοφῶς	_____	_____
καλῶς	_____	_____
μάλα	_____	_____

Translate the following sentences into Greek.

❡ ἄνθρωπος, –ου, ὁ = human being, person | διδάσκαλος, –ου, ὁ = teacher | εἰμί = to be | ἔχω, ἔξω (or σχήσω), ἔσχον = to have | ὀργή, –ῆς, ἡ = anger | πλοῦτος, –ου, ὁ = wealth | σοφός, –ή, –όν (adj.) = wise | χορτάζω, χορτάσω, ἐχόρτασα = to feed

1. Service is greater than wealth. (Use ἤ.)

_____

2. Service is greater than wealth. (Use a genitive of comparison.)

_____

3. We know that forgiveness is stronger than anger.

_____

4. I know that experience is the wisest teacher by far.

_____

5. Forgiveness fed the people more than possessions.

_____

Chapter 24

Write the contracted forms for the following uncontracted forms of φιλέω.

φιλέω   _____   φιλέουσιν   _____

φίλεε   _____   φιλέειν   _____

ἐφιλεόμην   _____   φιλέεσθαι   _____

ἐφίλεε   _____

ἐφιλέομεν   _____

φιλεόμεθα   _____

φιλέεται   _____

φιλέετε   _____

Write the corresponding future active forms of the following present active forms.

Present Active	Future Active	Present Active	Future Active
μένω	_____	βάλλεις	_____
μένομεν	_____	βαλλέτω	_____
μένει	_____	βάλλει	_____

Translate the following sentences into Greek.

1. You (singular) will respond.

2. We baptized the soldiers with water. (Use a dative of means without a preposition.)

3. We baptized the soldiers with water. (Use ἐν + dative.)

4. Let the temple be found.

5. The soldiers were thinking that they were wise.

6. I hate and I love.

7. You (plural) will not find water at once.

Chapter 25

Write the contracted forms for the following uncontracted forms of νικάω.

νικάομαι   _____   ἐνικάεσθε   _____

νικάει   _____   νικαέσθων   _____

νικάομεν   _____   νικαέτω   _____

ἐνίκαε   _____   νικάεσθαι   _____

ἐνίκαον   _____   νικάειν   _____

ἐνικάοντο   _____

Indicate whether the following forms are interrogative pronouns or indefinite pronouns.

τις   _____   τίσιν   _____

του   _____   τίνος   _____

τίς   _____   τι   _____

τινά   _____   τοῦ   _____

τινῶν   _____   ἄττα   _____

Translate the following sentences into Greek.

¶ διδάσκαλος, –ου, ὁ = teacher | ὀργή, –ῆς, ἡ = anger | σοφός, –ή, –όν (adj.) = wise

1. Why do we philosophize?

_____

2. Let the wise man conquer anger.

_____

3. What teacher does not question?

_____

4. Certain teachers neither question nor philosophize.

_____

5. Philosophize (plural) and prosper!

_____

6. We will not hesitate to allow certain things to prosper.

_____

Chapter 26

Write the contracted forms for the following uncontracted forms of δηλόω.

δηλόω   _____   δηλοέτω   _____

δηλόομαι   _____   δηλόου   _____

δηλόουσι   _____   δήλοε   _____

ἐδηλοόμην   _____   δηλόεσθαι   _____

ἐδηλόομεν   _____   δηλόειν   _____

ἐδήλοον   _____

Translate the following sentences into Greek.

¶ διδάσκαλος, -ου, ὁ = teacher | εἰμί = to be

1. Knowledge is golden.

_____

2. The knowledge of the teacher is small. (Use a genitive of possession.)

_____

3. The knowledge of the teacher is small. (Use a dative of possession.)

_____

4. The enemies made themselves known.

_____

5. We will reveal the small things to the enemy.

_____

6. I think that the teachers will not see golden things.

_____

7. Let knowledge be loved.

_____

Chapter 27

Give the person and number of the following perfect active forms of λύω.

	Person	Number		Person	Number
λελύκαμεν	_____	_____	λέλυκας	_____	_____
λέλυκα	_____	_____	λελύκασιν	_____	_____
λέλυκεν	_____	_____	λελύκατε	_____	_____

Give the corresponding forms of the definite article and perfect active participle of λύω.

¶ βιβλίον, –ου, ὁ = book | δεσμός, –οῦ, ὁ = chain | χαρά, –ᾶς, ἡ = joy

Definite Article	Perfect Active Participle of λύω	
_____	_____	δεσμός
_____	_____	δεσμούς
_____	_____	δεσμοῖς
_____	_____	χαρᾶς
_____	_____	χαράς
_____	_____	χαρῶν
_____	_____	βιβλίον
_____	_____	βιβλία
_____	_____	βιβλίου

Give the person, number, and mood of the following forms of οἶδα.

	Person	Number	Mood		Person	Number	Mood
οἶδεν	___	___	___	ἴστων	___	___	___
οἶσθα	___	___	___	ἴστω	___	___	___
ἴσασιν	___	___	___	ἴστε	___	___	___
ἴσθι	___	___	___		___	___	___
οἶδα	___	___	___	ἴσμεν	___	___	___

Translate the following sentences into Greek.

¶ εἰμί = to be | ἐν (prep.) = in (+ dative) | ζωή, –ῆς, ἡ = life | τίς, τί (interrogative pronoun) = who, what

1. Is there happiness in life?

_____

2. Say (singular) what life is.

_____

3. Have you (singular) changed your mind?

_____

4. Let the mortals know peace!

_____

5. I do not know what is similar to peace.

_____

6. We think that the hour of happiness has approached.

_____

7. You (singular) have not testified.

_____

8. I know that the mortals have not lived in peace.

_____

Chapter 28

Give all six principal parts of your model verb λύω.

1	2	3	4	5	6
present active	future active	aorist active	perfect active	perfect m/p	aorist passive

Write the primary and secondary middle/passive endings.

Primary Middle/Passive Endings			Secondary Middle/Passive Endings		
	Singular	*Plural*		*Singular*	*Plural*
1st	_____	_____	1st	_____	_____
2nd	_____	_____	2nd	_____	_____
3rd	_____	_____	3rd	_____	_____

Translate the following sentences into Greek.

¶ εἰμί = to be | ὑπό (ὑπ'/ὑφ') (prep.) = under, by (+ gen.)

1. The struggle is not fulfilled by violence.

_____

2. The struggle has not been fulfilled by violence.

_____

3. Infinite violence grows.

_____

4. Be (plural) not afraid.

_____

5. Nature has not been protected by arrogance.

_____

6. We will complete the struggle.

_____

Chapter 29

Write the shortened forms of the following reflexive pronouns.

σεαυτοῦ _____   ἑαυτοῦ _____

σεαυτόν _____   ἑαυτῆς _____

σεαυτῇ _____   ἑαυτήν _____

ἑαυτό _____   ἑαυτῷ _____

Translate the following sentences into Greek.

¶ εἰμί = to be | λέγω, ἐρῶ (or λέξω), εἶπον, εἴρηκα, εἴρημαι (or λέλεγμαι),
ἐρρήθην (or λέλειμαι) = to say, speak | μαθητής, –οῦ, ὁ = student |
παιδεύω, παιδεύσω, ἐπαίδευσα, πεπαίδευκα, πεπαίδευμαι, ἐπαιδεύθην
= to teach | ποῖος, –α, –ον = what kind?, what sort? | πόσος, –η, –ον –
how many?, how much? | Σωκράτης, –ους, ὁ = Socrates

1. When Socrates had spoken, he was bound.

_____

2. When Socrates goes out, he will have taught the students.

_____

3. We did not say what sort of students Socrates had taught.

_____

4. How many students will Socrates have taught when we go out?

_____

5. What sort of things have you (plural) taught yourself?

_____

6. The neighbors bound themselves.

_____

7. Fulfill (singular) yourself.

_____

Chapter 30

Write the forms of your three model μ verbs for the following:

	δίδωμι	τίθημι	ἵστημι
1st pers., sg., present, act., ind.			
2nd pers., sg., present, act., imp.			
3rd pers., sg., present, m/p, ind.			
1st pers., pl., present, m/p., ind.			
present active infinitive			
present middle/passive infinitive			

Identify the gender, number, case, tense, and voice of the following participles.

	Gender	Number	Case	Tense	Voice
διδούς					
διδομένην					
τιθέμενοι					
τιθέν					
ἱστάν					

Translate the following sentences into Greek.

¶ βούλομαι = to want | θεός, –οῦ, ὁ = a god, God

1. The shepherds were giving glory to God.

_____

2. Don't (singular) place blame on the shepherds.

_____

3. I will not betray the commandments being given.

_____

4. We do not want to place blame.

_____

5. A god is standing the shepherd up.

_____

Chapter 31

Write the forms of your three model μι verbs for the following. For ἵστημι, use the 2nd aorist forms.

	δίδωμι	τίθημι	ἵστημι
1st pers., sg., aorist, act., ind.	_____	_____	_____
2nd pers., sg., aorist, act., imp.	_____	_____	_____
3rd pers., sg., aorist, middle, ind.	_____	_____	NA
1st pers., pl., aorist, middle, ind.	_____	_____	NA
aorist active infinitive	_____	_____	_____
aorist middle infinitive	_____	_____	NA

Identify the gender, number, case, tense, and voice of the following participles.

	Gender	Number	Case	Tense	Voice
δούς	_____	_____	_____	_____	_____
δομένην	_____	_____	_____	_____	_____
θεῖσα	_____	_____	_____	_____	_____
θέν	_____	_____	_____	_____	_____
	_____	_____	_____	_____	_____
στάν	_____	_____	_____	_____	_____
	_____	_____	_____	_____	_____
	_____	_____	_____	_____	_____

Translate the following sentences into Greek.

¶ διδάσκαλος, –ου, ὁ = teacher | δίδωμι, δώσω, ἔδωκα, δέδωκα, δέδομαι, ἐδόθην = to give | ἵστημι, στήσω, ἔστησα/ἔστην, ἔστηκα, ἔσταμαι, ἐστάθην = to set; stand

1. The army released the evil men.

_____

2. The child gave advice to the teacher.

_____

3. We will suffer the given misfortunes.

_____

4. The child stood.

_____

5. The heart suffered many misfortunes.

_____

6. Give (plural) misfortune to the teachers.

_____

Chapter 32

Give the corresponding subjunctive forms for the following indicative forms.

εἰμί _____   δηλοῦμεν _____

ἐστί _____   δίδωσιν _____

λύω _____   δίδοται _____

λύεται _____   ἔδωκα _____

λύονται _____   τίθεσθε _____

νικῶ _____   τίθενται _____

νικᾷς _____   τιθέασιν _____

φιλεῖς _____   ἵσταμεν _____

ἐφίλησαν _____   ἔστη _____

δηλοῖ _____   ἵστημι _____

Translate the following sentences into Greek.

¶ διδάσκαλος, –ου, ὁ = teacher

1. Let us fight the senseless crowd.

_____

2. Don't (singular) criticize the weak. (Don't use an imperative.)

_____

3. Let us not think that the weak are senseless.

_____

4. Shall we declare that an encomium is senseless?

_____

5. Shall I criticize the senseless teacher? (Don't use a future.)

_____

6. Let us not imitate the senseless teacher.

_____

Chapter 33

Translate the following sentences into Greek.

¶ γίγνομαι (Koine γίνομαι), γενήσομαι, ἐγενόμην, γέγονα, γεγένημαι, —
= to become | διδάσκαλος, –ου, ὁ = teacher | διδάσκω, διδάξω, ἐδίδαξα,
δεδίδαχα, δεδίδαγμαι, ἐδιδάχθην = to teach | εἰμί = to be | εὐδαίμων, –ον
(adj.) = happy | ἤ (conj.) = or; than | Σωκράτης, –ους, ὁ = Socrates.

1. I am not teaching in order to become rich.

_____

2. Socrates was poor so that he could be happy.

_____

3. Let the teachers not teach in order to condemn.

_____

4. Socrates will not teach to become rich.

_____

5. Let us strive to be more than mouths.

_____

Chapter 34

Give the corresponding optative forms for the following indicative forms.

εἰμί	_____	δηλοῦμεν	_____
ἐστί	_____	δίδωσιν	_____
λύω	_____	δίδοται	_____
λύσεται	_____	ἔδωκα	_____
λύονται	_____	τίθεσθε	_____
νικῶ	_____	τίθενται	_____
νικᾷς	_____	τιθέασιν	_____
φιλεῖς	_____	ἵσταμεν	_____
ἐφίλησαν	_____	στήσω	_____

Translate the following sentences into Greek.

¶ εἰμί = to be | Σωκράτης, –ους, ὁ = Socrates |
εὐδαίμων, –ον (adj.) = happy

1. Adversity could benefit the happy.

2. How could the forms of misfortune still increase?

3. May the recognition of adversity be useful. (Use an optative.)

4. Socrates might be crazy.

5. I wish that I were happy.

Chapter 35

εἰ γὰρ ἕξομεν τὴν ταπεινοφροσύνην, ἕξομεν τὴν ἀρχὴν τῆς σοφίας.
For if we will have humility, we will have the beginning of wisdom.

1. Change the above simple condition into a future more vivid condition.

2. Change the above simple condition into a future less vivid condition.

3. Replace the protasis of the above simple condition with a conditional
participle.

4. Replace εἰ of the above simple condition with a relative pronoun. Be sure to
change the person of the verb as well.

Translate the following sentences into Greek.

¶ εἰμί = to be | Σωκράτης, –ους, ὁ = Socrates |
εὐδαίμων, –ον (adj.) = happy

1. If we destroy the temple, we will destroy the holy things.

_____

2. If we should destroy the temple, we would destroy the holy things.

_____

3. If I destroy the political things, Socrates will be happy.

_____

4. If I should destroy the political things, Socrates would be happy.

_____

5. Whoever destroys the temple will destroy the holy things.

_____

6. When you (singular) destroy the temple, you destroy the holy things.

_____

7. When you (singular) destroy the temple, don't destroy the holy things.

_____

Chapter 36

εἰ γὰρ ἕξομεν τὴν ταπεινοφροσύνην, ἕξομεν τὴν ἀρχὴν τῆς σοφίας.
For if we will have humility, we will have the beginning of wisdom.

1. Change the above simple condition into a present general condition.

_____

2. Change the above simple condition into a present general condition with ὅταν.

_____

3. Change the above simple condition into a past general condition.

_____

4. Change the above simple condition into a present general condition with a
conditional participle.

_____

Fill in the following flowcharts.

Protasis (if clause)
ἐάν (ἤν, ἄν) +
Subjunctive

Apodosis (then clause)
Future Indicative   = _____

Apodosis (then clause)
Present Indicative   = _____

Protasis (if clause)
εἰ + Optative

Apodosis (then clause)
Optative + ἄν   = _____

Apodosis (then clause)
Imperfect Indicative   = _____

Translate the following sentences into Greek.

❡ εἰμί = to be | καλέω, καλῶ, ἐκάλεσα, κέκληκα, κέκλημαι, ἐκλήθην = to call | Σωκράτης, –ους, ὁ = Socrates

1. When necessity is present, the servant is present.

_____

2. When necessity was present, Socrates was present.

_____

3. Whenever the servant is weak, there is no bread.

_____

4. Call (plural) us whenever Socrates is weak.

_____

5. If Socrates was ever weak, we were present.

_____

Chapter 37

Translate the following sentences into Greek.

¶ διδάσκαλος, –ου, ὁ = teacher | φυλάττω (Koine φυλάσσω), φυλάξω,
ἐφύλαξα, πεφύλαχα, πεφύλαγμαι, ἐφυλάχθην = to guard

1. If the teacher were terrible, I would guard the child.

_____

2. If I had seen the terrible stranger, I would have seized him.

_____

3. If we were not terrible, we would not be seized here.

_____

4. If only the oath were not terrible.

_____

5. If only I had not seen the terrible things.

_____

Chapter 38

Fill in the following charts.

	Main Verb	Fear Clause
The subject fears that something *will* happen.	verb of fearing	μή + _____
The subject fears that something *will not* happen.	verb of fearing	μὴ οὐ + _____
The subject fears that something *has* happened or *is* happening.	verb of fearing	μή + _____
The subject fears that something *has not* happened or *is not* happening.	verb of fearing	μὴ οὐ + _____

	Main Verb	Effort Clause
The subject makes the effort that something happen.	verb of effort	ὅπως + _____ or ὡς + _____
The subject makes the effort that something not happen.	verb of effort	ὅπως μή + _____ or ὡς μή + _____

Translate the following sentences into Greek.

> ¶ βλέπω, βλέψομαι, ἔβλεψα, βέβλεφα, βέβλεμμαι, ἐβλέφθην = to see, look | διδάσκαλος, –ου, ὁ, = teacher | πράττω (Koine πράσσω), πράξω, ἔπραξα, πέπραγμα or (πέπραχα), πέπραγμαι, ἐπράχθην = to do | τάχος, –εος, swiftness | ταχύς, –εῖα, –ύ (adj.) = swift, quick | χαλεπός, –ή, –όν (adj.) = difficult, harsh

1. Make (singular) it that you praise the courageous ones.

_____

2. It being possible to hesitate, we entered.

_____

3. I am afraid that the teacher will be difficult.

_____

4. I am afraid that the teacher will not be difficult.

_____

5. See (plural) to it lest you hesitate to do courageous things.

_____

6. The teacher has swift eyes. (Use an accusative of respect.)

_____

7. I am afraid that we have not done courageous things.

_____

Chapter 39

Fill in the following chart.

Cautious assertion that something *is* or *was* the case.	μή + _____
Cautious denial that something *is* or *was* the case.	μὴ οὐ + _____
Cautious assertion that something *will be* the case.	μή + _____
Cautious denial that something *will be* the case.	μὴ οὐ + _____

Translate the following sentences into Greek.

¶ ἀλήθεια, –ας, ἡ = truth | διδάσκαλος, –ου, ὁ = teacher | μαθητής, –οῦ, ὁ = student | πόνος, –ου, ὁ = toil

1. The truth must be served. (Use a verbal adjective.)

_____

2. We must remember the truth. (Use a verbal adjective.)

_____

3. Perhaps the teacher is not wise.

_____

4. Perhaps the teacher will be difficult.

_____

5. Perhaps the teacher will not help the students.

_____

6. Perhaps we are teachable.

_____

7. You (singular) will never escape toil. (Use an emphatic denial.)

_____

8. Don't (plural) escape. (Use an emphatic prohibition.)

_____

Chapter 40

In accordance with sequence of moods, change the verbs in secondary sequence into the optative.

1. ἐφιλοσόφουν ἵνα γένωμαι εὐδαίμων.

2. οἱ φιλόσοφοι ἔλεγον ὅτι Σωκράτης βλάψει τοὺς μαθητάς.

3. εἴπομεν ποῦ ἐστε.

4. εἶδον τί πράττεις.

Translate the following sentences into Greek.

> ¶ ἀποθνῄσκω, ἀποθανοῦμαι, ἀπέθανον, τέθνηκα = to die | ὁράω (imperf. ἑώρων), ὄψομαι, εἶδον = to see | Σωκράτης, –ους, ὁ = Socrates | εὖ (adv.) = well | φιλοσοφέω, φιλοσοφήσω, ἐφιλοσόφησα, πεφιλοσόφηκα, πεφιλοσόφημαι, ἐφιλοσοφήθην = to philosophize

1. I said that we desired the cup.

2. Socrates philosophized in order to die well.

3. I saw where you met Socrates.

4. We will philosophize until we die.

5. He philosophized until he died.

6. He philosophized before he died.

Suggestions for Further Reading

I've finished the book. How should I proceed?

Congratulations. Now that you have learned the fundamentals of Greek, you are ready to start reading continuous Greek texts. The first task is to pick what you want to read. Three factors should determine your choice: interest, ease, and edition.

You will be much more likely to progress if you enjoy what you are reading. Choose, therefore, the authors who motivated you to learn Greek. If you want to read the New Testament, the Gospel of St. John is a great place to begin. If you want to read classical authors, choose a short work by your favorite author. There also exist many "intermediate" readers out there. These books include selections from multiple authors. If you like all of the authors or some of them, these books can be ideal for increasing your reading proficiency.

You should also be mindful of the difficulty of the text that you choose. If reading Pindar's verse was what motivated you to learn Greek, I salute you. I would, however, strongly caution you to start with another author, preferably a work in prose, as poetry is considerably more difficult to read. Choosing a work whose subject matter you know can also be helpful.

Finally, the edition you choose is of the utmost importance. Choose one that is designed for intermediate readers. These editions should have vocabulary and grammatical notes included, thus eliminating the need for you to carry around a separate dictionary and grammar. Preferably, the notes and vocabulary should be on the same page or on the page facing the text. Look for the words "Reader's edition" when searching for a text.

Below is a short list of editions, lexica (dictionaries), and grammatical aids that are particularly helpful to any student who has finished this textbook.

Readers and Editions

Plato Apology: Text, Grammatical Commentary, Vocabulary, by Helm
The Wars of Greece and Persia: Selections from Herodotus in Attic Greek, by Lowe

A Reader's Greek New Testament, 2nd edition, by Goodrich and Lukaszewski
A Patristic Greek Reader, by Whitacre

Lexica

Brill Dictionary of Ancient Greek, by Montanari and Goh
This edition is the best and most up to date large lexicon. It is large, so it is better when you need to thoroughly investigate a particular word. It is better to use a smaller dictionary when you are working through a text for the first time.
Liddell and Scott's Greek-English Lexicon, Abridged
This edition, or any other Greek to English paperback, is best suited for reading texts.

Grammatical Aids

Greek Grammar, by Smyth
This grammar is extensive and best used as a reference work.
Oxford Grammar of Classical Greek
This grammar is better suited for quick reference. It can also be used for a review.

Vocabulary

Words set in boldface are given a full paradigm in Appendix A.

ἀγαθός, –ή, –όν (adj.)	good
ἀγαπάω, ἀγαπήσω, ἠγάπησα, ἠγάπηκα, ἠγάπημαι, ἠγαπήθην	to love
ἀγάπη, –ης, ἡ	love
ἀγαπητός, –ή, –όν (adj.)	beloved
ἄγγελος, –ου, ὁ	messenger; angel
ἅγιος, –α, –ον (adj.)	holy
ἄγω, ἄξω, ἤγαγον, ἦχα, ἦγμαι, ἤχθην	to lead
ἀγών, –ῶνος, ὁ	assembly; contest, struggle
ἀγωνίζομαι, ἀγωνιοῦμαι, ἠγωνισάμην, ἠγώνισμαι, ἠγωνίσθην	to compete, fight, struggle
ἀδελφός, –οῦ, ὁ	brother
ᾅδης/Ἅιδης, –ου ὁ	death, the underworld; (later) hell; capitalized (Ἅιδης) when referring to the god Hades. The iota is sometimes written subscript, sometimes adscript.
ἄδικος, –ον (adj.)	unjust
ἀεί (adv.)	always
ἀθάνατος, –ον (adj.)	immortal
Ἀθῆναι, –ῶν, αἱ	Athens

αἷμα, –ατος, τό	blood
αἴνιγμα, –ατος, τό	riddle
αἱρετός, –ή, –όν (adj.)	to be chosen; preferable
αἱρέω, αἱρήσω, εἷλον, ἥρηκα, ἥρημαι, ἡρέθην	to hold; to snatch, seize
αἰσχρός, –ή, –όν (adj.)	shameful
αἰτέω, αἰτήσω, ᾔτησα, ᾔτηκα, ᾔτημαι, ᾐτήθην	to ask; (middle) to ask, claim
αἰτία, –ας, ἡ	cause, blame
αἰών, –ῶνος, ὁ	age, generation
αἰώνιος, –ον (adj.)	eternal
ἀκούω, ἀκούσομαι, ἤκουσα, ἀκήκοα, —, ἠκούσθην	to hear (+ gen. of persons, + acc. of sounds)
ἀλήθεια, –ας, ἡ	truth
ἀληθής, –ές (adj.)	true
ἀληθινός, –ή, –όν (adj.)	trustful
ἀλλά (conj.)	but
ἄλλος, –η, –ο (adj.)	other, another
ἁμαρτάνω, ἁμαρτήσομαι, ἥμαρτον, ἡμάρτηκα, ἡμάρτημαι, ἡμαρτήθην	to err; to sin
ἁμαρτία, –ας, ἡ	mistake; sin
ἁμαρτωλός, –οῦ, ὁ	sinner
ἀμήν (adv.)	verily, in truth; so be it
ἄν (partc.)	untranslatable particle used in conditions and clauses
ἀνά (prep.)	up (+ acc.)
ἀναγκάζω, ἀναγκάσω, ἠνάγκασα ἠνάγκακα, ἠνάγκασμαι, ἠναγκάσθην	to force, compel
ἀνάγκη, –ης, ἡ	necessity

ἀναμάρτητος, –ον (adj.)	unerring; blameless, without sin
ἀνάστασις, –εως, ἡ	a raising; resurrection
ἀνδρεία, –ας, ἡ	manliness, bravery
ἀνδρεῖος, –α, –ον (adj.)	manly, courageous
ἀνήρ, ἀνδρός, ὁ	man; husband
ἄνθρωπος, –ου, ὁ	human being, person, man
ἄξιος, –α, –ον (adj.)	worthy; worthy of (+ gen.)
ἄπειρος, –ον (adj.)	without experience of (+ gen.); unlimited, infinite
ἀπό (ἀπ᾽, ἀφ᾽) (prep.)	from (+ gen.)
ἀποδίδωμι, ἀποδώσω, ἀπέδωκα, ἀποδέδωκα, ἀποδέδομαι, ἀπεδόθην	to return, render; to define, explain
ἀποθνήσκω, ἀποθανοῦμαι, ἀπέθανον, τέθνηκα, —, —	to die
ἀποκαλύπτω, ἀποκαλύψω, ἀπεκάλυψα, —, —, ἀπεκαλύφθην	to uncover, reveal
ἀποκρίνω, ἀποκρινῶ, ἀπέκρινα, —, ἀπέκρινα, ἀπεκρίθην	to set apart; (middle and passive) to answer, respond
ἀποκρύπτω, ἀποκρύψω, ἀπέκρυψα, ἀποκέκρυφα, ἀποκεκρύμμαι, ἀπεκρύβην	to hide, conceal
ἀπόλλυμι, ἀπολῶ, ἀπώλεσα, ἀπολώλεκα, —, —	to destroy, lose
ἄρα (partc.)	then, next
ἀργυροῦς, –ᾶ, –οῦν (adj.)	silver
ἀρετή, –ῆς, ἡ	excellence
ἄρτος, –ου, ὁ	bread
ἀρχή, –ῆς, ἡ	beginning; first place, power
ἄρχω, ἄρξω, ἦρξα, ἦρχα, ἦργμαι, ἤρχθην	to rule (+ gen.); to begin; (middle) to begin

ἀσθένεια, –ας, ἡ	weakness
ἀσθενέω, ἀσθενήσω, ἠσθένησα, ἠσθένηκα, —, —	to be weak
ἀσθενής, –ές (adj.)	weak
αὖ (adv.)	again; moreover
αὐξάνω, αὐξήσω, ηὔξησα, ηὔξηκα, ηὔξημαι, ηὐξήθην	to increase
ἀφίημι, ἀφήσω, ἀφῆκα, ἀφεῖκα, ἀφεῖμαι, ἀφείθην	to cast off, release; pardon
ἄφρων, –ονος (adj.)	senseless; silent
βαίνω, βήσομαι, ἔβην, βέβηκα, βέβαμαι, ἐβάθην	to step; go
βάλλω, βαλῶ, ἔβαλον, βέβληκα, βέβλημαι, ἐβλήθην	to throw; put
βαπτίζω, βαπτίσω, ἐβάπτισα, βεβάπτικα, βεβάπτισμαι, ἐβαπτίσθην	to submerge in water; to baptize
βάπτισμα, –ατος, τό	baptism
βασιλεία, –ας ἡ	kingdom
βασιλεύς, –έως, ὁ	king
βελτίων, –ον	better
βιβλίον, –ου, ὁ	book, scroll
βίος, –ου, ὁ	life
βλάβη, –ης, ἡ	harm
βλάπτω, βλάψω, ἔβλαψα, βέβλαφα, βέβλαμμαι, ἐβλάβην	to harm
βλέπω, βλέψομαι, ἔβλεψα, βέβλεφα, βέβλεμμαι, ἐβλέφθην	to see, look
βουλή, –ῆς, ἡ	plan, counsel, council, direction
βούλομαι, βουλήσομαι, —, —, βεβούλημαι, ἐβουλήθην	to want

βραδύς, –εῖα, –ύ	dull; slow
βροτός, –οῦ, ὁ	a mortal man
γάρ (conj.)	for, for indeed
γελάω, γελάσομαι, ἐγέλασα, —, —, ἐγελάσθην	to laugh; to mock
γένος, –ους, τό	race; kind
γῆ, γῆς, ἡ (older form γαῖα, –ας, ἡ)	earth
γίγνομαι (Koine γίνομαι), γενήσομαι, ἐγενόμην, γέγονα, γεγένημαι, —	to come into being, become
γιγνώσκω (Koine γινώσκω), γνώσομαι, ἔγνων, ἔγνωκα, ἔγνωσμαι, ἐγνώσθην	to know
γλυκύς, –εῖα, –ύ (adj.)	sweet
γλῶσσα (or γλῶττα), –ης, ἡ	tongue; language
γνῶσις, –εως, ἡ	knowledge
γόνυ, γόνατος, τό	knee
γράμμα, –ατος, τό	letter; in plural "writings"
γράφω, γράψω, ἔγραψα, γέγραφα, γέγραμμαι, ἐγράφην	to write
γυνή, γυναικός, ἡ	woman, wife
δαίμων, –ονος, ὁ	divinity, spirit
δέ (conj.)	and, but
δέδοικα, plupf. ἐδεδοίκη	to fear (defective verb whose perfect = present and whose pluperfect = aorist or imperfect.
δεῖ	it is necessary (+ acc. and infinitive); there is a need of (+ gen.)
δειλός, –ή, –όν (adj.)	cowardly; lowborn
δεινός, –ή, –όν (adj.)	terrible, dreadful

δένδρον, –ου, τό	tree
δέομαι, δεήσομαι, —, —, δεδέημαι, ἐδεήθην	to need, lack; have need of (+ gen.)
δεύτερος, –ον, –α	second
δέχομαι, δέξομαι, ἐδεξάμην, —, ἐδεδέγμην, ἐδέχθην	to receive
δέω, δήσω, ἔδησα, δέδεκα, δέδεμαι, ἐδέθην	to bind
δή (partc.)	so, then; indeed
δηλόω, δηλώσω, ἐδήλωσα, δεδήλωκα, δεδήλωμαι, ἐδηλώθην	to reveal, make known
διά (prep.)	through (+ gen.); on account of (+ acc.)
διακονέω, διακονήσω, διηκόνησα, —, —, ἐδιακονήθην	to minister, serve
διακονία, –ας, ἡ	service
διάκονος, –ου, ὁ	servant
διαφέρω, διοίσω, διήνεγκα (διήνεγκον), διενήνοχα, διενήνεγμαι, διενέχθην	to carry across; to differ; differ from (+ gen.)
διδακτός, –ή, –όν (adj.)	able to be taught, teachable
διδάσκαλος, –ου, ὁ	teacher, master
διδάσκω, διδάξω, ἐδίδαξα, δεδίδαχα, δεδίδαγμαι, ἐδιδάχθην	to teach, explain
δίδωμι, δώσω, ἔδωκα, δέδωκα, δέδομαι, ἐδόθην	to give
δίκαιος, –α, –ον (adj.)	just
δικαιοσύνη, –ης, ἡ	righteousness, justice
διό (διὰ ὅ)	on account of which, wherefore
δοκέω, δόξω, ἔδοξα, δέδοχα, δέδογμαι, ἐδόχθην	to think, deem; to seem
δόλος, –ου, ὁ	craft; treachery

δόξα, –ης, ἡ	glory, power; opinion
δοξάζω, δοξάσω, ἐδόξασα, δεδόξακα, δεδόξασμαι, ἐδοξάσθην	to think; believe, judge
δοῦλος, –η, –ον (adj.)	servile; as substantive "slave"
δύναμαι, δυνήσομαι, —, —, δεδύνημαι, ἐδυνήθην	to be able
δύναμις, –εως, ἡ	power, might
δυνατός, –ή, –όν (adj.)	possible, able; strong, powerful
δύο	two
δῶρον, –ου, τό	gift
ἑαυτός, –όν, –ή	oneself
ἐάω, ἐάσω, εἴασα, εἴακα, εἴαμαι, εἰάθην	to allow
ἐγγίζω, ἐγγιῶ, ἤγγισα, ἤγγικα, —, ἠγγίσθην	to bring near; approach, be imminent
ἐγκώμιον, –ου, τό	encomium, eulogy
ἐθέλω (Koine θέλω), ἐθελήσω, ἠθέλησα, ἠθέληκα, —, ἠλεήθην	to want, be willing
εἰ	if
εἴθε	would that, used to introduce wishes
εἶμι	to go, come
εἰμί	to be
εἶπον	see λέγω
εἰρήνη, –ης, ἡ	peace
εἷς, μία, ἕν	one
εἰς (prep.)	to, into; toward (+ acc.)
εἰσέρχομαι, εἰσελεύσομαι, εἰσῆλθον, εἰσελήλυθα, —, —	to enter
εἰσοράω, εἰσόψομαι, εἰσεῖδον, —, —, —	to look at, see

εἶτα (adv.)	then, next
ἐκ (ἐξ) (prep.)	out of (+ gen.)
ἕκαστος, –η, –ον (adj.)	each
ἐκεῖνος, ἐκείνη, ἐκεῖνο	that; the former
ἐκκλησία, –ας, ἡ	church
ἐκφεύγω, ἐκφεύξω, ἐξέφυγον, ἐκπέφευγα, —, —	to escape, avoid
ἐλέγχω, ἐλέγξω, ἤλεγξα, —, ἐλήλεγμαι, —	to cross-examine, question, test
ἐλεέω, ἐλεήσω, ἠλέησα, ἠλέηκα, ἠλέημαι, ἠλεήθην	to have compassion or pity for one
ἐλεήμων, –ον (adj.)	merciful
ἔλεος, –ου, ὁ	pity, mercy
Ἑλλάς, –άδος, ἡ	Greece
ἐλπίς, –ίδος, ἡ	hope, expectation
ἐμός, –ή, –όν (adj.)	my
ἐν (prep.)	in, among (+ dat.)
ἕνεκεν (sometimes written ἕνεκα) (prep.)	on account of (+ gen.)
ἐντολή, –ῆς, ἡ	order, commandment
ἐντός (prep.)	within (+ gen.)
ἔξεστιν	it is possible (+ inf.)
ἔξω (adv.)	out, outside
ἐπαινέω, ἐπαινέσω, ἐπήνεσα, ἐπήνεκα, ἐπήνημαι, ἐπηνέθην	to praise, approve
ἐπεί (adv.)	when, since, after
ἐπειδή (adv.)	when; since
ἔπειτα (adv.)	then

ἐπί (ἐπ᾽/ἐφ᾽) (prep.)	on, upon (+ gen.); on, by, for (+ dat.); to, against (+ acc.)
ἐπίγνωσις, –εως, ἡ	recognition; knowledge
ἐπιθυμέω, ἐπιθυμήσω, ἐπεθύμησα, —, —, —	to desire (+ gen.)
ἐπιθυμία, –ας, ἡ	a desire, longing for (+ gen.)
ἐπίσταμαι, ἐπιστήσομαι, —, —, —, ἠπιστήθην	to understand, know; know how to (+ inf.)
ἐπιστήμη, –ης, ἡ	knowledge
ἐπιτυγχάνω, ἐπιτεύξομαι, ἐπέτυχον, ἐπιτετύχηκα, —, —	to happen upon (+ gen.); obtain (+ gen.); meet (+ dat.)
ἐργάζομαι —, εἰργασάμην, —, εἴργασμαι, —	to work, make; do
ἔργον, –ου, τό	work, deed
ἔρχομαι, ἐλεύσομαι, ἦλθον, ἐλήλυθα, —, —	to go; come
ἔρως, –ωτος, ὁ	love
ἐρωτάω, ἐρωτήσω, ἠρώτησα, ἠρώτηκα, ἠρώτημαι, ἠρωτήθην	to ask, question
ἐσθής, ἐσθῆτος, ἡ	clothing, garment
ἐσθίω, ἔδομαι, ἔφαγον, ἐδήδοκα, ἐδήδεσμαι, ἠδέσθην	to eat
ἔσχατος, –η, –ον (adj.)	furthest, last
ἕτερος, –α, –ον (adj.)	other
ἔτι (adv.)	still
ἔτος, ἔτους, τό	year
εὖ (adv.)	well
εὐδαιμονία, –ας, ἡ	happiness; prosperity
εὐδαίμων, –ον (adj.)	fortunate, happy
εὐθύς (adv.)	at once, immediately

εὑρίσκω, εὑρήσω, εὗρον, εὕρηκα, εὕρημαι, εὑρέθην	to find
εὐτυχέω, εὐτυχήσω, εὐτύχησα, εὐτύχηκα, εὐτύχημαι, εὐτυχήθην	to prosper
ἐχθρός, –οῦ, ὁ	enemy
ἐχθρός, –ή, –όν (adj.)	hostile
ἔχω, ἕξω (or σχήσω), ἔσχον, ἔσχηκα, ἔσχημαι, ἐσχέθην	to have, hold; to be able to (+ inf.)
ἕως (conj.)	while, as long as; until
ζάω, ζήσω, ἔζησα, —, —, —	to live
Ζεύς, Διός, Διί, Δία	Zeus
ζητέω, ζητήσω, ἐζήτησα, ἐζήτηκα, ἐζήτημαι, ἐζητήθην	to seek
ζωή, –ῆς, ἡ	life
ζῷον, –ου, τό	animal
ἤ (conj.)	or; than
ἡγέομαι, ἡγήσομαι, ἡγησάμην, —, ἥγημαι, —	to think, believe (+ inf. in indirect statement)
ἥδομαι, ἡσθήσομαι, —, —, —, ἥσθην	to feel pleasure, be pleased
ἡδονή, ῆς, ἡ	pleasure
ἡδύς, ἡδεῖα, ἡδύ (adj.)	sweet
ἡμέρα, –ας, ἡ	day
ἡμέτερος, –ον, –α (adj.)	our
ἡνίκα (adv.)	when; while
ἥττων (Koine ἥσσων), –ονος (adj.)	inferior, less
θάνατος, –ου, ὁ	death
θαυμάζω, θαυμάσομαι, ἐθαύμασα, τεθαύμακα, τεθαύμασμαι, ἐθαυμάσθην	to wonder, marvel

θεῖος, –α, –ον (adj.)	divine
θέλημα, –ματος, τό	will
θέλω	see ἐθέλω
θεός, –οῦ, ὁ	a god, God
θεραπεύω, θεραπεύσω, ἐθεράπευσα, τεθεράπευκα, τεθεράπευμαι, ἐθεραπεύθην	to care for, respect; (middle) to serve
θησαυρός, –οῦ, ὁ	store–room, treasure
θνητός, –ή, –όν (adj.)	mortal
θνητός, –οῦ, ὁ	a mortal
θυμός, –οῦ, ὁ	soul, spirit; temper
θύρα, –ας, ἡ	door, entrance
ἰατρός, –οῦ, ὁ	physician
ἴδιος, –α, –ον (adj.)	one's own, private
ἱερόν, –οῦ, τό	temple
ἱερός, –ά, –όν (adj.)	sacred, holy
ἵημι, ἥσω, ἧκα, εἷκα, εἷμαι, εἵθην	to throw
Ἰησοῦς nom., Ἰησοῦ gen./dat./ voc., Ἰησοῦν acc.	Jesus
ἵνα	so that (+ purpose clause); that (+ object clause)
ἵστημι, στήσω, ἔστησα/ἔστην, ἔστηκα, ἔσταμαι, ἐστάθην	to set; to stand
καθαρός, –ή, –όν (adj.)	pure, clean
καθώς (adv.)	just as
καί (conj. and adv.)	(conj.) and; (adv.) also, even
καινός, –ή, –όν (adj.)	new
καιρός, –οῦ, ὁ	due measure; season, opportunity
κακός, –ή, –όν (adj.)	bad, base, evil

καλέω, καλῶ, ἐκάλεσα, κέκληκα, κέκλημαι, ἐκλήθην	to call, name
καλός, –ή, –όν (adj.)	beautiful, fine, noble
καρδία, –ας, ἡ	heart
καρπός, –οῦ, ὁ	fruit
κατά (κατ'/καθ')	down from, against (+ gen.); in accordance with (+ acc.)
κενός, –ή, –όν (adj.)	empty
κέρδος, –εος, τό	gain, profit
κεφαλή, –ῆς, ἡ	head
κίνησις, –εως, ἡ	motion
κλεινός, –ή, –όν (adj.)	famous, renowned
κλέος, –ου τό	glory
κοιλία, –ας, ἡ	any bodily cavity; womb
κοινός, –ή, –όν	common; shared in common
κόσμος, –ου, ὁ	order; an ornament, decoration; the world
κράζω, κράξω, ἔκραξα, κέκραγα, —, —	to croak, scream
κρείττων, –ον (Koine κρείσσων, –ον) (comp. adj. of ἀγαθός)	stronger
κρήνη, –ης, ἡ	spring, well
κρίνω, κρινῶ, ἔκρινα, κέκρικα, κέκριμαι, ἐκρίθην	to separate; judge, condemn
κρύπτω, κρύψω, ἔκρυψα, κέκρυφα, κέκρυμμαι, ἐκρύφθην	to hide, conceal
κτῆμα, –ατος, τό	a possession
κύκλος, –ου, ὁ	circle, wheel
κύριος, –ου, ὁ	lord
λαλέω, λαλήσω, ἐλάλησα, λελάληκα, λελάλημαι, ἐλαλήθην	to chatter; say

λαμβάνω, λήψομαι, ἔλαβον, εἴληφα, εἴλημμαι, ἐλήφθην	to take, seize; receive; understand
λαμπρός, –ά, –όν (adj.)	shining, splendid
λανθάνω, λήσω, ἔλαθον, λέληθα, λέλησμαι, ἐλήσθην	to escape someone's notice; to forget (+ gen.)
λέγω, ἐρῶ (or λέξω), εἶπον, εἴρηκα, εἴρημαι (or λέλεγμαι), ἐρρήθην (or λέλειμαι)	to say, speak
λίθος, –ου, ὁ	stone
λογίζομαι, λογιοῦμαι, ἐλογισάμην, —, λελόγισμαι, ἐλογίσθην	to calculate; reflect, think
λόγος, –ου, ὁ	word, reason, story, account
λύπη, –ης, ἡ	grief
λύω, λύσω, ἔλυσα, λέλυκα, λέλυμαι, ἐλύθην	to loosen, unbind, release; to destroy
μαθητής, –οῦ, ὁ	student; disciple
μαίνομαι, μανοῦμαι, ἐμηνάμην, —, μεμάνημαι, ἐμάνην	to rage, be mad
μακάριος, –α, –ον (adj.)	blessed, happy
μάλα (adv.)	very
μάλιστα (supl. adv. of μάλα)	most
μᾶλλον (comp. adv. of μάλα)	more
μανθάνω, μαθήσομαι, ἔμαθον, μεμάθηκα, —, —	to learn; understand
μαρτυρέω, μαρτυρήσω, ἐμαρτύρησα, μεμαρτύρηκα, μεμαρτύρημαι, ἐμαρτυρήθην	to testify
μάχομαι, μαχήσομαι, ἐμαχεσάμην, —, μεμάχημαι, ἐμαχέσθην	to fight, battle
μέγας, μεγάλη, μέγα (adj.)	great, large
μείζων, –ον (comp. adj. of μέγας)	greater

μέλλω, μελλήσω, ἐμέλλησα, —, —, —	to be likely to (+ pres. inf.); be about to (+ future inf.); to hesitate to (+ present inf.)
μένω, μενῶ, ἔμεινα, μεμένηκα, —, —	to remain, stay
μερίζω, μεριῶ, ἐμέρισα, μεμέρικα, μεμέρισμαι, ἐμερίσθην	to allot, assign
μετά (μετ'/μεθ') (prep.)	among, with (+ gen.); after (+ acc.)
μετανοέω, μετανοήσω, μετενόησα, μετανενόηκα, —, —	to change one's mind; repent
μέτρον, –ου, τό	measure, moderation
μή (adv.)	not
μήποτε (adv.)	never
μήτε (adv.)	and not; μήτε...μήτε "neither...nor"
μητήρ, –τρός, ἡ	mother
μικρός, –ά, –όν (adj.)	small
μιμέομαι, μιμήσομαι, ἐμιμησάμην, μεμίμημαι, —, —	to imitate, reproduce
μισέω, μισήσω, ἐμίσησα, μεμίσηκα, μεμίσημαι, ἐμισήθην	to hate
μνημονεύω, μνημονεύσω, ἐμνημόνευσα, ἐμνημόνευκα, ἐμνημόνευμαι	to remember
μόνος, –η, –ον (adj.)	alone, only
μορφή, –ῆς, ἡ	form, shape
μωρία, –ας, ἡ	foolishness, stupidity
ναός, –οῦ, ὁ	temple
νεκρός, –ά, –όν (adj.)	dead
νέμω, νεμῶ, ἔνειμα, νενέμηκα, νενέμημαι, ἐνεμήθην	to deal out, distribute
νέος, –α, –ον (adj.)	new

νήπιος, −α, −ον (adj.)	childish; as substantive noun = a child
νικάω, νικήσω, ἐνίκησα, νενίκηκα, νενίκημαι, ἐνικήθην	to conquer, win
νοέω, νοήσω, ἐνόησα, νενόηκα, νενόημαι, ἐνοήθην	to think; know
νομίζω, νομιῶ, ἐνόμισα, νενόμικα, νενόμισμαι, ἐνομίσθην	to think, consider
νόμος, −ου, ὁ	law, custom
νοῦς, νοῦ, νῷ, νοῦν, ὁ	mind
νῦν (adv.)	now
νύξ, νυκτός, ἡ	night
ξένος, −η, −ον (adj.)	foreign, strange
ξένος, −ου, ὁ	stranger, foreigner
ὅδε, ἥδε, τόδε	this; the following
ὁδός, −οῦ, ἡ	road, way
οἶδα, εἴσομαι, (plupf. ᾔδη)	to know; know how to (+ inf.)
οἰκέω, οἰκήσω, ᾤκησα, ᾤκηκα, ᾤκημαι, ᾠκήθην	to live, dwell
ὁ, ἡ, τό	the
οἰκία, οἰκίας, ἡ	house, building
οἰκοδομέω, οἰκοδομήσω, ᾠκοδόμησα, ᾠκοδόμηκα, ᾠκοδόμημαι, ᾠκοδομήθην	to build up
οἶνος, −ου, ὁ	wine
οἴομαι, οἰήσομαι, ᾠήθην, —, —, —	to think, suppose
οἷος, οἵα, οἷον (adj.)	such as; of what sort
ὀκνέω, ὀκνήσω, ὤκνησα, —, —, —	to hesitate, shrink from
ὅλος, −η, −ον (adj.)	whole, entire

ὁμιλέω, ὁμιλήσω, ὡμίλησα, ὡμίληκα, ὡμίλημαι, ὡμιλήθην	to gather, unite; to associate with (+ dat.)
ὄμμα, –ατος, τό	eye
ὅμοιος, –α, –ον (adj.)	like, similar to (+ dat.)
ὁμοίως (adv.)	similarly, in the same way
ὄνομα, ὀνόματος, τό	name
ὀνομάζω, ὀνομάσω, ὠνόμασα, ὠνόμακα, ὠνόμασμαι, ὠνομάσθην	to name, call
ὁπότε (adv.)	when
ὅπως (adv. and conj.)	how, as (adv.); that (conj.), used to introduce purpose and effort clauses
ὁράω (imperf. ἑώρων), ὄψομαι, εἶδον, ἑώρακα (sometimes spelled ἑόρακα), ἑώραμαι (sometimes spelled ὦμμαι), ὤφθην	to see, behold
ὀργή, –ῆς, ἡ	anger
ὅρκος, –ου, τό	oath
ὁσάκις (adv.)	as many times as, whenever
ὅσος, –η, –ον (adj.)	how much, how big; as much as
ὅστις, ἥτις, ὅ τι (adj. and pronoun)	whoever, whatever
ὅταν	(ὅτε + ἄν) whenever
ὅτε (adv.)	when
ὅτι	"that," when introducing indirect statement; because
οὐ, οὐκ, οὐχ (adv.)	not
οὐδείς, οὐδεμία, οὐδέν (adj.)	no one, nothing
οὐκέτι (adv.)	no longer
οὖν (adv.)	certainly; then, therefore
οὐρανός, –οῦ ὁ	sky; heaven

οὖς, ὠτός, τό	ear
οὐσία, –ας, ἡ	substance, being; property, riches
οὔτε (adv.)	and not; οὔτε…οὔτε "neither…nor"
οὗτος, αὕτη, τοῦτο	this; the latter
οὕτως (οὕτω before consonants) (adv.)	thus, to such an extent
ὄχλος, –ου, ὁ	crowd, multitude
πάθος, –ους, τό	experience, suffering
παιδεία, –ας, ἡ	education
παιδεύω, παιδεύσω, ἐπαίδευσα, πεπαίδευκα, πεπαίδευμαι, ἐπαιδεύθην	to teach
παιδίον, –ου, τό	young child
παῖς, παιδός, ὁ, ἡ	child
πάλιν (adv.)	back, again
πάντως (adv.)	in all ways, completely
παρά (prep.)	from (+ gen.); beside (+ dat.); to, contrary to (+ acc.)
παραβολή, –ῆς, ἡ	analogy, parable
παραδίδωμι, παραδώσω, παρέδωκα, παραδέδωκα, παραδέδομαι, παρεδόθην	to hand over, to betray
παρακαλέω, παρακαλῶ, παρεκάλεσα, παρακέκληκα, παρακέκλημαι, παρεκλήθην	to summon; encourage, comfort
πάρειμι, παρέσομαι	to be present
πᾶς, πᾶσα, πᾶν (adj.)	all
πάσχω, πείσομαι, ἔπαθον, πέπονθα, —, —	to experience; suffer
πατήρ, –τρός, ὁ	father

παύω, παύσω, ἔπαυσα, πέπαυκα, πέπαυμαι, ἐπαύθην	to stop; (middle) to stop/cease (+ part.)
πείθω, πείσω, ἔπεισα, πέποιθα, πέπεισμαι, ἐπείσθην	to persuade; (middle) to obey (+ dat.)
πέμπω, πέμψω, ἔπεμψα, πέπομφα, πέπεμμαι, ἐπέμφθην	to send
πένης, –ητος, ὁ/ἡ	poor
περ (partc.)	indeed, truly; although; at least
περί (prep.)	(+ gen) concerning, about; (+ dat) around; (+ acc) around
περιπατέω, περιπατήσω, περιεπάτησα, —, —, —	to walk around
πέτρα, –ας, ἡ	a rock
πῆμα, –ατος, τό	adversity, misfortune
πίνω, πίομαι, ἔπιον, πέπωκα, πέπομαι, ἐπόθην	to drink
πίπτω, πεσοῦμαι, ἔπεσον, πέτωκα, —, —	to fall; fail
πιστεύω, πιστεύσω, ἐπίστευσα, πεπίστευκα, πεπίστευμαι, ἐπιστεύθην	to trust, have faith in (+ dat.) or (εἰς + accusative)
πίστις, –εως, ἡ	faith
πλείων, –ον (adj.)	greater, more
πλεονάζω, πλεονάσω, ἐπλεόνασα, πεπλεόνακα, πεπλεόνασμαι, ἐπλεονάσθην	to be superabundant
πλῆθος, –ους, τό	number; the multitude
πληρόω, πληρώσω, ἐπλήρωσα, πεπλήρωκα, πεπλήρωμαι, ἐπληρώθην	to fill, fulfill
πλησίος, –α, –ον (adj.)	neighboring
πλησίος, –ου, ὁ	a neighbor
πλούσιος, –α, –ον (adj.)	rich

πλοῦτος, –ου, ὁ	wealth
πνεῦμα, –ατος, τό	air, breath; spirit
ποιέω, ποιήσω, ἐποίησα, πεποίηκα, πεποίημαι, ἐποιήθην	to make; to do
ποιητής, –οῦ, ὁ	poet
ποιμήν, –ένος, ὁ	shepherd
πόλεμος, –ου, ὁ	war
πόλις, –εως, ἡ	city, city-state
πολιτικός, –ή, –όν (adj.)	civic, political
πολύς, πολλή, πολύ (adj.)	much, many
πονηρός, –ή, –όν (adj.)	wicked, evil
πόνος, –ου, ὁ	hard work; toil
πορεύω, πορεύσω, ἐπόρευσα, πεπόρευκα, πεπόρευμαι, ἐπορεύθην	to carry; (middle/passive) to go, walk
ποτε (adv.)	ever, once
ποτήριον, –ου, τό	cup
ποῦ (adv.)	where
πούς, πόδας, ὁ	foot
πρᾶγμα, –ατος, τό	matter, thing
πράττω (Koine πράσσω), πράξω, ἔπραξα, πέπραγμα or (πέπραχα), πέπραγμαι, ἐπράχθην	to do
πραῦς, –εῖα, –ῦ (adj.)	gentle, meek
πρίν (conj.)	before (+ inf.); until (+ subj. or past tense of indic.)
προέρχομαι, προελεύσομαι, προῆλθον, προελήλυθα, —, —	to go out, present oneself
πρός (prep.)	from (+ gen.); at (+ dat.); toward, against, to (+ acc.)

προσεύχομαι, προσεύξομαι, προσηυξάμην, —, —, —	to pray
πρόσωπον, –ου, τό	face
πρῶτος, –η, –ον (adj.)	first
πύλη, –ης, ἡ	a gate
πῶς (adv.)	how?
ῥῆμα, ῥήματος, τό	saying, word
σάρξ, σαρκός, ἡ	flesh
σῖτος, –ου, ὁ	grain, bread
σός, –ή, –όν (adj.)	your
σοφία, –ας, ἡ	wisdom
σοφιστής, –οῦ, ὁ	sophist
σοφός, –ή, –όν (adj.)	wise
σοφός, –οῦ, ὁ	wise man, sage
σπεύδω, σπεύσω, ἔσπευσα, ἔσπευκα, ἔσπευσμαι, —	to hasten; be eager to, strive to (+ inf.)
στενός, –ή, –όν (adj.)	narrow, confined
στόμα, –ατος, τό	mouth
στρατηγός, –οῦ, ὁ	general
στρατιώτης, –ου, ὁ	soldier
στρατός, –οῦ, ὁ	army
συγγνώμη, –ης, ἡ	pardon, forgiveness
συμφέρω, συνοίσω, συνήνεγκα/συνήνεγκον, —, —, —	to bring together, benefit; be useful
συμφορά, –ᾶς, ἡ	occurrence; misfortune
συνετός, –ή, –όν (adj.)	intelligent
σῴζω, σώσω, ἔσωσα, σέσωκα, σέσωσμαι, ἐσώθην	to save

Σωκράτης, –ους, ὁ	Socrates
σῶμα, σώματος, τό	body
ταράσσω, ταράξω, ἐτάραξα, τετάραχα, τετάραγμαι, ἐταράχθη	to shake; disturb
ταχύς, –εῖα, –ύ (adj.)	swift, quick
τε (conj.)	and
τέκνον, –ου, τό	child
τελέω, τελέσω, ἐτέλεσα, τετέλεκα, τετέλεσμαι, ἐτελέσθην	to complete, fulfill
τέλος, –ους, τό	end, fulfillment
τέρμα, –ατος, τό	end, limit
τέτταρες, –ρα	four
τέχνη, –ης, ἡ	art, skill
τηρέω, τηρήσω, ἐτήρησα, τετήρηκα, τετήρημαι, ἐτηρήθην	to observe, keep; protect
τί (adv.)	why
τίθημι, θήσω, ἔθηκα, τέθηκα, τέθειμαι, ἐτέθην	to put, place
τιμή, –ῆς, ἡ	honor
τίς, τί (interrogative pronoun)	who, what
τις, τι (indefinite pronoun)	a certain, some
τόπος, –ου, ὁ	place
τοσοῦτος, τοσαύτη, τοσοῦτο (adj.)	so much, thus much
τότε (adv.)	then, at that time
τρεῖς, τρία	three
τρέπω, τρέξω, ἔτρεψα, τέτροφα, τέτραμμαι, ἐτράπην	to turn; (middle) turn or betake oneself
τρέφω, θρέψω, ἔθρεψα, τέτροφα, τέτραμμαι, ἐτράφην	to nourish; rear

τροφή, –ῆς, ἡ	nourishment, food
τυγχάνω, τεύξομαι, ἔτυχον, τετύχηκα, —, —	to occur, to happen to (+ dat.); to happen to (+ part.) chance upon, obtain (+ gen.)
τύχη, –ης, ἡ	chance, fortune, fate
ὕβρις, –εως, ἡ	violence; arrogance
ὕδωρ, ὕδατος, τό	water
υἱός, –οῦ, ὁ	son
ὑπάγω, ὑπάξω, ὑπήγαγον, —, —, ὑπήχθην	to lead under; go away
ὑπέρ (prep.)	over, on behalf of (+ gen.); over, beyond (+ acc.)
ὑπό (ὑπ'/ὑφ') (prep.)	under, by (+ gen.); under, by (+ dat.); under, toward (+ acc.)
ὑποτίθημι, ὑποθήσω, ὑπέθηκα, ὑποτέθεικα, ὑποτέθειμαι, ὑπετέθην	place under, offer; (middle) to give advice to (+ dat.)
φαῦλος, –η, –ον (adj.)	cheap, base; evil
φέρω, οἴσω, ἤνεγκα or (ἤνεγκον), ἐνήνοχα, ἐνήνεγμαι, ἠνέχθην	to bear, carry
φεύγω, φεύξομαι, ἔφυγον, πέφευγα	to flee
φημί, φήσω, ἔφησα, —, —, —	to say, assert; οὔ φημί = to deny
φιλέω, φιλήσω, ἐφίλησα, πεφίληκα, πεφίλημαι, ἐφιλήθην	to love
φίλος, –η, –ον (adj.)	dear to (+ dat.); friendly to (+ dat.)
φίλος, –ου, ὁ	friend
φιλοσοφέω, φιλοσοφήσω, ἐφιλοσόφησα, πεφιλοσόφηκα, πεφιλοσόφημαι, ἐφιλοσόφηθην	to philosophize
φιλοσοφία, –ας, ἡ	philosophy
φιλόσοφος, –ου, ὁ	a philosopher
φοβέω, φοβήσω, ἐφόβησα, πεφόβηκα, πεφόβημαι, ἐφοβήθην	to put to flight; (middle and passive) to be afraid, fear

φόβος, –ου, ὁ	fear
φράζω, φράσω, ἔφρασα, πέφρακα, πέφρασμαι, ἐφράσθην	to explain; declare; devise
φρήν, φρενός, ἡ	heart, mind
φρονέω, φρονήσω, ἐφρόνησα, πεφρόνηκα, —, —	to think; to be prudent, wise
φρόνησις, –εως, ἡ	thought; practical wisdom, prudence
φυλάττω (Koine φυλάσσω), φυλάξω, ἐφύλαξα, πεφύλαχα, πεφύλαγμαι, ἐφυλάχθην	to guard; (middle) be on guard against
φυσικός, –ή, –όν (adj.)	natural, physical
φύσις, –εως, ἡ	nature
φύω, φύσω, ἔφυσα/ ἔφυν, πέφυκα, —, —	to produce, grow. This verb is transitive is the present, future, and 1st aorist; intransitive in the 2nd aorist, perfect, and pluperfect.
φῶς, φωτός, τό	light
χαλεπός, –ή, –όν	difficult, harsh
χαρά, –ᾶς, ἡ	joy
χάρις, –ιτος, ἡ	favor; grace; in acc., for the sake of (+ gen)
χορτάζω, χορτάσω, ἐχόρτασα, —, κεχόρτασμαι, ἐχορτάσθην	to feed, feed till full
χρεία, –ας, ἡ	need, want
χρῆμα, –ατος, τό	thing; in plural "wealth"
χρηστός, –ή, –όν (adj.)	useful, serviceable
Χριστός, -οῦ, ὁ	Christ
χρόνος, –ου, ὁ	time
χρυσοῦς, –ῆ, –οῦν (adj.)	golden
χωρίζω, χωρίσω, ἐχώρισα, —, κεχώρισμαι, ἐχωρίσθην	to divide, separate

χωρίς (prep. and adv.)	(prep.) without (+ gen.); (adv.) separately
ψέγω, ψέξω, ἔψεξα, —, ἔψεγμαι, ἐψέχθην	to criticize, reproach
ψυχή, –ῆς, ἡ	soul, spirit; life
ὦ (interj.)	O!, Oh! (always precedes a vocative)
ὧδε (adv.)	thus; here
ὥρα, –ας, ἡ	hour; season
ὡς (adv.)	as, like; + indirect statement "that"; introducing purpose and effort clauses "that/so that"; since
ὥσπερ (adv.)	as if, just as
ὥστε (conj.)	so that, so as; therefore
ὠφελέω, ὠφελήσω, ὠφέλησα, ὠφέληκα, ὠφέλημαι, ὠφελήθην	to help, assist